THE
CONSTRUCTION
OF EQUALITY

THE CONSTRUCTION OF EQUALITY

Syriac Immigration and the Swedish City

JENNIFER MACK

UNIVERSITY OF MINNESOTA PRESS

MINNEAPOLIS • LONDON

This book is supported by a grant from the Graham Foundation for Advanced Studies in the Fine Arts.

Illustrations in this book were funded by a grant from the SAH/Mellon Author Awards of the Society of Architectural Historians.

A version of chapter 2 was published as "New Swedes in the New Town," in *Use Matters: An Alternative History of Architecture,* ed. Kenny Cupers (New York: Routledge, 2013), 121–37. An earlier version of the Conclusion, including parts of chapter 3, was published as "Urban Design from Below: Immigration and the Spatial Practice of Urbanism," *Public Culture* 26, no. 1 (2014): 153–85; copyright 2014 Duke University Press; all rights reserved; reprinted with permission of Duke University Press, www.dukeupress.edu.

Every effort was made to obtain permission to reproduce material in this book. If any proper acknowledgment has not been included here, we encourage copyright holders to notify the publisher.

Published by the University of Minnesota Press
111 Third Avenue South, Suite 290
Minneapolis, MN 55401-2520
http://www.upress.umn.edu

ISBN 978-0-8166-9869-1 (hc)
ISBN 978-0-8166-9871-4 (pb)

A Cataloging-in-Publication record for this book is available from the Library of Congress.

Printed in the United States of America on acid-free paper

The University of Minnesota is an equal-opportunity educator and employer.

22 21 20 19 18 17   10 9 8 7 6 5 4 3 2 1

For

MY PARENTS

Contents

Preface

IN 2007, TWO SOCCER TEAMS from the Swedish town of Södertälje, the Assyrian Soccer Association team (Assyriska FF, Fotbollsförening) and Syrianska Football Club (Syrianska FC), faced one another in two so-called derbies (contests between two teams from the same city, town, or village). Syriac Orthodox Christian immigrants had established both teams as recreational clubs in the 1970s, and both now played in the third tier of the Swedish professional leagues. Over the years they had enjoyed varying levels of success, and these 2007 derbies represented the first time Assyriska FF and Syrianska FC had met on the field of play since 1989. In their obviously foreign names and in their open embrace of explicit rivalry, these teams gave human form to a cultural and, ultimately, an architectural and planning revolution. That revolution is the subject of this book, which concerns how, in the new and mobile Europe of today, immigrants are causing sea changes in the creation, use, and physical appearance of lived urban space.

In the days leading up to the derby matches, Södertälje was abuzz with speculation about who would win and be "best in town," how many goals each team would score, and whether the results would lead to fights between the fans of the teams. Many of these are probably typical points of discussion when a derby is played just about anywhere. More unusual were the debates about which group more accurately represented the true history of one Middle Eastern minority group, which fans were more dedicated to God, how many fans would be watching by satellite from abroad, and whether bad sportsmanship would lead to conflicts in churches and schools in the weeks to come.

These derbies involved far more than just local sports, and the hotly contested 2007 matches concerned much more than a mere athletic rivalry. The teams, although they play in an old industrial town on the outskirts of the Swedish capital, represent the diasporic Syriac Orthodox Christians. For them, as fans frequently told me, "Every match is the World Cup."[1] Their supporters all over the world agree, and hats, shirts, and banners with the teams' names and symbols can be found in far-flung locales from Midyat in southeastern Turkey to Boston in the United States.

In the summer of 2007, I began preliminary fieldwork in Södertälje, and, as I learned, the derbies, the two soccer teams, and the arena where they play represent just one of the many ways the Syriac Orthodox Christian global diaspora has intersected with and altered the local spaces of this Swedish town. During that summer, I directed and shot footage for an ethnographic film on the Assyriska FF soccer team's fan club, Zelge Fans. I heard again and again that Syriacs the world over consider Södertälje their global capital, and I met fans from four continents. At one of our first meetings, Elias,[2] a member of the Zelge Fans, told me, "The clubhouse is our cottage, the arena is our palace, and the cultural association is our home." Other Swedes I talked with expressly avoided the town, labeling it a "problem area" because of its reputation as a segregated place. Others were simply indifferent; Södertälje did not appear on their map of essential Swedish geography.

When I returned in the summer of 2008 for more extensive fieldwork, the importance of Södertälje for the Syriac Orthodox Christians became increasingly apparent. As Elias's thoughts suggest, soccer was just one of the practices and the arena just one of the spaces that this community had created in the town since their first members arrived in 1967 as refugees. Many now went so far as to consider Södertälje the property of the group, as another fan, Izla, pronounced when she told me, "We're the only ones here." They had developed an independent infrastructure in Swedish urban space.

During the fifty long years since they first came to Sweden, Syriac Orthodox Christians have adapted and built structures for domestic life, for religious services, for social gatherings, for celebration, for mourning, for political organization, for sports, and for much more. They have often done so in an environment that has been explicitly or implicitly hostile to their pursuits. First, they transformed existing spaces created during the Swedish welfare state's midcentury modern project, when architectural and urban standards were used in the pursuit of social equality. After establishing a stronger foothold in Sweden, the group pursued new plans and new building permits and hired architects to build some of its designs. They have, in effect, planned a Syriac–Swedish city from below.

In this complex place, I had to rely on interdisciplinary methods. I combined ethnographic approaches and participant observation with the traditional tools of historians and theorists of the built environment: formal analysis and archival research. I merged these orientations both to attend to the omission of everyday human interactions with space from top-down views of design policy and practices, and to emphasize the physical dimensions of space and of the creation of space absent in most ethnographic accounts. Exploring these connections was at once a boon and a challenge.

I uncovered documents related to planning and construction in Södertälje's city archive *(Stadsarkivet)*, building-permit archives *(Bygglovsarkiv)*, planning department archives *(Planarkiv),* and, more briefly, in the Mesopotamia Library at Södertörn University. These diverse historical materials also offered information about the stance of the officials who have been charged with evaluating, designing, and commenting on proposals. I explored such documents as original plans, letters of complaint, architectural drawings, community bulletins, and descriptions of new and renovation projects.

Fieldwork served as a central component of the project, even after production was completed on my ethnographic film. Beginning in mid-2008, I lived in Södertälje for more than fourteen months in the neighborhoods of Ronna and Rosenlund. I regularly used many of the Syriac spaces in the town. I attended church services and soccer matches; bought my food and had my hair cut at Syriac businesses; socialized in Syriac homes and cafés; went to weddings, funerals, and parties; and volunteered part-time with the Swedish Red Cross. From 2009 to 2010, I worked for one year as an intern at the Södertälje Municipal Planning Department. This allowed for continual access to urban planners and meetings about ongoing projects.

During this phase of the project, I conducted more than fifty interviews with people who had contributed since the mid-1960s to the development of the city's built environment. Interviews with early Syriac arrivals, including those who came on the storied "First Plane" from Lebanon in 1967, offered critical information about how they experienced the city in relation to their encounters with buildings and landscapes in Turkey and Syria, as well as about initial building projects. Interviews with planners, policy makers, and architects—some trained in Sweden, others trained in Iraq and Italy—offered insights into how Södertälje has been shaped both according to and against their specifications. In conversation with Syriac home owners, church leaders, soccer officials, wedding planners, and others involved in the consumption and commissioning of space, I learned about their projects and how they navigated government-sanctioned practices of space making in Sweden in the late twentieth and early twenty-first centuries. I carried out additional ethnographic research in 2015 and 2016 by revisiting many of the sites of my original research with informants and conducting supplementary interviews.

Another key research method involved formal analyses of the built environment. Mapping and site work at existing buildings brought into sharp relief the changes to spaces over time. Media and newspaper research, especially at the National Library of Sweden and through the Swedish Media Database, offered insight into key historical events and changes to spaces in Södertälje. Critical was my review of articles published in the local newspaper *Länstidningen Södertälje* from 1960 to 1986 (the year Swedish prime minister Olof Palme was assassinated), as well as of those published in the journals *Hujådå* and *Bahro Suryoyo* in the late 1970s and 1980s. (These two journals represent the Assyrian Federation of Sweden [Assyriska Riksförbundet, though the English term is their official translation of the name] and the Syrianska Federation [Syrianska Riksförbundet], respectively.)

Articles and advertisements in Swedish architecture and planning journals from the 1960s to the 1990s articulated the changing relationship between ideology and form in the country, especially with respect to public space and housing. Countless government reports, known as Statens Offentliga Utredningar (SOU; in English, Swedish Government Official Reports), portrayed the official stance on issues ranging from immigration policy to the provision of residential laundry rooms from the 1930s to the present.

As I investigated the motivations of the various actors involved in making Södertälje into a Syriac–Swedish city, I also analyzed how official planners and Syriac residents of the town talked about, initiated, and developed projects in and for the built environment. In the physical spaces that Elias described (as cottage, palace, and home), as well as many other spaces, Syriac acts and practices on and in the built environment have been revolutionary, changing the city while also necessitating new ways of working for planners and architects.

The Syriac Orthodox Christians' work in Södertälje requires new interpretations of how the city is built and who plans and designs it, along with new understandings of how such acts recalibrate European urban space. The design, construction, and use of Syriac spaces in Södertälje suggest that it is high time to rethink current understandings of segregation and how architecture and planning really happen in twenty-first-century Europe.

INTRODUCTION

Urban Design from Below

We thought that polar bears ran around on the streets here. We heard that it would probably be rather cold, but we didn't care. We wanted to try something new. We got the chance on the 13th of March 1967, when we flew here. We landed somewhere in Malmö. That was "the First Plane." And the first person to touch the ground from the plane, that was me. We had thought there would be so much snow, but when we came out, there wasn't so much snow, only a little bit of snow on the ground. We were, you know, a little frightened. . . . It was a little exciting.

—DAVID, Syriac entrepreneur in his late fifties

IN THE SPRING OF 1967, a group of Christians, mostly Syriac[1] Orthodox, traveled by air from Lebanon and landed in southern Sweden.[2] Through the intervention and with the approval of the Swedish Ministry of the Interior, the country's Labor Market Board (Arbetsmarknadsstyrelsen, AMS) had established a quota for stateless refugees, then living in Lebanon, to be brought to Sweden and sent a state-sponsored committee to Beirut in November 1966 to choose them.[3] After interviews with 305 applicants, 205 were chosen: primarily younger people who had previously emigrated from the mountainous area of southeastern Turkey known as Tur Abdin (Map 1), literally "the mountain of the servants of God." There, as a minority religious group, they had faced discrimination and persecution repeatedly during the nation-building projects of the twentieth century.

Whether it was snowing on that first day or not, the arrival of the diasporic Syriacs to Sweden represents the beginning of an epic. It changed the lives of the 205 people chosen to come, and it had a deep and lasting effect on the social and physical shape of the Swedish town where many of them, and eventually their family and friends, settled. In this book, I follow the Syriacs to Södertälje, on the extreme outskirts of Stockholm, the Swedish capital, where they now make up approximately 26 percent of the local population.[4] Here, the group has created a new cosmological node and gathering point that many now label the capital city of the entire Syriac diaspora. Despite its marginal Swedish location, the town is pivotal to the global Syriac imaginary; it is both Mesopotamia and Sweden at once, or "Mesopotälje."[5]

1

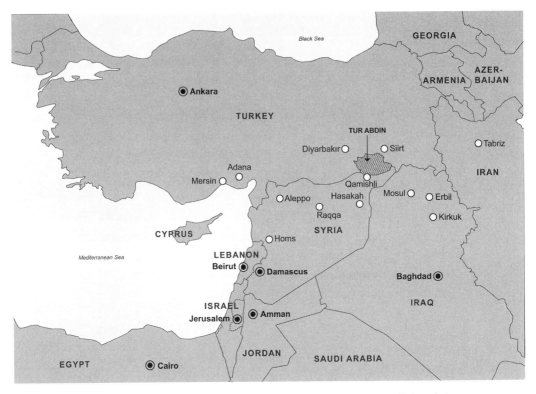

MAP 1. Map of the Middle East, showing major cities and the region of Tur Abdin.
Graphic design by Eliza Hearsum.

Critically, these social transformations have also required the town to undergo a
physical metamorphosis. Södertälje is a nexus of high modernist spatial and social
planning and a place where planners have long performed their role as agents of a
Swedish state seeking to redefine citizenship through the built environment. Since
the mid-twentieth century, Swedish planners have operated through a logic of space
making that uses architectural and urban standardization and uniformity as a means
to create parity among citizens. Among the sites produced under these conditions
and with these egalitarian agendas are the very locales where Syriacs, who arrived
with a heightened sense of their own difference, originally settled.

Processes of urban and social planning in Europe, however, have long been criticized. Today their idealistic visions for a utopian, egalitarian society are in crisis
because of a new set of perceived failures. In suburbs across the continent, the high-
rise husks of the bright modernist past—monuments to a society of the future that
never materialized—have become home to Europe's most recent arrivals: immigrants, who are increasingly ontologically linked not only to their geographies (on
the peripheries of major cities) but to the complicated, controversial discourses of
architecture and planning that created them. Unlike the suburbs of North America,

where individual homesteads, yards, and private cars were the imagined norm, these are the sites of a collective spirit expressed in a now-disparaged, common built environment.

Attending to the collision between the universalisms of modernist design and the particularisms of a group that has long self-defined as a minority, I take a close look at Södertälje and the buildings constructed there since the first Syriacs moved to the town in late 1967. I ask the following questions: Under what terms are new actors permitted to make changes to the urban environment? How have alternative *public spheres* expanded traditional notions of *public space*? How is equality reconciled with difference in the European city? Specifically, I focus on how architects, urban planners, and immigrant residents conflict and collaborate as they produce urban space according to differing agendas. Here, the story of public housing in Europe—especially as it intersects with immigration—aligns with none of the typical narratives of postutopian decline or grassroots resilience.

In this periphery that became a center, a universalism based in positivist conventions—reified in a Swedish planning and architectural practice that equated standardization with fairness—has interacted with forms of particularism that challenge these motives, a process that is also reflected in other Swedish and European suburbs today. As this development intersects with Sweden's international reputation as an ideal place for asylum seekers and immigrants, with traditions of humanitarianism and practices of multiculturalism that have been situated as a philosophical respect for difference, the perceived failures of these approaches have thus been damaging not only to the reputation of the projects themselves but to the self-image of the country.[6]

Segregation—ethnic or economic—is thus a particularly potent political problem in the Swedish milieu because social and spatial "solutions" to it have often been interlinked. This makes the country an ideal case study for considering how established relationships between equality and the built environment in Europe must be rethought, offering a much-needed alternative narrative about both segregation itself and "segregated neighborhoods." In Södertälje, then, buildings have not merely been constructed; rather, they have evolved as critical political acts, requiring both official designers and local residents to ask, Does equality require uniformity?

Waking from the Nightmare of Segregation

European modernist architecture and planning for suburbs have often been theorized as dystopic creation myths. Such negative narratives typically focus on the unfulfilled promises of activist designers to deliver equality and on the overscaled and generic formal qualities of the neighborhoods. Most damning, these areas are consigned to be territories of alienation, exclusion, and marginalization. Every time arson takes place, every time protest over social conditions is enacted, and every time criminal activity is reported in a European periphery, attention quickly turns to the "problem of the suburbs," whether in France, the United Kingdom, or the Nordic countries. Segregation and its specific geography outside city centers have long served as the supposed source of all manner of social, physical, and political problems.

Here, I offer a different perspective on European suburban architecture and planning by focusing on the generative capacities of "urban design from below," that is, the transformation of space at the urban scale through the slow accumulation of architectural projects that nondesigners initiate. I merge ethnographic and historical methods to examine how mid-twentieth-century European urban space-making practices—emphasizing formal uniformity and the supposed universalism of modernism as a means to create social equality—have been and are still being radically transformed as immigrants commission, design, and build new architectural projects. I focus on how physical changes to the city (enacted through initiatives "from below" but approved through official planning processes) have strengthened enclavization and have frequently required professional designers to rethink their assumptions and practices. Complicating the gloomy picture that has been endlessly reiterated in academic articles and books, popular accounts, and media coverage, I argue that segregated areas have served unnecessarily as scapegoats for other problems, and I draw attention to their often-overlooked generative potential.

The country of Sweden stands as a pinnacle of both a larger European "modern project" and its controversial aftermath. Swedish utopian aims for the built environment were more widespread (per capita) than anywhere else on the continent. In particular, the radically ambitious national project now known as "the Million Program" (*miljonprogrammet,* sometimes translated as "Million Homes Project") succeeded in constructing over one million dwelling units across the country from 1965 to 1974, when the population of Sweden was around eight million. Many of the suburban, high-rise "New Towns" created during the program were intended as middle-class—not social—housing, yet they nonetheless suffer from the intensely negative reputation of other housing areas across Europe that were explicitly intended for more vulnerable groups.

This has become particularly evident as these housing areas have become the domain of the numerous immigrants, refugees, and asylum seekers whom Sweden is internationally lauded for receiving but struggles to "integrate" domestically. Laments about suburbs prey on the self-confidence of a nation that imagines itself as the "best in the world" at planning for equality and humanitarianism. Architecture created through scientific principles specifically to provide both quality and equality has today become a domain mostly described in terms of social crisis and a need for intervention. I take a radically different approach to these concerns through a close-grained analysis of a Swedish town on the outskirts of Stockholm, where immigrants have been reshaping the urban environment physically and socially since their arrival in the mid-1960s.

Here, a pioneering group of newcomers encountered planning and integration regimes that sought to mesh them systematically into preexisting, hard-won structures of spatial and social life. Although utopian planning programs explicitly emphasized the erasure of difference, today this town displays ample visible evidence of its status as the global "capital" of the diasporic Syriac Orthodox Christians, who hail from across the Middle East. Long persecuted abroad for their minority religious beliefs, the Syriacs actively sought out the familiar safety of enclaves after their arrival in Sweden. This elective separation nonetheless fits neatly into accepted views about immigrants' negative social patterns.

Rather than accepting the terms of ongoing debates about segregation, which have been repeated from country to country and from decade to decade, this study foregrounds an underrepresented yet increasingly significant force in urban development. Using Södertälje as a case study, I ask how immigrants have altered the physical space of the built environment in ways that work against dominant design paradigms yet that often emerge through government channels. In this study of a new kind of planning process, I examine a series of immigrant-instigated projects and practices that developed in contrast to, but also in dialogue with, official planning and architecture. These architectural and urban interventions emerged from beyond professional design, yet they required legal approval through the planning process and the involvement of experienced architects. My research reveals that planners are more responsive to difference than earlier scholars have assumed, and it illustrates the ways in which the nightmare of segregation is already soothed by the realities of an unacknowledged but potent force: "urban design from below."

I therefore offer a new look into an old problem, noting that debates about how segregation should be solved have often focused on the very forces that are said to have created it: urban planning and architecture. This has occurred even as the designers who developed the urban environment in the mid-twentieth century frequently serve as the epistemological foes of their disciplinary descendants. Contemporary Swedish planners and architects seek to impose new paradigms on old spaces as they strive for justice in the urban environment. Despite their claims to the contrary, they most often do so in terms that echo their forebears. Equality, it seems, is still posited in terms of standardization, even as demographic conditions have shifted radically in Sweden and other European countries such as France and the United Kingdom. Planners use these methods, even as they try, ever more desperately, to incorporate forms of public participation that are often as limited in scope as they are superficial in outcome. Allowing immigrants' "voices" to be heard in public meetings has resulted in frustration on both sides, yet immigrants' inclusion has largely left the results of the planning process unchanged, even for major projects carried out over many years.

With a radical perspective on the boundaries of planning and architectural practice, this book focuses on what happens when immigrant actors react to the impotence of such professional solutions and the persistence of modernist design ideologies as they plan, design, and implement their own urban forms and formations. While stigmatized neighborhoods and unemployment are unequivocally problems for politicians, planners, and social workers, the difference between social exclusion and an enclave of choice is often difficult for Swedish planners and architects to see.

Paradoxically perhaps, new structures and enclaves that actually (and sometimes intentionally) accentuate difference—the nominal scourge of both past and present planning—offer something that top-down Swedish planning has been unable to deliver. In Södertälje, the architecture of difference serves as an unexpected contributor to true integration, creating a new planning praxis along the way. Rather than recycling the methods and approaches used in the past to work against segregated areas, lessons for urban planners and architects can instead be found in the processes that have created these dynamic new neighborhoods, the zones of the European future.

From Pretzel Town to Mesopotälje

On its streets and on the Internet, the town of Södertälje has acquired a variety of nicknames. These labels illustrate—in affectionate or disparaging terms—its commercial aspirations, its history, and, increasingly, its remarkable ethnic and cultural diversity. Some portray it in a positive light: "Pretzel Town" commemorates the town's local baked specialty (*kringla,* a sweet pretzel) and its bygone sale by "pretzel ladies" *(kringelgummor)* to passengers traveling on trains, and "SödertälYEAH!" uses English in an attempt to appeal to tourists and businesspeople. Others offer strictly negative assessments, such as "Tokstan" (Crazy Town, from *tokig,* "crazy," and *stad,* "city"), a reference to the mentally ill who lived in group homes in the town during the 1960s; or "Slöddertälje," which links a colloquial word for "mob" or "riffraff" *(slödder)* to the town's name. More recently, with the widespread arrival of immigrants from Turkey, Syria, Iraq, and Lebanon, nicknames have included "Little Baghdad," "Syriatälje," "Mosul-on-Stockholm,"[7] and "Mesopotälje."

Established in its earliest form in the seventh century, Södertälje is today a forty-three-minute commuter rail trip from Stockholm Central Station, and thousands of passengers travel to and from the town every day (Figure I.1). Lying at the junction of Lake Mälaren and the Baltic Sea, the town served as a critical meeting point for travelers as early as the Middle Ages. Since 1819, a picturesque canal has permitted the passage of both pleasure boats and floating cargo transits.[8] By the early part of the twentieth century, Södertälje was also well known as a bathing resort, attracting visitors from across the region but raising complaints from residents, who felt that their guests carelessly treated the city as a watery playground.[9]

As the bathing business wound down after World War II, industry took its place as Södertälje's primary economic base. Two companies predominated, then and

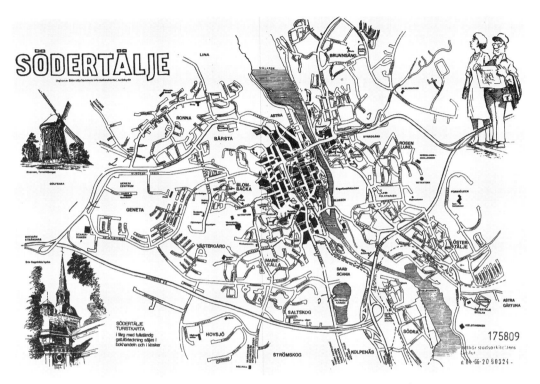

FIGURE I.1. Tourist map of Södertälje, 1984. Source: Stadsarkivet, Södertälje.

now: the pharmaceutical giant AstraZeneca, which long had facilities for both research and development activities and the production of medicines in the town (and
still has one of the world's largest pill factories there), and the automotive company
Scania AB.[10] Both occupy large swaths of the town's land, depicted as expansive gray
zones on official maps. This industry-dependent economy made Södertälje a prime
candidate for expansion during the Swedish state's Million Program. Helping attract
workers for its factories, the town acquired five new satellite suburbs during the
program: Fornhöjden, Geneta, Hovsjö, Ronna, and Saltskog (Map 2).[11] Modernist
multifamily housing and "rational" planning characterized these new areas, and they
shifted the geographic center of gravity toward the town's peripheries.

As Södertälje was remade into an *industristad* (city of industry),[12] Sweden's population of foreigners exploded, the newcomers coming both as laborers and as refugees or asylum seekers. The first Syriacs arrived in Sweden from Lebanon in 1967,
and three families were placed in Södertälje later that year.[13] By the mid-1970s, the
steady increase in Syriacs began to trouble the local authorities, yet efforts to quell
the trend of immigrants moving to the town proved futile. The closure of the West
German–Turkish guest-worker program in 1973 and conflicts in Cyprus and Lebanon made Sweden an attractive destination for thousands more, even as Södertälje's
industries suffered with the economic downturn of the 1970s.

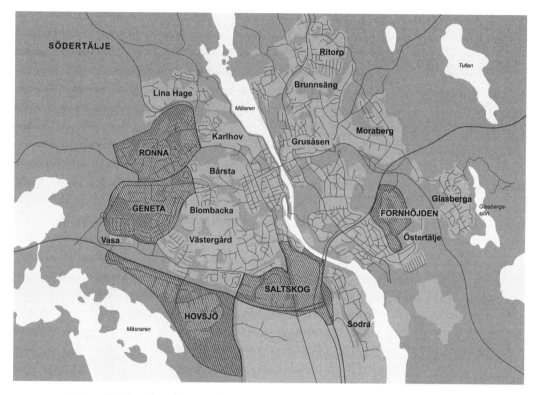

MAP 2. Map of Södertälje, showing the town's Million Program neighborhoods. Graphic design by Eliza Hearsum.

By the latter part of the 1970s, the Syriacs had become a significant presence in the town, which was attractively located close to Stockholm and had thousands of new but empty apartments. Most Syriacs concentrated in the high- and mid-rise apartment blocks of Million Program neighborhoods that had been intended for the now-departed industrial workers. This "segregation" was quickly rendered a major source of distress for planners (a concern that continues to the present day) and eventually led to the town's new reputation as an *invandrarstad* (immigrant city).[14] Even so, Södertälje lacks the extraordinary heterogeneity of other Swedish peripheries, where people from fifty to one hundred countries often live together in one neighborhood.[15] Specific identity groups increasingly dominate certain zones, however. In Stockholm, for example, Somalis concentrate in Rinkeby and Tensta, while Iranians form an ever-greater proportion of Kista's population. Södertälje's highly clustered population thus represents a potential future for other Swedish suburban locales.

Syriacs have also appeared to trouble the authorities in other ways. An early conflict emerged in the 1970s as some Syriacs rejected the designation *assyrier*, a Swedish term (equivalent to the English *Assyrian*) that predated their arrival and that officials bestowed upon the entire group in 1967. Over time, Syriacs acquired the label *assyrier/syrianer* in official Swedish parlance, a compound name that acknowledges continuing tensions between the group's two major contingents. On the one hand, the *assyrier* (an ethno-nationalist designation) claim Assyrian heritage; they are (in Sweden) largely Syriac Orthodox Christians, but smaller numbers of other Christian groups are also included in their ranks. On the other hand, the *syrianer* (an ethno-religious designation) base their identity primarily on their Syriac Orthodox Christian religion, though more recently many have also claimed Aramaean roots, as *araméer*. Bifurcated Södertälje reflects this, as many Syriac institutions in the town, from soccer teams to cultural clubs, come in twos.

Despite these conflicts, and the town's location on the extreme periphery of a European urban center, many Syriacs identify Södertälje as the capital of their worldwide diaspora. A steady stream of Syriac soccer fans, the religious faithful, and even honeymooners come to the town for a cultural experience. Satellite broadcasts in Neo-Aramaic Suryoyo extend from television stations in Södertälje to viewers in nearly eighty countries around the world.[16]

This global attention has increased Södertälje's reputation as a prime landing spot for Middle Eastern Christians more generally, precipitating a net population increase of just over eight thousand Syrian and Iraqi nationals from 2003 to 2015.[17] As I was told countless times, the town accommodated more refugees from Iraq than the United States and Canada combined, leading international journalists to marvel at this "town with a well-used welcome mat."[18] In April 2008, Anders Lago, at that time the mayor *(kommunstyrelsens ordförande)* of Södertälje, spoke at a session of the U.S. Congress to explain how this was possible. As a news report on Al Jazeera English on August 21, 2007, began, "The joke goes that Iraqis can't find Sweden on a map, but they all know how to get to Södertälje."[19] More recently, the town has absorbed a disproportionate number of the hundreds of Syrians coming to Sweden every month, fleeing the civil war in their home country.[20] Both Syrians and Iraqis frequently identify as Assyrian, Aramaean, Syriac Orthodox, or a combination, but they have been the target of new complaints—such as those concerning petty theft and general ignorance about how to live in Sweden—both from majority Swedes[21] and from Syriacs who arrived earlier.

Positive representations of Södertälje as a safe haven for Syrian and Iraqi asylum seekers and unlimited international humanitarianism are countered by extremely negative, often inflammatory local and national media coverage that highlights immigrant unemployment, organized crime, and low-quality education in schools where Swedish is supposedly a second language. A 2015 police report from Oslo, Norway, used Södertälje as a cautionary tale, claiming that the Syriac group living there was "a parallel society that works virtually as a separate state within a state. They have their own institutions, norms, laws, and regulations that have greater significance and influence on people's lives than the fundamental values in effect in

Sweden."[22] Anti-immigration parties that usually focus on Muslims have been active in the town, although Syriacs are Christians. In Södertälje, public arguments against new Syriac building projects recall the Islamophobic comments used against mosque building and veiling elsewhere. This prejudicial discourse snags the thread running through the supposedly secular nation-state of Sweden and its politics of integration and tolerant multiculturalism.

Today, nonresidents are often better acquainted with Södertälje's much-maligned suburban satellites than with its well-used canal and scenic downtown waterfront, complete with a boardwalk and resident ducks. The town's high-rise public housing holds a greater share of its public image than does its quickly developing stock of low-rise, luxury, single-family homes. Thanks to the international and national media's decision to focus on certain events, many people see Södertälje as a troubled city where cars burn openly on the streets, mafias control the local economy and make it a "black hole" for non-Syriac businesspeople (as one restaurateur in Stockholm described it to me), refugees live in overcrowded apartments, and a mentally ill man stabbed a young girl to death as she was on her way home. The Syriacs' ethnic segregation is considered unequivocally negative, and Södertälje is often presented as a worst-case scenario for integration politics. In February 2016, an unpublished police report was widely cited in the national media, identifying Sweden's "most dangerous areas" and including three neighborhoods in Södertälje as a "nearly lawless territory."[23]

For residents, however, such dramatic depictions are often remarkably disconnected from their everyday realities. Syriacs are "best in class" among immigrants, the Syriac journalist Rakel Chukri claimed in 2005.[24] As its many nicknames indicate, Södertälje complicates traditional categories. Just as it is a peripheral town, a capital city, and a suburb in one urban space, Södertälje is simultaneously a site of nostalgia, planning for the future, and cultural negotiation. Södertälje is a place where the collisions between differing visions of urban life are visible, particularly in the built environment; as such, it can lead the way forward in understanding how such processes develop in other European metropolitan settings.

Segregation or Enclavization?

Analyses of both segregation and suburbs are topical within social science, architectural and urban history, urban studies, and practice-based research in architecture and planning. Anthropologists have interrogated questions of identity, citizenship, and belonging in an increasingly plural Europe, from Berlin to Paris to London.[25] Cultural geographers have examined new territories of exclusion and alienation, sociologists have investigated immigrants in connection with questions of labor or housing, and political scientists have studied racism and the rise of xenophobic political parties on the national stage.[26] I connect to important works like these as

I examine relationships between policy and the symbolic dimensions of contemporary "segregated" spaces across the fifty years of Syriac presence in Sweden.

While ethnographic works on immigration in Europe often focus on Muslims, foregrounding the role of religious difference, my study instead concentrates on a Christian group. Their struggles to use and make space illustrate that xenophobic reactions to immigration have, in the end, less to do with disparities of faith and more to do with fear and control of "otherness" in general. The broad strokes of this study are thus drawn against the dismal backdrop of the rising power of one political party that is relatively new to the national stage, the anti-immigration Sweden Democrats (Sverigedemokrater); current moral crises over refugee reception; and high levels of unemployment among recent arrivals to Sweden. Even so, as I investigate how architecture and planning—from the scale of the neighborhood to that of the building—critically reshape everyday life in the city, I avoid the doomsday scenarios that often characterize accounts of immigrant-dominated Swedish neighborhoods. Enclavization is not always a negative force, and those who are geographically segregated are not always on the social margins.

The spatial politics of neoliberalism also inform my investigation of Sweden's move from an ever-expansive welfare state to one increasingly influenced by market forces. Here, individual versus group rights are often at the fore for both native-born and immigrant residents. The withdrawal of the Swedish state has reduced public investment in space and created what Brett Christophers terms a "monstrous hybrid"[27] in the Swedish housing market, and such tendencies and attitudes infiltrate other areas that were historically dominated by government action.

Following in the footsteps of anthropologists Setha Low and Michael Herzfeld, I am careful to attend to the tragedies of the social worlds destroyed by and the "evictions" resulting from the new power of the market.[28] At the same time, I argue that the state's attention to private investors and actors has sometimes unintentionally generated new space-making opportunities for immigrants. In this sense, I follow Margaret Crawford's caution that discourses of the public sphere and public space are "dominated by a narrative of loss . . . loss [that] is primarily perceptual, derived from extremely narrow and normative definitions of both public and space."[29] In this vein, I utilize an expanded definition of *public space,* including gathering spaces that may be privately owned or operated through public–private partnerships.

I specifically address the shifting relations between official urban planning and resident spatial practices, linking them to issues of power, hierarchy, legibility, and diversity. Rather than offering a strictly "urban anthropology"—one that takes place in the city—I view changes to the physical city as critical social and cultural acts themselves: an anthropology of the urban.[30] Drawing on urban planning theorist Leonie Sandercock's pioneering work on how planning and difference can be partners, I heed her call to challenge the "heroic model of planning" and move toward a new, more inclusive and flexible "postmodern praxis."[31] In this, I am also inspired by the work of planning theorist Abdul Khakee on the interface between immigration, urban planning, and participation in Sweden and by case studies from Lisa Kings and Lina Olsson that suggest that new forms of interactive planning practice are appearing in other Swedish peripheries.[32]

As Farha Ghannam writes in her ethnography of residents of modernist housing in Cairo, residents are "selectively appropriating modern discourses and images and using them to control and/or empower certain social groups."[33] I link this to Herzfeld's notion of "cultural intimacy,"[34] arguing that the Syriacs have selectively participated in the identity politics of the Swedish nation while also creating their own ideological and physical spaces. The acts and forms that the Syriacs conceal from Swedish planners and the confusion and shame that such planners experience as new class divisions emerge in their society despite their efforts to the contrary produce a dynamic that is at the core of this book.

Another key focus is on how the case of Södertälje demonstrates a need for new understandings of center–periphery relations. Raymond Williams described the "structures of feeling"[35] that reinforce class divisions: the city is portrayed as a site of corruption, and the countryside is posited as a bucolic idyll. I consider how logics of official planning are reconfigured as alternative publics turn these categories on their heads. Viewing the Greater Stockholm urban region holistically and ignoring traditional notions of center and edge, I draw on Thomas Sieverts's notion of "cities without cities," where these boundaries are blurred, making the country and the city symbiotic.[36] If the suburb is cast as external to the urban center, Södertälje redefines this by inverting such categories. Center–periphery relations repeat themselves at several scales. Just as the most important Syriac buildings are found not in the town's older center but on the edges of its edges, both geographically and symbolically, so, too, is Södertälje both a town on the extreme outskirts of Stockholm and the Syriac diasporic capital.

As I move from the scale of the city to that of its architecture, I connect symbolic and formal expressions in the built environment to forms of what Pierre Bourdieu labels "distinction."[37] Choices about the elements of the house and the neighborhood, for instance, offer residents opportunities to demonstrate their class positions. In Södertälje, Syriacs blend sculptures and paintings displaying themes from ancient Assyria and Orthodox Christianity with the latest consumer goods found, for example, at interior-design expositions at the Stockholm International Fairs pavilion or seen on subtitled versions of the American program *Extreme Home Makeover* on Swedish television. In so doing, they redefine their homes as spaces of distinction that separate them, both in status and in form, from the "classless" (but stigmatized) Million Program dwellings that they inhabited in earlier years.

New buildings also offer evidence of Syriacs' intentions to remain in Södertälje and to modify their relations with the Swedish state and its discomfort with the spatial separation or concentration of identity groups. Historian Abidin Kusno writes, "The city, while embodying the state, is forming and transforming national unity."[38] I link this to political theorist Giorgio Agamben's notion of the refugee as a "border concept." Agamben argues that the refugee "unhinges the old trinity of state/nation/territory" that defines "nativity."[39] Both domestic spaces and institutional structures (such as churches and social clubs) have been built with expensive materials and after long-winded negotiations with municipal planners, project architects, and even contractors, who have sometimes resisted building as clients' drawings prescribed. Syriac building projects uncouple nation and state, opening up new dialogues. As the Syriacs (who were once refugees or asylum seekers) redefine the meaning of home and nation in Sweden, they also recalibrate what it means to produce space in a condition of exile.[40] This creates a new form of *diaspora space*— a term typically used to describe large-scale social networks across oceans—that is both local and urban.[41]

Further, these complex projects are built not merely for today but for the children and grandchildren to come, further solidifying Södertälje's status as the Syriac capital. Anthropologist Annika Rabo writes in her study of Syriac family networks, "In many of the interviews, it's not 'Sweden' that is identified as the homeland but rather Södertälje. . . . There is no doubt that Södertälje is perceived to be the center of '*syriansk/assyriskhet*' [*syrian/assyrier*-ness]."[42] Each new building, whether made for one family or for the entire community, remakes the itinerant Syriac diaspora— defined as a community in motion—as a settler society.

Writing in the Swedish newspaper *Expressen,* Rakel Chukri once said that Södertälje was "as close to a capital as any stateless ethnic group has been able to have,"[43] and the Syriac journalist, filmmaker, activist, and author Nuri Kino has stated that "Many Södertälje Christians themselves don't understand how special their town is until they travel to other countries."[44] Refugees fleeing conflicts in Syria and Iraq and landing in Södertälje, then, follow the lead and the narratives already established by Syriac predecessors who came from Turkey, Lebanon, and elsewhere. As in every other capital, nationalist forms of expression in the built environment, and changes as newer residents arrive from abroad, have been necessary in Södertälje.

Critical to these spatialities of membership are ideas of "publics" and "public spaces," and I draw in particular on the theories of Jürgen Habermas and his interlocutors.[45] Habermas's ideal public sphere is built out of the rational consensus occurring in open, democratic debates. Yet, according to political theorist Nancy Fraser, to believe that such forums are "accessible to everyone," "of concern to everyone," and "pertaining to a common good or shared interest" is naive.[46] She contends that Habermas "fails to examine other, nonliberal, nonbourgeois, competing public spheres,"[47] assuming a "space of zero-degree culture."[48] Fraser's "*subaltern counterpublics,*" comprising "women, workers, peoples of color, and gays and lesbians,"[49] are omitted from these conversations—and often from the very spaces in which they occur.

Swedish planners of the mid-twentieth century sought explicitly to expand the public sphere through a welfare state that achieved universality through the elimination of class differences. When the Syriacs arrived to this precocious new world, they were already defined as an alternative public, both in their countries of origin as a religious minority and again in Sweden as "refugees" and later as perennial "immigrants." While these categories may appear to be rigid in state discourse, I consider how the Syriacs bent and reshaped both publics and public spaces after their arrival. Their building projects have been predicated on "urban ethnic encounters"[50] between planners and residents; at the same time, they have reconfigured the boundaries of both groups.

Literary and social critic Michael Warner contends that the public is developed through "participation," does not require a test for admission, and always has "unclear addressees."[51] This makes time and embodiment forms of "poetic world making," leaving the boundaries of membership open and flexible.[52] The Swedish categories in which Syriacs were organized after their arrival in this nation-state—in the midst of a national process of anxiously codifying both its citizens and its spaces—ultimately have little effect on these immigrants' ability to participate in new forms of "poetic" city making. Warner contends that "counterpublics are *spaces* of circulation in which it is hoped that the poesis of scene making will be transformative, not replicative merely."[53] If immigrants are regarded as subalterns in the context of Swedish society writ large, then Syriac publics constituted through uses, claims, and the creation of the built environment may transform the larger social worlds through which their varying memberships pass.

Public space may function similarly, with the Swedish planners' idealistic notions of imagining playing out against the material, urban, and spatial needs of immigrants. This links the study to the writings of philosopher Michel de Certeau and sociologist Henri Lefebvre. For de Certeau, "spatial practice" is temporary and opportunistic; Lefebvre sees it as permanently transformative, with space and society as mutually constitutive.[54] I therefore also connect to notions of "everyday urbanism."[55] This theory argues in part that relevant, innovative forms of contemporary urbanism are generated through spatial practice, often without designers. The "high" politics and planning and "low" occupation and use of the city should thus be seen in dialectical terms.

As I concentrate on the perceived failures of modernist urbanism and public housing projects in particular, I recall cultural historian Celeste Olalquiaga's thought that modernism has "aged . . . leaving only the *dusty shells of its dreams behind.* In the midst of this obsolescence, however, new ways of life emerge, more skeptical of those visions that represent the world as moving in only one direction."[56] I apply this view to the broader scope of European suburbs of the twenty-first century, arguing that their center–periphery relations and the agendas of both experts and users are being remade.

Scholars such as James Holston and Faranak Miraftab provide key theoretical tools to consider "insurgency" in the context of city making.[57] Drawing on lessons learned from explorations of the urban triumphs of those living in favelas or slums, I consider such adaptive and emergency approaches among Syriacs in Södertälje. My analysis departs from these traditions, however, in that I include new architectural projects that have traveled through the official ledgers of the Swedish planning regime. This extends the study beyond such insurgent acts and into the realm of formal design. While Lefebvre offered his notion of "differential space" as a corrective to the "abstract space" of capitalism,[58] I here employ the concept as it unfolds in a semisocialist context. In Södertälje, immigrant "users" have become producers of space, questioning the regulatory assumptions that made welfare-state cities and that continue to govern them.

Recent architectural and urban histories of European social housing and modernist urban planning have explored architects' and planners' agendas in relation to design discourse, collaborations between the state and social scientists, and the politics of design.[59] I draw on these studies as I examine how spaces were planned with specific ideological intentions about citizenship, and I link them to the forms that resulted in their use, transformation, and design by alternative publics. Rather than treat the design and construction of the built environment and social factors as separate spheres, I examine how immigration to Europe has necessitated the expansion of traditional understandings of European public space, monuments, and residential architecture. I use ethnographic, architectural, and urban methods to rethink questions of segregation, studying both the development of the city's social and physical forms as a dialogue between "designers" and "residents," and the slippage between these categories.

Chapter Overview

Questions of equality and clashes over its definition are critical for understanding both the conflicts and constructions in the built environment of Södertälje and the way segregation became the bane of the city, the scourge of its planning, and the target of so many new social and spatial programs. Chapter 1, "Standards and Separatism: The Swedish Million Program, Syriac Enclaves, and Equality," examines the contrasts between agendas for architectural and urban space of the twentieth-century Swedish welfare state and the urban traditions of the Syriacs. I provide an overview of the so-called Million Program, built from 1965 to 1974, which saw Sweden develop one million new dwelling units for the burgeoning middle classes at a time when the population of the country approached only eight million. I argue that the program sought to enforce social equality through formal uniformity, a cultural inclination still evident in the aisles of the Swedish multinational furniture chain IKEA. Having experienced discrimination and persecution in the Middle East, the Syriacs carried with them to Sweden architectural and urban forms—such as residences in close proximity to family members—that reflect those that allowed their survival throughout the twentieth century. These tendencies were emboldened in the 1970s when agents of the Swedish state, carrying out new policies of "integration" (rather than assimilation), encouraged Syriacs to retain cultural markers. I focus on the contradictions between definitions of equality in Swedish policies and among Syriac immigrants, offering insight into the early and ongoing disparities in attitudes toward ethnic enclaves.

Chapter 2, "Visible Cities, Invisible Citizens: Service and Citizenship in the *Centrum*," zooms down to the urban scale of the city of Södertälje. As the dreams of the welfare state faded with the economic crises of the 1970s, New Towns became ghost towns. Syriacs moved to Södertälje's empty Million Program neighborhoods by the thousands. As nativists sought to battle them in public space, police and other authorities encouraged the group to become invisible, and Syriacs retreated to Södertälje's new satellites, resuming their familiar historical pattern of protective enclaves. They adapted welfare-state spaces—such as the Workers' Educational Association (Arbetarnas Bildningsförbund), remodeled for use by a Syriac nationalist club, and a Lutheran church in the town center, retrofitted for Orthodox practice—retaining forms and programmatic functions but shifting their meanings and primary clientele. This suggests that "generic," modular modernist architecture and urban design were more successful at accommodating difference than has typically been acknowledged.

From the 1980s onward, Syriacs shed the identity of passive recipients of social programs and disciplinary spaces and emerged as the active designers of a new urban landscape. In chapter 3, "Making Mesopotälje: Sacred and Profane 'Diaspora Space' in the City," I examine theoretical constructions of diaspora space—a term usually used solely as a metaphor or to connote expansive, pan-oceanic geographies—in connection with Syriac monumental architectural spaces for the Syriac Orthodox Church and for the Assyriska and Syrianska soccer clubs, sacred and profane respectively. These social institutions developed during the 1970s and 1980s, but it took decades to build dedicated physical spaces for their activities. Today, these spaces are the sites where visiting Syriac honeymooners and soccer fans congregate and where, I argue, diaspora space becomes material. Center–periphery relations, both across the city and globally, are reshaped in these sites.

Critically revisiting the classic ethnographic topics of weddings and funerals, chapter 4, "'Södertälje Is a Theater': The Performance of Propriety and Ritual Infrastructure," focuses on both permanent spaces and temporary spatial practices associated with these significant ritual moments linking community, family, and religion. Over time, the Syriacs' repeated visible and audible uses of the city for these rites of passage began to contrast with the imposed silences of the 1970s and 1980s, redefining everyday life through new infrastructure. Urban spaces have become backdrops for a role-playing game with an ever-attentive audience, as Syriacs metamorphose between audience members and stage actors and continually reinscribe social expectations about personal bodily and social propriety. While many members of the group continue to reside in modernist enclaves and, according to planners' definitions, are "segregated," new ritual spaces and practices reshape the geographies of their city as members of the diaspora settle, wed, and die.

In chapter 5, "Greetings from Hollywood! Enclaves and Participation 'from the Ghetto to the Mansion,'" I focus on several new and controversial Syriac-dominated neighborhoods of custom-designed and formally elaborate single-family houses. In the 1990s, more flexible forms of planning reflected the emerging political shift to the right and its attendant focus on individualism while also addressing the long-standing Swedish desire for single-family houses, partly suppressed during the Million Program. The logistical space created through new flexible plans, however, was implicitly intended for middle-class majority Swedes. The new Syriac-dominated neighborhoods that emerged instead have confounded planners, requiring them to rethink their understandings of the links between poverty and ethnic segregation and to reformulate the boundaries of participation in the planning process. Syriac architectural displays of difference and affluent enclaves—segregated by design—have also enabled new forms of professional practice.

In chapter 6, "Safety in Numbers: Tolerance and Norms in Syriac Design," I examine how the so-called Swedish Standard—where national norms defined both rational design and questions of taste and beauty—intersects with new forms and standards that Syriacs have developed in houses, churches, banquet halls, and other buildings in Södertälje. In conversation with architects, interior designers, and clients, I focus on how questions of tolerance and norms in building construction relate to larger debates about what forms should be allowed to appear in the city, how taste and distinction are expressed in the built environment, and who may contribute to the urban image. While designers describe their projects as occurring between two systems, they also laud the projects as spaces of release from the strict oversight of an otherwise-intransigent planning process. This architecture of difference uses imported materials and innovative appearances that have thereby become metaphors for debates about nationalism and citizenship.

In the aggregate, the Syriacs' discrete projects have changed the way the city functions, both in material space and in the practices of the town's experts, a development that I theorize as "urban design from below." In the conclusion to the book, I outline this phenomenon as a space between the "top-down" (designs and plans created through official means) and the "bottom-up" (forms of community activism without an effect on the *form* of physical space), as so-called "users" become planners and designers. The conclusion compares change in Sweden—seen as representing best practices for both design and immigration policies—to suburban transformations elsewhere. Discrete projects commissioned by immigrants have altered one town and its urban form overall and over time, building by building. As urban design from below crosses the lines of specific religious and ethnic identities or nation-states, it underscores the fact that city plans—often developed for universal citizens, whether they are found in Stockholm, Paris, or London—are revolutionized through new formations of the public. As I link this case to emerging patterns of construction and destruction in other cities, I point the way forward to understanding how enclaves may be a productive force in the future of European societies and cities. This new approach to planning (not as a custom but as a mode of thinking) through urban design from below will shape the urban twenty-first century in meaningful, generative, and wonderfully unfamiliar ways.

CHAPTER ONE

Standards and Separatism

The Swedish Million Program, Syriac Enclaves, and Equality

CAN DWELLING BE A PRACTICE OF CITIZENSHIP? Can design create social equality? As Syriac Christians arrived in Sweden from across the Middle East in the late 1960s, they were unaware that Swedish planners and politicians had recently answered these questions in the affirmative. Syriacs came to Scandinavia after escaping centuries of persecution and everyday discrimination associated with their minority religious identity. In such settings, they often resided in villages in small, tight-knit groups, subsisting on agriculture or the sale of handicrafts. Homes and village enclaves centered on relations with the extended family and on the church, in stark contrast to the prevailing Swedish models with which they were to come into contact.

After the rise of the Turkish national state in the early twentieth century, violent attempts to eradicate minority groups after World War I gave way to everyday economic hardships and social stigmatization by the 1950s and 1960s. Many Syriacs escaped through emigration. A prosperous stronghold for Christianity, Lebanon became their "Switzerland of the Middle East," but naturalization there was not possible.[1] When the World Council of Churches offered 205 stateless Christians in Beirut, most of them Syriac Orthodox, the chance to relocate to Sweden, council representatives described it as a land of fellow believers. Religion had long been the Syriacs' defining group identity, and Sweden thus seemed to represent an opportunity for cultural acceptance and safety available in neither Turkey nor Lebanon.[2] Many had mythical visions of their new host nation as a land of polar bears, snow, Christians, and job opportunities.

The Sweden to which the first Syriacs landed in 1967, however, was on a path toward its own form of utopia, one in which Christianity did not figure prominently.[3] Here, equality was largely predicated on the erasure of class differences and on a social order in which the secular nation-state trumped both family and locality. With seeds in the 1930s, the Swedish welfare state as a national project reached its heyday in the 1960s, taking physical shape in what is now known as the Million Program, the national housing scheme that built one million dwelling units from

1965 to 1974. Its uniform housing and "rationalized" neighborhood plans formed didactic spaces where modern citizenship would be practiced in specific ways. The Million Program served as the zenith of governmental physical intervention, and measures to distribute a new Swedish prosperity continued into the 1970s, drawing on extensive normative research.

As the state ordered away squalor and poverty through social and spatial planning, new forms of sanguine nationalism arose in a Sweden now so prosperous that it could afford to give charity (and housing) to others. Politicians considered the once-fragile modern project robust enough to share, but they intended to choose its beneficiaries methodically and to receive newcomers meticulously. In this spirit, the national government deliberately transformed the previously unregulated influx of temporary foreign workers into a strictly managed immigration regime during the late 1960s, ostensibly requiring work permits before arrival from 1967 onward.[4]

As a quota system offered safe haven to refugees while controlling their numbers and permitting their orderly processing (via training camps) into the welfare state, Sweden's global reputation as a bastion of humanitarianism gained currency, becoming a source of national pride and even self-righteousness. The country practiced "assimilation" into the 1960s; immigrants would merely require indoctrination before getting on with their new (Swedish) lives.[5] Refugees arrived as *utlänningar* (foreigners), but the reception regime developed from the assumption that newcomers would, naturally, want to be Swedes themselves.[6] Residing among Swedes in the physical spaces of the Million Program would buttress this already-convincing argument.

Across the Middle East, however, Syriacs typically lived as a minority ethnic and religious group in enclaves. This ensured their safety from the considerable and repeated threats coming from beyond the walls of their villages or neighborhoods. As this association between seclusion and security reemerged in Sweden, it collided with both discourses and forms of then-current Swedish planning, especially the links between spatial and social equality and the belief that newcomers should be geographically dispersed. Here I explore why (to use Ulf Björklund's key phrasing) Syriacs moved "north to another country,"[7] investigating how the Swedish "norm" and "standard" met a group for whom social and environmental isolation was a way of life.

While these two competing spatial logics were both posed in opposition to forms of violence—the dirt and chaos of urban poverty on the one hand, genocide and persecution on the other—they operated according to differing principles. Swedish efforts centered on categorization and distribution; the Syriac approach emphasized enclosure, withdrawal, and the hermetic. As Swedish officials sought to introduce physical and social norms to newly arrived Syriacs, they imagined themselves as giving them the gift of equality, freeing them from the entrenched structures of their recent past. For Syriacs, this magnanimity appeared genuine, but the philosophy of distribution—particularly when Swedish officials sought to keep members of the group from concentrating in one place—clashed with their own approaches to domestic life. As the First Plane[8] with Syriacs shut off its engines on the tarmac in southern Sweden in 1967, cranes were lifting prefabricated concrete panels to form the walls of new Million Program housing elsewhere. The stakes of equality were critical for both groups, but their spatial and social manifestations differed radically.

Cleaning "Dirt Sweden"

In the early twentieth century, Sweden was one of Europe's most impoverished nations, with an extremely low housing standard. A lack of electricity and running water met overcrowding to produce what one 1938 radio series termed "Dirt Sweden."[9] Arriving en masse from the impoverished countryside to urban centers, migrants found jobs but miserable living conditions in cities unprepared for their arrival.[10] Because of this accelerated urbanization, which occurred later but proceeded faster than in most other European countries,[11] shantytowns peppered the landscapes of many Swedish urban zones. Magnus, a young Swedish planner, told me, "Even all the way up to the 1950s, you could get paid to collect rat tails, which was proof that you'd killed rats." Urban squalor was pervasive.

Political foundations for a new society were laid as the Social Democratic Party (Socialdemokraterna) rose to national power in 1932. They remained at the helm until 1976, a lengthy interval giving them ample time to enact wide-ranging policies. But not until after World War II was the *folkhem* (literally, "people's home")—the Swedish term that came to encapsulate the early welfare state—transformed from a metaphor wielded by visionary politicians into a social, economic, and urban reality. The Social Democratic politician Per Albin Hansson first used the term in an address to the second chamber of Parliament on January 18, 1928:[12]

During celebrations and even sometimes on everyday occasions, we happily speak of society—the state, the municipality—as though it is for all of us the common home, the people's home *[folkhemmet]*,[13] the citizen's home *[medborgarhemmet]*. . . . The foundations of the home are camaraderie and a feeling of togetherness. The good home knows no privileged or neglected ones, no favorites and no stepchildren. No one looks down on anyone else there. No one tries to gain at another's expense; the one who is strong does not oppress and exploit the one who is weak. In the good home, equality, consideration, cooperation, helpfulness prevail. If applied to the great people's and the citizen's home *[folk- och medborgarhemmet]*, this would mean breaking down all the social and economic barriers that currently divide citizens into privileged and neglected, into rulers and dependents, exploiters and exploited.

Swedish society is not yet the good citizen's home *[medborgarhemmet]*. Certainly, a formal equality predominates: equality in political rights. But it remains a class society socially, and a dictatorship of the few prevails economically. . . . If Swedish society is going to become a good citizen's home, class differences must be eliminated, social welfare must be developed, economic leveling must occur, the workers must be given a share of economic management, democracy must be implemented and applied even socially and economically.[14]

Hansson's *folkhem* eventually stood for the new and increasingly socialist direction in which the Social Democratic leadership took Sweden during the twentieth century.[15] Even so, in 1938 a pact between trade unions and companies was signed, known as the Saltsjöbaden agreement, and the "spirit of Saltsjöbaden" described the atmosphere of consensus and cooperation between labor and capital that then emerged. This collaboration became a key pillar of the *folkhem*. As a metonym, *folkhem* illustrates Swedish successes in remaking the country from a place of class and housing disparities to a new modern welfare state whose socioeconomic differences have ostensibly been leveled.[16]

The new "classless" society of the *folkhem* would also work against the discriminations of inheritance that had spawned revolutions across Europe. Sweden's leaders hoped to avoid such ruptures and to alleviate the human miseries of industrialization through a systematic approach and "comprehensive planning."[17] Everyone would have work that paid the bills, and everyone would have rights, such as access to public education.[18] Rather than living in the tenements of New York or the slums of London, citizens of the modern Swedish state would have modern Swedish lives in modern Swedish apartments.[19] Social Democratic dreams were increasingly viewed through the Technicolor hues of financial prosperity, and the diminutive size of the country made comprehensive intervention viable.

As these reforms progressed, the Social Democrats routinely utilized the *folkhem* as a powerful rhetorical tool. In her seminal book *Att lägga livet tillrätta* (To set life right), historian Yvonne Hirdman describes its social resonance:

That the native land was likened to a home was, in actual fact, nothing new within the Swedish labor movement. The image of workers as the stepchildren of society—as though they were, like Cinderella, exploited and scorned without having any rights—is an old image. But it had constantly been a negative image: the country is not yet "the good home." The term *folkhem,* on the other hand, is a positive, utopian emblem.

Certainly, it can—and should—be described as a metaphor for the entire Social Democratic construction. It was an image of a society as an immense fellowship, where solidarity and helpfulness would prevail. It was also an image of the sensible, and thereby of the socialist, in the sense of an economically and socially just society.[20]

This model of justice struck an unusual balance: it coupled socialist programs with democratic politics and selected forms of capitalist enterprise to produce the so-called Swedish Middle Way, a unique balance of economic and political systems predicated on a new classless consumer society.[21]

In this political space, as ethnologists Jonas Frykman and Orvar Löfgren write, "The word *class* became an unpleasant and old-fashioned expression. To the extent that one talked about class, it was mostly about the growing middle class, which sometimes seemed to include most of the old bourgeoisie, the new middle strata, and even parts of the working class. Many regarded the middle class as the seed of the future classless Sweden."[22] This also reflected a Swedish past that, unlike that of other European countries, did not privilege strict social hierarchies.[23] The country had long had a relatively small group of influential nobles and a strong tradition of peasant empowerment that included land ownership. Folding agrarian structures into the new *folkhem* was natural, as Eva Österberg writes:

> Unlike those in most European countries, many peasants in Sweden owned their own land from the Middle Ages onward. They were continuously represented in the Parliament from the sixteenth century. The main conflict in the society was fundamentally about relations between state power and the peasants, not between peasants and the feudal nobility or between the state and the citizenry.[24]

These traditions helped focus state action on the leveling of the disparities between existing socioeconomic classes. The Social Democrats would be, if not the creators of the social spirit, at least the ones who reframed and put it into a new order for the modern era, as Frykman and Löfgren write:

> The feeling of class neutrality, of impartiality and government representation, is a phenomenon that gives civil servants a special position. They play an important role in the formation and continuation of ideas about the classless *folkhem*. Here, a bridge was created between senior doctors and postal workers, between deputy directors and railroad conductors.[25]

In this Social Democratic vision, then, differences based on family, education, or profession would be eliminated,[26] and prosperity would be delivered to all. Architects and designers were central to this development, allowing a radical social, political, and material transformation that took place in Sweden from the 1930s to the 1960s.

A confluence between policies for the spatial and the social allowed the state to intervene in everything from consumer tastes to family structures to reproduction. Eventually, carefully researched designs for the built environment evolved from visionary experiments into everyday ways of life in Sweden, extending from the *folkhem*'s housing of the 1930s, 1940s, and 1950s and ultimately reaching their apex

in the construction of the Million Program from 1965 to 1974. As the Social Democrats made the provision of housing for everyone—not just the disadvantaged—
a centerpiece of their policies, they made this *people's home* a literal one for a new
Swedish middle class.

"Le Corbusier with a Shot-Glass of Aquavit"

Given widespread overcrowding in cities and dilapidated dwellings, politicians
quickly turned to the construction of a new built environment as a key tool for
eliminating class differences and to counter Sweden's low birth rate. Two prominent
Social Democrats in particular argued for the family home as a site of intervention:
the Nobel Prize–winning sociologist Alva Myrdal and her husband, also a Nobel
Prize winner, the economist Gunnar Myrdal.[27] In their 1934 book *Kris i befolkningsfrågan* (Crisis in the population question), the Myrdals argued for the replacement
of much of the existing housing stock, writing, "Controlling births is in fact the
individual families' method to try to 'solve' overcrowding's social problems. . . . This
is a liberal economic solution to the problem, where the 'individual initiative' has
taken the place of public regulation."[28] In their view, the state should encourage
families to expand through the provision of affordable, high-quality housing. For
the Myrdals, the physical environment was an inseparable part of the practice of
socially engineering ideal citizens.

Such reframings of the housing question coincided with the professionalization of
urban planning across Europe, remaking what was a gentleman's avocation into a
new tool of state power, as illustrated in the Swedish Town Planning Acts of 1907 and
1931 and in the 1931 approval of new building ordinances (replacing those established
in 1874).[29] Suddenly, overcrowding, low-quality housing, and other by-products of
the urbanization that came in the wake of late-nineteenth-century industrialization
could be tackled with pragmatic and potent tools.[30] Urban planning would solve
the massive Swedish housing shortage and come to the aid of the embarrassing
number of citizens living in poverty, creating in the process a new modern state
worthy of international admiration—a utopia.

Although "Garden City" models emphasizing a balance between city and country
gained popularity,[31] they required large swaths of land for self-sufficient communities
with common property and copious green space.[32] This limited their effectiveness
for the production of mass housing, creating space for ideas from the pan-European
group Congrès internationaux d'architecture moderne (CIAM). For CIAM, creating
modern cities meant replacing old urban centers with carefully planned, high-rise,
multiuse buildings and green space, sunlight, and fresh air.[33] The result, as anthropologist James Holston describes, would be "a city of salvation."[34] Most important
for Swedish planning was CIAM's "Functional City," divided into four types of
zones: housing, work, recreation, and traffic. Strict spatial separation would eradicate

and sanitize the medieval city of heterogeneous uses and winding streets, just as Swiss architect Le Corbusier's unrealized 1933 plan for Stockholm razed most of the historic city to make way for high-rise buildings and open space.[35]

CIAM's ideas gained currency in Europe in the period following World War II, offering a model to replace urban fabric ruined by bombings and battles. Sweden had remained neutral during the war and escaped its destruction, yet functionalism still achieved prominence, owing to the emerging sense that it could have a strong common agenda with Social Democratic politics.[36] As architectural historian Johan Rådberg notes:

> Both architects and politicians saw as their objective the eradication of nineteenth-century urban environments, which were regarded as expressions of an unjust social system. The backyards and the garbage cans, the wooden shacks and the bedbugs, everything had to go. Instead, they would build modern, rational, hygienic housing. For politicians, it was an important symbolic issue, a way to show that they were serious about promises to build a better and fairer society. Then the functionalist urban development project—"cities as ocean liners"—fused with the political project— "*folkhemmet.*"[37]

For different reasons, then, design ideas being used to rebuild war-ravaged Europe also suggested methods for making new urban centers and mass housing in Sweden. The emphasis on the large scale in functionalism also implied multifamily living.[38] But this needed to be sold to the public.

To this end, the didactic and spectacular 1930 Stockholm Exhibition of Arts, Crafts, and Home Industries opened with great fanfare, introducing functionalist ideas and new consumer goods to the Swedish population. As cultural geographer Allan Pred writes, "Here was the summer-long spectacle as national project. Here a program for progress was made concrete. Here a politically charged ideology was given material expression."[39] While architectural historian Henry Russell Hitchcock and architect Philip Johnson called this "the International Style" two years later,[40] this was not by any means an *international* exhibition, being limited to Swedish designers. As one visitor reportedly described it in a 1930 journal interview, "It's international but with a Swedish aroma; one might say Le Corbusier with a shot-glass of aquavit."[41] The exhibition celebrated the dawning of the modern Swedish nation for audiences both at home and abroad.

Marketing functionalism as necessary for the social evolution of the Swedish nation, the exhibition aimed specifically to alter the taste of modern consumer-citizens. However, "*Funkis,*" as the fairgoers immediately nicknamed functionalism, was treated with suspicion, as visitors scornfully labeled the exhibition and its buildings "*Lådstan*" (Box City) and "*Rakstugan*" (the Barbershop, but also a play on the literal meaning of *rak,* "straight," and *stuga,* "cottage").[42] Despite the negative public response to *Funkis* during the exhibition, the architects and influential intellectuals behind the project—Uno Åhrén, Gunnar Asplund, Wolter Gahn, Sven Markelius, Gregor Paulsson, and Eskil Sundahl—published their functionalist manifesto, *acceptera,* in 1931.[43] The movement, they contended, was not merely one of aesthetic taste; rather, as indicated by the title, it should be "accepted" as a way of life. Recognizing the potential interplay between design and the social agendas of the modern Swedish state, they wrote, "The most important thing is that *society takes care of certain elements in the lives of individuals* that were formerly their own responsibility or that did not exist at all."[44] As a de facto campaign promise from the Social Democrats,[45] then, the exhibition illustrated designs for Swedish cities and homes that would shape not only furniture and lighting fixtures but the lifestyles, behaviors, and subjectivities of the nation's citizens.[46]

Standardization—enabled through streamlined, machine-age production—operated as a key link between consumption and citizenship: a new market where collective tastes should trump individual ones. Helena Mattsson and Sven-Olov Wallenstein remark that Åhrén explicitly made this connection in 1929:

> Personality has two parts, he suggests, the universal and the individual, and the first represents the "classless" object (the commodity outside of the logic of fetishism), while the second is the consumer item in its "fake" form. In other words, individual taste can, quite easily, be satisfied through standardization to the extent that the consumer develops the universal side of his personality, all of which will lead to the formation of a subjectivity rooted in the collective.[47]

Standard forms also supported a key polemic of *acceptera,* as the authors argued that three housing types would dominate in the future: the rented apartment, the single-family home, and "*the family hotel,*" also known as the collective house *(kollektivhuset).*[48] The last type also permitted common spaces for certain functions, such as kitchens, improving upon poor conditions and creating cooperative living environments at the same time.

Scaling Up and Down

Both designers and politicians endorsed this confluence between architecture and social engineering, but not until after World War II was Sweden sufficiently stable to experiment with new relations between the individual and the collective at the urban scale. Promoters considered the unbuilt periphery of Swedish cities a key site for potential experimentation, yet concerns surfaced about the willingness of the recently urbanized Swedish public to move there, as the authors of *acceptera* acknowledged: "Many have believed that they would be living in a cabin in the forest when they moved out to the suburbs. But as the sites must be exploited so intensively, buildings, not nature, will predominate. . . . And, above all, let us not believe that because we are living on the periphery of the city we are farmers."[49]

Beginning in the 1940s and 1950s, efforts moved toward the creation of "rationalized" suburbs, drawing on the Garden City, CIAM, and German *Siedlungen* (housing estates)[50] models to create housing and neighborhood spaces with collective functions and program pieces, from health clinics to post offices to laundry rooms. Lena Magnusson Turner notes that "the housing question became a part of population politics, and housing was built on the basis of ideas about public education and healthier lifestyles."[51] Urban planning offered an opportunity to create new public spaces for the new public sphere, as one national government report accentuated:

> The city plan and the environment for daily life that it creates cannot provide only comfort and beauty but can also contribute to the development of the desirable features of citizenship for a democratic community. One means that the goal of city planning policy is, ultimately, to create the conditions for "the good life" through a good environment.[52]

In this spirit, peripheries formed the tabula rasa missing from urban centers; there, discrete citizens could be sculpted into collectives at multiple scales: national, municipal, and neighborhood. New plans meant that a modern life could be built without visible class differences.

With the Stockholm subway system on the cards as early as 1941, "neighborhood unit" planning—developed in 1929 by the American Clarence Perry—offered an attractive model for disseminating these ideas (as self-sufficient satellites) along new transit lines.[53] Perry's neighborhood units would house populations of between six thousand and ten thousand, with prescribed distances between housing and schools, the dedication of 10 percent to open space, and employment on site.[54] The symbiotic unions of residents and space in the neighborhood unit—translated into Swedish as *grannskapsenhet*—joined the planning apparatus of the Swedish state in parallel with new national laws emphasizing the political collective and the spatial standard as key partners. A 1946 proposition allowed state loans for housing construction but required borrowers to adhere to the standards outlined by the government.[55] The Building Act of 1947 introduced the municipal planning monopoly, allowing each municipality to reject plans for public—and private—developments if they were not beneficial for the larger society, and a new statute in 1948 allowed municipal planners to determine the placement of buildings on publicly or privately owned sites. The growing power of governments—both state and municipal—privileged the public good over individual rights and sought increasing control of the physical environment.

In this vein, Swedish planners developed what came to be known as ABC cities (*arbete, bostad och centrum,* "work, housing, and town center"), a transit-oriented system to be developed simultaneously with the Stockholm subway line in the 1950s and intended to create jobs on site for at least 50 percent of working residents. The Stockholm General Plan of 1952 famously sought to make this a municipal policy, and Vällingby, a Stockholm suburb that opened in 1954, served as the ABC poster child, attracting international attention.[56] New services around its town square included civic institutions such as schools and day-care centers and commercial functions such as stores and a movie theater.[57] Many residents found employment in Stockholm rather than locally, however, and Vällingby's planners' larger ambitions were forestalled as only 25 percent of the population were employed locally in what was "more accurately a metropolitan district linked by the underground transport system."[58] Even as the ABC city lost its A, collective urban planning with the neighborhood unit remained.

As the fixed distances and approved program pieces of neighborhood units surfaced as a working paradigm at the urban scale, appropriate consumption and practices within the home came to be equally important. In 1944, the Swedish state provided funding for women's groups to open the Home Research Institute (Hemmens forskningsinstitut), whose work would "rationalize" housework through scientific research.[59] Researchers included not only architects and engineers but also home economists, nutritionists, chemists, and sociologists who studied domestic labor in private homes and conducted laboratory experiments that mapped movements in kitchens and recorded workers' breathing, through facial masks, during dishwashing.[60] Regulations and building norms published in 1950 in informational pamphlets described the best ways to rip off a paper towel and to organize flatware, along with measurements and specifications for materials (detailing, for example, the placement of cabinets, stainless-steel countertops with spill-preventing lips, and the lengths of the countertops) (Figure 1.1).[61] This research, which was intended "to arrive at a limited number of standard sizes and shapes with extensive possibilities for variations," also led to the development of optimized floor plans for housing (Figure 1.2).[62]

Following these prescriptions, the government agency known as the National Housing Board (Kungliga Bostadsstyrelsen, or Bostadsstyrelsen) published formal guidelines in its brochure series *God bostad* (Good housing), including dimensions for everything from unit sunlight to the size of the kitchen sink. The series was reissued several times from 1954 to 1976 and continued on with other topics into the 1980s. Ultimately, the guidelines became more than recommendations: developers who accepted public financing were required to incorporate these standards, allowing the Swedish national government a heavy hand in shaping not only plans but interior dwelling spaces.[63] Standardized rooms also allowed standardized refrigerators, bathtubs, and other consumer goods. The pieces of a collective puzzle were now cut, missing only an apparatus for their widespread distribution and placement.

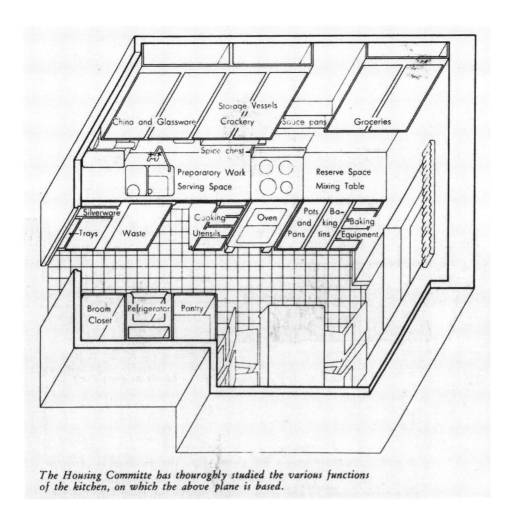

China and Glassware Storage Vessels Crockery Sauce pans Groceries

Spice chest

Preparatory Work Reserve Space
Serving Space Mixing Table

Silverware Cooking Oven Pots Ba- Baking
Utensils and king
Trays Waste Pans tins Equipment

Broom Refrigerator Pantry
Closet

*The Housing Committe has thouroghly studied the various functions
of the kitchen, on which the above plane is based.*

FIGURE 1.1. Optimized kitchen diagram and model kitchen, as printed in Hald, Holm, and Johansson, *Swedish Housing*, 39–40.

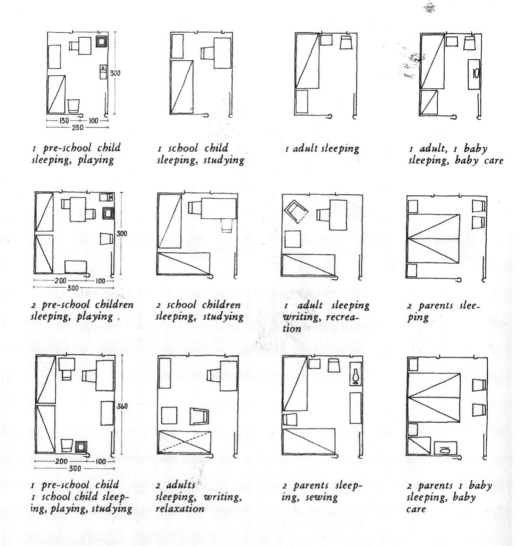

1 pre-school child sleeping, playing

1 school child sleeping, studying

1 adult sleeping

1 adult, 1 baby sleeping, baby care

2 pre-school children sleeping, playing

2 school children sleeping, studying

1 adult sleeping writing, recreation

2 parents sleeping

1 pre-school child 1 school child sleeping, playing, studying

2 adults sleeping, writing, relaxation

2 parents sleeping, sewing

2 parents 1 baby sleeping, baby care

From the bedroom studies. The plans show three different sizes of bedrooms furnished for different family members and different functions. The aim is to arrive at a limited number of standard sizes and shapes with extensive possibilities for variation according to different needs. (All measurements are given in centimeters. One inch equals about 2 1/2 centimeters.)

FIGURE 1.2. Standardized floor plans for apartments, as printed in Hald, Holm, and Johansson, *Swedish Housing*, 38.

The Million Program

In the early 1960s, Sweden found itself on a firm financial footing with increasingly affluent urban-dwelling citizens. Many of them—unlike the Stockholm Exhibition visitors—expressly sought access to these new innovations, yet the extreme housing shortage had contained them in small, low-quality spaces. Standardization techniques, world stability, and a strong Swedish economy had not kept pace with political or consumer will. Karl-Olov Arnstberg argues that "Swedish Social Democratic housing politics start in earnest with the breakthroughs of the 1930s and, thereafter, the housing question remains at the center of the political debate, virtually without interruption, for four decades."[64] As these long-standing visions were made into actual concrete, the Million Program turned utopian dreams into reality.[65] The project constructed one million dwelling units for a population then under eight million.[66]

A state research project involving the architect Lennart Holm served as the tipping point, producing the influential government report *Höjd bostadsstandard* (Raised housing standard) in 1965.[67] Holm and his collaborators urged the national government to construct 1.5 million dwelling units from 1960–1975.[68] Opposition parties had damningly made the "queue society" a focus of their rhetoric, arguing that Social Democrats had failed to address the long waits for housing in the climate of shortage.[69] Following first this pressure and then Holm's specific advice, the government introduced legislation that eventually became known as "the Million Program." The Swedish Parliament adopted the bill in 1965, promising one million dwelling units in ten years. This was not "social housing" for the poor, the disadvantaged, or the old (as in other European countries such as France and the United Kingdom). The Million Program would house the new Swedish middle class, making homes for the average citizen.

While removing the A (*arbete*) from the ABC equation, the Million Program otherwise adhered to the earlier model, typically producing transit-oriented developments and maintaining social collectives and formal standards. Building one million dwellings for fewer than eight million citizens would have a comprehensive effect on society, lending a coherent physical form to a Social Democratic welfare state that now linked equality and standards. The new Type Approval Unit established in 1967 at the National Board of Planning "meant that one building detail or building type could be approved nationally, and the possibility for local variations ended."[70] Two-thirds of the dwelling units were built in multifamily structures, where apartments would be affordable. Most would be publicly owned and leased to tenants.

New technologies for producing housing en masse in the building industry made this viable, with suburbs as the key sites of experimentation. The rise of the crane as a building tool during the 1950s, together with innovations in industrialized and prefabricated building components, created the possibility for efficient, large-scale construction.[71] Advertisements in architectural periodicals informed tradespeople that, for example, "concrete builds a better society" (Figure 1.3), suggesting that their work was to build not just dwellings but new social worlds.

Betong bygger bättre samhälle

Blå Rand cement med hög och jämn kvalitet — en väsentlig faktor för betongvaruindustrins insatser för ökat industrialiserat byggande

Betongvaruindustrin omfattar i dag ca 800 fabriker och sysselsätter 7—8.000 arbetare. Produktionsvolymen har ökat med mer än 50 % under tiden 1953—62 och omfattar tillverkning av bl.a. rör, olika byggelement — bjälklag, tak, pelare och väggelement —, block, takpannor, plattor m.m. Cementa har nyligen utgivit en katalog över betongvaru- och elementfabriker i Sverige, vilken kan rekvireras från Cementa, Box 248, Malmö 1.

Genom att använda prefabricerade element för olika ändamål kan byggnadsverksamheten i hög grad ratio-

naliseras med mindre åtgång på arbetskraft och förlängd byggsäsong som resultat.

Dagens industrialiserade byggande kräver förstklassiga material. Cementa har genom rationell tillverkning och distribution av cement med hög och jämn kvalitet kunnat bidra till betongvaruindustrins snabba expansion.

Cementa svarar för 80 % av den svenska cementproduktionen och kan genom sitt väl utbyggda distributionsnät tillhandahålla löscement från 36 platser över hela landet.

FIGURE 1.3. "Concrete builds a better society." Advertisement for Cementa Corporation in the periodical *Arkitektur* 12 (1966): back cover.

Social Democratic politicians had many instruments at their disposal in their efforts to control these processes. For instance, state loans encouraged large-scale projects, with a 1969 law giving financial breaks to construction companies building one thousand units or more. The significant scale led to a more monolithic design, as Thomas Hall writes:

> Housing production was regarded primarily as a question of technology and economics, not of architecture. What a good home should look like had been established in the national norms; provided these were fulfilled, by definition the standard would be acceptable. This meant that all efforts could be concentrated instead on improving the speed and efficiency of production. Many architects saw themselves as coordinators rather than designers. Around 1960 ideas about "production-related planning" began to circulate. A major planning goal, perhaps even sometimes *the* planning goal, was to design areas that lent themselves best to "rational" building.[72]

Interiors followed suit, as guidelines from *God bostad* (Good housing), published in 1960, meant that, for example, kitchens were created within a sixty-centimeter module, including cabinetry, sinks, and countertops (Figure 1.4).[73] Behind their uniform doors, then, residents lived in units with a limited range of floor plans and used standardized dishwashers, washing machines, and refrigerators. These norms promoted economy and efficiency in construction, but they also reinforced ideas of social equality founded on formal homogeneity.[74] Everyone would have the same things; there would be, echoing Hansson, "no stepchildren."

At the urban scale, Million Program neighborhood units explicitly blurred the boundaries between domestic and communal space. In the new suburban neighborhoods, residents would identify themselves with the *trapphus,* or stairwell, that they shared in an apartment building and use a common laundry room fitted with the latest machinery, booked in advance for regulated slots of time. Their children would play on communal grounds. Construction with large machinery typically required a flattened ground plane outside the buildings. Rational landscaping implied limits on the diversity of plant species, which led to mass orders for trees and other vegetation.[75] Making this streamlined future as quickly as possible, builders had to cut some corners.

A new sense of collectivity among previously disparate people was to emerge through the everyday use of space and objects. Sweden was no longer the nation with the worst housing in Europe but was now the society of the (high) standard. Residents, like citizens, had both rights and responsibilities, so the blocks incarnated the new Swedish state in miniature form. Both the public realm and public space had been radically expanded: the traditionally private was achieved only behind the closed doors of a bedroom in a municipal apartment at night.

SIS 83 41 10 Bänkskåp SA6, diskbänksskåp

Beteck-ning	Bredd dm
SA6 : 1	8

SIS 83 41 11 Bänkskåp, SA7, diskbänksskåp

Beteck-ning	Bredd dm	Variant
SA7 : 1	14	v
SA7 : 2		h

SIS 83 41 12 Bänkskåp SA8. bakskiveskåp

Beteck-ning	Bredd dm
SA8 : 1	1

SIS 83 41 13 Bänkskåpskombinationer SD

Kombination SD4

Innehåller 7 kombinationer av bänkskåp för diskbänkar och arbetsbänkar. Varje kombination kan erhållas i ett antal bredder och som vänster- och högervarianter.

SIS 83 41 14 Väggskåp SB1

Beteck-ning	Bredd dm	Höjd dm	Luck-hängning
SB1 : 1	4	10	v
SB1 : 2			h
SB1 : 3		11	v
SB1 : 4			h
SB1 : 5	6	10	v
SB1 : 6			h
SB1 : 7		11	v
SB1 : 8			h

SIS 83 41 15 Väggskåp SB2

Beteck-ning	Bredd dm	Höjd dm
SB2 : 1	8	10
SB2 : 2		11
SB2 : 3	10	10
SB2 : 4		11

SIS 83 41 16 Väggskåp SB3, medicinskåp

Beteck-ning	Bredd dm	Höjd dm	Luck-hängning
SB3 : 1	3	6	v
SB3 : 2			h

SIS 83 41 17 Högskåp SC1, skafferiskåp

Beteck-ning	Bredd dm	Höjd dm	Luck-hängning
SC1 : 1	6	24	v
SC1 : 2			h
SC1 : 3		25	v
SC1 : 4			h

SIS 83 41 18 Högskåp SC2, skåp för kylskåp

Beteck-ning	Bredd dm	Höjd dm	Luck-hängning
SC2 : 1	6	24	v
SC2 : 2			h
SC2 : 3		25	v
SC2 : 4			h
SC2 : 5	6	24	v
SC2 : 6			h
SC2 : 7		25	v
SC2 : 8			h

SIS 83 41 19 Högskåp SC3 och SC4, städskåp

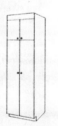

Beteck-ning	Bredd dm	Höjd dm	Luck-hängning
SC3 : 1	6	24	v
SC3 : 2			h
SC3 : 3		25	v
SC3 : 4			h
SC4 : 1	8	24	—
SC4 : 2		25	—

FIGURE 1.4. Furniture diagrams from the revised edition of *God bostad,* Kungliga Bostadsstyrelsen, *God bostad i dag och i morgon,* 56.

Governmentality *på svenska*

In just half a century, Sweden transformed from an impoverished, peripheral Nordic nation with a rural economy to a modern, urban welfare state with an increasingly complex program of social, economic, and physical planning. The Million Program served as the crowning achievement of the Social Democrats' modern project, as the social and architectural visions of the 1930s of creating a classless and well-housed Sweden seemed to be arriving by express delivery. As Harry Sandberg, mayor of Stockholm, argued in a speech in 1932, "The dwelling, the home, is the foundation of family formation, which in turn is the prerequisite for every society's construction, assistance, and development. Good housing nurtures good citizens and happy communities."[76] By the late 1960s, Sweden's "good democratic citizens"[77] could live in affordable apartments, cook in kitchens so efficient that housewives had time to join study circles, watch the same (two) television channels, and shop at stores with identical stock.

Norms, standards, and modules recalibrated citizenship for a new urban Sweden, becoming a form of what Sally Engle Merry theorizes as "spatial governmentality"[78] (connecting space to Michel Foucault's notion of governmentality).[79] According to Foucault's analysis, citizens are molded into docile subjects of the state through carefully designed discourses and disciplinary practices. Spatial governmentality in 1960s Sweden emerged in Social Democratic efforts to shape citizens through the built environment, using buildings, landscapes, furniture, and public spaces as means of communication.

As the Million Program was under construction, "good housing" was making "good citizens." Or, as cultural critic Per Wirtén writes, "Everything would be good. No one should do badly: not the workers who built it, not the children who played on the car-free playgrounds, not the parents who cooked in large modern kitchens and ate lunch on attractive balconies."[80] The Swedish state made conformity desirable by making it affordable, distributing it to all, and rendering the following of norms synonymous with being modern. If the Social Democrats had fulfilled their promises, the price of admission to this mid-twentieth-century utopia was spatial and social conformity. Not only should the sinks be homogenous, but so should the citizens washing dishes in them.[81]

How then did Sweden deal with deviations from this standard arriving from abroad, with immigrants who disrupted the closed boundaries of a society in which citizens had been, in effect, cataloged through census taking and reprocessed through a new urban education? Swedish life had just been, to call on Hirdman's term, "set right" when the small group of Syriac pioneers appeared on the scene. Mass-produced consumer goods for the modern era were being promoted by the state, new public transit was in progress, and a post office and health clinic appeared in every New Town square. In 1967, immigration was still a new part of political discourse, and migrants were often treated as exotic beneficiaries of Swedish generosity.

As Syriacs occupied apartments in newly minted Million Program neighborhoods, they were initially mostly unaware of the symbolic messages contained in these dwellings, with their scientifically perfected spatial arrangements and appliances. As cultural geographer Moa Tunström explains, "Similarity in physical expression can be linked to both an increased standardization and industrialization of construction, as well as to similarity as a positive social ideal—or that one's value is not determined by the appearance of the house where you live."[82]

But the towers, concrete, and large open spaces between buildings that served as evidence of a Swedish triumph in the long fight against poverty and low housing standards were to Syriacs merely welcome shelter. Quickly, they began to question their forms of spatial governmentality, which emphasized the erasure of social difference through dwelling-based practices of citizenship. These dwellings operated through a spatial logic that emphasized the centrifugal—providing to all—over the centripetal, hermetic neighborhoods and villages to which Syriacs were accustomed. Increasingly, Syriacs drew on their own experiences and memories of urban and rural life outside Sweden, where marking—rather than expunging—social difference, together with spatial enclosure and withdrawal, were the keys to survival.

From the Millet to the Sword

In his 1991, partly autobiographical novel *I fikonträdets skugga* (In the shadow of the fig tree), Bahdi Ecer decries the eroding connections between Syriacs in Sweden and their homelands.[83] Inspired by the Swedish author Vilhelm Moberg's story of the starving Swedes of Småland who journey to America in the nineteenth century, *Utvandrarna (The Emigrants),* Ecer's parable draws on his own family history to detail a village life of precarious agricultural subsistence and codependence, where the built environment became critical for protection as trust between Christian and Muslim neighbors ruptured violently.

The territories of the Ottoman Empire (circa 1300–1922) included Tur Abdin and the adjacent lands now regarded as the Syriac homelands. Yet this was a Muslim empire. Within it, the Syriacs—known as *Süryani*—lived under conditions of limited autonomy as participants in the so-called millet system, which predated but continued during Ottoman times.[84] Organizing groups by religious identity, the millet system required payment of duty to a local leader, or *aga,* to ensure continued safety.[85] Recognized as the *Süryani Kadim Millet,* the Syriacs lived as a minority-faith group, with internal courts that used their own religious laws.[86] As the Södertälje journalist Stefan Andersson wrote in 1983, "Since ancient times, therefore, the *assyrier* have regarded themselves as belonging to a community within a community. Such a stance may be ever so inappropriate in a modern industrial society—the stance is nonetheless firmly rooted."[87] The millet system established the Syriacs early on as socially and physically isolated.

As the Ottoman Empire declined in the late nineteenth century and then col-
lapsed during World War I, however, a new order arrived under the so-called Young
Turks. This group of reformist intellectuals defined itself in opposition to their
Ottoman predecessors, regarding the latter's laissez-faire approach to ethnocultural
diversity as outmoded.[88] The Young Turks demanded a secular Turkey as rationalized as its European counterparts.[89] In this spirit, they also set about defining who
belonged to the Turkish nation. Those groups identified as minority millets under
Ottoman rule were reframed as Turks and were to be culturally assimilated by any
means necessary.

With both actual and alleged alliances made between Christians and anti-Turkish
powers, including Russia, the new Turkish government especially feared minority
groups' desires for political autonomy. Tragically, their reactions included such violent measures as the forced expulsion of Greeks and savage acts of ethnic cleansing carried out against the Armenians, Syriacs, and other Christians in the wake of
World War I. These events, which left an open wound on the country that has yet
to heal, achieved a mythic status among Syriacs, for whom they are known in
Suryoyo as *Seyfo,* meaning "the Year of the Sword."[90] While the armed forces and
Kurdish warlords perpetrated many of these acts, ordinary villagers (previously the
Armenians' and Syriacs' neighbors) also participated, producing for the Syriacs an
irrevocable loss of trust in both the Turkish national government and in the non-
Syriac elements of their local urban and village communities.

Current estimates conclude that approximately two-thirds of the total Christian
population of Turkey was killed during the *Seyfo* genocide.[91] For many of the Armenian and Syriac Orthodox Christians' contemporary descendants, this remains by far
the most significant historical moment in Turkey. With the partial obliteration of
their community, these attacks disenfranchised the group and created a continuing
social instability and sense of threat, leading to their eventual dispersal across the
Middle East and migration to Europe. The recent violent rise of the Islamic State in
Iraq and Syria has included the brutal takeover of traditional Syriac strongholds (including Mosul, Iraq, in the summer of 2014) and the destruction of historic Assyrian
imperial sites (such as the bulldozing of the three-thousand-year-old city of Nimrud
in March and April 2015).[92] These developments and the continuing civil war in Syria
have been seen to confirm suspicions that Syriacs will never be able to return to these
territories, buoying permanent emigration as a key part of the group's identity.

Jakob, in his late seventies, is a Syriac businessman, Assyrian nationalist, and
church leader living in Södertälje and the father of five children. His story, which
he relayed to me in his home in 2010, is representative of the Syriacs' conditions just
before they came to Sweden. For him, the journey began when he was twelve years
old in the 1940s. His brother had deserted from the Turkish army, fleeing across the
border to Syria, from where he could not return, so the family migrated one by one
in order to reunite with him. Jakob said, "We went by foot, since there were no

cars. We walked to Qamishli from Midyat. It wasn't so far. Before we moved, it was very common for us to walk there, to walk over the border. We gave half a Turkish lira to the border guard, and we got to cross." This made the move to Syria relatively uneventful.

As an adult in Qamishli, Jakob developed a construction business, specializing in carpentry, and married another Syriac, Katrin. They had three sons and two daughters. Though the family's everyday life was mostly peaceful, many of Jakob's relatives emigrated to Europe from Syria and Turkey. They were persistent in asking him to follow:

> I was in the building industry for four years, and then I started to get letters from relatives in Germany, Holland, and Sweden encouraging me to go to Europe. They wrote, "If you can manage to get here, it's good." After I decided to go, I changed my mind and decided to stay, since my firm was doing really well. I sent letters to my friends, who are also my relatives, and I wrote, "I want you to stop sending me letters. I have left the thought of migrating behind me."

Even so, Jakob became increasingly concerned about the conflicts developing between Christians and Muslims in Lebanon in the late 1970s. He said, "They killed each other on the basis of your ID card. If they got ahold of a Christian, they killed him." For Jakob and other Syriacs, these local-level clashes over religious differences recalled the earlier genocides, even if they were geographically far away.[93] Eventually, fear prompted Jakob to reconsider his decision, and he gathered information, writing to relatives and visiting his sister in the Netherlands.

When Jakob ultimately informed Katrin that he wanted to emigrate, she resisted, saying, "Why should we go and start all over again? Why should we destroy everything when the work is going so well and the children are in school?" But Jakob insisted that they leave Syria. As he recounted, he told her, "*Walla* [I swear by God] that we're going to go. *Khalas!* [Enough!] I'm not staying in this region anymore."[94] He sold his belongings and procured visas for the entire family. As we talked about this experience in his well-appointed living room, he remarked, "It wasn't difficult to get a visa, like it is now [in 2010]."

The door to immigration was ajar, but Jakob's anxieties about its possible closure motivated him. He said, "My oldest brother, who died last year, said, 'This country [Syria], this place, this soil will never be ours.' He pointed out that everyone else was in the process of leaving Syria and said, 'We'll be the last ones here in the end, and then it will be difficult to get a visa.'" The departure of other Syriacs also had implications for security. As Naures Atto writes, "Aware there was safety in numbers, Assyrians/Syriacs who were more determined to continue to live in the *athro* (homeland) tried to convince others not to leave, too. To live next to an empty house meant to be in a very vulnerable position."[95] Their pleas became largely ineffective as more Syriacs departed, worsening the position of those who remained. Furthermore, while "a growing 'concept of Sweden'"[96] was traveling through the Syriac communities of the Middle East, a harder-line Swedish immigration regime appeared to be on the horizon, a reaction to popular characterizations of Syriacs as "the most unforeseen and . . . least welcome group of immigrants" in the 1970s.[97]

In spite of his rationally and carefully made decision, Jakob described the Syriacs' exile from the Middle East and dispersal across the globe with melancholy:

> All the *assyrier*'s lives and situations are the same. My brother died in Midyat and is buried there. My father died in Qamishli and is buried there. My other brother [is buried] in Aleppo. My mother and my brother are buried here in Sweden. Two of my sisters [are buried] in Amsterdam. We have wandered our whole lives. We have never established ourselves in one place, because we didn't have a country and because the Muslims were always persecuting us. This is our life.

If Syriacs' global diffusion has been most visible in death, their exceptionally strong family ties (a focus of most studies of the group)[98] make this condition even more emotionally and practically difficult. As their geographic bonds disintegrated within the national spaces of Syria, Turkey, and beyond, Syriac families atomized and scattered across the world.

Subaltern Community Space

The Syriacs' traditional homeland in the mountainous region of Tur Abdin lies in the southeastern portion of modern-day Turkey, on the borders of contemporary Iraq and Syria and peppered with villages and towns (Map 3). In springtime, the region's prodigious open fields are covered in a swath of red poppies, with the outlines of numerous stone churches on every horizon. The remnants of many Syriac villages are now abandoned or repossessed by Kurds. In a few others, at the end of dusty country roads or in the shadows of the major cities, Orthodox ways of life are still visible. Most Christians in Midyat and the surrounding *Süryani* villages speak Suryoyo, known in Tur Abdin as Turoyo (the mountain language), in reference to the region.

Hard evidence of the demographic shifts of the twentieth century exists throughout the region today. The metalworking shops that were once the domain of Syriacs are now run by Kurds in Mardin, and only small remnant Syriac populations exist in some villages. As political scientist Thomas Smith points out, "In many cases, the physical space they [Christians] had occupied was 'Turkified,' as state agencies redistributed vacated properties to Muslim refugees from the Balkans."[99] While Islamic State takeovers of space in Syria and Iraq in the 2010s have been rapid and violent, these more-insidious and slow-moving repossessions began long ago.

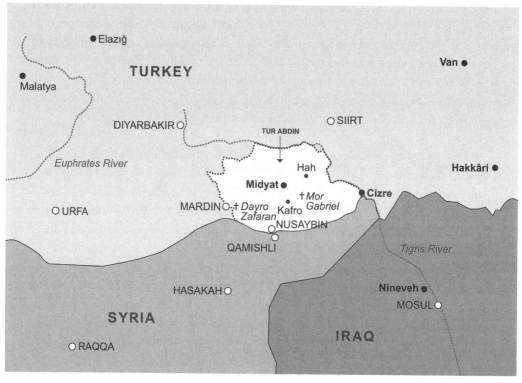

MAP 3. Map of Tur Abdin, northeastern Syria, northwestern Iraq, and southeastern Turkey showing the major villages, towns, and monasteries. Graphic design by Eliza Hearsum.

Despite these social shifts, the many surviving, if not functioning, Syriac Orthodox churches bear witness to an earlier history and offer evidence of the previous social and spatial importance of the church to the towns (Figure 1.5). At least one hundred churches and eighty monasteries once existed in the region.[100] Professor of liturgical science Hans Hollerweger describes this landscape as populated by "the bearers of an uninterrupted tradition from the beginnings of Christianity until the present day,"[101] outlining how churches built in local limestone now serve as the vestiges of a once-prominent group.

Fragrant wildflowers and expansive vineyards in the springtime are a testament to the fecund setting in the warmer seasons, when many residents sleep on rooftops. Hollerweger notes that village churches also followed this seasonal pattern: "*Beth Slutho* ('The House of Prayer') is the outdoor area beside or in front of the church, where daily common prayers are said during the summer."[102] When telling me their departure and arrival stories, several Syriacs who grew up in Tur Abdin described how the church and *Beth Slutho* provided key community space for both prosaic and festive occasions.[103] Here, prayer was held three times a day; the rites of baptism,

FIGURE 1.5. Church in the village of Hah, Tur Abdin, 2009. Photograph by author.

marriage, and funerals were performed; and the local priest (often an important figure in the life of the village) had his base.

As conflicts between Christians and Muslims intensified in the early twentieth century, the tangible site of the church served as an important safe haven for discourse: it was the only space where the Syriac minority religion could be fully expressed without retribution from either the Turkish state or fellow citizens. This safety for words in the church became bodily when, as Andersson writes, "during the war, many of them [churches] served as fortifications. A large proportion of the Christians who survived [during the *Seyfo*] were able to do so because they could take refuge in churches and monasteries."[104] The social and spatial haven of the church reinforced feelings of togetherness and paved the way for future enclaves. As Father Johannes, a Syriac Orthodox priest in Södertälje, told me, "Because of the massacres against us, the only thing that could keep us together was religion. It was the church. We have no government, no one to help us. We try to live by our own efforts, using our own minimal resources. That's why it is very important for us to stay together." In the increasingly precarious political field of Turkey, the church saved lives and served as a crucial public space for a vulnerable Syriac subaltern public, both during and after the *Seyfo*. These associations continue in the diaspora.

Domestic Distress

In 2009 I traveled with two companions toward the village of Hah in Tur Abdin to see a famous church. On the way, we noted several Kurdish paramilitary members walking in a group by the side of the road, carrying guns. Nervously, we continued and, shortly thereafter, arrived at a fork in the road where several people were hanging around a schoolyard. Not knowing which way to turn, we asked for directions. Within seconds, we acquired a fourth passenger, someone who would "help us to find the way." This turned out to be a man in fatigues with a machine gun, who sat behind me with his weapon as we drove down a road between agricultural fields.

Anxious small talk peppered the trip, which lasted only a few minutes, until our arrival. The army lieutenant (I had by now learned) called to some of his lower-ranking soldiers, also carrying machine guns. The group escorted us into the church's courtyard, surrounded by high stone walls. Scenes from various Hollywood films flashed through my mind. Rather than lining us up for execution, however, the soldiers located the wife of the church's caretaker, who produced the key to the church and allowed us to enter. The army contingent then left, and we enjoyed both a tour and afternoon tea with the caretaker's wife as we overlooked both farmland and a makeshift soccer field from the church's upper story. The lieutenant had also invited us for tea in the gun tower, which was visible from the rooftop of the church, but we left Hah without saying goodbye.

The ongoing conflict between the Turkish military and Kurdish separatists (most attached to the Kurdistan Workers' Party, the PKK) in the Tur Abdin region represents a central feature of contemporary everyday life there. In Hah, this was highly visible, with the prominence of the gun tower (emblazoned with the Turkish flag), a military barricade preventing unauthorized automobile traffic, and the constant presence of soldiers. "But nothing ever happens here," the caretaker's wife said.

At the same time, the villages of Tur Abdin offer more than mere vestiges of a time before the PKK. Here, life revolves primarily around subsistence agriculture. The picturesque vineyards sweeping the countryside have been a major source of livelihood, even as the Syriacs have become increasingly dependent on trade with outsiders. Within the village, families farm for themselves, following a long tradition that Fuat Deniz describes:

> The villages were divided into units called *bavik,* and inhabited by descendants of the same ancestors, including those who joined through marriage. . . . The small community had a low degree of diversity and high degree of self-containment, a common life together with family and friends that lasted a lifetime. Life was characterized by stability.[105]

The Syriacs' concentration in the remote, mountainous region of Tur Abdin facilitated these social structures. It also meant that the regulatory power of the state had practical limitations: while Christians were required to hold a theoretical loyalty to the Turkish state, the church held even more social power within the Syriac community. This was how the Syriac Orthodox followers understood their church when they emigrated to Sweden.

Given the geography of the region and its rugged landscape, with mountains and sharp passes, the roads winding through them (many developed for transport with animals rather than vehicular traffic) became more easily traversable only recently. The great difficulty of traveling between places meant that many people remained in their villages except when they had to sell agricultural products. Even in the nineteenth century, villagers had tried when possible to go in groups, since the dangers of wildlife and robbers were compounded for solo travelers.[106]

Typically surrounded by agricultural fields, the houses in Tur Abdin's villages were generally grouped together in small, protective enclaves and were primarily constructed out of local limestone (Figure 1.6). In places such as the village of Hah,

FIGURE 1.6. Partially abandoned village of Kafro, 2009. A new settlement on a much larger scale is located directly adjacent to the old village; here returnee emigrants have built homesteads in stone with money earned abroad. Photograph by author.

where the Christian families lived together in a part of the town called the "Castle," neighbors frequently shared walls with one another, in part for defensive purposes.[107] Everyone shared the outhouse. In some more prosperous village settings, houses were completely detached.

In the late nineteenth century, Christian villages were scattered across the Tur Abdin region, along with some Muslim villages, but the balance between Muslims and Christians in these villages has shifted radically since then. The large Kurdish contingent in this region, which initially collaborated with the new Turkish government in the early twentieth century, quickly transformed into targets of its "Turkification" programs.[108] This affected both Kurdish and Syriac individuals and their spaces, as they were increasingly expected to adopt a standardized identity as Turkish citizens. James C. Scott describes how states employed surnames as a technology of power to create a uniformity of identity among citizens.[109] In the new Turkey headed by Mustafa Kemal Atatürk, all citizens were required to take a Turkish surname. This policy was extended to territories, and villages were retitled with Turkish-language names.[110] With tensions between Christians and Kurds at a new high, the taxonomy of citizenship in the modern state included neither of them as separate groups, further deteriorating their internal relations and provoking increasingly anxious conditions in the Tur Abdin region.

Urbanism in Tur Abdin

When anthropologist Ulf Björklund arrived to begin fieldwork in Södertälje in the late 1970s, he worked almost exclusively with Syriacs who had grown up in Turkey in the Tur Abdin region. Within this group, some had come from the region's villages, and others had emigrated from its two major urban centers: Mardin and Midyat (Figure 1.7). Even this difference of origin among members of the group led to variations in their attitudes and experiences during the initial period of settlement in Sweden. Explaining that a *şauto* is an area "corresponding approximately to a residential block or quarter of a town"[111] and known as *mahalle* in Turkish, Björklund writes:

> The whole of Midyat comprises four *şautoto* (plur.) and a *şuko* with shops, workshops, etc. In the 1960's the Christian population of Midyat numbered five to six thousand (as against one thousand Muslims).
>
> In its unofficial sense a *şauto* denotes the neighborhood unit[112] in which one traditionally lives, surrounded by relatives and well-known neighbors, and where women especially spend much of their lives in dense female-dominated networks for intercourse and cooperation. Much of the daily lives of the somen [*sic*], the young girls, and children is centered in the walled court—*dırto*—around which the houses are typically built. During the hot season people eat and sleep in the yard, the big

beds standing usually on the roof of lower parts of the house. At least certain *ṣauṭoṭo* have constituted relatively exclusive neighborhood units, where dogs constantly remind every outsider that he is on foreign territory.[113]

Exclusive definitions of family, neighborhood, and the larger urban community appeared in these boundaries. Perhaps invisible to outsiders, the social meanings of each level in this hierarchy of urban enclaves were nonetheless made material in these physical forms.

In the towns of Mardin and Midyat, "Syrian Orthodox culture has left its mark on stone carving, filigree work, weaving, woodwork, the arts of the goldsmith and coppersmith, and many other local handcrafts."[114] Furthermore, town dwellers there firmly believed that their urban condition elevated their social status vis-à-vis friends, relatives, and even enemies in villages. Björklund writes:

> All the established Midyat families were united in a feeling of shared cultural competence and civilized ways of life, setting them apart from all "*maq-qıryaoṭo*," "(people) from the villages." This boundary between "*bajariye*" ("towns-people," "civilized") and

FIGURE 1.7. Urban landscape of Midyat, showing outdoor bedframes used for sleeping on rooftops in the summer, 2009. Photograph by author.

on the other hand "*kurmanciye*" ("villagers," "uncivilized"; literally "Kurds"), also cuts right across the division Suryoye–Tayye.[115]

While the two towns permitted lifestyles unavailable in the countryside, those who lived there had different roles in the group's local political, economic, and religious cosmology.

Mardin (meaning "fortress" in Suryoyo) was once a major Syriac outpost. From a distance it resembles Pieter Bruegel the Elder's sixteenth-century painting *The Tower of Babel,* with contours of houses, cafés, shops, and government buildings rising over its prominent hill, from which the Mesopotamian valley and northeastern Syria are visible. Proximity to the Syrian border means that more Arabic than Turkish is spoken, and sales to travelers serve as an important source of revenue.[116] Streets and alleyways teem with small shops, where purveyors sell candy, nuts, soap, and hammered copper pans, among other goods. Some *Süryani* silver- and goldsmiths still operate storefronts, where they peddle the handcrafted jewelry for which the Syriacs are well known. *Süryani* wines are also available. The town's main Syriac Orthodox church is the Church of the Forty, completed in 569. Near to Mardin lies the important monastery of Dayro Zafaran (the Saffron Monastery), which has been on the site for over 1,500 years, preceded by a temple built by sun worshippers.[117]

Historically, however, the major Christian town of Tur Abdin was Midyat, to the east of Mardin (see Map 3). The town, settled as early as the ninth century BCE, was originally called Matiate on account of its cave dwellers.[118] Its distinctive contemporary skyline of minarets and church spires attests to the mixture of religious groups that have populated it over the centuries. A prominent central traffic circle includes a column decorated with both a Christian cross and a Muslim crescent. Midyat was the seat of the archbishop of the Syriac Orthodox Church beginning in 1478 and once contained eight Christian churches and only two mosques. As Hollerweger notes, "It was coupled with the nearby town of Estel, which boosted its Muslim population and, with the emigration of the Christians, rapidly reversed its ratio of mosques to churches."[119]

The monastery of Mor Gabriel, founded in the fifth century, is located to the southeast of Midyat (see Map 3). Receiving visitors from all over the world and home of the archbishop, Mor Gabriel gained international attention in 2008 when the Turkish government fought to seize some of its land. According to some accounts, this Turkish government action (prompted when Kurds claimed territory that repatriated Syriacs contended was theirs) was retribution against members of the diaspora who had lobbied foreign governments to push for the 1915 killings to be recognized internationally as genocide.[120]

The court case became a symbol of the continuing encroachment by the Turkish state on the land and heritage of the Christians in Tur Abdin.[121] Björklund observed in 1981, "Christians now exist as a small minority among the Kurdish

Muslim population, but only 75–100 years ago certain parts of Tur ʿabdin were heavily dominated by the Christians."[122] The situation has become only more extreme, although the recent arrival in Turkey of Syriacs and other minority groups from the conflicts in Syria and Iraq has the potential to change the social mix again. If many struggled to make their way to safe havens from war-torn Syria in the 2010s, Syriacs like Jakob emigrated in the other direction just a few decades earlier by simply crossing the Turkish border.

Peasants' Dreamland

When Ecer's novel reaches the 1960s, the character known as "M" leaves with others for Syria to escape impending military service, a move much like that of Jakob's older brother. Syria is described there as "a country that, they had heard from historians, their ancestors lived in and ruled, although it was long ago."[123] M was reacting to the Turkish state's compulsory service for young men, during which Christians were often given the most unpleasant and dangerous assignments. Considering both the political context and what often appeared to be a death sentence, Syriacs did what they could to avoid military service. Some did not appear when called up for duty. Some parents altered their sons' birth dates to allow them more time to grow and gain strength before their military service commenced.[124]

Like M, Jakob and several other older Syriacs I spoke with in Södertälje had migrated, or attempted to migrate, to Syria and other neighboring countries. The country represented new freedoms as a land both steeped in their glorious past and promising them a luminous future, as Ecer conveys:

> Syria, the land of kings and the gentlemen's battlefield.
>
> Syria, the grain's earth and the migrating birds' meeting point.
>
> Syria, the businessmen's Venice and the prisoners' hideout. The peasants' dreamland. The camel's resting place.
>
> Syria, the foreigners' colony, the gold mine of wealth, and the home of poverty.
>
> Syria, the prophets' parade park and the angels' landing strip.
>
> Syria, God in heaven has made you so flat. In your soil, gold grows as in no other land.
>
> Syria, I want to reach you, I want to visit you, M had said. He was still anxious to realize his dreams.[125]

This pull toward Syria also reflected larger political differences between that country and Turkey in the twentieth century. Syria had been a French mandate until 1946, and Syriacs considered France's Christian heritage an advantage.[126] Likewise, the French, acknowledging the precariousness of the border condition, encouraged Christians to come across and settle this sensitive territory.[127]

Upon arrival in northeastern Syria, a region the Bedouins and other groups had populated without establishing permanent settlements, the Syriacs began to develop urban outposts.[128] During the 1920s they developed two cities comprehensively: Qamishli (or Qamishlo in Kurdish), a new urban center founded in 1926; and Hasakah, which had become a provincial capital for the region of Al-Jazira by the 1950s (see Map 3). When Jakob's family reconvened in Qamishli, they found a new level of comfort in everyday life:

> Qamishli felt much bigger. It felt like we had come to a major city, and there were so many of us there, maybe 80, 85 percent of the population in Qamishli was Christian. In Midyat, there were so many Muslims around us, but in Qamishli we were more. In Midyat, we were around two thousand households; in Qamishli, we were a hundred thousand. The churches were much more beautiful, and we felt more at home. In Qamishli, almost all of the national civil servants were Christian. We went to the city hall, the city council, and the county courthouse and spoke Suryoyo. It felt like we were coming into the church because we spoke Suryoyo when we went in there. All of the civil servants were our relatives. Today, it's not like that at all.

While the boundary between Turkey and Syria remained contested well after the French mandate ended, the Syriacs' position remained key in the region.[129]

Here, as in Hasakah, the Syriacs established a stable community, living in houses with courtyards, a typical form of dwelling space in the Middle East. By the mid-twentieth century, Qamishli and Hasakah also had apartment buildings. In the 1960s, Turkey maintained its policies of nationalism and secularism by force, but Syria's attitude toward its Christian minorities was less interventionist. Even as the Syriacs became more urbanized in Syria, many made their fortunes as farmers. After the mandate ended, agricultural expansion in this area was rapid during the 1950s, with Syriacs leasing land from Bedouins or from the national government.[130] Given this hands-off approach by the Syrian state, a secular, minoritarian nationalism was much more viable than in Turkey. Little by little, however, Syriacs were joined by a growing number of Kurds, who, with the Christian departures for Europe, came to dominate.[131]

As the governments of ostensibly Muslim and ethnically Arab states turned a blind eye, an Assyrian nationalist group known as the Assyrian Democratic Organization (ADO) was established in Qamishli on July 15, 1957. ADO began as an underground movement among intellectuals seeking an independent Christian state; it transformed into a worldwide organization with a newsletter and publicized gatherings.[132] ADO developed as colonial empires all over the world were disintegrating in favor of new nation-states. Following Benedict Anderson's theories of nation building, for the Syriacs, "the nation is always conceived as a deep, horizontal comradeship,"[133] signaling a splintering of minoritarian "imagined communities" from newly formed, postcolonial countries like Syria.

ADO looked to the ancient Assyrian Empire as the source of their nationalist legitimacy, arguing that the Assyrians were continuous, autochthonous residents of the land between the Tigris and Euphrates Rivers and should have their own autonomous state. The group's website today reveals that these aims have not changed: "The *Assyrian Democratic Organization is a national, political and democratic movement* having for objectives the safeguard of the existence of the Assyrian people and the realization of its legitimate national aspirations (political, cultural, administrative) in its historic homeland."[134] While the Syrian government eventually cracked down on such illicit forms of ethnic nationalism, Syria at least offered more room for such sentiments than did Turkey.[135] This was particularly true in the far-flung territories of the Hasakah region, where the Syrian state did not yet have a firm grasp on governance.[136] These contexts would later migrate to Sweden along with the Syriac community, informing conflicts within the group as it interacted with a new political regime in Sweden.[137]

Safety in Enclaves

The young Syriac migrants from Tur Abdin who arrived on the First Plane had originally relocated to Lebanon because of a difficult economic climate, bitterness, and fear in the wake of ethnic violence in the earlier part of the century, as well as because of the everyday discriminations that had taken their place since then. By the 1960s, up to fifty thousand Christians were living in Tur Abdin.[138] Arriving in Sweden, the group had a strong sense of its own difference. Benjamin, a Syriac author in his midsixties, arrived on the First Plane. He described his confusion upon landing:

> It was spring. But it was still snowing. That was unbelievable for us who had just come from warmer countries. I mean suddenly to end up in a country where there was still snow on the ground. That was extremely strange. And I remember the drive from the airport so vividly. We were on our way to a place where we would be assembled. For the first time, we saw women and girls who were bicycling and people who were standing up against walls and sunning themselves. We thought they were completely crazy. It was so strange, this first meeting with the new country. And actually . . . it stays with you. You never forget such an impression.

As they were transferred to the small southern Swedish town of Alvesta and then to the Labor Market Board (Arbetsmarknadsstyrelsen, AMS) refugee camp, the Syriacs stoically underwent processing, thinking it the first step toward a long-elusive religious freedom. David, an entrepreneur, described the methods with bitterness:

"Something that we were unaccustomed to was that we had to shower together. All the men would be showering and a woman walked in between the men. That was something that we felt was wrong. Finally, there were doctor's examinations of all the men and all the women." Syriacs experienced these forms of management in this unfamiliar country as morally shocking and physically harsh, a stark contrast to the expectations of benevolent humanitarianism that had developed when they were chosen from the applicant group in Lebanon.[139]

Once in residence in the camp, the Syriacs waited many frustrating months for word on their fate. They "wanted to work and to send money to their relatives. Instead, they ended up at school desks in a refugee camp."[140] Transforming Syriacs into "good democratic [Swedish] citizens"[141] worked well in the eyes of the authorities, however. After completing the Syriacs' Swedification,[142] civil servants divided them into groups and dispersed them across the country, offering them manufacturing jobs and housing according to prevailing spatial logics. Some were placed in Gothenburg, others in Örebro, and still others in Stockholm. The Swedish authorities strategized to promote assimilation by placing no more than three families in each town.[143]

Syriacs, however, had already begun to worry about separation in the camp, and forced geographic distribution was "increasingly intolerable."[144] They were accustomed to a deeply interlinked community life and to banding together against external threats. Sonya Aho writes:

> For the *assyrisk/syrianska* minority's existence and survival, being close to the group, family, friends, and relatives is vital. Being close to the group is a decisive factor, not least of all in order to maintain their ethnicity, their minority's culture, language, and religion. For thousands of years they have managed to preserve their distinctive nature and language by living in larger groups in relatively isolated mountain areas. Therefore most *assyrier/syrianer* choose to continue to live close to other *assyrier/syrianer*. It is perhaps even more important for group survival to live close to each other in the diaspora.[145]

Given the heightened sense of safety of that living in enclaves in Ottoman and Turkish contexts provided, as well as their isolation from family and friends, the Syriacs coming from Alvesta felt immediately uncomfortable when such assemblages were not allowed. As Deniz explains:

> The will to live close to each other does not develop in exile but reflects the group's long tradition of being segregated. Housing segregation is thus both a strategy for coping with life in exile and an expression of a historical segregation [that] corresponds with the group's social interaction and their ways of socializing, which are based in the family and in intensive family relations. In the homeland, interaction within the

family and among relatives in the villages was a necessity because of the society's agrarian structure and for security in the hostile environment. The group was forced to collaborate and interact because of this. They often lived by themselves; they did not mix with the Muslim majority population but were instead segregated by village or by neighborhood. The group's residential segregation in Sweden can be seen as a continuation of the historical tradition of segregation and as a relic of the structure of the Tur Abdin.[146]

The isolation of Syriacs in Sweden expressed a continuing understanding of symbolic differences—religious but also sociocultural—between this group and other Swedes.

As the Syriacs left the Middle East, they also disrupted their patterns of living, slowly making it harder for the members of the group who remained to feel safe in their enclaves. This was true even in the cities of Mardin and Midyat. By the 1970s, the effects of emigration were heavily felt in Tur Abdin. For example, in Ecer's novel, one character describes Mardin as it was at that time:

> It was Tur Abdin's capital, Mardin, the *syrianer*'s heart and Turkey's star. Caravans and horses' hooves were always heard on the mountain roads. It was not long ago that the *syrianska* people enjoyed all this. Now no further noise from the church bells is heard. The River Euphrates flows slowly toward the sea. The people migrated to the West.[147]

Despair and loss are deeply ingrained in the physical territory of the towns and the villages and in neighboring Syria. As seeds on an ever-stronger wind, Syriacs had blown across their former region and gathered to grow in Chicago, Australia, the Netherlands, and, of course, Sweden, where Syriac desires to live together in enclaves—a spatial logic emphasizing withdrawal—were anxiously read through a new lens. There, the Swedish welfare state, with its emphasis on social equality through formal uniformity and spatial distribution, rejected enclaves on ideological grounds.

Standards and Separatism

If a refugee is already a "border concept," according to political theorist Giorgio Agamben, this figure also "unhinges the old trinity of state/nation/territory" that defines "nativity."[148] This decoupling of nation and state opens up new ways of thinking about space, access, equality, and rights. Inured to geographic isolation and possessors of a proud particularism, Syriacs were reluctant to accept the terms of equality that the Swedish nation-state had materialized in building norms and the associated efforts to disperse the Syriacs geographically. "Unhinging" the Swedish desire to erase their otherwise obvious difference from the landscapes of quality housing and town centers in which they were offered shelter, Syriacs retained their diasporic nationalism and understood themselves, again, to be a minority. Difference was their calling card. Continuing their membership in fiercely ideological groups such as the ADO, they recalled lost homelands and earlier experiences of social and spatial exclusion while experiencing new ones in Sweden.

Despite the explicit differences between Swedish aims for a classless society and the Syriac sense of minoritization, the majority Swedish and Syriac social worlds coexisted mostly peacefully during the 1960s. Putting the country's urban squalor on a dusty shelf of memories, Swedish economic prosperity produced a willingness to cooperate with immigrants in both political and urban space. Sweden transformed itself internationally to a proud benefactor for deserving individuals from abroad and a technological giant able to build a million dwelling units in ten years. Even today the country's humanitarianism and design aesthetic—reflected, for example, in the Swedish International Development Agency (SIDA) and in the IKEA furniture chain, respectively—remain synonymous with its identity abroad. Within its borders, the Social Democratic, utopian national project of the twentieth century—founded on linking building standards to social equality and the dispersal of resources—remains discursively strong, even if it increasingly exists more in myth than in reality under more recent neoliberal leadership.[149]

A collision was, however, on the horizon in the 1970s. With their own histories of difference packed on the plane from Lebanon, Syriacs arrived in a country that had not fully settled upon its approach to foreigners. Sweden increasingly linked respect for difference to the promotion of difference, while still wanting immigrants to be Swedish members of the classless urban world that the Million Program made material. Critically, officials also aimed to avoid clusters of immigrants congregating in specific geographic locales.

Foucault writes that modern disciplinary logic operates through "tactics of distribution, reciprocal adjustment of bodies, gestures and rhythms, differentiation of capacities, reciprocal coordination in relation to apparatuses or tasks";[150] it also "arrests or regulates movements; it clears up confusion; it dissipates compact groupings of individuals wandering about the country[side] in unpredictable ways; it establishes calculated distributions."[151] In this spirit, the Swedish welfare state expected Syriacs not only to accept the new norms of social equality developed through careful government research but also to adopt the spatial logic of distribution requiring them (ostensibly for their own benefit) to relinquish their desires to concentrate, to withdraw, or to be different.

Despite their Swedish indoctrination, however, Syriacs remained committed to their own spatial logic of enclosure as outsiders—by design—from the dominant society, just as they were in the Syriac millet in Turkey and in underground political organizations in Syria, avoiding spatial governmentalities and disciplinary distributions when possible. As Syriacs were finally given some measure of freedom to carry out the lives the Swedish state had so carefully prepared for them, they began to devise ways to reunite and settle together, working to determine the best possible location. According to Björklund's account, three Syriac men living in Nyköping decided to start the search:

> So they packed themselves into their second-hand Volvo Amazon and began to make excursions in the geography of Sweden (or the geography of Assyrian Sweden). The destinations of their trips were places with names that still sounded strange to them: Eskilstuna, Örebro, Växjö . . . , where they met Suryoye who had had similar experiences to their own. The idea of moving together to a common place was soon greeted with much enthusiasm by Assyrians throughout the country.
>
> But where? Many wanted to live closer to Stockholm and all the opportunities offered by a great city. Where did they have any fellow-countrymen in the vicinity of Stockholm? Well, there were a few living in Södertälje. Having reconnoitered in that direction they found the prospects promising.[152]

Only seventeen Syriacs (who were members of just three families) had been placed in Södertälje after their time in the AMS camp,[153] but the group began to form their new Syriac center in that town. Sending word of their new lives back to their relatives and friends in Turkey, Syria, and beyond, this call was enthusiastically answered in the mid-1970s. Working against Swedish efforts to assimilate them by separation, they renewed their historical tendencies toward enclaves, even as these settlements increasingly became a problem for the Swedish authorities and a crisis to solve.

What happened when a family of eight accustomed to symbiotic village living moved to an apartment in a high-rise building on the outskirts of a metropolitan area, an apartment designed for a Swedish middle-class family of four and surrounded by neighbors who kept to themselves? How were the public spaces of Swedish modern citizenship used and transformed by separatist Syriacs? As difference turned from questions of class to considerations of ethnicity during the 1970s, planning was increasingly charged with solving immigrant segregation through its discursive opposite: integration.

CHAPTER TWO

Visible Cities, Invisible Citizens

Service and Citizenship in the Centrum

Trumpets will be blown on Thursday, when the eagerly awaited and festive
inauguration of Ronna Centrum will happen—an eagerly awaited sounding of the
trumpet because the business center is the last piece of the puzzle for a
neighborhood that is nearly complete. People have already moved in there and have
had a hard time getting their shopping done for more than a year. But now all of
these problems are over. . . . Ronna will finally be finished!

—BOSCO, "Ronna blir självförsörjande: 9 butiker för 1.800 hushåll,"
Länstidningen, November 30, 1965

On December 2, 1965, the new shopping and citizen-service center known as Ronna
Centrum opened to great fanfare in Södertälje. A full-page advertisement had appeared in the local paper, *Länstidningen Södertälje* (often abbreviated as *Länstidningen* or *LT*), two days before, including a site plan with the locations and names
of its new businesses and services: recreational facilities and meeting spaces for organizations and clubs, a health-care center, a bakery, a post office, a dry cleaner, a
fishmonger, a florist, two hair salons, and two grocery stores (Figures 2.1 and 2.2).

Ebullient descriptions of this "hypermodern shopping city"[1] were filled with optimism about this achievement in social and physical planning, a novel form of public
space for an advanced twentieth-century society. Under the subheadline "Rational
Center," the newspaper proudly informed locals, "All the shops are situated in a
relatively small area, making it possible for you to plan your shopping so that it
takes as little time as possible."[2] Ronna Centrum's opening echoed the promises of
spatial efficiency made in modernist European urban design, as the Million Program's uniform planning required standardized public spaces to complement the
domestic ones then being built across Sweden.

The *centrum* (town center) represented a critical component of most Million Program neighborhoods; it was the place where modern citizens would engage with and
express their modernity.[3] The *centrum* would offer pedagogical centers, shopping,
health facilities, social clubs, and more. As the advertisement promised, the design
for Ronna Centrum followed suit, incorporating the latest ideas about commerce

RONNA
CENTRUM

ÖPPNAR DEN
2 DECEMBER
KLOCKAN 10.oo

1. Södertälje stads Fritidsgård
2. Södertälje stads Mödravårdscentral
3. Herrfrisörsalong
4. Salon Majvi
5. W. Karlssons Kemiska Tvätt
6. Be-Ge:s Tobak
7. Ronna Blommor
8. Ronna Livs
9. Församlingslokal
10. ABF:s Studielokal
11. Posten
12. Starcks Konditori
13. Lindbergs Fiskaffär
14. Konsumhallen

FIGURE 2.1. Plan of services in advertisement for Ronna Centrum's inauguration, December 1965. *Länstidningen,* November 30, 1965, 7.

Högtidlig invigning. Vädret var kyligt när stiftelsen Telgebostäders direktör Olov Lekberg höll invigningstalet.
Arkivfoto: Thomas Brandt

FIGURE 2.2. Inauguration of Ronna Centrum in 1965, reprinted in *Länstidningen* on the neighborhood's fortieth anniversary, December 1, 2005. The caption reads, "Festive inauguration. The weather was chilly when the Telgebostäder foundation's director, Olov Lekberg, gave the inaugural speech." *Länstidningen* i Södertälje AB. Photograph by Thomas Brandt.

and social services. The *centrum* would encourage interaction and create a space of identification for community members in Ronna, as others like it were doing across Sweden.

Though some residents had moved in earlier, the unveiling of the *centrum* also marked the official inauguration of Ronna at large: a new neighborhood built in what had been nearly uninhabited farmland. As the Million Program radically shifted the country's urban geography by suburbanizing virgin land like this, it altered Södertälje fundamentally, representing "one of the most thorough urban developments in Sweden."[4] Five new neighborhoods were constructed in the town: Ronna, Geneta, Saltskog, Fornhöjden, and, in the early 1970s, Hovsjö (see Map 2), each with a template town center. Given that workers in downtown Södertälje businesses were using outhouses into the 1940s, the Million Program's hygienic, modern, and comprehensive neighborhood services were received with the jubilation of trumpets that accompanied Ronna's opening.

As these major architectural, urban, and demographic transformations occurred in Södertälje, the town exchanged its identity as a bathing resort along a historic waterfront, surrounded by farms, for something more industrial. In the postwar period, Södertälje had rapidly become a center of production for the pharmaceutical company Astra AB (now AstraZeneca), founded in 1913, and the automobile and truck maker Scania AB, founded in 1891. By the end of the 1960s, these two companies employed two-thirds of the town's population. Södertälje became known as a "city of industry"[5] and its 4,500 industrial employees in 1950 doubled to 9,000 by 1960. Workers were lured to the town from other parts of Sweden and from other European countries, especially Finland.[6]

Employees of Scania referred to the prosperous 1960s as "job-hopper times,"[7] with the onus on employers to offer salaries and benefits to keep their valuable workers on-site. In Södertälje, the state funding, attractive loans, and political structures of the Million Program were thus seen as welcome interventions with a direct and positive effect on the local economy, allowing businesses to provide housing with modern standards.[8] An initial emphasis on rooms in so-called bachelor hotels quickly evolved into the creation of units for nuclear families, a move that further helped retain employees. The "Industry Group" quota allotted new housing to the companies but also allowed them to evict workers if and when their jobs ended.[9]

In the early 1970s, however, the music of continuous Swedish progress, structured social engineering, and regulated immigration suddenly stopped. As a vital organ in the body of Swedish industrial progress, Södertälje's extreme dependence on the fortunes of industry left it on life support when those fortunes flatlined. Its Million Program areas, intended as showpieces for a new progressive society and a beacon of Södertälje's luminous future, seemed to darken overnight as they rapidly emptied. The local media shrilly decried the growing number of "unrented apartments," blaming the municipality's planners for poor foresight. As New Towns became ghost towns, who would live on Södertälje's urban periphery? The answer quickly came.

The first Syriacs had arrived in Sweden in 1967, just two years after Ronna Centrum's inauguration and at the height of the boom years. As the grim realities of the 1970s took hold, local employers laid off their workers; many Finns, Greeks, and Yugoslavians left Södertälje. Yet Syriacs—who were motivated to migrate to Sweden by more than merely economic concerns—continued to arrive in unprecedented numbers. For many members of the town's existing population, who had just seen their jobs evaporate, the Syriacs were unwelcome. Most came as asylum seekers, but increasingly harsh newspaper headlines described them as "illegal immigrants" or a "mass invasion."[10] Racist letters to the editor of *LT* promoted nativist groups such as Keep Sweden Swedish (Bevara Sverige Svenskt, BSS).[11]

As the tide of negative public opinion crashed against the shores on which they had only just arrived, Syriacs established themselves in Södertälje's Million Program areas—especially Ronna and nearby Geneta. Södertälje had literally bet its farms on a Million Program increasingly under attack in the 1970s. As conflicts pitted majority Swedes, Finns, and Syriacs against one another and Syriacs against themselves, town centers became battlefields for a social and spatial revolution that would remake and redefine public squares, streets, and meeting rooms. Architectural historian Helena Mattsson notes, "The critical narrative of the suburbs, as the new locus for the welfare state, told a story of inhabitants caught in a misanthropic architecture that destroyed human individuality."[12] The Million Program has become the definition of failed Swedish social and spatial planning in exactly these terms, with areas in Södertälje no exception. The Syriacs' changes (continuing into the present day), however, suggest that such criticisms should be reevaluated.

Reconfiguring these meticulously planned territories, Syriacs redesigned urban space from below in *unplanned* ways. At a time when citizens, residents, and refugees could no longer rely on the promises of the state, Syriacs reclaimed public spaces designed for a Sweden that assumed an ethnically monolithic nation, reshaping public life in the process. These "users" have ultimately redefined the public space of Swedish modernism par excellence—the *centrum*—while working within it, as an examination of their symbolically potent but physically sedate transformations demonstrates.

From Farm to Hypermodern Shopping Center

The boom years of the 1960s suggested never-ending Swedish economic growth. The dream of a million new dwelling units was becoming a reality, and politicians capitalized on the fulfillment of their lofty promises. Social Democratic visions of a Sweden without class conflicts had delivered success. This allowed the welfare state to infiltrate the everyday lives of citizens on an unprecedented scale and scope, providing amenities from health clinics to post offices to high-tech laundry rooms in the basements of new apartment blocks. Improved income equality promoted a sense of national belonging.

The Swedish public sphere had expanded from a mere "moral order"—regulations defined by politicians and implemented by bureaucrats—to, in philosopher Charles Taylor's terms, a "modern social imaginary," whereby citizens understood themselves to belong to a newly retooled Swedish nation.[13] If the Million Program engendered a moral order among disparate people through the built environment, that moral order seeped into collective consciousness through everyday urban activities and became part of something larger: a modern social imaginary. New microlevel societies of the neighborhood unit and its public spaces regulated the everyday. The town center, or *centrum,* served as the symbolic and geographic core of the neighborhood unit.

As the first comprehensively designed Million Program neighborhood in Södertälje, Ronna followed national prescriptions for public space almost to the letter, but its radical development in the 1960s also extended the processes of urban development already underway in Södertälje twenty years before its inauguration. Until the mid-twentieth century, its land use comprised small-scale agricultural production—chiefly vegetables and flowers—along with a forest.[14] Ronna's subdivision into plots allowed single-family homes to be built on the southern side of what eventually became the neighborhood. Until the early 1960s, it had no other housing types.

Political infrastructures that developed in Södertälje during the early twentieth century facilitated the mass housing of the Million Program era. A public–private housing corporation proposed in 1915 became AB Bostäder in 1916. Not until March 10, 1948, however, did the city council approve a completely municipal housing company: Telgebostäder.[15] As Södertälje shifted from being popularly defined as a "recreation city" to a "city of industry" in the 1950s, the new and rising presence of laborers—many of them immigrants from Finland, Greece, or Yugoslavia—produced a critical housing shortage. With the support and influence of Scania, Telgebostäder developed new neighborhoods in the town's periphery to address this concern.[16] Here, the separation of functions was paramount in planning, and high-rises were included as early as 1952, in the plans for the Grusåsen area.[17]

In the early 1960s, planners identified Ronna as a possible site for development, with Telgebostäder its primary developer from 1962. At this time, Sverre M. Pettersen of the City Planning Office described the topography of the area in the description of the plan:

> The terrain climbs upward from Strängnäsvägen to a forest-covered, elevated section north of Bårsta Gård. Continuing to the north, the terrain sinks again into a dell, which stretches between Karlhov and Bårsta School. North of this dell, the ground rises—rather steeply in some places—up toward a higher elevation along the border of the Lina grounds.

For this challenging terrain, designer Fritz Voigt drew plans for high- and mid-rise multifamily apartment blocks amid copious open space, reminiscent of CIAM's "tower in the park" models. Plans for the earliest section of the new neighborhood, Ronna Gård (Ronna Farm, named after the bygone farm), were finalized in 1962, and construction of the town center began in 1963 (Figure 2.3).[18]

When completed in 1969, the Ronna neighborhood contained just one major road: Robert Anbergs Väg (Robert Anberg's Way), named after the town council's chairperson from 1940 to 1962. While bifurcating the neighborhood, the single road limited automobile access, following prescriptions for traffic separation and safety. On the eastern side, high-rise apartment buildings of seven stories were configured in three staggered lines, with woodlands embracing them on the northern side (Figure 2.4). To the west, in a subdivision labeled Ronna Park, mid-rise buildings of three stories were situated in closer proximity around rectilinear outdoor spaces. Another small zone constructed in 1969, dubbed Västra Ronna (Western Ronna), introduced a zone of row houses and detached houses. The differing housing typologies marked internal borders and reflected historical divisions between farm and forest.

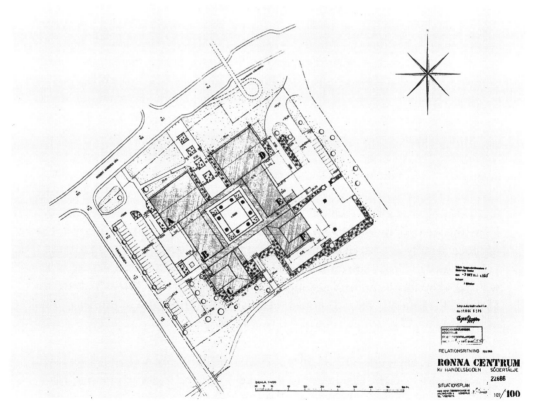

FIGURE 2.3. Site plan for Ronna Centrum, October 7, 1964. Stamped by Fritz Voigt Arkitektkontor AB. Source: Södertälje Kommun.

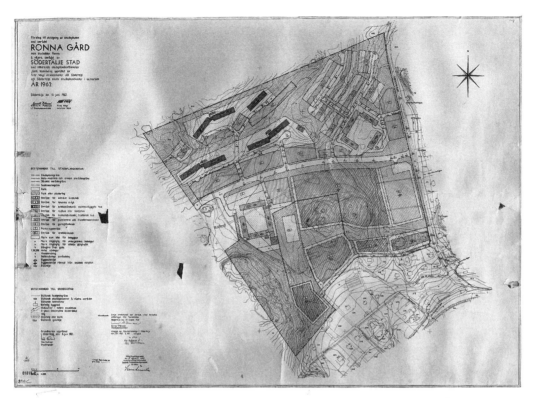

FIGURE 2.4. Plan for extension of Ronna Gård, 1962. Signed by Sverre Pettersen (city planner) and Fritz Voigt (architect). Source: Södertälje Kommun.

Voigt designed Ronna Centrum as a full-service public space that would provide social and commercial amenities to the entire neighborhood. Plans included a post office, quarters for a chapter of the Workers' Educational Association (Arbetarnas Bildningsförbund, ABF), a church, a library, a fishmonger, a flower shop, two grocery stores, and men's and women's hair salons. Schools and youth centers were also included (Figure 2.5). As in earlier models and in other Million Program developments across Sweden, the town center served as the nucleus of the neighborhood and, symbolically, of then-current welfare-state planning ideologies.[19] Ronna Centrum combined services for citizenship and consumption in one space.

The *Centrum*: Town Square of the Million Program

As the physical armature of the expanded Swedish public sphere, new collective spaces of the Million Program explicitly blurred distinctions between public and private, domestic and communal, and civic and commercial. Rather than occupying private, single-family houses, residents lived in multifamily apartment blocks and

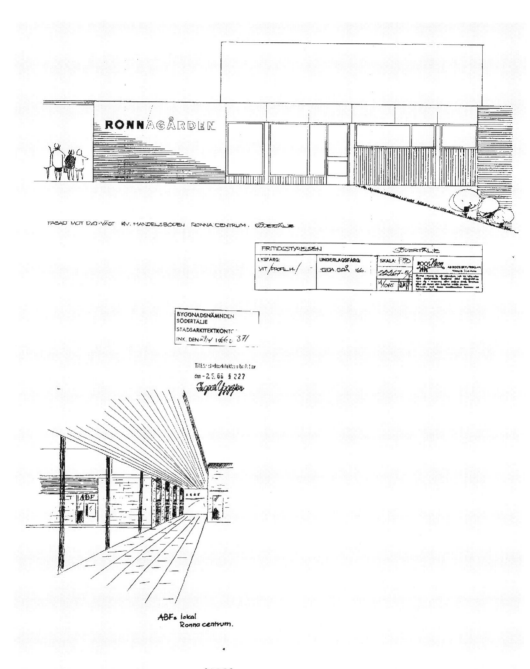

FIGURE 2.5. Drawings for the social services included in the 1960s plans for Ronna Centrum. Youth Center (Ronnagården) and the Arbetarnas Bildningsförbund (Workers' Educational Association, ABF). Stamped by the city architect on October 26, 1965, and May 2, 1966. Source: Södertälje Kommun.

identified themselves with the *trapphus,* or stairwell, that they shared with others. After booking and using a meticulously proportioned, common laundry room fitted out with the latest machinery, they were responsible for cleaning it.[20] Their children would play together outside on carefully designed grounds. With residents, like citizens, having both rights and responsibilities, these new public spaces incarnated the late-modernist Swedish state in miniature form, and the *centrum* was at their heart.

Ronna Centrum culminated decades of experiments with *centrum* planning. While the earliest Swedish town centers contained only a minimum of commercial and community structures, Årsta Centrum, designed by Uno Åhrén in the 1940s and completed in 1953, initiated an expanded concept for town center designs.[21] Broadened programmatically in Vällingby in 1954, the *centrum* then became a regular urban design feature. The government-sponsored Collective Housing Committee report entitled *Samlingslokaler* (Community centers), published in 1955, reinforced this agenda.[22] Achievements in workers' rights had increased leisure time, and the report reflected political anxieties about how this time would be used. The *centrum* was seen as a way to provide appropriate activities.[23]

By the 1960s, *centrum* design expressed Social Democratic beliefs in the direct correlation between productive practices of citizenship and urban planning.[24] Like Ronna's, New Town centers united residents who did not share a stairwell but lived in the same neighborhood unit. Johan Rådberg writes, "The leading idea was that suburban life would be made more comfortable [and] richer in content by being complemented with community services. Under this collective heading, they included day care centers, community centers, laundries, kiosk shops, etc."[25] Here, neighbors could happen upon one another while shopping and have a quick chat or attend a planned meeting or event.

In Södertälje, these national planning trends held great sway. A caption for a diagram (Figure 2.6) published in a 1965 edition of the community magazine *Din egen stad* (Your own city) states, "Like a heart and a vital nerve, a *centrum* is often located in the middle of a new housing area to serve the inhabitants' material and cultural needs."[26] The accompanying article explains that the typical *centrum* should, among other functions, provide spaces for community organizations, a Workers' Educational Association (ABF), church, post office, hair salon, flower shop, self-service grocery store, neighborhood health clinic, and library. Located around a new town square, the article argues, the *centrum* would reduce dependency on the downtown and modernize public life. The plan for Ronna Centrum followed this plan almost exactly.

As the welfare state became a way of life rather than merely a utopian vision, town centers like Ronna's also became receptacles for a Swedish modern social imaginary. Here, the public was redefined, along with public space, where an expanded understanding of the collective enlarged the spaces to be shared. As Hans-Erland Heineman wrote in 1975:

FIGURE 2.6. "Vi bygger och bor: Hur ett nytt område kommer till" (We build and live: How a new area is created). Diagram for template town center, *Din egen stad* (June 1965): 14–15. Courtesy of Jonas Nordin. Source: Stadsarkivet, Södertälje.

In pre-war Sweden the two were strictly separated—the public street and the private home were two different worlds. In Sweden today, almost all community functions are to be found . . . in a form characterized by fluid boundaries between public and private, the general and the individual: indoor environments of this kind include the office landscape, the nursing landscape, the educational landscape, the hypermarket, and the "house of culture," while outdoors the unfenced villa or row house area, and the new shopping centers and service facilities are tending in the same direction. . . .

These attitudes are to be seen . . . as a general protest against the propensity of the affluent society to think in terms of belongings and possessions, rather than services, contacts, and personality development.[27]

Blurring the public and private domains, the *centrum* was thus imagined as a heavily programmed, indoor–outdoor space that would encourage interaction and a sense of equality among modern Swedish citizens, provide opportunities for condoned forms of consumption, and create a physical and social space with which community members would identify.

Service Space for Citizens

Basking in the political and economic security of the 1960s, debates about the *centrum* focused increasingly on the notion of "service": the functions and goods required to run a household and to develop one's personhood outside the dwelling itself. The 1964 national government booklet *God bostad i dag och i morgon* (Good housing today and tomorrow) (a revised edition of *God bostad*) described the importance of programmed public space: "Improved housing standards mean not only better housing, but also increased space for all the other functions that are related to housing, not the least of which are the arrangement of collective amenities and chances to use your spare time in an enriched way."[28] This gave the *centrum*—ostensibly a mere recreational and commercial space—a specific didactic purpose within the structure of the larger society. Here, leisure and shopping would be pedagogical.

On April 14, 1967, the national government's Service Committee initiated research on this topic, producing seven reports from 1968 to 1973.[29] In the first, the committee described how the need for service arose out of a radical change from multigenerational households to nuclear families (with one or two children) over the period from 1920 to 1965.[30] For the committee, service comprised the following elements: (1) child care; (2) services for the elderly, ill, and disabled; (3) recreation and culture; (4) food; (5) household maintenance; (6) laundry and clothing care; and (7) goods distribution and sales. Since most were traditionally imagined as women's (unpaid) labor, service provision was also part of larger efforts to bring women into the paid workforce.[31] The authors also discussed traffic planning and organized activities for all ages.[32]

Even though most Million Program New Towns were built in peripheral locations, the *centrum* was to be as central to each neighborhood as its name implies. In a 1965 edition of the Swedish journal *Arkitektur,* Allan Westerman notes the effects of the increasing size of retail stores on the design of town centers, and the centers' critical social role:

> The concentration of functions was regarded as providing a better sense of orientation and as facilitating the integrated design of the entire urban area, a design that, through the architectonic environment's qualities, could affect a person in a positive way, could enrich her everyday existence, and could create a feeling of belonging to a group.[33]

The *centrum* would lend a pedagogical purpose to free time, reinforce equality and sameness among citizens, and blur the space between the public and private as it strengthened the Swedish modern social imaginary.

By 1975 this role had shifted, following, as Ingegerd Ågren describes, the transformation of the "welfare society" into a "service society," a stark change from before World War II. Ågren suggests that the *centrum* and its services occupied an ever-greater role in the life of the local neighborhood:

> Since the 30's, the concept of "service" has gradually altered, having been broadened from services fairly closely linked to the dwelling, such as the care and minding of children, and services related to the upkeep of the dwelling and to catering, which were

organized and paid for by the tenants and were often linked with the idea of "collective" multi-family houses, to cover a much wider system, in which the community is actively committed, by legislation, planning, financial support, and administration, to extend all-round assistance to the inhabitants, and provide the necessary conditions for a sense of community, social contacts, recreation, and activities that will develop personality.[34]

The 1971 Municipal Reform merged around 2,500 towns, boroughs, and rural districts extant in 1950 into just 278 municipalities of eight thousand or more residents by 1980.[35] Even as this centralized planning control, social institutions remained decentralized in the town centers. The global oil crisis of 1973 illuminated Sweden's uncomfortable dependency on international economic fortunes and its impotence in determining its own fate, which had immediate repercussions for the programs—and spaces—most beloved by Social Democratic planners, including the *centrum*. Exacerbating the crisis was the Swedish state's decision to decommission neighborhood-level services in the 1970s. For instance, only centrally located libraries would now be offered, and budgetary cuts forced community youth centers to reduce their hours.[36] Increasingly, there was no public in public spaces like Ronna Centrum.

The provision of retail space, together with social functions, recalls the idea that Million Program housing was not "social housing" for the needy. Rather, the neighborhoods were part of efforts to eliminate existing forms of socioeconomic and gender inequality.[37] Mats Franzén and Eva Sandstedt describe how the Service Committee's report from 1970 emphasizes this relationship between ideology and space:

> In 1968, residential service is defined as a set of functions. . . . [The] 1970 [report] is not satisfied with this list, instead emphasizing that service also affects the social environment, and therefore "service must also be addressed from ideological points of departure." Such a point of departure is that housing services contribute to "community and equality within and between generations and between people with different interests and in different social and economic situations" and that it "increases the opportunities for the individual to influence the shape of the common environment."[38]

Their analysis suggests that the impending period of austerity may have inadvertently produced an ideological return to the spirit of the 1955 report on assembly spaces,[39] stressing communal activities and appropriate, educational forms of leisure. The economic, political, and demographic shifts of the 1970s thus engendered new questions and conflicts to which the architecture and planning of the earlier period had difficulty responding. As town centers like Ronna Centrum were being transformed, they were also absorbing the frictions of these broader changes.

Even during the ten years of the Million Program, however, many of its New Towns began to lose their initial sheen, with criticism being focused on excessive standardization and oversimplified planning. Their signature facades—often gray concrete with green trim—signaled more a climate of melancholy and less an image of "homes of the future" after only a few years in the Swedish sun and snow. Furthermore, the amenities meant to surround them remained unfinished: playgrounds were unbuilt, vegetation failed to thrive, and bus and subway lines did not run. The criticisms, when combined with the economic crisis sweeping the world in the 1970s, had a devastating effect on Södertälje, with its deep dependence on industry. As residents of Ronna waited or relocated, other structural changes were afoot.

Integration, the Swedish Order of Things

In *The Order of Things,* Michel Foucault analyzes taxonomies as a technology of power, using the Swedish botanist Carolus Linnaeus and his classification of plants as a prime example.[40] Foucault does not, however, discuss Linnaeus's extensive work on categorizing people.[41] Sweden's philosophy of "integration," which emerged in the 1970s, drew on related understandings of unchanging ethnic, racial, and cultural groups.[42]

While making immigrants into Swedes had been the goal of the philosophy of assimilation practiced in the 1960s, new legislation in 1974 adopted a new policy—integration—stating that "ethnic, linguistic, and religious minorities' chances to maintain and develop their own cultural and religious life should be promoted."[43] A parliamentary declaration followed in 1975, arguing that "immigrants and minorities should be allowed to choose to what degree they want to take on a Swedish cultural identity or to maintain and develop the original identity."[44] Provisions linked this "original identity" to offerings such as "home-language" *(hemspråk)* provisions that began in the 1977–1978 school year, through which children of immigrants were given government-supported instruction in their parents' native language(s). While these policies created official political space for difference, they were nonetheless predicated on a hard taxonomy of cultural categories.

The disjuncture between these seemingly humanitarian policies that emerged in the 1970s and their less savory outcomes appears in cultural geographer Allan Pred's classic study of Swedish racism, *Even in Sweden,* published in 2000. He argues that most "positive" forms of contact between minority and majority Swedes occur through the cultural commodification of difference, such as in food or music: a move from "biological racism" to "cultural racism" that he labels a "refined replacement."[45] In her work on Norway, anthropologist Laurie McIntosh discusses the "impossible presence" of African men in the Norwegian nation, where "race-thinking" pigeonholes them into a state of invisibility and a continuous lack of belonging.[46] In a similar vein, anthropologist Lena Sawyer argues that "ethnicity" superseded earlier discourses about "race" in Sweden.[47]

Though the philosophy of integration allowed more room for alternative life-styles, it nonetheless simultaneously reified cultural expectations, a theme often seen in relation to so-called immigrant-dense suburbs.[48] In her seminal work from 1997, cultural geographer Irene Molina comments on the dark undertones of the integration model and the "urban racialization" that it created in the city:

> In the racial-hygiene discourse of the 1930s, vagrants, gypsies, the mentally ill, and even women were the deviant elements of society. They were the Other and should be disciplined. The equivalent today are "immigrants" who will be integrated. Although the differences between these two different epochs are fairly extensive, the idea of the Other never ceased; it only came to include other groups.[49]

The integration regime encouraged and appeared respectful of difference, but, in these views, it actually reinforced a secondary mode of citizenship for immigrants. These attitudes have taken an ominous turn today through the rise of far-right, anti-immigrant political parties to European national governments. The Sweden Democrats (Sverigedemokrater, SD), a party originally built out of the neo-Nazi movement, first won parliamentary seats in 2010, garnered nearly 13 percent of the Swedish vote in 2014, and has had polling numbers approaching (and occasionally surpassing) 20 percent since that election. While ostensibly arguing against immigration in favor of "helping people where they are," the SD's racist platform emphasizes the reification of Swedes and Others and the notion that their boundaries can never be transgressed or shifted.[50] In Sweden, in other words, the philosophy of integration has created what anthropologist Paul Silverstein terms a "new savage slot";[51] it has opened and closed to define Others.

Shifts in immigration policy during the 1970s also placed greater restrictions on both who could come to Sweden and under what conditions they could remain.[52] Critically, a new national law required immigrants to secure a residence permit before arrival, ending the era of the "spontaneous" labor-migrant arrivals of the 1950s and 1960s.[53] Several groups were exempted, however. Citizens of Denmark, Finland, and Norway were still allowed to move and work freely in Sweden through the 1951 joint Nordic agreement. Even so, as concerns about the rising number of immigrants occurred in parallel to discussions about how to make room for women in the job market, other forms of labor immigration ended in 1972.

Political refugees and family members of earlier migrants were also exceptions to the new rules. For the former, the 1951 United Nations Convention Relating to the Status of Refugees has served as the primary point of reference for international refugee law since the end of World War II.[54] The Migration Agency labels the 1980s "the decade of the asylum seeker," but the groundwork was laid in the 1970s. First, a large number of Chileans sought asylum in the aftermath of the 1973 coup d'état. Immigrants from other areas arrived after the breakdown of the Soviet Union or in response to environmental disasters.[55] In 1960, 299,879 foreign-born people were living in Sweden (4 percent of the total population of 7.5 million). By 1970, the number was 537,585 (6.7 percent of 8.1 million).[56]

Even as integration became the dominant doctrine where foreigners were concerned, the modern social imaginary of Sweden remained homogeneous and isolated, both domestically and abroad. The welfare state sought to erase economic and class differences but did not address ethnic inequalities.[57] Franzén and Sandstedt point out that the focus, from the 1970s onward, was on supporting weaker groups in society and working against the perceived growing problem of segregation, neither of which was present in the 1960s literature.[58] Strict cultural categories made the treatment of foreigners "separate but equal" in practice, but the spatial implications of these policies remained unclear.

These emerging frictions chafed painfully as new arrivals appeared without a formal invitation. As refugees in the late 1960s, Syriacs encountered the benevolence of an affluent Sweden whose economy seemed to promise eternal prosperity. Conflicts emerged when this closed system allowed outsiders to seep into the Swedish mainstream—a leak that quickly became a full-fledged deluge as Syriacs arrived "spontaneously." By the mid-1970s, Syriacs were recast from innocuous laborer-refugees helping build the welfare state to unsolicited "immigrants" or "foreigners" threatening the Swedish modern project.[59] The public of welfare-state spaces was defined a priori as a non-Syriac one, and the crisis of the Syriacs' unplanned arrival erupted as they used planned streets and services. Though the welfare state succeeded in creating a powerful modern social imaginary that still shapes Sweden today, to be trapped in what Abidin Kusno terms a "violence of categories"[60] was to be forever othered and, by proxy, to be excluded from redefining the spaces of modernity.

Ronna, Capital of Assyria

As structural shifts around planning, administration, and immigration occurred in the 1970s, popular perceptions of Million Program areas became negative, and Social Democratic boosters and politicians were pressed to admit failure. New areas were still being built, prompting laments in public research reports.[61] With one million dwelling units in the balance, a public relations catastrophe loomed, but the evidence spoke for itself: those who had the resources to leave Million Program areas were doing so, en masse.

Popular opinion, however, blamed not civic leaders but, rather, the Million Program's designers for the welfare state's inability to deliver on its promises. As Ingemar Johansson writes, "It was actually more common in the Swedish debates of the early 1970s that architects were incriminated for the new society's failings rather than the politicians or the contractors."[62] In response, and in a radical move away from Million Program top-down planning models, the Swedish Parliament approved a housing policy in 1974 that placed a new focus on "tenant influence and housing democracy."[63] But approximately twenty-five thousand new apartments were already empty across Sweden by 1976, and one municipal housing company had gone bankrupt.[64] Despite the explicit emphasis of the Million Program on creating equality through a perfected built environment, New Towns like Ronna became the stigmatized domain of those with few other options: the mentally ill, the elderly, alcoholics, and, finally, immigrants.

In Södertälje, the national trend was magnified. The town's enthusiastic participation in the Million Program meant that its suffering was amplified. The downturns for Scania and Astra met the paradigm shift concurrently taking place in production and industrialized labor, requiring fewer workers. While the building boom of the 1960s produced a sizable new housing stock for workers, many had left by the time the majority of the dwellings were available. In Ronna, many of the area's large number of Finns returned to their home country.[65]

Södertälje's numerous "unrented" (the term preferred over *empty*)[66] apartments dealt a heavy blow to the town's reputation and created a financial crisis for Telgebostäder, for which each empty apartment meant lost revenue. Local leaders received this situation with increasing trepidation, and the problem was frequently discussed in the media.[67] As plans were announced in 1975 to spend 2.5 million Swedish kronor for renovations to several just-completed neighborhoods, the white flag of surrender seemed be waving high. As Södertälje journalist Ingegerd Asp-Lundström wrote that year, "It is no secret that, for instance, Ronna, Geneta, and Saltskog [all Million Program neighborhoods] are problem areas."[68]

On September 16, 1976, an editorial in *LT* debated solutions to the housing crisis and included a cartoon visualizing the problem (Figure 2.7). The cartoon depicts a long queue of prospective residents waiting to enter a storefront offering "Housing close to the ground"; the shop window contains three small, traditional houses with pitched roofs and a sign, apparently taped onto the glass, reads, "Six years' waiting time." Another apparent proprietor looks on from an adjacent door, where his company's sign reads, "Södertälje Housing Market." His window features highrise blocks and three signs: "1300 apartments for rent," "Available now!!!," and "Sale." The contrast made palpable the climate of panic in a town that had just invested heavily in architectural modernism's promises, only to find itself vulnerable to market forces that had not been predicted.

Of most concern in the early 1970s was the ongoing construction of the new neighborhood of Hovsjö.[69] Knowing that there would be few tenants to populate it, Telgebostäder considered abandoning the project in its half-built state, but the cost proved higher than continuing.[70] With few tenants, however, the neighborhood suffered from disuse, careless upkeep, and petty crime even in its earliest days. In its lofty ascent and precipitous collapse, Hovsjö mirrors the Million Program both at large and in its perceived failures during the 1970s.

FIGURE 2.7. Cartoon from *LT,* published on September 16, 1976. The storefront on the left offers "six years' waiting time" for "housing close to the ground." The shop on the right is called "Södertälje Housing Market" with signs declaring, "Available now!" "1300 apartments to rent" and "Sale." *Länstidningen* i Södertälje AB. Artist unknown.

What were meant to be the shining beacons of the triumphs of the welfare state (and the *folkhem* that preceded it) evolved into embarrassingly visible symbols of its failures. In 1980, Hans Asplund (son of architect Gunnar) wrote that it was time to say "Farewell to functionalism!"[71] As the cities of the future had evolved into the "problem areas" of the present, a new suburban dystopia of monotonous housing, social alienation, and undesirable ethnic segregation took its place.[72] The *centrum* was no longer the nucleus of a new modern world; instead, it was a symbolic void at the center of a lost dream.

Uniting in the Association

Economic collapse, the unrented apartment crisis, and Million Program malaise peaked in the mid-1970s. Södertälje media reports frequently bemoaned the loss of residents to neighboring communities with vacant single-family homes, which were regarded as more desirable than the town's multifamily high-rises. Articles about the constant arrival of Syriacs often appeared in newspapers on the same day, sometimes on the same page. Yet journalists failed to draw a connection between the two. Even so, Syriacs themselves understood the calculus, and the empty apartments of Södertälje became a considerable pull factor, drawing them from across Sweden. Many arrived on their own, and others came as the State Immigration Board (Statens

Invandrarverk), which was created in 1969, assigned asylum seekers and refugees to the town.[73] Large Syriac family networks that had disbanded in Turkey, Syria, and Lebanon reconstituted in Södertälje, particularly in Ronna.[74] The neighborhood became the center of Syriac life in Sweden.

Even though the Million Program became a negative symbol for Swedish planning and architecture, its high quality represented a new form of utopia for Syriacs. Björn, a Swedish man in his sixties who had spent considerable time with the group during the 1970s, described this contrast to me in 2009:

> It was so new, this Million Program that was ugly from the beginning in my middle-class Stockholm. But they [the Syriacs] often declared that "This is paradise. Cold water. Hot water. Bathtub. Shower. All of that. Refrigerator. Freezer." They were hillbillies from the Third World.

As they lived the Million Program dream—now a nightmare for the Swedish nation—some Syriacs also legitimized their use of the neighborhoods' institutional spaces as they organized in an association *(förening),* a particularly Swedish form of social club. The Assyrian Association (Assyriska Föreningen) was founded in 1971.

Named from the word *förena* (to unite), this government-supported arrangement—usually based at the local level—had its roots in working-class social movements of the eighteenth and nineteenth centuries.[75] In Sweden, these groups quickly lost their revolutionary, antiestablishment orientations as the state recast and promoted them as sanctioned social clubs. For this reason, Million Program town centers contained dedicated meeting spaces, as Franzén and Sandstedt explain:

> In Sweden, it is above all the separate associations that have come to use meeting rooms, so it is primarily an internally organized public that is supported by the state through these spaces. In a broader perspective, these meeting rooms are a form of state support for these associations.[76]

Each association delimited its own appeal, encouraging a small number of people to meet regularly around a common interest.[77] Some focused on personal interests such as handicrafts or art, bird-watching, gardening, or sobriety; some attracted people who wanted to discuss a particular topic, such as a common medical problem or child rearing; and some became an extension of labor unions. As they met in the *centrum,* participation in an association formed a key element of a modern social life.

When the first groups of Syriacs learned about Swedish ways of life in the AMS refugee camp, they received explicit instruction in creating federations and associations.[78] Organizing in a recognizably Swedish way permitted them to capitalize financially on the new doctrine of integration, since the immigrant "federation" *(riksförbund)* promoted a non-Swedish cultural identity that the state supported socially and financially, with local branches, "immigrant associations" *(invandrar-föreningar),* working in direct collaboration.[79] This intersected in intriguing ways with the Syriacs' already well-developed sense of themselves as a subaltern public. Syriacs coming from Turkey, for example, declined to join existing Turkish associations in order to form their own groups instead.[80] Svanberg and Tydén write, "It is also usually argued that immigrants should form associations in part to maintain and expand their own distinctive nature and identity, and in part to be a contact point with the authorities."[81]

True to these expectations, Syriacs used the association to legitimize themselves within the Swedish welfare-state bureaucracy, though this form of political and social organization worked against Syriac traditions, as sociologist Fuat Deniz writes:

> The formation of councils through democratic elections, discussions, and decisions about various issues were distant from the group's hierarchical social organization. The [Syriac] group came to a country whose popular-movement traditions and democratic history stretched several hundred years back in time. To form associations according to this model with elected councils, which was a historical tradition and a given for Swedes, was something new and unfamiliar for most *assyrier/syrianer.*[82]

Some Syriac leaders quickly understood, however, that establishing an association would help in the quest to attain group rights in Sweden and that forming associations could also be a potent and lucrative endeavor. Furthermore, they would be following a successful local lead: the cultural association Finlandia (established in 1952) appeared to be powerful and remained the largest immigrant association in Södertälje throughout the 1970s.[83]

Benjamin, who had taken part in the lessons in the camp in Alvesta, described the increasing appeal of the association and how it would allow Syriacs across Sweden to reconnect:

> When we were going to establish the Assyrian Federation of Sweden *[Assyriska Riks-förbundet],* we traveled around to different municipalities and informed others about what we knew and what we had learned about the society. And we promised them that if they set up an association, we would help them, we would make calls for them. And we did. After about a year, in 1977, we established the federation. It was in Södertälje, but the federation had associations all over Sweden.

The Assyrian Association of Södertälje began renting an underground space in Ronna Centrum in the 1970s.[84] This gave the neighborhood a new importance in the Syriac social imaginary. As parish priest Father Johannes told me, "The association was in Ronna, and everyone was in Ronna. So, clearly, it felt like Ronna was the place of possibility."

Beginning in the fiscal year 1975–76, all national-level immigrant associations were offered financial support from the Swedish state. This sponsorship required that an association have over one thousand members spread over a large geographic area, a democratic organizational structure, and a focus on handling the specific issues of that immigrant or minority group.[85] Municipal organizations could instead receive financial support locally. According to a report published by the State Immigration Board and Labor Market Department in 1990:

> The immigrant associations fill an important social function. They are a kind of home base where you can meet people who speak the same language, or read newspapers from the homeland. Newly arrived immigrants can discuss phenomena that seem strange in the new country. The associations help their members and new arrivals to understand how the society works in different contexts. For immigrants who have lived in Sweden for a long time, the associations have another function, which is that they help them to retain contact with their language and their culture and try to make sure that the immigrants' children also take part in the common cultural inheritance.[86]

With increasing importance and visibility in public life, the Assyrian Federation of Sweden began publishing a monthly journal known as *Hujådå* (meaning "union" in Suryoyo) in May 1978.[87] The editors of the inaugural issue chose the confluence of Syriac Orthodox Easter celebrations—the major holiday of the year for the group— and the First of May, a major Swedish workers' holiday, as its release date. Published in Suryoyo, Swedish, Arabic, and Turkish, the magazine's articles followed the lead of new Swedish integration politics, emphasizing the importance of being simultaneously culturally Syriac and full members of Swedish society.

The Assyrian Association, the Assyrian Federation of Sweden, and what later became known as the Syrianska Federation (established in 1978) flourished during what was otherwise a moment of crisis for the Swedish social welfare state. While political support for immigrant associations continued, public opinion about immigrants' arrival and presence shifted. Once received systematically and with the cheerful self-respect of a magnanimous benefactor, immigrants were now portrayed as a drain on the Swedish economy, for which welfare was predicated on clear boundaries of membership. Even as public opinion came to see Million Program neighborhoods as unwanted urban detritus, the anchoring of the Assyrian Association in Ronna Centrum eventually became an irritant—both for some residents of Södertälje and for others outside it. Ronna had become the headquarters for the *assyrier* in the group, and, in effect, the capital of a new diasporic Assyria.

"Our Immigrants" or "Illegal Immigrants"?

In 1975 and 1976, Syriacs migrated to Sweden in unprecedented numbers. Most made their way to Södertälje, giving the city thousands of new residents in just two years. Unlike their predecessors, they did not come through a quota program. Instead, the media labeled them, at best, "our" immigrants[88] and, at worst, "illegal" immigrants.[89] A retired city council member active in Södertälje's politics at the time described this to me as "caravans from Arlanda [the primary Stockholm airport] arriving every day." Södertälje's local paper carried numerous stories about the issue, eventually suggesting that organized smuggling was underway.[90] One article detailing a "mass invasion of *assyrier*" noted that "the municipality is deeply strained" and then stated, "Every morning, ten *assyrier* come to the police station in Södertälje and ask to be allowed to stay here. They have been attracted here by relatives, whose letters have described how good it is in Sweden."[91]

What attracted them was not just a better life. Generous Swedish immigration policies and the burgeoning Syriac Orthodox community pulled them to Södertälje, but push factors were at work as well. In 1973, with its economy in crisis, Germany closed its borders to guest workers from Turkey, ending a bilateral agreement enacted in 1961.[92] Many workers there were Syriacs who chose to move on to Sweden rather than return to the Middle East. The coup d'état in Cyprus in 1974, followed by the Turkish invasion, worsened the position of minority Christians in Turkey itself, encouraging even more Syriacs to leave that country.

The earlier Syriac immigrants had received a measured reception; in contrast, the authorities now struggled to respond to this unplanned, "unregulated" immigration. As journalist Per-Erik Persson described the situation in Södertälje in 1975: "The personnel at the Bureau of Information are working under pressure to help the new immigrants cope with life; the police have been forced to expand their immigration department."[93] Proposals were aired to assemble "spontaneously immigrated" Syriac volunteers willing to be housed in a nationally supported "investigation camp," where their children would also receive special instruction.[94] The Syriac population in Södertälje was estimated at four hundred in early 1975; they numbered approximately three thousand by March 1976 as journalists described a "new immigrant wave" flooding Södertälje.[95]

A major debate then ensued about whether Syriacs were actually "refugees" according to Geneva Convention definitions, leading to limited deportations in 1976. In a speech in Stortorget (the major downtown public square in Södertälje) that year, the Syriac Orthodox archbishop argued rhetorically that it would be better to execute the Syriac asylum seekers at the airport than to return them to Turkey.[96] The pages of *LT* included provocative titles like "Kill Us Rather Than Deport Us!"[97] and "Rejected *Assyrier*: The Government Is Splitting Our Families."[98]

In 1975, the State Immigration Board weighed emergency responses to an unmanageable number of asylum applications. Granting amnesty to many of those already in Sweden, the board created a new refugee category outside the restrictive definitions of the Geneva Convention in 1976, bestowing "B-Refugee" status on 1,200 Syriac asylum seekers in the so-called *nollställningsbeslut* (resetting decision).[99] Another 2,000 Syriacs were granted B-Refugee status later in the year.[100] The authorities assumed that these measures, coupled with a new law requiring Turkish citizens to obtain a visa before entering Sweden, would end spontaneous migrations. Border enforcement continued to be less than successful, however, as the power of the regulations in law far surpassed their effectiveness in practice. Although no additional B-Refugee amnesties were offered and the number of Syriac immigrants coming to Sweden did decline, many continued to arrive during the late 1970s and early 1980s.[101]

Complicating matters, the new Syriacs began from a rather different position than their predecessors. The quota refugees had spent months in Alvesta under official tutelage, learning about welfare-state institutions and acquiring Swedish-language skills, but newcomers were not instructed about Swedish codes of public behavior. Their understandings of public space came from Tur Abdin and the cities of Syria and Lebanon. Varying visions of urban life, and their supporters, came into physical and rhetorical conflict as Syriacs became increasingly visible in public space, especially in the *centrum.*

Whose Public Space?

In *Unsettling Europe,* published in excerpts in the *New Yorker* during the 1970s and then in book form in 1980, American journalist Jane Kramer examined immigration in Europe through portraits of individual immigrants living in four European settings, including Södertälje. There, the downtown pedestrian mall was the site of clashes between immigrants and majority Swedes, particularly as they understood the use of public space differently:

> No Swede ever really stops to *enjoy* Gånggatan [*sic*].[102] The Swedes are a private people, and it is not their style to use the middle of the town for socializing. They are scandalized when new *invandrare,* taking the mall for a kind of plaza, descend on Gånggatan for strolling and gossiping and drinking and the kind of amiable loitering that goes on all the time in the middle of a southern European village. The sight of an *invandrare* family all dressed up for a leisurely evening paseo on the mall seems to distress the Swedes nearly as much as the sight of a gang of tough young Greeks or Yugoslavs hanging around at night under the Gånggatan street lamps on the prowl for Swedish girls—and in their own way the Swedes let the *invandrare* know it. Lately the stores on the mall have hired guards to keep their doorways clear and break up nighttime scuffles. The cafeteria in the department store called Domus, which is owned by the Stockholm branch of the country's consumer movement, has put up signs in six languages warning people who come to gossip over a cup of coffee that they are permitted

the use of a table for only half an hour. The Södertälje *invandrare* learn about Sweden by learning, trial and error, the rules of Gånggatan.[103]

The street that Kramer analyzed still exists today as a primary downtown public space, created in 1969 through an urban-renewal project. Like the earlier immigrants in Kramer's piece, Syriacs used the public spaces they found in Södertälje in ways that often made earlier residents uncomfortable, producing rancorous rumors. As Syriac men were seen walking down public streets in suits and ties on weekdays, some residents asked if they bought clothes with Swedish tax money and why they were dressed up anyway. When Syriacs bought small shops and kiosks, resentments built about their perceived wealth relative to the working-class majority Swedes of Södertälje. The Syriacs were said to be even more disrespectful behind closed doors, where they supposedly grew vegetables in their bathtubs, having no other use for them.

In the early 1980s, social tensions in Södertälje precipitated the production of a six-part documentary series on Swedish Public Television (SVT, Sveriges Television). Entitled *Klyftan* (The divide), it concerned Södertälje and immigration, with a focus on the Syriac group. Interviews with majority Swedes illustrated their expectations about the use of public and semipublic spaces. For example, in a segment entitled "Södertälje—City in the World," shown on February 2, 1982, one Swedish resident of Ronna complained that Syriacs used laundry rooms when others had already booked the times and threw trash from balconies. She was particularly incensed, however, about one issue:

RESIDENT: During the summers, they stay out on the lawn. They eat breakfast, dinner, everything. They gather in heaps on the lawn. That bothers us a lot, for our children's sakes also. We have to pick up everything that they throw there: paper, scraps of food, everything like that.

INTERVIEWER: Don't Swedes eat outside?

RESIDENT: No, we don't. Not like that anyway. We have a coffee together on the playground, but not like them with entire families. They might be twenty or thirty, maybe even more, on the lawns in the summers. That is what bothers us so much.[104]

The welfare state relied on tacit codes of public behavior, such that breaking rules of use for the laundry room, the lawn, or the pedestrian street made Syriacs, for some majority Swedes, unwelcome guests in the People's Home.[105] Perceived disruptions of the moral order in public spaces implied, often in racist terms, a potential threat to the Swedish modern social imaginary.

With tensions mounting, and with a looming potential for ethnic violence like that dominating the news from the United States, France, and other locales, bureaucrats sought to disrupt stereotypes and rumors. A municipal brochure, for instance, offered information about the Syriacs' background, illustrating their move from Turkey to Million Program Sweden (Figure 2.8). Likewise, in the free municipal paper *Ditt Södertälje,* an article in the October 1980 edition was entitled, "Our *assyrier/ syrianers* background." One picture (Figure 2.9) showed a Syriac woman washing clothing in Turkey, with the caption "Laundry day: You don't need to book a time."

The ascendant Syriacs also changed the social position of the Finns, as seen in one 1980 Swedish television program.[106] In it, a group of Finns sit around a coffee table, drinking vodka and coffee. One man describes the arrival of the Syriacs, saying proudly, "The Finns have moved one flight up." His wife says, however, "It's clear that they get more social welfare than the Finns." Her husband replies, "If someone else goes to Social Services, they wave with a cold hand." The woman responds, "But that's because they are coming as political refugees. They need more help for that reason. But they don't get more than what's usual. They don't get a fruit and wine subsidy."

Some residents of Södertälje did in fact believe that Syriacs received a special welfare benefit to buy fruits and vegetables, since they did so in quantities that

FIGURE 2.8. Pages from the government-issued brochure *Folkgrupp i Södertälje* (Ethnic group in Södertälje), emphasizing the contrast between Tur Abdin villages and Million Program Sweden. They are labeled "From Basibrin outside Midyat in southeastern Turkey . . . ," ". . . to Södertälje." Source: Private collection.

Gabrielsklostret,
Tur Abdin. (.h.)

Taggigt ris och
plåtburkar på
murkrönen tjä-
nar som skydd
och.alarm

Klosterskola

Tvättdag. Man
behöver inte
boka tid. (nedan.)

Foto: Stig Hellmers

Södertälje-politikerna
i Turkiet:
Det feodala
systemet återspeglas
i Södertälje

FIGURE 2.9. Images from an article in the municipal magazine *Ditt Södertälje*, "Our *assyrier/syrianer*'s background," October 1980: 6. The main headline reads, "The feudal system is being reflected in Södertälje." Photographs by Stig Hellmers. Source: Stadsarkivet, Södertälje.

earlier residents considered highly unusual. A major Swedish newspaper described this conflict over public comportment in 1981:

> The Swede who is called "Masen" stands and sells fruit by the boxful to the immigrants. The Swedish hawkers do not like this. Fruit should be sold by the kilo and not by the box! . . . In the middle, among all the boxes and the people, "Masen" stands and watches over his business. He gets irritated when the customers put their fingers on his tomatoes. "One is of course a little bit of a racist. . . . But at the same time, we make money from them. I have to admit that they're good customers." Many Södertälje residents are amazed that the immigrants don't have the same eating habits as Swedes. A rumor has spread that says that the immigrants receive a "fruit subsidy."[107]

Food preparation in large quantities for extended families did not figure into the analysis. Instead, such purchases became yet another example of inappropriate behavior in Swedish public space.

Media reports linked Syriac comportment in urban space to anxieties about their territorial domination in Södertälje. A Swedish security guard described the situation in the 1970s in a radio program from 2008: "People thought that they got everything for free. . . . They talked too loudly, they had gold chains and ties on in the middle of the week. . . . The *assyrier* wanted to take over the entire city. It was like we Swedes didn't have space anymore."[108] Many Syriacs, however, understood these disparities as merely a difference in sartorial standards. One man, for instance, argued that Swedes did not understand that refugees were, by definition, persecuted but were not necessarily impoverished and that they wore their best clothing for meetings with authorities to demonstrate their respect for them. He also noted, however, "It did not take long before we realized that these clothes were not the way it was done in Sweden. And then we began to tell each other: 'Okay! So there are different rules that apply.' And we put those clothes aside and wore typical Swedish clothing."[109]

Rumors flew on the Syriac side as well, as they believed that the authorities might be stealing money from them. The Red Cross or World Council of Churches was said to have constructed "luxurious" neighborhoods for them, as Björn told me:

> The thought was that there were international organizations that had thought about the *assyrier* and financed the construction [of the Million Program]. And that's why they thought that the Swedes manipulated things, and that the Swedes wouldn't admit that that's how it really was. They thought the Swedes just pretended that it was difficult to get housing.

In reality, Syriacs populated what would otherwise have been a modernist ghost town, rejected by Swedes and abandoned by Finns. As the number of Syriacs in Södertälje exploded in the mid-1970s, they further concentrated in the neighborhood, slowly becoming Ronna's majority ethnic group and numbering approximately ten thousand to twelve thousand people by the early 1980s. During this decade, they began to establish themselves within the community structures, especially the *centrum*.

Rumbles with the *Raggare*

The Assyrian Association's rental of the clubhouse in Ronna Centrum from 1977 marked a key initial phase in changes to the area's identity.[110] The group used the space for social gatherings, card playing, and discussions about Syriac history and politics during the day. Community celebrations, such as weddings and the celebration of the Assyrian New Year on April 1, took place at night. In this way, the group utilized the spatial structure of Ronna, established with Social Democratic ideals of community engineering for the Swedish state, for their own nationalist purposes. When Finlandia moved from Ronna Centrum to a space vacated by the Recreation Administration in downtown Södertälje in 1980, the Assyrian Association claimed the larger space they left behind.

Syriac commercial activities flourished in Ronna in parallel. In his 1983 book, journalist Stefan Andersson mentions that "*klanledaren* [the clan leader] Chamoun Ganno rented a workshop in Ronna. He started manufacturing wooden shoes there, which were sold for a significantly lower price than for similar wooden shoes in the Swedish stores."[111] Little by little, Syriacs began to operate the stores and other services of the *centrum*. One grocery store, for instance, retained its name but offered an increasing supply of goods and wares from the Middle East.

The anchoring of Syriacs to the spaces of Södertälje was regarded as a provocation by the so-called *raggare*,[112] the anti-immigrant youth gangs who rode around Sweden in large American cars from the 1950s until the 1980s. In the mid-1970s, they drove regularly to Södertälje. A conflict now known as "Sweden's first race riots"[113]—between a group of *raggare* and a group of Syriacs—took place in downtown Södertälje at the Bristol Hotel on June 18, 1977. One *raggare* yelled, "Look, there are *svartskallar* [a racial epithet used for all immigrants; literally, "black heads"] sitting in there!" and pointed to a group of Syriacs sitting in the hotel's restaurant. A major fight ensued, and fourteen people were hospitalized, but just one arrest was made. One headline in the local paper screamed, "Saturday Night's Riots Only the Beginning: Police Fear Continued Race Conflict."[114] After this, fights between *raggare* and Syriacs occurred regularly. Blockades on the roads the *raggare* used to enter the town had limited effect.

During the so-called terror night of August 23, 1980, *raggare* burned several Syriac businesses.[115] Public protests took place. In a supposed effort to curb the violence, police advised Syriacs to avoid appearing in large groups, attending services at Syriac Orthodox churches to spread this message.[116] One Syriac man, George Baryawno, described, in a Radio Sweden documentary, how they adopted strategies of invisibility:

We learned that we needed to hurry up and adapt. We had to integrate. We had to stop walking around in groups in the town so that we wouldn't be seen. We got different spaces. Cafés were created then just so that we could hide. Many associations were formed, many clubhouses were opened just so that we could gather in different, secluded places. We had no other option at that time. That was something that the police were pointing out to us all the time through interpreters. And even the social authorities, they used to say quite openly during meetings in the churches or in the associations that we had to avoid going around in groups. Somehow they wanted us to be invisible because it wasn't common for more than two–three people to walk around together in town: to be seen. But we had the habit from our homelands of being in large groups, regardless of where we were, and then to talk a little bit loudly. And we usually sat in different cafeterias and so on, and there were some disruptions. And all of this was of course pointed out by the authorities.[117]

As Swedish officials explicitly encouraged the Syriacs to make themselves invisible, Ronna Centrum, where the Assyrian Association operated from behind the opaque walls of clubhouse spaces, became all the more important. There, Syriacs could congregate in large numbers and dress as they wished without attracting negative attention.

In their campaign of provocation, the *raggare* also claimed that Syriacs walked around Södertälje wearing T-shirts bearing the text "We're going to take over the town!"[118] When a reporter for Radio Sweden interviewed two *raggare* and a police officer about this rumor, each admitted that he had never seen such a T-shirt himself. One *raggare* said, however, "But I've heard about it from so many people that it must be true." The police officer continued with this ominous comparison: "The Jews owned a lot in Germany, and Hitler had the people behind him. The *assyrier* own a lot here in Södertälje. They buy up a lot of shops. They have more money than the Swedish people have ever had. So there are of course parallels."[119]

The *centrum*, with its many shops, highlighted the terms of the conflict, and memories of Ronna Centrum as a battleground are strong. One man in his fifties, David, told me:

They knew that we [the Syriacs] were most organized in Ronna, and these *raggare* got permission to operate a clubhouse in Ronna, parallel with our clubhouse. They wanted to drive the people out, to drive them insane. They hate all foreigners. Anyone who is anything other than Swedish, they hate them. How could they give them permission to operate a clubhouse so close to where the people were gathered?

David described the two groups engaging in daily fistfights there over several months, a battle over Ronna Centrum that was framed in nationalist terms by both groups. He said that the *raggare* affiliated themselves with the sentiments of groups like

"Keep Sweden Swedish!," while the Syriacs sought to maintain their association.[120] According to David, the *raggare* eventually withdrew after many fights. With this Syriac victory in the multiyear battle for Ronna Centrum, its public spaces rebranded the much-maligned Swedish welfare-state spaces of the Million Program.[121] In 1970s Södertälje, styles of dress, the quantities of produce purchased, and loitering were interpreted as "non-Swedish" uses of the city, an affront to the rules of Social Democratic decorum. In Ronna Centrum, the Syriacs developed a parallel city, a space that had fallen off the map of majority Swedish national geography. Here they could be invisible—but public—at the same time.

New Swedish Public Space

From the critical vantage point of the 1970s, the *centrum* and its service spaces appeared to be not only architectonically but socially rigid. As Tom Avermaete and Dirk van den Heuvel describe, European welfare-state architecture was then regarded as "too bureaucratic, too much one-size-fits-all, and too reformist."[122] As new local residents have changed such spaces, however, the hidden flexibility and power of their apparent genericness has become evident. This practice has continued into the present day, as Syriacs have altered Ronna Centrum to reflect their own needs, little by little, through urban design from below.

In Million Program planning, the town center offered a standardized module, and the new modern social imaginary of the Swedish welfare state (as both demos and ethnos) envisaged these urban squares as reinforcing ideals of public behavior. Despite the increased visibility of the Syriacs in Ronna Centrum over time, its initial architectural design has prevailed. Today, Ronna Centrum functions almost exactly as Voigt proposed. Although apartments were added on upper levels in the 1990s, the *centrum*'s structural walls and window placements remain largely untouched and unchanged since 1965. As majority Swedes became Ronna's minority, however, the absence of the universal subject intended to inhabit these spaces nonetheless permitted the inward seepage of a particularized identity, remaking the *centrum*'s spatial and symbolic roles.

The modernist flexibility of Ronna Centrum—a flexibility designed to ensure that the same town center was distributed to Swedish citizens across the country—has allowed Syriac spaces to adapt. New signs and color schemes, symbols, markers, and physical displays have altered Ronna Centrum's surfaces, attesting to these transformations. Rather than a library, a post office, and the Swedish supermarket chain Konsum, Ronna Centrum has housed Syriac cultural clubs, along with a grocery store, Ronna Livs, that sells almost entirely Middle Eastern products (Figure 2.10). A "multicultural health clinic" opened in 2011 (taking over the former Oasen club space) as Ronna Vårdcentral, offering medical practitioners who speak Swedish, English, Suryoyo, Arabic, and Romanian.[123]

FIGURE 2.10. Olive bar, baklava station, and butcher at a grocery store in Ronna, 2011. It occupies the original position of a grocery store in the 1965 plans. Photograph by Danielle Barsoum.

Parishioners transformed St. Olov's, the Swedish Lutheran church in Voigt's original design, into the Syriac Orthodox church St. Gabriel's, with only its new altar space reconfiguring the building's footprint (Figure 2.11). This satellite church serves many of the elderly residents of Ronna, who prefer to worship closer to home. Hairdressers, located in the same salon spaces of the original design, specialize in the complicated hairstyles that women are expected to commission for the numerous formal occasions of the Syriac community. Here, as one young Syriac woman about to attend a wedding excitedly told me in 2010, "the hairdresser who just came from Syria" has some tricks up his sleeve to make you look "like you just came from Damascus." Thus, even as most of the original physical form of Ronna Centrum remains, Syriac territorial claims have reconfigured it over time. Ronna Centrum's modular structure, so prized as a beacon of welfare-state "service" and so integral to the development of citizens and consumers for the Swedish nation-state, has evolved through urban design from below.

FIGURE 2.11. Interior of St. Gabriel's Syriac Orthodox Church, 2009, formerly St. Olov's [Lutheran] Church. Photograph by author.

The "generic" architectural forms for which Ronna Centrum has been critiqued, together with its strong and specific social programs, have paradoxically made it flexible, more universally adaptable than even its architects and planners had intended. While these spaces were designed to reinforce—through the new modern social imaginary of the welfare state—scientifically standardized and condoned ideals of leisure and recreation, the absence of the imagined universal (Swedish) subject required their modification. *Nysvenska* (New Swedish) signs, hair treatments, and forms of religious practice have shifted the *centrum*'s symbolism and clientele, even as most of its walls, programs, and pavements remain as they looked upon inauguration in 1965.

Uses or Users?

More than forty years have passed since the dual forces of the Social Democratic Million Program and the arrival of the Syriacs carved a new urban identity into Södertälje's landscape. The New Towns constructed for the training of Swedish citizens now form its primary urban image, even as living in a "segregated" Million

Program neighborhood is nearly synonymous with having a "foreign background." Among all municipalities in Sweden, Södertälje had the second-largest proportion of residents in this category (51.9 percent), as well as the third-largest percentage of foreign-born residents (38.2 percent) in 2016.[124] Whether Little Baghdad, Syriatälje, Mosul-on-Stockholm,[125] or Mesopotälje,[126] these satellites add architectural form to journalists' descriptions. For outsiders, Ronna and the other Million Program New Towns *are* Södertälje.

In tandem, Södertälje's town centers—where New Swedes are redefining public life—are portrayed as only perilously public. Contemporary Swedish media and anti-immigration party depictions frequently and damningly refer to Ronna as a "segregated" space where the tensions of the 1970s have only worsened: the opposite of the classless utopia inaugurated there in 1965. In these views, its *centrum* is a hornet's nest, its physical infrastructure openly criminalized through gangs and associations that are actually illegal gambling parlors or fronts for illegal trade. Abetting this perspective in Ronna Centrum are high-profile incidents like the 2005 "Ronna Riots," sparked when Syriac teenage boys allegedly harassed a Finnish-Swedish girl, calling her "whore" as she passed through the *centrum,*[127] and the murder of the beloved Assyriska FF soccer player Eddie Moussa and his brother Yaacoub in Oasen (a former social club in the *centrum*) in July 2010. When Ronna Centrum's architectural plans are represented publicly today, it is no longer to herald an optimistic new society, at it was fifty years ago, but to portray the scene of a crime (Figure 2.12). This Ronna Centrum is a very dangerous place.

Tasked to solve these problems, Södertälje's urban planners have embarked on such endeavors as the European Union initiative URBACT/RegGov, active from 2008 until 2011 in Ronna. Defining Ronna from the outset as a "deprived urban area," representatives argued that Ronna Centrum should be either demolished or radically renovated. The final report stated, "The impoverishment of service that has happened since the end of the 1980s has affected social life in the entire neighborhood with negative consequences. Fewer people come to the *centrum* to meet each other, to shop, and to do errands."[128] Proposals for public art projects, galleries, and architect-designed houses were intended to draw majority Swedes to Ronna, and the idea of erasing the *centrum* became an attempt to eliminate, simultaneously, an undesired Syriac ethnic concentration. In this sense, planners have sought to undo the work of police in the 1970s, who were apparently successful in ordering the Syriacs to disappear from public view. But this story has more than one side.

In a brochure for prospective tenants, Graflund's, a housing company, described Ronna as "a child-friendly and car-free area, with many playgrounds and green spaces on your doorstep. . . . Here, you have almost everything you need at a comfortable distance, such as nursery schools, schools, shops, and bus connections." Meanwhile, the Swedish Union of Tenants (Hyresgästföreningen) and St. Gabriel's Church have used the spaces of Ronna Centrum to organize the community for "cleaning days,"

FIGURE 2.12. Diagram of crime scene in Oasis Club in Ronna Centrum, in which Eddie and Yaacoub Moussa were killed in July 2010, as included in an *Aftonbladet* article about the crime. Mattias Carlsson and Eric Tagesson, "Här har tre mördats—på sex månader" (Three have been murdered here—in six months), *Aftonbladet,* July 2, 2010. Graphic design by Paul Wallander.

when residents pick up trash, as well as to host wildly successful family festivals that continue well into the night.

Resident representations of public life in Ronna, such as those by the journalist Nisha Besara, who grew up there, do even more to contradict pessimistic portrayals. In a 2006 article entitled "Ronna—Sweden's Chinatown," Besara worked against seeing Ronna as monolithic, arguing that residents are extremely diverse, even though most are Syriac Orthodox Christians.[129] Highlighting the neighborhood's family-friendly atmosphere and its unique status as the only true ethnic enclave in Sweden, she concluded:

> There are countless, neat strips of row houses. Fantastic, huge, pompous villas. And a host of cozy, three-story buildings. A concrete town center and leafy jogging trails. A suburban feeling and domestic idyll, all in one. In Sweden's only Chinatown. My Ronna is completely different from the neighborhood that is conveyed in politics and the media.[130]

While Ronna is not simply Besara's bucolic suburbia, neither is it the dystopia that politicians, planners, and other journalists imagine as they describe crime and segregation. As the Swedish national model of integration encouraged Syriacs to retain cultural markers—to be separate but equal—met coercive suggestions from local police to disappear, Ronna Centrum became a space of release. The standardized social and commercial infrastructure built for the universal, midcentury Swedish citizen became a key (and surprisingly flexible) public space for a subaltern group identity predicated on difference.

Homi Bhabha writes, "The borderline engagements of cultural difference may as often be consensual as conflictual; they may confound our definitions of tradition and modernity; realign the customary boundaries between *the private and the public,* high and low; and challenge normative expectations of development and progress."[131] In Ronna Centrum, a consensual but conflictual dialogue occurred between official, municipal urban planning and the unofficial use and transformation of urban spaces. On the one hand, Million Program designs would develop "good democratic citizens"[132] through engagement in comprehensive planning and the "service" spaces of the welfare state's town centers. On the other, an immigrant group needed institutional spaces to maintain another national identity, simultaneously New Swedish and diasporic Syriac: a public not imagined in the original plans.

In Ronna Centrum, sanctioned forms of Social Democratic leisure occur almost exactly as their Million Program designers originally intended: neighbors meet, do their shopping at Ronna Livs, go to hairdressers located exactly where they were in 1965, and attend a Syriac Orthodox church where Lutheran services once were run by the Church of Sweden. This is a community within a community, just as its architects and planners designed it, and it thus continues to resemble its town-center

counterparts in other Swedish and European peripheries. Practices of spatial governmentality that were intended to encourage user uniformity have thus transformed as
centrum spaces have gained new clientele, while, at the same time, the broad strokes
of their intended programming have been retained.

Thus, the major discrepancy between Ronna Centrum's plan and the reality is
not in its uses but in its *users*. If the Swedish state defined public space as the space
of operation for a classless society, the *centrum* served as a centerpiece. But Ronna
Centrum—once considered merely a single unmarked, classless territory among
many and belonging to all Swedish citizens—has instead become the visible, specific
domain of a minority ethnic and religious group. As similar social and physical
transformations take place in the suburbs of other welfare states and provoke similar
anxieties for citizens and policy makers, Ronna Centrum illustrates a new mode for
European public space.

In Ronna Centrum, urban design from below has allowed the New Swedes paradoxically to instantiate difference in spaces originally designed for sameness. This
shift in the *centrum's* users has resulted in a hybrid zone. Here, the planned ideologies of citizenship in a Scandinavian state and a Middle Eastern diaspora have
intermingled, even as the original form of this important welfare-state leisure and
commercial space remains, perhaps curiously, the same. In this sense, its designers'
intentions—to create a space of equality for all Swedish citizens and a flexible space
for modern living—were a remarkable success.

CHAPTER THREE

Making Mesopotälje

Sacred and Profane
"Diaspora Space" in the City

IN MAY 2009, I boarded a plane from Istanbul to Stockholm, noticing the elegant attire of several fellow passengers, including one man with a neatly trimmed white beard, clad in red, and traveling with associates in business suits. Suddenly, I recognized one member of his entourage. I had met Gabriel a few days earlier when he guided me at the Saffron Monastery (Dayro Zafaran), outside Mardin. As luck would have it, he was assigned to the seat beside me.

Gabriel and his group were traveling to Södertälje for the consecration of the new St. Jacob's Syriac Orthodox Cathedral. The distinguished man in red was Filüksinos Saliba Özmen, the archbishop of Mardin. The cathedral would now become the largest Syriac Orthodox church in Europe, and Gabriel told me the archbishop had been eager to accept this invitation to ordain the space. With a tinge of sadness, he described the dwindling population of Syriacs in Turkey, where the monastery now operated mainly as a tourist destination. To come to Sweden, then, was a way for the archbishop to take part in the living religion in this new center of Syriac life, Södertälje.

Gabriel had never visited Sweden, although his uncle was one of the earliest Syriacs to settle in Södertälje and still lived there. He and his fiancée met at the monastery after her escape from war-torn Iraq, and she had been living in Södertälje with her mother for several months after receiving asylum in Sweden. He thus knew a great deal about the town's history and spaces, despite never having been there himself. At the baggage belt after landing, the archbishop and his group waited as leather cases with velvet linings appeared among the Samsonite hardsides and Fjällräven backpacks. They gingerly carried the gift they had brought for the event— a painting of Dayro Zafaran—through the terminal.

Syriac Orthodox bishops and priests from Syria, Turkey, and the United Kingdom, along with officials of the Church of Sweden, ordained St. Jacob's Cathedral on May 17, 2009, with the mayor of Södertälje and other local politicians in attendance. A stand outside sold commemorative baseball hats, mugs, scarves, and candles, all emblazoned with the English-language text, "17 May 2009 The Church consecration of Mor Jacob Nsibinoyo in Södertälje, Sweden," with an image of the church and a translation of the text in Syriac above it. Both the Swedish press and Suryoyo-language satellite television stations broadcast the event, drawing national and global attention to this small Swedish town on the extreme periphery of the capital (Figure 3.1).

The consecration was the culmination of a long process of Syriac spatial settlement occurring through the construction of significant buildings. Custom-designed, purpose-built Syriac spaces, both sacred and profane, now serve as monuments for and by this diasporic community whose members have spread all over the world. Individual—and eventually iconic—building projects have remade Swedish urban territory at large, transforming this peripheral, undistinguished, industrial town and ostensible suburb into a conspicuous, modern focal point in the Syriac geographic imagination through a process of urban design from below.

Diasporas are typically defined as ethnic groups in motion, expelled from a geographic territory as a result of the trauma of forced migration, making a missing

FIGURE 3.1. Crowds inside the church for the consecration of St. Jacob's Syriac Orthodox Cathedral, 2009. Photograph by author.

homeland central to their sense of identity.[1] Anthropologist Engseng Ho labels the diaspora the "society of the absent"[2]—a group for whom mobility rather than settlement plays a key role. Syriacs in Sweden today constantly refer to lost spaces in ancient Mesopotamia and regions of the contemporary Middle East. In this sense, they constitute a "society of the absent," yet they rarely express a hope to return to these territories. Syriac Sweden has become a settler society instead.

"Diaspora space"[3] has often been articulated metaphorically: through voyages across large swaths of geographic space—often oceans—over long periods of time, such as Paul Gilroy's "Black Atlantic"[4] or other rhizomatous forms of cultural production.[5] Such diaspora spaces are *dislocated,* exceeding both the time and territory of the urban environment. When articulated in bodily practice, they remain diffused as "*chaorders,* chaotic orders," according to Pnina Werbner.[6] "Diaspora cities,"[7] meanwhile, are diverse urban centers where members of one group have concentrated among others.

Syriac Södertälje invites reconsideration of the definitional limits of both diaspora space and diaspora cities. The integration politics of the 1970s encouraged Syriacs to spread themselves across Sweden even as they were also asked, locally, to retreat to Million Program neighborhoods like Ronna, Geneta, and Hovsjö. In the 1980s and 1990s, their growing need for gathering spaces—religious and recreational—solidified their presence in these peripheral New Towns architectonically. Cumulatively, these building projects remade Södertälje, reshaping this suburban town into a national capital "without a country."[8] The area has since drawn Christians escaping civil war in Syria, thousands of Iraqis, and other Syriacs from within Sweden and across Europe, while also disturbing the clearly defined categories through which Swedish policy makers had earlier attempted to manage its immigrants.

With Middle Eastern Christians comprising at least 30 percent of Södertälje's total population by 2016, this suburban city has become key to the Syriac group's cosmology. A place to be revered and visited, it is the sun around which the Syriac moon revolves. Ho remarks that "land has unique properties precisely because it is immobile, and it thereby contains the potential for moral transformation."[9] As most Syriacs extol their lost homelands but nonetheless assume continued settlement in Sweden, they consider investment in significant new architecture for their diasporic community life to be an endeavor in need of neither explanation nor justification. The productive frictions developing since the 1980s between a mobile Syriac group and the immobile land of Södertälje—particularly when religion and soccer are concerned—have transformed the town from a site of exile to a place of pilgrimage: Mesopotälje, an urban and global center.

Architecture, beyond acting as merely an expression of the Syriacs' expanding presence in the town, has also produced new forms of conspicuity and aggregation despite the repeated calls from Swedish local and national authorities for minority groups to avoid concentration and expressions of distinction. As Södertälje has nevertheless evolved into the Syriac capital, each building makes the Syriacs increasingly visible while also reinforcing their autonomous forms of difference. Today, Syriacs are not just a key social influence on the local community; rather, they are a society of the *present* that shows its conspicuous independence from the greater Swedish whole both architectonically and visually.

"God's House Is Closed for Vacation?"
The Social Space of the Church

The small Syriac Orthodox Christian group living in Södertälje in the late 1960s found themselves unmoored on a foreign shore without one of their major social anchors: the church. Before emigration, it had served as a "symbol"[10] and gathering point for the group, providing political power since the days of the Ottoman millet, as well as access to education. The church also held great social importance, as David, a distinguished fifty-eight-year-old entrepreneur with a successful chain of Stockholm salons and cafés, described:

> The church is our collective power, more or less. Many people go to church not because they are religious, but to meet other people. That need is very strong even today. People have become Swedes in part, but they miss the old traditions at the same time. The church played an important role in keeping the group together, and it still does.

Echoing these sentiments, anthropologist Annika Rabo argues that the church allows Syriacs to maintain unity in the diaspora, without which they would "disappear."[11]

With her shock of white hair, severe looks for late arrivals, and motherly yet disciplinary demeanor, it is fitting that fifty-nine-year-old Maria works as an elementary-school teacher. She claims to be the first Södertälje Syriac to hail from Syria rather than Turkey. In her hometown of Qamishli, Maria participated actively in her church, singing in the choir and serving on the advisory board. In Qamishli she met Afram, who later went to Sweden on the First Plane. Their exchange of love letters over several years led to his proposal, and they married in Lebanon and quickly continued to Södertälje in 1970. Apart from her husband and his family, she had no relatives there and was isolated by her lack of Swedish-language skills, making the loss of the church even more acute. Eventually, she and Afram tried to find a solution:

> So, on the first Sunday, okay, there was no church. On the second Sunday, I began to miss the church, to miss the choir. Then I said to my husband, "I want to go to church." We had not yet established ourselves as *assyrier*. We had no church, no associations. We had nothing. But I wanted to go to church, and he said, "Okay, we'll go to church." Then we went to the church in the square, the one called St. Ragnhild's

[Church of Sweden], and I was really surprised about one thing. There was a note on the church door: "The church is closed for vacation." My husband explained to me what a vacation was because I didn't know about that either. "It's summer, and many factories are closed, many shops are closed, and the church is also closed." "What? God's house is closed because of vacation? I don't get that at all!" He started laughing.

Despite the comedy and Maria's clear pleasure in retelling the story, the lack of a church was socially traumatic, exacerbating her sense of disorientation in this new Swedish urban setting.

Eventually, Syriacs began to hold religious meetings in apartments, with rituals conducted informally in the absence of a priest.[12] Maria remembered these gatherings nostalgically, noting that they helped ease her isolation. Whereas earlier interfamilial disputes and histories fell by the wayside in the context of early migration, this spirit of cooperation changed with the arrival of additional Syriacs in the 1970s.[13] Maria described this:

> Between 1970 and 1974, many people came to Södertälje, and it wasn't just us here anymore. People from Örebro moved here. People from Norrköping moved here. People from Eskilstuna moved here. People from Gothenburg, they moved. These families were strong. Families were growing. Children were born here. They needed a priest to baptize them. They had children who were marrying, and they needed a priest. You don't want to do that in the Church of Sweden. Then they asked the patriarch—they wrote to him—and said that we needed a priest. In all of Sweden, there was no Syriac Orthodox priest.

Parents, wives, children, and friends arrived in Södertälje, rendering ad hoc religious practices less viable, and, with the surge of thousands more coming from abroad in the mid-1970s, the Syriac population far exceeded the capacity of any living room. Meeting in a neutral space, free from the progressively more complicated web of familial ties and social obligations, also became increasingly necessary.

In 1969, the growing population prompted the patriarch to organize the official visit to Sweden of Afrem Aboodi (then a monk, later bishop); he recognized the serious problems presented by the absence of a Syriac priest and a dedicated space for worship.[14] The families reuniting in Södertälje required formalized wedding services, funerals, christenings, and ceremonial events around major holidays, especially Easter and Christmas. After many requests, the patriarch finally dispatched Priest Yousef Said from Iraq to Södertälje in 1970.[15] The jubilation of Syriac residents coincided with new Swedish support for "immigrant churches," a form of financing that also provided a salary for the new priest in 1971.[16] Björklund notes that his arrival also altered the geography of Syriac Sweden:

The priest settled down in Södertälje and had already begun his ministrations. From this time onwards there was a Syrian Orthodox congregation in Södertälje. Even if at the start the congregation did not possess a church of its own, services could still be held (the Swedish Church [Church of Sweden] provided premises) every Sunday, christenings and marriages could be performed, etc. It is obvious that this was an important factor for future settlement.[17]

Said's arrival lent Södertälje a new importance for Syriacs, who had been doubly dispersed through international migration and the Swedish refugee reception regime.[18]

Benjamin, a sixty-three-year-old man who established himself first as a political activist and sometime soccer player and then as a journalist and poet, described how the rooting of the church to a local territory—in the persona of the priest—drew other Syriacs, including himself, to Södertälje:

> I moved to Södertälje in the beginning of 1971. I had been among those at the AMS camp in Alvesta, Småland. From there, I moved to Gothenburg, so I was in Gothenburg for two and a half or three years first. Then I moved to Södertälje. At that time, there weren't many of us really, just a few families who lived in Södertälje. And then, little by little, when the church had been established and a priest was on site, it attracted the many other *assyrier* who were living in other municipalities to move.

Older people depended on the church for social contacts, as they did not work or go to school. Many Syriacs revealed that their move to Södertälje emerged out of (a sometimes begrudging) filial obligation. For Benjamin, his mother's needs prompted his move to Södertälje for an extended period during the 1970s before he relocated to a suburb of Stockholm. He said:

> My mother moved to Gothenburg with me, and there were no other *assyrier* there. She was very isolated when I worked, and it was very difficult for her. I wanted her to have contact with others, maybe with the larger families, and they were in Södertälje, so we moved there.

For Benjamin, the presence of the church trumped his own desires to live elsewhere, since he knew the church would provide his mother with social outlets. Likewise, the Syriac entrepreneur David initially resisted moving to Södertälje in favor of a more exciting life in Stockholm but was forced to reconsider:

> My parents were so extremely religious that they went to church almost every day, and I couldn't oppose them, and that's why it was Södertälje. Then it became a common thing, that you felt at home in Södertälje. At first, I thought it was only farmers who lived here in Södertälje, when I lived in Stockholm. "No," I said, "never Södertälje!"

Then I started to realize that I had my friends, my relatives, my association, my church, you know. Sometimes, when you reach a certain point in your life, you need those anchors. And that's why I moved here, to Södertälje.

While Södertälje initially appeared to be an albatross of responsibilities and obligations that would strangle his independence, David's desire to connect not only with his parents but with the growing community of Syriacs in the town made it increasingly appealing, as it was for many other Syriacs both within Sweden and abroad.

The Spatial Politics of Integration

From skirmishing with anti-immigrant *raggare* in public spaces to being labeled "illegal immigrants" during the 1970s, Syriac exclusions from majority societies in the Middle East seemed to be echoed in a Sweden that was not as welcoming as they had expected.[19] After their dispersion and expulsion from their homelands, they were, paradoxically, greeted with new forms of dispersion in Sweden. The Swedish philosophy of integration meant that officials encouraged Syriacs to retain cultural practices, and, as informants described, directives to disappear spatialized their separation in Million Program neighborhoods. Critically, as they were asked to atomize, infrastructure for religious practice continued to evade them, being regarded among Swedish officials as an undesirable draw that might encourage a tendency to congregate and sediment spatially. Even so, while the Syriac priest had established the church socially, the need for a sacred oasis was acute in what increasingly appeared to be the hostile desert of everyday life in urban Sweden.[20] By the late 1970s, Syriacs numbered over four thousand in Södertälje, with more across Sweden, pressing the issue.[21]

The attitude of Syriacs toward the church in 1970s Södertälje reflects its established role in other settings. George is in his fifties and came to Södertälje with his brothers in the early years. In Tur Abdin, he lived close to the Syrian border and traveled frequently to trade in Qamishli, where he stayed in the town's church, Mor Yakub:

Mor Yakub was our haven. It was a place to spend the night. Officially, it's still like this: if you travel somewhere and have no family members nearby, you can stay at the *dayro* [monastery]. They will give you food and drink, and you can stay there. There are no fixed prices, you give what you want to the church. Usually, those who come from Europe can afford it, and then they give something. Otherwise, you can stay for free.

Churches and monasteries facilitated business transactions for the itinerant Syriac trading community when they acted as free hostels, in addition to their historically protective roles as safe refuges for the open expression of a minority faith and during times of turmoil.

As temporary measures during the 1970s, the Church of Sweden provided access to various Södertälje churches, including St. Ragnhild's in the historic downtown and St. Olov's in Ronna, and the Baptists also provided space (see Map 4 and Figure 3.2). Despite the abundance of Swedish churches, these short-term rentals meant constant moves around town, since Syriacs had difficulty securing regular times in the same space. The Lutheran floor plans and minimal altar spaces of borrowed churches also made Orthodox services difficult, and their maximum capacity was far too low. As Father Johannes told me:

> For major holidays, we had St. Ragnhild's Church in the center, the largest. That could take up to six hundred people, not more. We weren't allowed, I mean. There might be eight hundred people who came, but we weren't allowed. Those who were seated could be up to six hundred people, end of story, no more. But that was only during holidays. The rest of the time, we went around to almost every church in Södertälje.

Eventually, the Mission Church, slated in 1975 for demolition, became the Syriacs' primary meeting space.[22] Located, as many described, "behind the police station" in central Södertälje, this new church solved a major ongoing problem. As outlined in a newspaper editorial, it would allow Syriacs "to feel at home—not as Swedes, but as who they are."[23] The offer clearly echoed the philosophy of integration then being popularized, as the piece continued:

> To afford immigrants the possibility of participating in "our" social life, while retaining their cultural traditions, it is necessary to give them the possibility of continuing to live on with their faith. One of the biggest problems is that there are no suitable places where they can have their gatherings and their parish activities. Usually, immigrants do not have the economic resources to acquire places that can be decorated and formed as their religious exercises demand.[24]

The anonymous author of this *LT* article argues that the Syriac community should be provided with the opportunity to build but also suggests in quietly pejorative language that the group is, in a sense, not modern—and not modernist—because of the need to "decorate."

Indeed, temporary solutions persisted, despite the fact that the Syriacs had the second-largest membership of all religious organizations in Södertälje by 1979.[25] Borrowing and renting spaces left the group vulnerable, always mobile and dependent on the benevolence of others, especially when the demolition of the Mission Church approached in 1980.[26] One Swedish bishop described their itinerant worship as a larger social problem: "When immigrants don't have a foothold in their

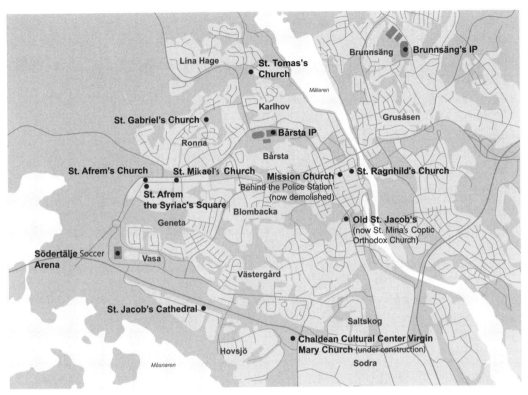

MAP 4. Map of Södertälje, showing the locations of churches and soccer fields. Graphic design by Eliza Hearsum.

traditions, it creates insecurity. And then we get bad immigrants."[27] Again, the politics of integration—emphasizing static notions of identity—echoed through the halls of this missing spatial home.

Beyond its protective role, the Syriac church represented a primary means for Syriacs to establish themselves socially, all the more critical in diaspora. As Benjamin explained:

It has always happened that when a few *assyrier* have gathered somewhere, they're interested in building a church. That's more or less the only thing we had a right to in our old homelands, so it's a tradition that we moved with us. The only chance we had to organize was under the umbrella of the church.

In their dubious circumstances and in keeping with these traditions, Syriacs began to plan more seriously for a dedicated church building by the late 1970s, actively searching for a site from 1979 to 1981.[28] In 1980, they asked the municipality for a site to build a church for more than one thousand worshippers.[29]

I den lånade kyrkan i Södertälje vigs Ibrahim och Ismune. Ibrahim är bror till Simon Düzgün som tjänstgör som diakon — d v s biträder prästen under vigselakten.

Vigseln är ett sakrament och både bruden och brudgummen får för en kort stund bära den krona som symboliserar Kristi krona — men det innebär också att bruden och brudgummen tar ansvar för varandra och visar varandra respekt.

Vigselförrättare är korbiskop Yusef Said, han har studerat i Heidelberg och Irak. Sedan 1974 arbetar han som präst och översättare i Sverige. Biskop Said är utsänd av patriarken i Damaskus som representerar jakobiterna d v s den syrisk-ortodoxa kyrkan.

FIGURE 3.2. Photographs of a Syriac Orthodox wedding service in a borrowed Swedish Lutheran church, published in Knutsson, *Ashur eller Aram.*

Other residents and politicians in Södertälje argued that a new church would permanently root the group to the town and would attract further Syriacs, both of which were considered undesirable outcomes.[30] Others offered a more measured response, suggesting that "if it doesn't double in-migration to the municipality and worsen the crises in the economy, schools, and housing environment, a place for such a church should be prepared," while arguing simultaneously that "immigrant groups should be made aware of the consequences of their accumulation. A voluntary distribution [of Syriacs across Sweden] would be a suitable demand."[31] Some were explicit about fears that the local majority Swedish population would be displaced. As these debates raged on, however, the Syriacs' frustration ended in a threat: "We'll occupy the Mission Church if we don't get a space before it's demolished."[32]

As early as 1979, officials suggested the disused Skeppsholm's Church in Stockholm as a possible venue, to be shared with a music group.[33] Echoing the notion that integration should also require immigrants to disperse, the municipality considered that "for Södertälje's part, it would have been good if the *assyrier*'s religious center had been Stockholm. Today, some are drawn to Södertälje because the municipality is the principal city of the church."[34] The Skeppsholm's Church proposal would counteract that trend, but Syriacs argued against what would have been a highly impractical commute of nearly forty kilometers. Daily worship would be impossible, which would have drastic effects on elderly parishioners. Desmond Carragher, secretary of refugee affairs for Sweden's Free Church Council, agreed:

> The number of *syrianer* has of course increased fivefold since 1975, when the demolition of the Mission Church was first discussed. A suggestion has been made that the *syrianer* should organize in Skeppsholm's Church in Stockholm. But it is, of course, completely unthinkable that thousands of people should need to travel to Stockholm every Sunday.[35]

The proposal lost further ground, and attention returned to a possible new, purpose-built church.

Despite this, many local authorities assumed that the Syriacs would be unable to finance the construction of a new church. Carragher offered the group a subsidy and identified a more dubious reason for their difficulties: "This is not an economic but rather a political question. I think that they [representatives of the municipality] are afraid that Södertälje will become something of a center *[högsäte]* for all the *syrianer* in Sweden if a church is built there."[36] Jakob, a Syriac man now in his seventies, described how the Syriacs themselves had also amassed money, saying, "When we moved to Södertälje, they were in the process of building St. Afrem's in Geneta, and everyone took part and helped economically. They knocked on our door, too."

These anxious discussions centered on whether permitting the construction of a church would solidify and expand ethnic concentration in the town. For officials, a potential Syriac architectural expansion signaled new concerns about the group's need to sediment and aggregate. By 1980, one journalist wondered, "Why hasn't the municipality found a space or a plot of land for the *syrianer*? Is the municipality afraid that the *syrianer* are becoming too well-established in the city?"[37] A local government commissioner, Lennart Svensson, denied this:

> No, we consider it a duty to help the *syrianer* find a church space, but we haven't been able to find a suitable alternative yet. The boiler room in Ronna was on the table, but that has proven to be much too small. And the plots available in Geneta have too many problems, with parking places, among other things. At the moment, this looks rather hopeless, but we are ready to continue the negotiations.[38]

In a city with vast land resources at its disposal, these claims appear disingenuous. They were perhaps based in the esoteric logics of fear, with the analysis appearing just before the "terror night" of August 23, 1980, when *raggare* burned down several Syriac businesses.[39] Voices suggesting that Syriacs be spread around Sweden became louder. Integration now meant that immigrants should maintain their cultural identities but not live in enclaves together. This further argued against the church project. After a long journey sailing against the winds of public debate, however, the group in 1981 purchased a site originally zoned for parkland on Klockarvägen in Geneta, where they ultimately succeeded in building what is now St. Afrem's Syriac Orthodox Church (Figure 3.3).[40]

Münir, a Syriac civil servant in his forties whose parents arrived from Turkey in the early years, offered this explanation for the Syriacs' interest in the Geneta site: "We had a chance to get land there, and there were a lot of Syriacs who lived around there. Besides, Geneta was centrally located in the middle, you know? It was Ronna then Geneta then Hovsjö." This space on the edge of the planners' view of Södertälje was, in other words, situated at the social and geographic heart of the growing Syriac community.

Swedish architect Per Hörlin of Casa Arkitektkontor AB, a suburban Stockholm firm, designed a building for several hundred worshippers (an unthinkable number for a village church in Tur Abdin).[41] As a monument to Syriac triumphs over the hardships of arrival, its opening in 1983 also signaled their intentions to stay. Suddenly, an essential sacred space for this community in exile—both the first purpose-built Syriac space in Sweden and the first Syriac Orthodox church in Europe—appeared in a strip that planners had seen as a mere buffer zone.

Becoming Visible

Upon opening in 1983, St. Afrem's had the extremely discreet exterior Hörlin had designed, with a subdued brick facade and an unobtrusive cross on the eastern side

FIGURE 3.3. Exterior facade, St. Afrem's Syriac Orthodox Church, 2009. Photograph by author.

recalling the sober materiality of Lutheran churches (Figure 3.4). Its nondescript, rectangular form appeared more warehouse than holy space. If Syriacs were encouraged to disappear from public view in the 1970s, this building—in spite of its grand scale—reflected that agenda architecturally. The church's location on this buffer strip gave it prominence on Klockarvägen, but the area itself remained an ostensibly insignificant periphery of Södertälje. David described how these initial gestures required changes over time:

> We got a place, land, in the Geneta neighborhood, and we built our own church there with our own impetus. It was some Swedish architect who built it, but we weren't satisfied. It was not our culture that he designed. But afterward, some people remade the church. It was really important to establish that this is our culture, and this is how it should look. In the beginning, it was a mere industrial building that they built. The Swedish architect really had no clue about our traditions.

The tensions between the parish's expectations and the architect's assumptions (real or perceived) resulted in a predicament for the group: their new church was constructed, but it remained marked with formal foreignness.

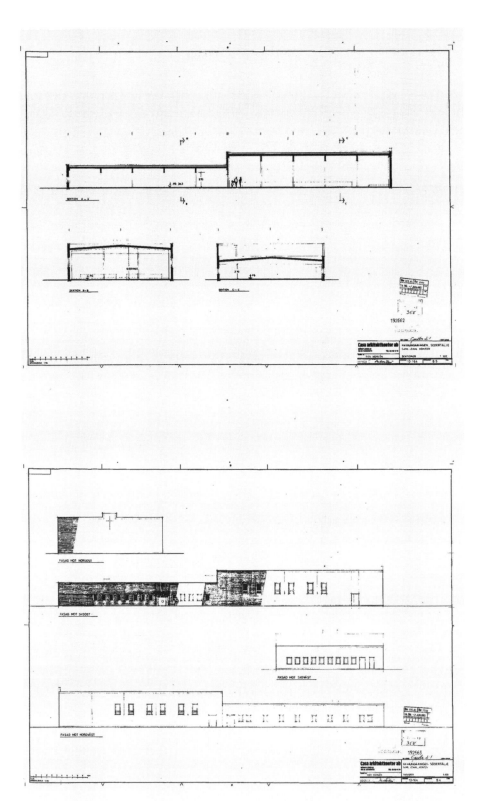

FIGURE 3.4. Original sections and elevations, St. Afrem's Syriac Orthodox Church.
Casa Arkitektkontor AB, 1983. Source: Södertälje Kommun.

As David mentioned, this demure public face belied what eventually became an ornate interior, as Syriac craftspeople redesigned the austere space. Sculptors originally from Midyat carved intricate reliefs and columns; Shabe BarAbraham carved the altar.[42] Detailed biblical paintings and quotations covered ceilings and walls, and stained glass depicted important scenes and saints (Figure 3.5). Münir recollected the scope of this work:

> I remember how the older gentlemen worked on the altar. Everything by hand! There was so much activity there. And we saw, little by little, how there were more and more stones, and they eventually took form. On the outside, it was plain brick, and on the inside it was plaster on the altar. Unbelievably beautiful! The older gentlemen's handicraft and knowledge! For the most part, they were illiterate, but they knew so much on the artistic side, about handicraft.

Accepting a stark contrast between its bland exterior and an interior that parishioners themselves were remaking after their Swedish architect had finished the design, St. Afrem's held Christmas services in December 1983. While daring to build an expensive

FIGURE 3.5. Interior, St. Afrem's Syriac Orthodox Church, 2009. Photograph by author.

and critically needed community structure, the decision to present a subdued face to the urban environment clearly extended beyond mere financial considerations.

As the Syriac group continued to expand, representatives of the church grew increasingly bold in their proposals to the town's official planners. In 1985, the parish applied for a permit to construct a slim brick bell tower along the main facade and to ring the bell daily at 8:00 a.m. and 4:00 p.m. (Figure 3.6). In issuing the permit, Dan Björklund, director of environmental protection, responded, "There are many shift workers who live in the neighborhood, making ringing the bell early in the morning unsuitable, especially on weekends. The bell tower will be constructed at least one hundred meters from the closest residential building."[43] Björklund also stipulated maximum decibel levels and warned that permission to use the bell would be revoked if there were complaints or if "sanitary reasons" required. Adopting the disguise of a functionalist church accoutrement, the tower conformed to welfare-state standards of architectural discretion: clad in brick and bearing the two-dimensional cross of the Church of Sweden rather than the three-dimensional Orthodox version.

These initial additions led to more daring renovations. In 1988 a large-scale, block-letter sign was added with the name "Syrianska Ortodoxa Kyrkan" (the name St.

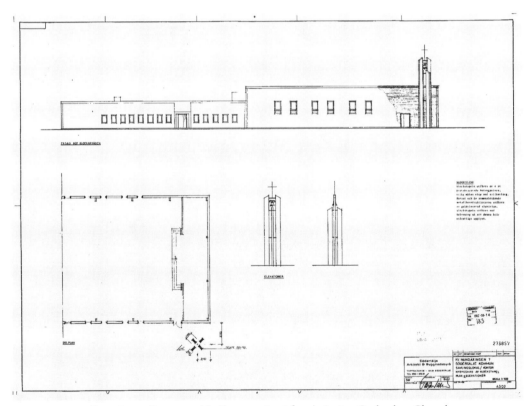

FIGURE 3.6. Drawings of proposed bell tower, St. Afrem's Syriac Orthodox Church. Södertälje Arkitekt och Byggnadsbyrå, 1985. Source: Södertälje Kommun.

Afrem's was added in the 2010s), using the group's preferred designation—*syrianska*—rather than the more neutral *syrisk*. Later, the parish received permission to construct a barrel vault over the altar and a pitched roof over the offices, finally distinguishing the structure as a Syriac site formally.[44] Eventually, three Orthodox-style crosses decorated a delicate barrel vault over the nave, and a pitched roof on the western side covered the offices and the areas used for social functions. An onion-domed cupola with a clerestory cast daylight onto the worshippers, and a monumental entryway covered the south door.

The Syriacs' changes functioned aurally as well. As St. Afrem's bell began to call parishioners to prayer, it also worked against the intended functional divisions of the surrounding urban plans and brought a form of hybridity to the neighborhood. Religion—assigned a muted identity as one social function among many in the Million Program town center—instead entered the domestic space through sound, just as Dan Björklund had feared.

In this sense, although the Swedish urban planners who designed Geneta in the 1960s imagined it as the New Town satellite of Södertälje, changes in the neighborhood's identity and form offer parallels to many other contemporary European urban settings. Indeed, these concerns from the 1980s recall the successful referendum to ban new minarets in Switzerland in 2009, as well as recent debates on calls to prayer in Sweden (as recently as April 2013), France, Germany, and beyond. As the "unplanned," major institutional structure of St. Afrem's began to remake a strictly regulated Million Program New Town, the debates surrounding it suggested other concerns lurking under the surface in the surrounding Swedish community. Its unified form masked an internal Syriac debate that simmered slowly during the 1970s, erupting violently in Södertälje at the turn of the decade: the "name conflict."[45]

The Name Conflict: *Assyrier* or *Syrianer*?

On September 30, 1980, more than one thousand mourners formed "the most significant funeral procession that Södertälje has ever experienced,"[46] for a twenty-eight-year-old man named Aslan Noyan, who had been murdered. Many considered the Assyrian Democratic Organization (ADO) culpable. Noyan was said to have been planning to expose negative information about ADO to Swedish authorities that day.

Eighteen months later, on March 19, 1982, Swedish Television asked, "Why was Aslan Noyan murdered?"[47] Claiming that ADO sought to establish a nation-state around Kirkuk, Iraq, the program compared the organization to a Soviet politburo, using a graphic illustration of underground cells in twenty countries.[48] The Assyrian Federation of Sweden (Assyriska Riksförbundet), created through Swedish governmental policies, was now regarded as a cover for insurgents. Gabriel Afram, its leader in 1982 and a self-professed member of ADO, denied these charges, saying, "The only thing we hope for is to get minority status where we live."[49]

Though they had initially urged Syriacs to develop associations and federations, some majority Swedish officials harbored suspicions about their success in doing so, citing their background in nondemocratic societies as evidence. Fuat Deniz writes that this and "a series of incidents raised Säpo's [Swedish Security Police] suspicions or qualms that ADO was running some sort of subversive operation."[50] Or as SVT host Birgitta Bergmark gravely informed the television audience on the program:

> In Södertälje, Syriacs began to form their own associations in the early 1970s. Those were public communities and not at all secret like ADO. Eventually, there were associations across the country, which were linked under the Assyrian Federation of Sweden. . . . Many members did not know that the Assyrian associations were in fact run by the underground ADO. In this way, the Assyrian Federation of Sweden became ADO's public face.[51]

In public discourse, the once-benign "immigrant association" was now malignant, and to the horror of majority Swedes, they themselves had apparently encouraged its creation.

The so-called name conflict between Syriacs identifying as either *assyrier* or *syrianer* appeared to be at the heart of the troubles, as the latter blamed the former for the murder. Linking the name conflict to the supposedly subversive direction in which the associations had gone, SVT blamed the Swedish government:

> It's difficult to see this as merely a local conflict in a local association. With a larger perspective and from all legal descriptions, [such conflicts] must be seen as a result of the confrontations that had been allowed to grow to such a degree. For example, in many cases, ADO members had become a sort of intermediary between society and the group. And they achieved a kind of power position, and Swedish society regarded them as specially favored, and, by all accounts, they were. And then, within this, there was the political question: namely, the various attitudes toward Assyrianism within the group. Sweden has been very careless about the naming issue.[52]

Swedish officials stood by helplessly as a split appeared in what the integration regime had categorized as one unified identity group, since, when the Syriacs had first arrived, they had all been labeled *assyrier*. With more Syriac families in Sweden, the group's increasingly complex factions, national backgrounds, lineages, and attitudes toward history unraveled the unified discursive tapestry that Swedish officials had tried to weave. Many identifying as *syrianer* now dared to take exception to a name they had never truly accepted.

The Assyrian Federation argued that the name conflict began in 1975 when some reclaimed their emic word for Syriacs: *Suryoye,* which was then "Swedified" as *syrier* and, later, *syrianer.*[53] The church regarded a separation between ethnicity and religion as threatening, leading the Assyrian Federation of Sweden to write in its magazine, *Hujådå,* that "the reason for the name conflict is consequently not just a question about naming but also a question of power. The church has capitalized on the Suryoyo [later Syrianska] Federation's and the older generation's lack of awareness and ignorance about the naming question."[54] An Assyrian ethnicity was more inclusive than for these *Suryoye,* they charged, since "a religion can never represent a person's entire identity."[55] As *assyrier,* they could be Syriac Orthodox, Syriac Protestants, or Syriac Catholics, and they could also be Chaldeans. Yet the *syrianer* considered this attempt to forge links to a pre-Christian group a sacrilege and expressed skepticism for its historical accuracy.[56]

In 1976, the patriarch dispatched Afram Aboodi, by then a bishop, to inform all the Syriacs in Sweden that the church prohibited its members from calling themselves Assyrian.[57] This stance directly opposed Swedish state policies, as interpreted by the Assyrian Federation of Sweden:

> Although we do not make any territorial claims, the name *"assyrier"* has national connotations. For this reason, the church wants to avoid confrontations with the governments of Iraq, Syria, and Turkey in the case that the name *"assyrier"* would affect areas in their territory, i.e., ancient Mesopotamia. This is the primary reason for the emergence of a name conflict among the *assyriska* people in Sweden.[58]

The conflict worsened, bringing an ineffectual visit from the patriarch himself to Södertälje. Perhaps it was not yet clear that most Syriac Orthodox émigrés would ultimately remain in Sweden, and the governments the patriarch represented feared dissent upon their potential return.

Conversely, the *syrianer/Suryoye* charged that the *assyrier* were counterfeiting their ethnicity. Alleged connections to the ancient Assyrian Empire were at best a misrepresentation and at worst a fabrication, they said; the actual Assyrians had either expired when the empire fell or were the modern Nestorians. The patriarch used another approach in a letter to the Swedish National Board of Health and Welfare (Socialstyrelsen) on August 22, 1977:

> A certain discussion concerning the name of our church has occurred. Some say *syriskortodox,* others say *assyrisk-ortodox. The correct name is* syrisk, *the name of the church or community,* because the church does not belong to any nation but includes various nations, with Jews, Arabs, Indians, Persians, and other peoples of the Orient, in addition to *araméer* and *assyrier.*[59]

In 1980, a new patriarch, Ignatius Zakka I Iwas, took a harder line, charging Bishop Aboodi to threaten that anyone claiming to be an *assyrier* would not be allowed to hold baptisms, weddings, or funerals in the church. In 1981, a census of members in

Sweden began via a form entitled "Application for Admission to the Syriac Orthodox Church in Scandinavia and England." It included the following lines:

> I accept the Syriac Orthodox Church's patriarch as the primary leader of the church
> and the Syriac Orthodox Council of Bishops' (Sinod's) decisions from 81/11/03–81/11/15
> to reject and to disallow any organization for the *Syriansk* people *(Suryoye)* that go
> under the names *Assyriska* and *Arameiska.* Thus, I certify with my signature that I do
> not belong to any of the above-mentioned *Assyriska* or *Arameiska* associations, [and
> that] in any other case I am aware that I can be expelled from the church by its leader-
> ship and thereby lose membership in the church.[60]

Those identifying as *assyrier* quickly understood the underlying political motivations of the census and the larger context of the conflict. For example, the Suryoyo
Association had published an article in the June–July 1979 issue of *Bahro Suryoyo*
implicitly claiming Aramaean descent, declaring, "The *Assyrier* [sic] were barbaric,
but the *Arameer* [sic] were civilized [written incorrectly as *diviliserade*] and proud of
their language and their sciences."[61] Conflicts between ancient civilizations enabled
a protracted division based on unresolvable, differing interpretations of history.
Over time, the name conflict defined Syriac urban development in the town as, two
by two, parallel institutions for *assyrier* and *syrianer* were created.

A Sacred "Tax House"

In 1990, the group had worshipped in St. Afrem's for seven years, but the fissures
of the name conflict had become ravines. Tensions between Syriac families in Södertälje had increased along with the group's size. Maria explained her own position:

> I stopped going there [to the church in Geneta]. I disagreed with them. Those who
> are left in St. Afrem's, when they call themselves *syrianer,* they do not want to go
> back to the roots before Jesus. They want to start with Jesus, Christianity. But those
> who are *assyrier* are proud to be descended from the Assyrian people, not only from
> Jesus. What happened to the people before? You have to think. Everyone didn't die
> at once. Everyone wasn't born when Jesus was born. There were people in the area
> we're from. I'm proud to have roots from there. But they don't want to have it that
> way. If you even mention the word *assyrier,* then you have sinned. That's the tension.

Any pretense of peace dissolved over the treatment of Bishop Julius Abdulahad
Gallo Shabo, expelled from the church on March 31, 1990, for "subversive activi-
ties." A letter sent on July 13, 1990, from the "Syriac Orthodox Church's Central
Board" to Swedish national authorities, the police, and the Södertälje town council

represented the faction that had ejected Shabo. Indicating that the patriarch intended to hold a special synod on September 17, 1990, to put the conflict to rest, it stated that he had directed that no unapproved priests—including Shabo—could give sermons for any of the sixteen Syriac Orthodox congregations in Sweden.

The spaces of St. Afrem's became the cauldron in which this bitter stew of families in conflict reached its boiling point. Like Maria, members calling themselves *assyrier* stopped attending services and canceled their membership, and Shabo became their religious leader. As Maria explained, "Those who called themselves the *assyrier* received him, agreed with him, supported him, didn't want him to be deported—not by the authorities, not sent back. They wanted him." But the group's hasty departure from St. Afrem's did not allow time for deliberate spatial planning. After initially renting an apartment in the Blombacka neighborhood in 1990, the group—eventually called "St. Jacob's of Nsibin congregation" (named after the town Nusaybin in Tur Abdin on the Turkish border with Syria)—later borrowed spaces in Södertälje from the Church of Sweden, the Pentecostals, and the Swedish Catholics, resuming the pattern of earlier years.

When St. Jacob's parish finally approached the municipality about a new space, they justified their request on the basis of overcrowding in St. Afrem's rather than on the name conflict. An application for building permission, dated January 24, 1991, explained that between 5,500 and 6,500 Syriac Orthodox Christians now lived in Södertälje, served by only one church.[62] The St. Jacob's group alone had approximately 2,000 members over the age of seven, according to their November 8, 1990, application for an official organization number.[63] Eventually, they received approval to renovate a building in central Södertälje on Almen block, steps away from the Södertälje Centrum train station.

Originally an office building constructed in the 1930s, the building had later been remodeled as a gas station, which had closed after the Swedish switch to right-hand driving in the 1960s rendered its site plan untenable. Most recently, it had been the premises of the Swedish Tax Authority and was known as the "Tax House." As Father Johannes, the group's priest, told me:

> We had no money to buy anything or to build a church. We looked for a suitable space, but there were none. For a whole year, we traveled around every Sunday with our suitcases in our hands. One day here, one day there. There were at least 400 to 500 people who usually came to church. And the churches available for rental, Swedish churches, could hold a maximum of 150 to 200 people. And at least 400 came, so that meant that 200 people were outside the whole time. They couldn't come into the church. We were forced to look around. So it was then that the Tax Authority had moved to their new, fresh space. Then we bought this at a very high price. Then we renovated it. We took away all the walls.

The congregation sought permission to make radical changes to the building, as well as to the local development plan, which was at that time zoned for business activities or housing. In the group's application to the municipal building committee, they wrote:

> The building will be used for religious/sacred activities. The purpose of these activities is to meet the sacred, religious, spiritual, cultural, and social needs of churchgoers and children. This building will be a central meeting point for our youth, especially to bring them in from the streets and in that way to protect them from evil. Here, there will be a place for everyone: for the old who do not have a place to gather, especially women who live partially isolated and alone.[64]

Knowing that their efforts were being observed from St. Afrem's, the St. Jacob's group was particularly anxious to overcome the considerable obstacles. Jakob, a board member in his seventies, described this:

> We heard that the other church did not think we could handle it, that we would not get anywhere because we are composed of small families and were therefore more fragmented. They, the *syrianer,* consisted of large families. My family is very large. Many of us are in the other church, and many of them tried to convince me to switch with that argument: that our church was made up of small families. But I said that I would never abandon my church after everything we went through together.

The creation of a physical space as an institutional home for St. Jacob's legitimized it in the eyes of both the Swedish authorities and their rivals. Together with their official organization number, the renovated building provided evidence that the split from St. Afrem's was not only permanent but successful and that the group now had a physical node around which to assemble. This was buttressed when, in 1996, the patriarch consecrated the new bishop, Dioscoros Benyamin Atas, to lead the group still assembled at St. Afrem's.

The two churches with two bishops (and two Syriac Orthodox dioceses) operating from Södertälje ultimately helped solidify the town's bifurcation into institutional enclaves for *assyrier* and *syrianer,*[65] yet the new congregation felt pressure to build a church equal to St. Afrem's even as they revamped the Tax House. While its site was considered ideal, the building itself was not. The replacement of load-bearing walls with columns allowed a larger space for church services but blocked views. A parish leader recounted:

> It was obviously a bit difficult and a challenge to transform a Tax House into a church. But since we were angry and upset about not having our own church, about having

been ostracized, and also that we always got fines when we parked at the Swedish churches, we all became carpenters! I did as much as I could myself as a carpenter, but I did not have much time because we were often in meetings with the municipality. But there was no shortage of carpenters, they were plentiful! When you are banished and you get something that makes you happy, you gain strength. We worked until the middle of the night without getting tired. My cousin carved all the benches for free. Everyone in the congregation was very pleased with the results.

Ad hoc solutions were still visible when the church left these premises in 2009. For example, despite a formal entrance on the street, many people entered from the small parking lot at the back. There, the inscription "S:t Jacob av Nsibins Församling" had been hand-painted in white block letters. Inside, shrines were jammed into niches around structural elements; the church had a corner platform for the choir and an asymmetrical nave (Figure 3.7). An austere basement party space held christenings, engagement parties, Bible study, and other youth-oriented activities.

While men and women typically sit separately during Orthodox services, the irregular floor plan complicated this. The load-bearing columns obscured the altar from some seats and made the choir mostly invisible, although their call-and-response vocal contributions could be heard. Still, this space could hold more churchgoers than any of the Church of Sweden options. As Father Johannes said, "This space

FIGURE 3.7. Interior of the former St. Jacob's Syriac Orthodox Church, just before a service, 2009. Photograph by author.

holds 480 Swedes, I usually say, or 600 immigrants, because we sit a little closer together." To maximize capacity, pews filled the room.

Parishioner donations and investments in marble baptismal fonts, iconographic oil paintings, embroidered velvet curtains for the altar, and a sound system alleviated but did not solve the problems with this ad hoc church. Father Johannes acknowledged these shortcomings:

> The actual physical space was very important for us as a cultural space as well. We took away the non-load-bearing walls on the second floor, so that became a gathering space, too. But the space only fulfilled about 50 percent of our needs, and we had problems with parking the whole time.

The secular Tax House was not quite fit for its new sacred job, and over time, dissatisfactions among the congregation were pervasive. Though they spent millions of Swedish kronor on the renovations,[66] Father Johannes explained:

> We were aware of the problems and already thinking about building a new church right from the beginning. When we bought this one, it was just to be able to come to our own church, to have our own space. But even then, we were thinking that we would buy something and went and checked around. Ideally, we wanted to expand, but there was no room, there was no chance.

While St. Jacob's parish no longer had to "carry [their] bags around," this transitional church accommodated "only 50 percent" of the group's needs. The result paled in comparison to the rival St. Afrem's church, which, despite being almost ten years older, had a greater capacity and an increasingly dominant symbolic presence on Geneta's skyline. For both the purposes of liturgical function and representational flare, the search for a site and the collection of money to build again had begun—before the paint was even dry at Almen.

The consecration of the purpose-built, costly St. Jacob's Syriac Orthodox Cathedral in May 2009 marked the end of this process. The social institution of the church would again be anchored to the urban environment of Södertälje, as Jakob told me:

> It was obviously very special for us to build something so big from the ground up. The people's support made us stronger. We received support from Germany and throughout Europe, and many said that our people had never done anything so great—neither in Europe, nor even in Turkey.

Pride in the project therefore extended well beyond the simple triumph of a local parish building its own sanctuary. Encompassing the global public, it elevated the status of St. Jacob's parish and Södertälje at large through this material "diaspora space."

Sited in an industrial district, the enormous white church lies in the middle of a block on Hantverksgatan. Rather than acting as a traditional geographic node, then, the church reshapes the social geography of this hinterland of the Hovsjö neighborhood. Situated behind the Assyrian Cultural Center and a desert of chain-link fences, gravel parking lots, and large driveways, it distinguishes itself from its surroundings (Figure 3.8). The cross-shaped windows, which Father Johannes has claimed as his own design, are the most prominent decorative feature. Large black lettering identifies the building as "S:t Jacob av Nsibin Syrisk Ortodoxa Katedral Södertälje" in Swedish, with the translation in Syriac underneath (Figure 3.9). The large foyer contains letters from the Estrangela and Serto scripts of the Syriac alphabet, which alternate with small mirrors to form a sculptural mural. In the domed basilica, where worship takes place, the ornamentation is exclusively Christian, including saints and biblical quotations, paintings, and decorations around the altar. The white walls and subdued decor follow the Orthodox tradition.[67]

FIGURE 3.8. Exterior, St. Jacob's Syriac Orthodox Cathedral on consecration day, May 17, 2009. Photograph by author.

FIGURE 3.9. Installation of new signage, St. Jacob's Syriac Orthodox Cathedral, 2009. Photograph by author.

Many churchgoers expressed admiration for this restraint. Ayla, a thirty-year-old woman whose acting talents have made her locally famous, said this white interior "makes it look much more like a cathedral than a church." Others proudly contrasted it with the "flashy" St. Afrem's. Some suggested that the two buildings differed because the craftspeople available in the early 1980s had died or were too frail to work. Painters and sculptors were hired from Germany instead. In the banquet hall on the other side of the building, wedding receptions, coffee after church services, and other social activities take place among reliefs of Assyrian warriors and kings in their chariots, lions, and mythological creatures. Here, Christian symbolism is absent.

The cathedral includes classrooms for Bible study and youth-group meetings, offices for church officials, meeting spaces, a library, an archive, apartments for visitors, and a reception hall for the bishop, among many other spaces. Controversially, St. Jacob's officials gained permission to create a special sanctuary for deceased priests and bishops in a small separate building.[68] This burial space demonstrates Syriac intentions to remain, not only in this expensively constructed church building but in Sweden. Departed bishops and priests will be interred here for ages to come, as they previously were in Tur Abdin.

New Pilgrimage Sites

Today, onion domes and three-dimensional Orthodox crosses adorn St. Afrem's. The building's roofscape is visible from a great distance, its colorful lighting illuminating Geneta's night sky. The name "S:t Afrem" now appears above the earlier gold lettering. The Syriacs are no longer invisible. Rejecting their liminal conditions in temporary Swedish spaces, they defined new material diaspora space from within the group. As monuments to the Syriacs' transformation of Södertälje at large, St. Afrem's, St. Jacob's, and other churches mark its reconstruction from an estranged host city to a new hometown and capital, Mesopotälje.

The progressive architectural establishment of the Syriac Orthodox Church in the city of Södertälje transformed not only the local urban landscape but also Middle Eastern Christian geographies—within Sweden and globally. Over the course of fifty years, what began as uncomfortable, ad hoc, and spatially creative solutions driven by necessity became serious social and economic investments in visible, large-scale structures.[69]

A spatial sojourn from informal meetings in living rooms to the design and construction of new Syriac pilgrimage sites reflects the church's importance, the group's growing size, and, ultimately, its internal factions. As in the villages of Turkey and the cities of Syria, purpose-built churches serve as central spatial nodes for this community, in Geneta beginning in 1983 and Hovsjö beginning in 2009. Even so, these new diaspora spaces need not be mapped onto the existing cartographies of urban Europe. When Syriacs rejected the opportunity to worship at Skeppsholm's Church, they signaled their commitment to Södertälje as a new urban nucleus. This logic also remade—for Syriacs—the Swedish capital of Stockholm into a periphery. Instead, Södertälje, a marginal town, became the group's capital through urban design from below.

The Sacred in the Profane: The Soccer Arena as a Place of Worship

On September 24, 2007, a broadcast about the Assyrian Soccer Association team (Assyriska FF, *Fotbollsförening*) on the Al Jazeera English television channel began with the following words:

> Football [soccer] has often been described as a religion in itself, stadiums modern places of worship, and the fans the congregation who put all their faith into their idols. But how many teams can claim they have followers who sing their songs in Assyrian, a branch of Aramaic, the language of biblical times?

Bishops and priests regularly attend matches, and players wear white warm-up jerseys featuring prominent red Christian crosses; the religion of soccer for this team stems from more than fan euphoria for Assyriska FF. Together with its archrival, Syrianska FC, the two teams represent the divide of the name conflict and have been competing against each other discursively and on the field since the 1970s. Both also claim to represent the entire Syriac "nation," making each match the local equivalent of a World Cup match.[70]

As an urban monument, their stadium, Södertälje Soccer Arena (Södertälje Fotbollsarena), celebrates the long journey of the teams from informal "kick-arounds"[71] to two of the premier soccer organizations in Sweden (Figure 3.10). Constructed as a partnership between Assyriska, Syrianska, and the municipality, the arena opened in 2006, with 3,500 seats, 3,000 standing-room spaces, and ten VIP lounges (one of which is usually occupied by priests and bishops during the matches). Syriacs from around the world now worship at this bricks-and-mortar shrine to their national teams or have watched them play there via the Södertälje satellite and Internet television stations Suryoyo SAT, Suroyo TV, and Assyria TV.[72]

While the original players established Assyriska and Syrianska more for pleasure than for competition in the 1970s, both teams have now played in Sweden's top

FIGURE 3.10. Södertälje Soccer Arena, as seen from the parking lot in front of the Scania Rink, 2009. Photograph by author.

division. Policy makers have celebrated their rise as an example of successful immigrant integration in Sweden. And while both teams may accept the label "immigrant team," they have larger aspirations.[73] Soccer has often been portrayed as a social resource in other European contexts, particularly for the children of immigrants, and specific individuals have usually been cast as role models (such as international star Zlatan Ibrahimović, the Swedish son of Bosnian immigrants; or Zinadine Zidane, whose Kabyle Berber parents immigrated to France from Algeria). Assyriska and Syrianska, on the other hand, are said to represent the advances of the Syriac group at large, as they also foster feelings of unity like those of other national teams.[74]

When Assyriska FF represents the Assyrian nation, flags displayed during the matches contain nationalist symbols, such as the ancient Assyrian god Ashur, the Babylonian Ishtar Gate, and the Assyrian sunburst flag. Syrianska FC represents a religious nation of Syriac Orthodox Christians, and, more recently, Aramaeans; their flags, with a red background and a yellow winged sun, appear prominently among fans adorned in a similar palette.[75] The patriotic intentions of these "national team[s] without a country"[76] are highly visible in such displays (Figure 3.11).

FIGURE 3.11. The stands at Södertälje Soccer Arena during an Assyriska FF match, 2009. Photograph by author.

Summertime social life in Södertälje revolves around soccer matches, where fans
from Sweden and abroad converge. Tom, a businessman in his fifties with a strong
Boston accent, was visiting from Worcester, Massachusetts, in 2007, and he told me,
"I follow Assyriska like I follow my own Red Sox," watching via satellite on Suroyo
TV. By his side was Ilona, a lawyer from Los Angeles who had relocated to Sweden
to live in the center of Assyrian cultural life. She told me, "Do you know what
they've done? Assyriska has put us back on the map. People go to the Louvre and
think we are only a part of history. Assyriska has made us a part of current history."

When promoted to Allsvenskan, the top Swedish division, in 2004, Assyriska
received text messages, faxes, and telephone calls from seventy-eight countries.[77]
With success, the teams transformed from ethnically homogeneous recreational clubs
to professional organizations with players from diverse ethnic and national backgrounds. They have also inspired many imitators—locally, nationally, and globally—
while the soccer teams play from the territories of Södertälje. These successes have
had spatial consequences.

The Golden Age of Bårsta

When the Syriacs first arrived in Södertälje, the town's successful hockey team,
Södertälje Sportklubb, represented it professionally. Soccer was far off the radar of
most residents in 1967. Million Program planners envisioned soccer as just one
of many recreational sports, as evidenced in the 1968 plan for section nine of the
Geneta neighborhood (Figure 3.12), which includes separate areas for tennis, soccer,
and other sports articulated in bushy, semicircular partitions.

The first Syriacs quickly established informal soccer clubs to allow members to
maintain social ties during a tumultuous period. Assyriska began in 1974 as an off-
shoot of the Assyrian Association, established three years earlier. Mirroring the
group's church rentals during the same decade, they did not have a dedicated space
for matches and borrowed existing fields on a rotating basis, such as one in the
neighborhood of Brunnsäng. Eventually, Assyriska began to use Bårsta IP (Bårsta
Idrottsplats, Bårsta Sports Field) as its home stadium (Figure 3.13).

The older generation and young adults who grew up during this time remember Bårsta fondly and nostalgically as the site of folk festivals (*folkfester*; literally,
"people's parties"). The matches at Bårsta were more than mere sporting events,
offering music and food and giving both players and fans a regular chance to get
together. The author Benjamin, who became a player for Assyriska in its earliest
incarnation, recalled, "It was a way to maintain contact, to break our isolation. It
had a social function, playing soccer."

Younger women who attended many matches as teenagers also recalled Bårsta IP's
importance for Syriac courtship and matchmaking. Ishtar, twenty-seven, and Temra,
thirty-three, argued that most women considered it more important to look good

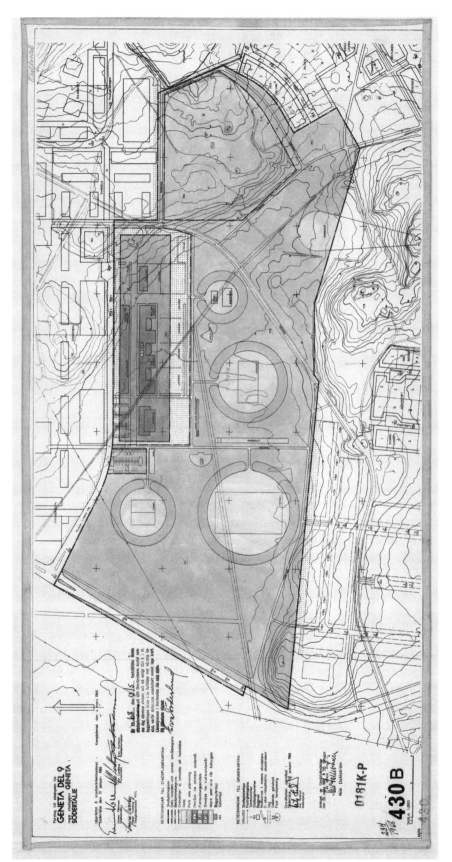

FIGURE 3.12. "Plan for Geneta Section 9, 1968. Source: Södertälje Kommun.

FIGURE 3.13. Bårsta Sports Field, 2008. Photograph by author.

than to demonstrate interest in the game. Bårsta's form facilitated this; the open spaces between the stands made it possible to circumambulate throughout the match. Ishtar and Temra referred to this as "the catwalk" *(catwalken),* where women were chosen, "like from a catalog." Although they claimed that men, in contrast to women, actually came to watch the match, this ritual suggests the equal (if less conspicuous) participation of men as judges of the catwalk's participants. I asked if they took part, and Temra sheepishly said, "Yes, a little bit."

As the teams became more popular, articles in *LT* during the 1970s attested to the festive atmosphere and throngs of supporters that distinguished these games from those of other teams.[78] This visibility—like their appearances in groups downtown—triggered complaints from others in the local community, and some claimed that these "people's parties" were merely chaotic melees. One letter to *LT* from an anonymous writer using the name "FAIR PLAY" in 1980 defended the team, stating:

> Matches in Södertälje with immigrant teams as participants are thought of as often ending in disturbances and fights. But we shouldn't simply complain about hot-tempered immigrants. During the match between Assyriska and Cosmos, the *assyrier* brought their own guards with them, who managed the audience. A great initiative![79]

The large size and active participation of Assyriska's audience clearly provoked anxieties among some majority Swedes. Yet the teams, like the church, increasingly became an institutional force around which the group could organize and for which local financial and logistical support from Södertälje was available.[80]

Climbing the Ladder

At Södertälje Soccer Arena today, greeting friends and family from the moment of arrival (whether at the bus stop behind the arena or in the parking lot across the street) serves as a key part of match attendance. Fans then buy tickets and enter through turnstiles into an exterior outdoor space. Ascending one of several staircases, they proceed through a short tunnel on the mezzanine level, where they are released into the seats and can choose to go up or down. Direct lines of sight from the stands make this arrival experience theatrical and public. Visitors enter on the opposite side. Assyriska fan merchandise is available in a small shop on one corner, and Syrianska has their shop on another. Each team's offices are located behind their gift shop, effectively bifurcating the arena into Assyriska and Syrianska sections.

When the halftime whistle blows, and often before it, fans file out of the arena's stands to the ground-level zone to converse. Others remain on the upper level, where snack shops swell with customers and conversations take place as roving audience members greet one another. These salutations have become essential elements of the game experience, and departing from an Assyriska or Syrianska match involves socializing in motion. Fans convey their joy or sorrow to one another in short, casual conversations and with knowing looks as they exit the arena.

Assyriska FF and Syrianska FC have become critical elements of both family and youth culture among Syriacs and other Middle Eastern Christians in Södertälje, such as those who identify as Assyrian but are not Syriac Orthodox. Even in early years of Syriac settlement in Södertälje, many parents regarded sports as a positive influence on their children, an inclination that was also encouraged through municipal support for teams. One man in his thirties named Ashur, who has been heavily involved in the Assyriska FF fan club Zelge Fans, told me that soccer allowed him to express pride in his national identity. He had tried ice hockey, he told me, but his parents became alarmed about the costs when he outgrew his newly purchased protective gear after just one year. Soccer required only cleats and shin guards, so they encouraged him to play that instead.

As more and more Syriacs played soccer in Södertälje, the teams enjoyed increasing success, rising through the Swedish divisions at a steady clip.[81] Beginning in the low-level Swedish Division VII in 1975, Assyriska played in the top-level Allsvenskan division in 2005 and has lately played primarily in Superettan, the second division. Syrianska FC, created in 1977 as the Suryoyo Sports Club (Suryoyo Sportklubb [SK]), has had even more success, playing in Allsvenskan for three years from 2011 to 2013 but in Superettan since then. With these moves, the teams' match schedules have become prominent fixtures of everyday life in Södertälje, and there is a palpable sense of emptiness in other parts of the town during matches. Practice fields are frequently illuminated at night, constantly reminding residents of the presence of the teams.

A National Arena

Even as Assyriska FF's growing triumphs transformed the team into a success story for Swedish immigration politics and this "integrated" minority group, the dilapidated state of the beloved Bårsta IP belied this status. While playing in Allsvenskan, Assyriska was required to host its "home" games at Råsunda Stadium in Solna, a northern suburb of Stockholm, frustrating fans with its alien atmosphere and long commute. Afram described what had became a long-term battle for a new stadium:

> When we got into Division I [the third division], we went to the municipality. Every time, we fought with the municipality. We wanted to have a nice arena, but the municipality was poor. They were always complaining about money, that they didn't have any money. They didn't want to take responsibility. Every party promised us before the elections: "We are going to renovate. We are going to build a soccer arena for Södertälje and for Assyriska." They promised year after year but did nothing. In the end, they built the arena, together with Assyriska, because the National Soccer Commission didn't approve Bårsta as an arena for Allsvenskan.

The Assyriska team, in effect, had played for its arena, being so successful in the leagues that their wishes could no longer be ignored.

When the teams and municipality finally built Södertälje Soccer Arena in Geneta, they chose a site adjacent to the ice-hockey stadium known as the Scania Rink (Scaniarinken, named after Scania AB). Before that, the site had been a parking lot where, Ishtar told me, "Everyone in Södertälje did their driver's training." Situated at the junction of the E20 freeway and Strängnäsvägen, the arena is also adjacent to a big-box shopping district. Today, the arena's roof hangs suspended over the home fans' section, visible from a great distance behind the large and colorful storefront of the grocery store Coop, the state liquor store Systembolaget, the MIO furniture showroom, and others.

Designed to hold 6,400 people, the new arena set an attendance record of 8,453 during a match in 2009.[82] It was quickly nicknamed "Jallavallen," a combination of *jalla* ("hurry up" in Arabic) and *vall* ("pasture" in Swedish, a word often used in connection with lower-league soccer fields to reflect their grassy, informal character). Numerous team sponsors have banners along the edge of the field, including such companies as Barolo Restaurant (a popular postgame hangout) and Ninve

Jeans (a clothing company taking its name from the ancient Assyrian imperial city Nineveh).

Though Assyriska's requests for a better space were finally fulfilled in the new arena—a source of pride for the community—emotional attachments to the space of Bårsta IP had been underestimated. Higher security standards and separate entrances for home and visiting fans at the arena prevented the circumambulation that had so long characterized matches. I frequently heard nostalgic laments about the old days at Bårsta, and about how there was now "another feeling" during matches. Distancing the arena from the group, for instance, Ishtar told me, "I don't like it. It's not really us, you know. It's too nice. We don't even dare to throw our nuts anymore." Ninos Sharro, then the head of Zelge Fans, made similar comments in an interview for the team's website on September 11, 2008:

> Personally, I miss the passionate and exotic atmosphere that once distinguished Assy-riska's matches. Nut chewing and the spontaneous dancing have disappeared. . . . The classic media image of Assyriska with the nut chewing, the kebab, the dance, and the raki has disappeared as the new Assyriska has taken shape. The new arena has played a big part. I remember that it was still there until the last match at Bårsta IP, but today no one wants to sell nuts anymore. When I was younger, I remember that the most fun we could have was to go to the matches and just hang out. The soccer part came second. I was too busy greeting people, thinking about how I could jump over the fence to avoid paying the entrance fee, and so on.[83]

As Ishtar and Ninos recognized, the new physical space of the arena required radical changes to the group's social traditions at soccer matches. Assyriska's success transformed not just their team's public profile but their bodily engagement with the arena itself and with one another.

The "catwalk" of Bårsta IP has also been, in effect, eliminated at Södertälje Soccer Arena, since the two major stands are not connected to each other (Figure 3.14). Despite this, many women in their twenties and thirties wear dresses, high-heeled shoes, and careful makeup to matches and, Temra and Ishtar noted, do their best to walk in front of the stands as many times as possible. Temra herself was generally uncomfortable at matches in the new space and rejected this spatial practice, despite the fact that she was consistently an elegant and fashion-conscious person. On one rare visit to the arena, she sighed, "I don't belong with these people anymore." In a weary voice, she said that she had simply grown tired of "performing."

The team fan clubs, Zelge Fans and Gefe Fans, are renowned for their energetic support of Assyriska and Syrianska (respectively), their faithful attendance, and their willingness to travel to away matches.[84] They also manage the fans at large, cheerleading at games and organizing events and parties.[85] While most fan-club members are young men, many younger women and teenagers participate actively, wear match

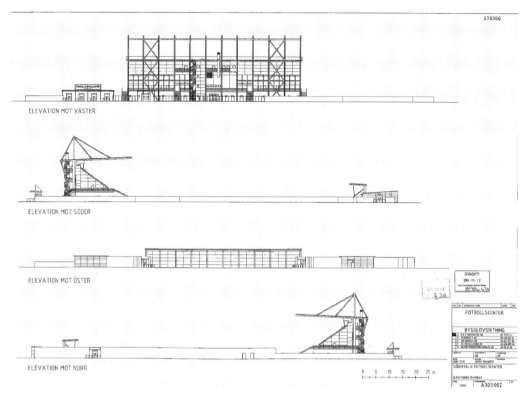

ELEVATION MOT VÄSTER

ELEVATION MOT SÖDER

ELEVATION MOT ÖSTER

ELEVATION MOT NORR

FIGURE 3.14. Elevations overview, Södertälje Soccer Arena (here called Södertälje Soccer Center), 2004. Design by Jerry Ramnitz Arkitekt AB. Source: Södertälje Kommun.

jerseys, and sit with the rest of the club in the designated cheering section. Thirteen-year-old Meryam proudly said that when the chants are in full force, she yells too, "Just like the guys!" Despite her critical comments about nut chewing, Ishtar regarded the new arena as a place where gender roles were neutralized, saying, "The differences don't exist anymore during the match." Temra disagreed, however, claiming that women still go to Södertälje Soccer Arena to take part in something on men's terms, losing themselves completely for two hours while acting a part for potential suitors. This disagreement indicates that the new arena has made the boundaries of game-time gender relations much more fluid.

Whether or not courtship rituals and expectations for women have changed since the early days at Bårsta, women often sit together at home games. Baby carriages and young children, typically accompanied by women, are plentiful at most matches. Although Nahrin, a Syriac housewife in her thirties, and I had attended many matches together, I did not in fact realize that her husband was also attending these matches until she mentioned once that he was there. She told me that he always sat "with the guys" and that they usually drove to matches in different cars. The game was not a date or a family outing for them and their two children (always with her) but was instead a time to meet independently with male or female friends and relatives.

Visibility in this extremely public place also demands propriety in other ways. For example, Sanharib, a friend from my first research trip in 2007, had recently become engaged to Belinda, a young woman from a traditional Syriac family, when I began fieldwork a year later. Although Sanharib and I had remained friendly in smaller social settings, I was surprised when he greeted me coldly at the first soccer match that I attended after returning. I complained to Temra, who informed me that with his betrothal, Sanharib "has eyes on him" and was no doubt nervous about how to behave. I asked if the engagement was common knowledge, and she said, "Everyone knows. This kind of thing spreads very quickly." Temra continued, "He has obligations now. He has to greet tons of people." For Sanharib, the space of the arena, where he had once been an enthusiastic fixture in Zelge Fans, was now a forum for his new role as fiancé. With the crowd watching more than the game, appropriate behavior in the stands was required.

A death in the family also demanded specific comportment at the arena. For example, Izla, a nurse in her early thirties, wanted to attend a match after an older relative of her father's had passed away. She was concerned, however, that others might consider her presence "ugly" (but added that she would attend if her father did). Likewise, Simon, in his early twenties and the main cheerleader for the Assyriska matches, once sat alone at a match in a section populated almost entirely by women. Both the location and his mood departed radically from his typical behavior, and he looked angry throughout the match. I said hello to him, and he acknowledged me but did not smile. Confused, I asked Ishtar about this. She also thought it was strange, so she asked Sanharib, her brother, who informed us that Simon's grandmother had died. Public propriety allowed Izla and Simon to attend matches after the deaths of relatives, but they were required to do so according to certain logics. Moving through the turnstile and into the stands is to accept rules about public behavior that take shape in new, soccer-specific spatial practices.

In this sense, Södertälje Soccer Arena emphasizes functionalist spatial ideologies, especially concerning crowd discipline and internal zoning. As it separates home and away teams and regulates the social world of fans' encounters with the field and one another, it also creates a socially disciplinary space. With the elimination of the catwalk and other courtship traditions, the arena even begins to negate the gendered imbalances of Bårsta. The arena thus makes possible the integration of the fractured parts of a resistant Syriac aggregate internally while ostensibly celebrating its separatist successes. In a sense, the arena proves that the architectural technologies of the welfare state and its spatial tools of separation remain effective, even here, in the heart of a community resisting those technologies.

Derby as Public Event

Mirroring the tensions over the divided spaces and social worlds of St. Afrem's and St. Jacob's parishes, the Assyriska FF and Syrianska FC teams have developed a major rivalry. Syrianska was considered, until recently, to be the "little brother" of the two, given its later formation and slightly lesser degree of success initially. It finally surpassed Assyriska in 2010, when it advanced to Allsvenskan and then qualified to remain there for the following two years, while Assyriska was demoted after just one year in Allsvenskan.

Among sports fans, two teams from the same town playing each other is known as a "derby," a term also used in Swedish. As both teams have a home and an away game, this happens twice each year.[86] Syrianska and Assyriska have played in the same division several times over the past decade: Division I (the third division) in 2007 and Superettan in 2009, 2010, 2014, and 2015.[87] This has created an exciting yet mildly dangerous event every season when they have played each other.[88]

The soccer rivalry exacerbated tensions over the name conflict, yet the teams had avoided the direct clash of a derby while playing in different divisions. Ishtar lamented its influence:

> We're the same people, we live in a very little town, but we never collide. Same people, same parties, same songs, soccer, same religion. But, after high school, you stop hanging out with *syrianer* if you're an *assyrier*. We do the exact same things at different times in different places. When we see each other in restaurants and cafés, you can almost count what the majority of the people in each café call themselves.

School was generally a neutral zone for the name conflict, but children who attended matches talked about how much they feared going to school after the derby.

Since the turn of the twenty-first century, choices about identifying as *assyrier* or *syrianer* have been less loaded than in the past in most social settings. These personal identity choices, however, remain threatening in the context of sporting events, which present opportunities to disparage the other side holistically. For example, Ishtar excused people calling themselves *syrianer* when it was people she liked, such as one of her best friends and her brother's wife, saying, "Oh, that's what they call themselves, but it's a personal choice." When discussing the group in the context of their behavior at soccer matches, however, she described *syrianer* as "uncivilized" or "barbarians."

Such negative characterizations were not limited to the *assyrier* side. Gabriella is a twenty-eight-year-old woman who came from Tur Abdin via Syria and had been living in Sweden without a residence permit for more than eight years. Her sister Kristina, thirty-three, married a local Syriac man and quickly had two children with him, but even she had not yet been granted permanent residence, and their

ailing mother had recently been denied asylum as well. Attending soccer matches
and daily church visits to St. Afrem's in Geneta or St. Gabriel's in Ronna relieved
some frustrations.

On our way to attend a Syrianska FC match together, Gabriella, Kristina, her
husband Afram, and I were parking when a car with an Assyriska FF flag drove by
the arena, honking. Kristina and Gabriella scoffed. Gabriella immediately said,
"They don't believe in God. They're not good Christians." *Syrianer* sometimes call
assyrier "cows," referring to an Assyrian icon that links the group to a pre-Christian
history. But when Syrianska fans began chanting the name of the group in Syriac,
"*Suryoye! Suryoye! Suryoye!*" the Zelge Fans adopted it, too, saying, "What do they
think? We're not?" When Syrianska won a derby in 2007, several Assyriska fans
claimed to be happy about the outcome, saying, "They would destroy the town if
we'd won." Claiming a civilized role for themselves, they cited the ringing of the
St. Afrem's Church bells after the match as a demonstration of the *syrianer*'s poor
sportsmanship, as well as an uncomfortable confirmation of just which side that
church was on.

When it was Assyriska that triumphed in a 2009 derby, a spontaneous party took
place at the Assyrian Cultural Center, but arson destroyed part of the building shortly
after the event concluded. Assyriska FF fans decried the "barbaric" Syrianska FC
supporters as culpable for the crime, while several Syrianska fans, including Afram
and Kristina, suggested that "shady" Assyriska fans had actually ignited the fire
themselves. For many people, this intragroup rivalry trumps success in the Swedish
leagues. Or, as one Assyriska fan said to me, "I don't care if we're in Allsvenskan,
I just don't want to play against Syrianska." If these teams represent competing
nations, they attempt to settle both the name conflict and the truth of their history
on the soccer field.

The Arena as Temple, Theater, and Monument

In the off-season, tensions around soccer reduce to a slow simmer, but Södertälje
Soccer Arena remains a prominent physical presence on the town's skyline, with its
enormous red trusses piercing the horizon on the edge of Geneta. As it sits covered
in snow and ice, the season begins for nationalist history lectures indoors at the
cultural centers and associations and for winter parties, even as off-season discussions about previous or upcoming soccer seasons occur frequently.

As the immigrant community has progressed from small groups of exiles battling
loneliness and disorientation to populations able to field elite teams of professional
players, the informality of the past has given way to a highly regulated present in
which Assyriska and Syrianska are annually either participants in the top division
in Sweden or contenders for positions in it. A settler monument, Södertälje Soccer
Arena represents the successes of the teams even as it solidifies their continued

bifurcation in architectural terms, with two team offices and two team gift shops on opposite sides of the structure. The teams alternate their home and away games, and special efforts are taken to ensure that fans do not meet after matches, such as when Zelge Fans delay their return after an away game in order to avoid fights in the parking lot.

As neighbors of the arena have complained about match noise levels (echoing those who wrote about "hot-tempered" Syriacs in the past), others have expressed irritation over the use of municipal funds to construct the arena, arguing that it caters to only one of the town's ethnic groups, despite its catch-all name.[89] These "national" teams are said by their detractors to use private spaces paid for, in part, by the public.

Literary theorist Roland Barthes writes, "At certain periods, in certain societies, the theater has had a major social function: it collected the entire city within a shared experience: the knowledge of its own passions. Today it is sport that in its way performs this function. Except that the city has enlarged: it is no longer a town, it is a country, often even, so to speak, the whole world."[90] While some local residents of the town feel excluded from Södertälje Arena, followers worldwide see the team and its arena on the satellite channels every game day. These events draw visitors and fans of Assyriska and Syrianska from the United States, Germany, Turkey, and beyond to this peripheral suburban strip in Geneta. Even as they remain divided within it, the arena, like the churches before it, signifies a spatial triumph for the Syriac group, where urban design from below has allowed them to remake the geography of the town and the place of soccer within it. As a national monument for two nations, the arena anchors the social institution of soccer, long important for the group, to a new diaspora space.

Conclusion: Diaspora Space in the City

Expensive, ornate, and with capacities in the thousands, individual monumental spaces for the Syriac Orthodox Church and for soccer clubs in Södertälje are now pilgrimage sites. Today they always have Syriac visitors present, from the Syriac Orthodox patriarch and priests from Syria and Turkey to doctoral students from Canada and lawyers from the United States to soccer fans and honeymooners from Germany and Holland. They visit, hoping to pray with the congregation at St. Jacob's or St. Afrem's or to yell chants of support for Syrianska FC or Assyriska FF from stands awash in a sea of hoodies bearing Christian crosses or Ashur banners. Södertälje—socially and geographically marginal from a Swedish point of view— has become a central node for the worldwide Syriac community, a larger circle in a Venn diagram than any other homeland. This is diaspora space made material.

The representation of Syriac minority identities within the Swedish soccer leagues, along with their worship in recognizably Christian (yet Orthodox) ways, also seems to demonstrate a success story for Swedish integration politics: Syriacs are separate but equal within these systems. Yet other, less-successful claims on space have come from politicians and church members, such as unrealized attempts to rename several of Södertälje's streets after Syriac figures and places. These failed efforts may demonstrate the current limits of efforts to make diaspora space.

For example, the Liberal Party (Liberalerna, formerly Folkpartiet and Folkpartiet Liberalerna) politician Metin Hawsho, a Syriac, argued that street names should reflect Södertälje's current population, a move that would, he told me, "create unity" and a feeling of "safety." His December 2008 motion to the town council to rename streets and squares in Södertälje highlighted these psychological justifications.[91] As he further explained to me when we met in 2009, "If you have a street with a Syriac name, you have a feeling of belonging in the total image of Södertälje. You are included in a different way. It makes you care about the city in another way. 'I belong to the city, and the city belongs to me.'" An initial application to rename Klockarvägen as St. Afrem's Road was denied, but proponents succeeded in retitling the nearest bus stop in 2004, and an adjacent plot of grass became S:t Afrem Syrerns Plan (St. Afrem the Syriac's Square). A small, reflective sign marks this minor victory (Figure 3.15).

One parish priest expressed his hopes that the renaming of the square would, despite the initial failure of the larger effort, lead to further urban rechristenings, a long-term strategy that municipal officials had apparently recommended. The sign on this square has, however, occasionally been defaced, and motorists on Klockarvägen honked when I approached it (after a derby) in the company of Nisha, an *assyrier* who interpreted, "You see how crazy they are! They're being mean because we want to take a picture of the sign!" Since the pictures were blurry, Nisha advised me to return in the daytime. "But don't come on a Sunday. There are so many people here then, and they'll kill you!"

When I told Nisha about the idea to change the street's name, she replied, "The *syrianer* want to make a special neighborhood, you know, like a Chinatown. They think their ethnic group is superior to the country where they're living." When I asked if the *assyrier* were doing the same thing, she incorporated the language of official Swedish immigration politics, saying, "We would never do that! The *assyrier* know that integration is very important. We want to have success here." When I asked why it was then important that *assyrier* marry other *assyrier,* she said, "We believe in integration but not assimilation." Even so, the construction of St. Jacob's next to the Assyrian Cultural Center suggests that Hovsjö has evolved into a parallel Assyrian enclave.[92] Major monuments may unite the diaspora, but they also bifurcate the city.

Despite this split, Södertälje is a Syriac town within a European nation-state, acting not just as a new hometown but as a new urban homeland. David described its importance:

FIGURE 3.15. Signage at St. Afrem the Syriac's Square, opposite St. Afrem's Church and adjacent to the bus stop, 2008. Photograph by author.

> More and more people have begun to see that Södertälje has opened up for our community. We have our churches, our cultural associations, our TV stations here, and our soccer teams. It is from here that our face turns outward. Our roots are going to be here, and we are going to fight for this community.

Sacred and profane architectural projects have slowly made this marginal place into a central node in the diasporic cosmology.

As Södertälje's reputation as a haven for Christians has spread across the world, the thousands of Middle Eastern Christians lately arriving from Syria and Iraq have also begun to affect the town physically. These new groups, like their predecessors, create their own diaspora spaces. For example, St. Tomas's parish comprises Iraqi Syriac Orthodox Christians, who began by renting time at the Swedish St. Mikael's Church in Geneta Centrum. This Arabic-speaking group could not follow sermons at the other Syriac churches, where they were conducted in Suryoyo and classical Syriac. Their new church in the neighborhood of Lina Hage lies directly across the street from a Swedish church that was constructed in the 1990s (Figures 3.16 and 3.17).[93]

FIGURE 3.16. Exterior, St. Tomas's Syriac Orthodox Church, under construction, 2011. Photograph by author.

FIGURE 3.17. Exterior, St. Tomas's Syriac Orthodox Church, decorated for the patriarch's visit to Sweden, 2015. Photograph by author.

Now complete, it welcomed the visiting patriarch during his Swedish visit in 2015, just like St. Afrem's and St. Jacob's.

Another group of Iraqi Christians—a Chaldean Catholic parish—currently plans to build a new church in Hovsjö with support from the Catholic Diocese of Stockholm (Stockholms Katolska Stift), and they currently borrow space.[94] While Josef, a Syriac building-permit officer in his thirties, described its siting at the entrance to the neighborhood as a "portal" that Hovsjö desperately needed, one Swedish resident criticized this, saying, "The new church they're building is going to make it hard to change things in Hovsjö. It's like saying it's an Iraqi area. Building it there is like building a sign. It's going to solidify the structure of the community." While Christians increasingly atomize into different factions in Södertälje, the town's reputation as a space of release from the anxieties and dangers of war and minority life elsewhere gain ground. Today, not only Syriac Orthodox and Chaldean Catholics but also Syriac Catholics, Armenian Catholics, Coptic Orthodox, and Mandaeans practice their religion from spaces in Södertälje.[95] These diaspora spaces create additional social landmarks for Middle Eastern Christians around the world.

Rather than Ho's "society of the absent," Syriacs have become a prominent society of the present in Södertälje. Each site that the Syriacs have constructed operates across several registers. The churches and soccer arena are positioned in marginal spaces of the town, where their conspicuity—and associated noise, parking, and late-night revelry—is assumed to be less disturbing to the majority Swedish community. As megastructures, these works of architecture also operate at a larger scale than most other buildings in Södertälje. Furthermore, aesthetic decisions like nighttime illumination and increasingly bold signage produce a sense of difference because they mark the sites as iconic and exclusively Syriac. Separating itself from the emphases on visual discretion and sameness of the midcentury modernism surrounding them in Geneta and Hovsjö, this architecture offers a glimpse into how a diasporic migrant community has—conspicuously—established itself socially (and perhaps paradoxically) as settlers.

Declaring their intentions to remain in Sweden through the design, planning, and construction of expensive new community buildings, each architectural project illuminates a new star in the ever-larger constellation of the Syriac world in a form of urban design from below. These feats of planning and architecture have also disrupted the traditional Swedish strategy of immigrant integration—a politics predicated on sharp social boundaries uncomfortably wedded to geographic dispersal; this minority group was encouraged to retain certain features of their cultural difference but, at the same time, to spread themselves across Sweden. As they rejected the oversimplification of an ethnic category applied from above and created an enclave in the process, they produced Mesopotälje, where diaspora space is urban, monumental, and conspicuous.

CHAPTER FOUR

"Södertälje Is a Theater"

The Performance of Propriety and Ritual Infrastructure

BABILONIA NEVER CRIED WHEN SHE TALKED ABOUT IT. She looked down, she smiled painfully, she clutched the crucifix hanging from her neck, she played Amy Winehouse at top volume in her car, but she never cried. She knew a decision was looming. She had delayed it for years. It had almost become a permanent part of her, this deferred choice: to tell her family about the love of her life, of whom they would certainly disapprove, or to let the secret, nearly eight years old, go untold and so lose him.

The situation demanded absolute discretion. Several of her closest friends and even her sister had no idea. She did not want to burden them with the secret that she was in love with a man originally from Iran. She assumed that many of them would chastise her anyway. Kaveh, her boyfriend, was mostly understanding about her need for extreme discretion. When the couple entered public places, however, his tolerance faded, leading to several arguments and straining their relationship. She told me of one such case: "I never let him hold my hand on the platform for the commuter rail in Stockholm Central Station." When Kaveh asked to hold her hand there, she reminded him, "But someone from Södertälje might see us. That's where everyone takes the train home." He repeated his request, and she refused again, making him angry. With embarrassment, she described how her fear trumped his need: she simply could not make their relationship public in this space. For Babilonia, this platform in the middle of Stockholm was where the city of Södertälje began.

For the Syriac community, Södertälje today is a city that, in practical terms, lacks urban anonymity in public and private spaces. In every café, on each street corner, and even behind the wheel of a car, behavior is being observed, discussed, calibrated, and evaluated according to Syriac standards of acceptability. For Babilonia, this visibility emerged on the platform of the train that she took from visits with Kaveh, whom she met while studying at Lund University in southern Sweden and had hidden from her parents since then. Once she had hurt him deeply, panicking in a park in Stockholm when she saw a Syriac acquaintance there having a picnic. She

135

froze, stopped touching him, and insisted they leave. The fight that ensued lasted for several days and nearly ended their relationship.

Negotiations between Syriac private and public space are performed in a role-playing game with ever-attentive spectators, where "Södertälje is a theater," as Babilonia explained. Alternating between audience members and actors, each person knows how to react to the proper and improper behavior of others in the city. As the stage for these spectacles, the town contracts and expands—sometimes all the way to Stockholm—to assume the various shapes of a social world with specific rules for dramaturgy. A young woman must consider whether she wants to be seen with a male friend at a café; it may be rumored that they are having a relationship. In the arena during a derby, a fan of Assyriska FF must think twice before greeting a fan of Syrianska FC, even though he or she might be a friend in other contexts; the two could be accused of betrayal. Babilonia could not touch Kaveh at the station or in a public park in Stockholm.

Syriac norms for public comportment in Södertälje have shifted dramatically since the 1970s, when the police and politicians explicitly told members of the group to avoid congregating in the city's streets, strengthening the development of parallel spaces hidden underground in Million Program town centers or behind demure church facades. Even though Swedish officials' instructions produced a city that was more symbolically ghettoized than it otherwise might have been, today's Syriacs do not restrict themselves to these spaces. The enclaves that they were asked to create have expanded to the scale of the town, itself often described as "segregated." A minority group originally seen as guests—and asked to disappear rather than publicly disturb the social codes—Syriacs now form a dominant pillar in Södertälje's urban social life. Rather than adapting to the standards that Swedish authorities tried to impose upon them (or to the condoned public life of the spaces of the Million Program), Syriacs now conform to social and spatial norms of their own.

Benchmarks for Syriac public behavior are enforced through what Michel de Certeau and Henri Lefebvre label "spatial practice"—both within the historic built environment of this Swedish city and in more recently constructed Syriac spaces.[1] For de Certeau, spatial practice is temporary and opportunistic; Lefebvre sees it as spatially and socially transformative. Temporary Syriac spatial practices in Södertälje have produced new urban patterns that, over time and with repetition, have changed expectations for how, when, with whom, and in what clothing Syriac bodies should appear—and even how the spaces around these bodies should be decorated. Spatial practice also affects the construction of new buildings for a ritual infrastructure, as Swedish civil servants and Syriac clients clash over what is "appropriate" during planning meetings for banquet halls and churches. Here, seemingly mundane issues like loud music and parking echo the tense discussions that happened over church bells in the 1980s.

Swedish welfare-state planners emphasized classless spaces in both domestic and public life, and minimalist Swedish spatial practices for wedding and funeral rituals followed suit. In contemporary Södertälje, in contrast, Syriacs have often valued a maximalist way of life, especially around the celebration and mourning of family members.[2] High-volume wailers who cry at funerals and lavish weddings for five hundred to eight hundred guests require a ritual infrastructure that has reshaped the town at large. Using some of the same spaces as majority Swedes, however, Syriac events are not mere contrasts to their counterparts; instead, they comprise a "cultural intimacy"[3] that accepts some features of the didactic Swedish urban landscape while rejecting others.

Whereas the Million Program itself outlined explicit rules for spatial decorum, predefining uses for public spaces and prohibiting loitering or large gatherings on lawns through social enforcement, Syriac propriety manifests differently as a culturally intimate revision of these attitudes. Here, elaborate spatial practices and "conspicuous consumption"[4] within a new ritual infrastructure are—not paradoxically—paired with expectations of modesty and chastity, together providing evidence that one is a good daughter, a good Christian, a good widow, or a good family. This has transformed Södertälje socially and physically, both through temporary uses of existing spaces and in specifically Syriac buildings and interior designs for social functions.

As new Syriac architecture sometimes makes the group's presence uncomfortably conspicuous for majority Swedes, Syriac internal performances in and through the built environment suggest that—perhaps like the welfare-state disciplinary mechanisms they have often sought to upend—only a limited heterogeneity is supported within the autonomous, aggregated body of the Syriac community. New ritual infrastructures activate subjectivities of gender, religion, and politics that work in dialogue, mostly tensely, with Swedish welfare-state morality and its standardized built environment. In Södertälje, a minoritized Syriac ritual protocol is being enacted, built, and planned in this "segregated" city through urban design from below.

The Right Match

In 2008, Babilonia and I went to the Södertälje theater Oktoberteatern to see one of the earliest performances of *iamjustagirl,* a one-woman show starring the Syriac actress Yelda Hadodo. The story revolved around boxing, a secret relationship between a Syriac woman and a Swedish man, and her ensuing identity crisis: "I don't know which Nina is appropriate. I am only Nina. But it's not enough. I can't just be Nina. There's no place for her. I have always been Nina in the company of someone else." The ticket sales agent Ticnet described the show as follows:

> Nina is twenty-seven years old and works in a bridal shop. Every day, she dresses couples about to wed, even as she does not dare to choose Mr. Right for herself, since he is Swedish. In the evenings, she relieves tension in the gym. *iamjustagirl* is a monologue about a young *assyrisk* woman's ponderings about how she should live her life.

Can one be an independent woman and, at the same time, marry and have a family? Or does one have to choose one over the other? How free are we really, and what or who makes our choices in life?[5]

After the performance, Babilonia and I walked into Wayne's Coffee in central Södertälje, and Babilonia quickly whispered, "I'll tell you something in a minute if you remind me." She later revealed that, as we walked into Wayne's, she had made eye contact with several women around her age who had also been at the play. They had communicated solidarity with their eyes, since they have all had similarly secret relationships. Publicly, they appeared to be perennially single, "because we don't have a ring," but in certain circles, it was common knowledge that all of these women "have had stories with men they weren't supposed to be with." Tales of inappropriate love occurred many times in my conversations with Syriac women.

Endogamous marriage is the only kind that is explicitly condoned in Syriac Södertälje, but these rules affect men and women differently.[6] Many women told me that Syriac men frequently dated Swedish women semi-openly, sometime for years, only to marry a Syriac woman. One popular trope describes a Syriac man who begins a serious relationship with a Swedish woman, promising commitment. He confines their meetings to Stockholm, never bringing her to Södertälje or introducing her to his parents, although she may meet friends and younger family members. Later, the man initiates an official courtship with a Syriac woman in Södertälje, telling his first girlfriend nothing. One day, the Swedish woman happens to call her boyfriend. Upon hearing music and shouting in the background, she asks, "Are you at a party?" He hesitates, finally answering, "Yes, I'm at my wedding." This call ends the man's illicit relationship, which may not have been especially secret, thrusting him into a new, condoned, public role in this Syriac city: as a husband and, eventually, a father.

While Nina's monologue from *iamjustagirl* outlines a continuing conservatism, an intended Swedish spouse scandalizes some families much less today than it would have in the 1990s. When I met thirty-year-old Izla at a soccer match on one occasion, she mentioned a "new boyfriend," whom she had met on Midsummer Eve. Knowing her family to be very nationalist, I asked if he was an *assyrier,* and she said, "No, he's Swedish." Concerned, she looked at me and said, carefully and slowly, "It's okay that he's Swedish," underscoring her family's approval. While stories of extra-ethnic matrimony—or exogamy with permission—are plentiful, public opinion in this most private of matters remains powerful. A Syriac marriage partner, Annika Rabo argues, helps members of the group retain their "ethnic and religious uniqueness" even as they participate in Swedish everyday life in other respects.[7] Syriacs marrying Syriacs are thus integrated rather than assimilated in Sweden.

Babilonia constantly moved between worlds, from Södertälje to Stockholm and back again. At her job as a teacher, she had one identity; at home with her family, she had another; with her boyfriend, a third. In Södertälje she followed her family's rules, but she expressed her independence from them elsewhere. Many of her Syriac friends and relatives liked visiting but did not want to live in Södertälje, she explained, where "the community is watching you" and "you have to behave better than you otherwise would."

Panoptic forms of Syriac social control—particularly over the dating lives of young women—have been pervasive in Södertälje since the 1990s, though the rules have recently loosened somewhat. Even young women seen having coffee with male cousins were once accused of breaking the rules of chastity, making Syriac-dominated cafés public places. Other cafés became locales for, as Ishtar told me, "secret lovers or teenagers who smoke cigarettes." The clientele of what she called these "mostly Swedish spaces" would not damage anyone's reputation by circulating information about their behavior.

In the 1990s, rumors circulated that covert spies representing St. Afrem's Syriac Orthodox Church were on local patrol, reporting back about the men with whom the young women were seen and at what times of the day they were in town. Another rumor charged that one parish priest had forbidden the public consumption of a certain unforgivably phallic Swedish popsicle, admonishing in a sermon, "It's unsightly when girls eat Calippo ice cream." These rumors reinforced a sense that there were "eyes on the street" with an ominous mission.[8] A young woman seen drinking alcohol, in the wrong company, or at a nightclub, ran the risk of being branded as sexually promiscuous and shaming her entire family.

Even in the less stringent context of twenty-first-century Södertälje, these public views of private relationships greatly affected one couple, Ninos and Layla, before their preengagement. Dating privately for four months, they met at his apartment, talked on the telephone, or played cards with his family. Ninos, who had spent most of his teenage years in southern Sweden and did not know the codes of Södertälje intimately, found sneaking around to be difficult and tedious. The couple's betrothal had merely been a way for him to date his girlfriend openly. As he told me, "We're not engaged. There were no rings exchanged or anything. There is no difference for me." On the other hand, he acknowledged that it made Layla "much more relaxed."

To remain a virgin until one's wedding day is without question the most important performance of chastity for a woman, but behaving correctly in public space—on the street, in cafés, at parties, in school—also has direct significance for her eventual marriage. Sonya Aho writes, "Girls cannot go out with whomever they want and to whatever extent they want. They always have to think about their reputation and their family's standing among the *assyrisk/syrianska* group."[9] Even a woman who breaks an engagement may be considered damaged goods. Marriage to the wrong woman can cast a negative light on a man's family, while a woman's family often worries about the groom's financial or social status, particularly since many Syriac women are housewives.

As I watched some women lighting cigarettes for their boyfriends (said to be gangsters) at a party at the Assyrian Cultural Center, my companion Nahrin, a housewife in her thirties, laughed and said, "They fly!" Women who change suitors often are known as "flying women." A widely used Swedish description of the practices of some minority groups—usually Muslim—is "honor culture," referring to the violence to which women are subjected if they break social codes.[10] Thirty-three-year-old Linda, a Syriac civil servant, has tackled "Syriac honor culture" in her work and discussed it on Suryoyo-language television, after having herself left a mentally disturbed husband. While physical abuse occurs, Linda argued that the most common form of punishment for a Syriac woman is negative gossip designed to ostracize her. Rumors can cause social death, leaving a young woman too tainted for marriage.

Most such attention is paid to the behavior of teenagers and younger women, however. Babilonia, in her early thirties at the time, announced once, "I am not nearly as interesting as a twenty-year-old would be." She also mentioned her surprise at the conservatism of many younger members of the Syriac community. She saw it as a paradox when younger people argued against premarital cohabitation, while some of the older generation said, "They should really try that out. It would be good for them. What's the problem?" She said attitudes had become more relaxed over time about Syriacs marrying non-Syriacs, although marrying a Muslim was still out of the question. She gave me a knowing look. These performances of female chastity and male financial security through actions in the city lead, eventually, to the right (or wrong) match. Eventually, this culminates in an even more complex (and expensive) public spatial practice: the wedding itself.

My Big Fat Syriac Wedding

To the chagrin of many Syriacs, a new reality television program on the commercial Swedish television channel TV3 appeared during the fall of 2011: *Mitt stora feta syrianska bröllop* (My big fat *syrianska* wedding). Playing on stereotypes about immigrants while also presenting previously undisclosed Syriac wedding traditions for the titillation of Swedish audiences, the series followed several couples on the road to matrimony. One pair required Burberry-patterned wedding invitations and rented a fleet of expensive cars for the entire bridal family.[11] Depicting extravagant receptions for hundreds of guests and multiple Syriac bridezillas, the series featured decked-out banquet halls as the key infrastructure for this community tradition, capitalizing on the stark contrast between these weddings and the typically smaller, more sedate Swedish nuptials.

Compared to the stories I heard about earlier times, these portrayals accentuated the changes in the spaces and services used for Södertälje's Syriac weddings since the 1970s. One Syriac woman in her midfifties, Gülli, came from Midyat to Södertälje by way of Stuttgart and today lives in Ronna in a high-rise apartment building. She described the preparations for her husband's brother's wedding in the late 1970s, which was held in Mission Church, the borrowed church "behind the police station." She said, "I made the food myself. There weren't so many Syriacs in Södertälje then, maybe one hundred in total, so we had to make all the food ourselves. Even the stuffed grape leaves." These time-consuming preparations took a toll on family members, who became the "infrastructure" not provided elsewhere in the majority Swedish society.[12] This responsibility grew increasingly onerous as the Syriac group expanded and events increased in size and scope.

The Assyrian Association in Ronna Centrum also hosted weddings, baptisms, and parties that, at the time, were considered enormous. One Swedish man recalled:

> I remember a guy who belonged to this major family group. They had a huge party in the space. It was full. There were tons of people. If I say there were one hundred, it would not be an exaggeration. It was maybe two hundred when Jakob got married. It would be regarded as a shitty party today. At that time it was huge, and that was *the* major family.

Expectations for the number of wedding invitations extended to family members expanded both as the diaspora gained a foothold in Södertälje and as the Syriacs' economic conditions improved. But for this Swede, the early Ronna Centrum parties already represented a magnitude that dwarfed those of the majority society.

In contemporary Sweden, many couples choose to live in a long-term state of engagement known as *sammanboende,* or *sambo,* without marrying. From a long-term perspective, wedding celebrations of the agricultural Swedish past, when men and women ran homesteads together and produced children out of necessity, shifted radically as the country urbanized.[13] Priest and historian Lars Bondeson states that almost 50 percent of children born in Stockholm in the mid-nineteenth century were born out of wedlock; only 25 percent of women were married.[14] As welfare-state ideologies took root, this trend continued. Marriage was increasingly unnecessary in an industrialized society. Low-key weddings with minuscule receptions were regarded as a tasteful, modernist version of the countryside celebrations, reinforcing social preference for a lack of ostentation.[15] In contrast, Syriac weddings, where the guest lists are often ten times that of their Swedish counterparts, are social and spatial performances, and cohabitation before marriage is exceptional. Syriac families must, in fact, officially condone a relationship before it can be carried out openly on the city's streets.

At a Christmas party in the Assyrian Cultural Center, friends, relatives, and some strangers watched in amusement as nineteen-year-old Alexandra danced next to her boyfriend of two years, pretending to be oblivious as he danced with friends. Their relationship was widely known, but they had not started the sanctioned process of betrothal in private. Ishtar told me that these rites were imminent, saying, "They'll be coming to her house soon." In the high-pressure theater of Södertälje courtship, protocol demanded that they act like strangers—strangers who just happened to dance next to each other all night.

Betrothal has developed into an expensive and serious business, occurring over at least two meetings between the families. The first, which takes place at the young woman's parental home, is often described as "coming for coffee." For Ninos and Layla, the meeting began at 9:00 p.m. and lasted until 11:30 p.m. The Issas, Ninos's family, brought a large bouquet of flowers, while the Hannas, Layla's parents, prepared a nighttime snack with fruit and pastries. Layla made the coffee but refused to follow the protocol completely, ignoring the dictate requiring her to put salt in Ninos's cup (if he drinks it anyway, it means he really likes her). She felt this was unnecessary.

At a second meeting a few days later, the man's family confirms its approval of the relationship, offering the bride-to-be a necklace with a diamond-encrusted cross on it. Ninos's family knew something of these rituals but, since they had not lived in Södertälje for long, thought the two meetings were one. Layla found this ignorance humorous, being herself completely fluent in the rites of courtship as a longtime resident of the town. The necklace was an important symbol to wear on Södertälje's streets, indicating that other men could no longer consider her. While Ninos may not have considered the shift very significant, for other Syriacs it meant he and Layla were now officially together for life.

While Layla guided the Issas through the betrothal successfully, a rift emerged at Christmastime, nearly dissolving the engagement. The Issas visited the Hannas to offer their holiday greetings, taking a necklace worth five thousand Swedish kronor for Layla and sweets wrapped in cellophane and ribbons. Shortly afterward, however, Ninos's sister Nisha mentioned a "crisis in the family" that was causing their mother, already frequently in ill health, great emotional stress. Uncharacteristically, she refused to divulge any details. A few days later, she explained that Layla's mother was offended that the Issas had not brought presents decadent enough to fulfill their obligations. For instance, she felt that they had failed to present an adequate number of the customary lavish trays of candy and cookies expected at the event. She had suggested that her daughter break off the relationship. Ninos tried to reach Layla by telephone, but she would not take his calls.

Additional gifts were offered, and Layla and her family returned to their previously welcoming behavior. The engagement was on. Though these exchanges took place in private, public propriety required that this holiday ritual be performed in the correct way. Through their son's engagement to a local woman whose family was well versed in such traditions, the Issas, who were relative newcomers to the town, learned a painful lesson as they were evaluated according to Södertälje's stringent Syriac social standards and spatial practices.

"The Customer at the Center"

> Cleopatra Banquet Hall is for you who value high quality, exclusivity, and unique
> solutions for your special event. We work under the mottos "The customer at the
> center" and "Nothing is impossible." Our employees' creativity has no bounds.
> In every respect, we will take care of your wishes and dreams and convert them
> to reality.
>
> —Cleopatra Banquet Hall Facebook page, http://www.facebook.com/Cleopatrafest/

Syriac weddings today represent not merely religious affirmations of individual couples but major public events, and the wedding industry that has developed in Södertälje since the 1970s makes the parties as lavish and entertaining as possible: a theater
of love using columns, curtains, flowers, and lights. With PowerPoint presentations
and animation, professional wedding consultants demonstrate a wide range of possible visions and a portfolio of the previous events they have styled. They know they
must compete with one another for clients who are typically both savvy and fashion
conscious. One suggests Doric columns around the table of honor (where the bride,
groom, best man, and maid of honor will sit on a platform during the dinner) and
mirrored place mats to reflect colored lights. Another recommends a smoke machine
to envelope the bridal couple in a spectacular mist and centerpieces of flowers and
jewels sitting in faux-crystal vases. When hosting hundreds of guests—from across
town and around the world—each couple must find the right balance between
originality, luxury, tradition, and price.

Södertälje's lucrative banquet halls differ in size and profile while offering similar
services in a new Syriac infrastructure, with standardized lists of options from the
"welcome drink" to the flowers on the tables. Evocative names such as "Panorama,"
"Mona Lisa," and "Cleopatra" suggest the fantasy worlds partygoers enter as they
cross the threshold and take a champagne flute from an ornately balanced tower.
The Assyrian Association, the Syrianska Federation and every church also offer dedicated spaces for members and affiliates. St. Gabriel's in Ronna Centrum offers a basic
space underground, along with a diminutive one aboveground for smaller events,
while the massive banquet halls at St. Afrem's and St. Jacob's can accommodate hundreds of guests. This infrastructure has a regional reputation, and many of the spaces
are also used for the large weddings of other ethnic groups, such as Kurds.

Wedding planners and suppliers have also sprung up in Södertälje to capitalize
on this ever-expanding business. In the shadow of St. Afrem's in Geneta, for instance,
clients enter a party supply shop through a collection of Doric columns, "stone"
bridges, and ziggurats (all in Styrofoam) and are led past the rows of plastic baby
decorations for baptism parties (Figure 4.1). The event designers here show examples
of how they have transformed generic banquet halls (from Södertälje to Norrköping
to Damascus) into an ancient Greek agora or the Assyrian imperial city of Nineveh
(Figure 4.2). Lightweight materials make transport, construction, and disassembly

FIGURE 4.1. Stage sets at a wedding and christening boutique in Geneta, 2009. Photograph by author.

FIGURE 4.2. The table of honor at a Syriac wedding, 2009. Photograph by author.

extremely easy. Flower arrangements are composed to complement a bride's own adornment with veils, tiaras, and pearl necklaces. As wedding designers create stage sets for an ongoing performance for Syriacs locally and across the diaspora, this practice is reflected in parallel preparations of the body.

In Ronna Centrum on a typical Saturday, several women sit in a salon to have their hair styled in intricate braids and buns, while music from Syria streams from speakers connected to a TV showing videos. "I think he used a whole can of hair-spray on me," one woman complains to her friend when the stylist goes into the back room for additional supplies. Both spirits and expectations are high before a wedding. Relatives of the bride or groom enlist a professional hairstylist; the closer they are on the family tree, the more intricate a hairstyle they require. On Fridays and Saturdays, the most popular wedding days, the hairdressing salons in Södertälje are full.

Coiffures for guests follow a standardized, symbolic lexicon: an updo indicates an intimate connection to the couple, while friends or more distant relatives are blow-dried to wear their hair down. When her brother Sanharib's wedding approached, Ishtar told me that it would be inappropriate for her to have "homemade hair."[16] Sartorial choices about the evening gowns and semiformal dresses that the majority of women wear to Syriac weddings also follow a protocol. Short dresses signify a more distant relationship to the bridal couple than do the long dresses required for close friends and family members.

When I asked Babilonia for advice about what to wear to Sanharib's wedding, she counseled that length was only one issue. Also important was "the certain feel-ing" you get from each dress and its fabric, which must be silk, Thai silk, satin, or at least "something that shines," she said. For men, suits and ties are required. Bridal shops in Södertälje with names like Princessa and the Swan's House (Svanens Hus) are full of dresses in expensive materials like these, offered in a range of spectacular colors and patterns for both brides and guests.[17] Here, women giggle as they try on different looks and compare them to clothes worn at previous weddings, baptisms, engagements, and other parties. This reinforces a key Syriac spatial practice of dress-ing: a woman cannot wear the same dress to two major events. A bride may also host a number of makeup artists at her home for test drives.

Given that one's presence was generally required even at a distant relative's nup-tials, many Syriacs expressed their extreme boredom with the number of weddings they were obliged to attend. Summertime, the wedding season, only increased the intensity of this malaise. The solitary associated joy for many women was the oppor-tunity to buy a new dress. For some, however, especially those with atypical body types, this merely exacerbated their feelings of obligation and anxiety. These spatial practices forced them to adorn and feature their bodies in banquet halls, a New Swedish public place.

The Big Day

Drums pound in front of a high-rise apartment block in the Million Program neighborhood of Ronna, signifying the start of a Syriac wedding; a bride is being collected from her parental home. She emerges, surrounded by a group of female relatives who support her both with their arms and with their glances. The volume of the drumming increases, and the women ululate to its rhythm. They circulate slowly in front of the grey-green buildings, and all the neighbors can see and hear the proceedings from their windows. Finally, they arrive at a white limousine idling in a nearby parking lot, and the bride, unsmiling and walking stiffly, gets in.

At the church, the women are already dressed in a colorful array of formal gowns and smartly tailored suits. They stand in small groups, joking and talking with one another while waiting for the bride. This is the first moment for each woman's ensemble of hair, makeup, and dress to be seen publicly, so many women congratulate one another for their sartorial successes. These guests, usually the closest family members and friends of the couple, are only a small fraction of the hundreds coming to the reception. When the bride's car pulls up, these small groups become one large gathering extending outward from the foyer of the building. The bride emerges, the women ululate, and a blessing is shouted, with hands flapping repeatedly over the bride's shoulders and head.

The bride continues into the church, where she remains sequestered in the bridal room until the ceremony. As the guests seat themselves, some of the older women don lacy white veils on their heads—demonstrating their respect for God—and cross themselves. The ceremony begins, and the guests rise. The couple enters together and slowly approaches the altar, where witnesses (one man and one woman) are waiting with the priest and deacons. The bride and groom are blessed, say their vows, and are crowned separately as the priest sings prayers. Their official presentation provokes more ululations as they exit.

Decorative touches profess to distinguish each Syriac bridal couple, yet the uniformity of the proceedings makes each wedding nearly indistinguishable from the last. After the ceremony, guests go to the reception, while the couple travels around town in a car (usually a limousine), killing time. When the couple arrives at the reception, partygoers create an *allée* that guides them into the space, blessing them as they enter and air-tapping them with their hands. Such blessings continue throughout the night.

Syriac receptions begin with meze (small appetizers such as hummus, *muhammara,* and grape leaves) on the table. Dishes of nuts and empty containers for shells (obsessively emptied by wait staff) are placed on each table, along with a variety of sodas and several bottles of hard liquor, usually including raki. Some say that the number of meze (usually at least eight) is a marker of how luxurious the wedding will be. When planning her own wedding, thirty-two-year-old Ilona expressed concern that there were too few dishes for the size of the tables, provoking a discussion with her wedding planner. Working within the constraints of her budget, Ilona—on the advice of her friends—chose to adorn her reception tables with an assortment of name-brand sodas instead of offering the guests a welcome drink. Having the Swedish brand Spendrup's orange soda instead of Orange Fanta equates to owning a knockoff Chanel handbag; the conspicuous display of the original conveys a status that even an additional drink upon arrival could not outweigh.

At the reception, a rumor starts that the couple's limousine has been seen outside. A small group gathers in two rows from the front door to the door next to the room. After the bride and groom make their grand entrance and receive the crowd's blessing, accompanied by music and shouting, with the majority of guests on their feet, the celebratory mood shifts temporarily to a more sedate and sentimental moment, as the couple shares their first dance, followed by more dancing with relatives and friends.

The selection of the singer for a Syriac wedding exhibits both the couple's own personal tastes and their politics. Turkish music at a wedding reception, for example, may be interpreted as support for the Turkish government, potentially offending staunch Assyrian nationalists. When a woman whose parents grew up in Syria marries a man whose relatives are mostly in Turkey, such decisions can be very sensitive. Most wedding singers are able to perform in several languages, catering to the variety of traditions of a couple with roots in both Syria and Turkey or of a bride whose mother was raised with Kurdish as her first language. Music and folk dancing at weddings (and other Syriac parties) create "a common focus for attention, a center to gather around," and "an emotional state among the partygoers" that encourages "the creation of community and solidarity," as Syriac sociologist Fuat Deniz argues.[18]

At one wedding, Södertälje folk singer and restaurateur Aboud Zazi sounds plaintive as he begins, carefully building an atmosphere as he draws out the musical anticipation for several minutes. Catharsis occurs when the musicians behind him suddenly join in. The excitement in the room is palpable, and a few young women pull each other to the dance floor. This song is one to which both *assyrier* and *syrianer* will dance.[19] Quickly, the floor fills with guests who form a great circle for folk dancing, with everyone holding hands with those adjacent to them and following the same steps in the same rhythm. The longer the song continues, the larger the ring of dancers becomes.

During the reception, after we had been eating the meze for a while, Hilma, in her late twenties, turned to me and said, "You know, everyone's already full. We don't need any more food, but they're going to serve a *varmrätt* ["main course"; she said this in Swedish while otherwise speaking English] soon. When they serve it, no one will be able to eat it all, but if they didn't serve it, everyone would say, 'Oh, they're so cheap! They didn't even have a *varmrätt*.' So they have to serve it." Just as Hilma finished speaking, waiters and waitresses appeared with plates piled with grilled meats and vegetables, fried potatoes, and side dishes. She groaned. The bountiful abundance exhibited on the table—food in dishes that barely fit within the confines of its surface, name-brand sodas, and bottles of liquor that may not even be opened—serves less to satiate the appetites of the guests than to convey an atmosphere of unlimited wealth, an opulence that instantiates the socioeconomic status of the families.

After the dinner, music accompanies the bride and groom to the center of the dance floor, where they cut a cake, which may be exploding with sparklers. A sword in a sheath appears, and a small number of family members hold it while dancing individually for the bride and groom. The bride then dances with it for a short time, it is unsheathed, and the bride and groom hold it together to cut into the cake's top tier. After serving cake to each another, they then drink a toast, and waitstaff cut and serve cake to the guests. Dancing, drinking (primarily for men), and circulation by the bride and groom continue into the night.

"Yes, I Do!"

Most Syriac banquet halls (religious or secular) are located in urban areas originally zoned for commerce or industry. Daniel is a Syriac civil servant in his midforties who grew up in Södertälje. He noted, "There is not much in the common living room that we have changed, I mean in the center of Södertälje. Instead, we have built a lot in the private sphere, a house, or we've built some colossal building for an association. And then it is always out in the margins. It's never central. It is 'off' [said in English] in an industrial zone. It's in Geneta. It's in Ronna." Here, on the edges of the city, no neighbors complain about noise continuing until three in the morning or about the hundreds of cars descending on an area at once.

At these sites, sumptuous celebrations that work against the Swedish welfare state's prescriptions of sober propriety are effectively invisible to the outside community. For instance, Panorama Banquet Hall, with room for up to 550 seated guests, sits atop the automobile parts store Mekonomen in the industrial zone Viksängen. The Mona Lisa Banquet Hall (Mona Lisa Festvåning) hovers over a furniture store in the middle of a commercial strip in Geneta and can seat up to 600 people. Cleopatra, which opened in 2009, is located in the industrial district of Moraberg and holds up to 800 guests (Map 5). Advertising their services with interior shots and close-ups of food and decor, they never depict the exteriors, which are irrelevant—or even damaging—to a narrative of fairytales and happily ever after. These forgotten Swedish peripheries become, through temporary and transformative spatial practices and the creation of a new ritual infrastructure, new social centers for Syriacs during events through urban design from below.

When Sanharib and Belinda got engaged, most people expressed initial surprise before saying that it seemed strangely ideal: she was a close friend of his sister, so the

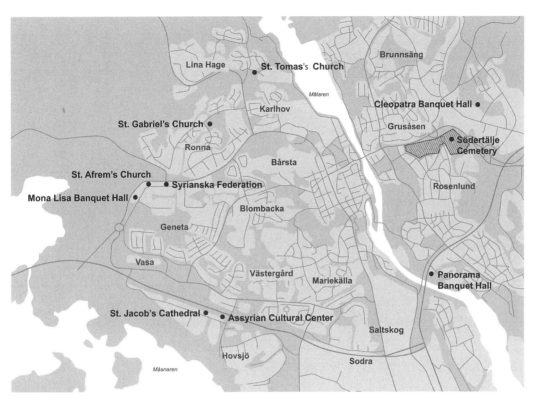

MAP 5. Map of banquet halls, social clubs, and cemetery. Graphic design by Eliza Hearsum.

couple had known each other for years. Yet difficulties emerged when they discussed their respective affiliations to the *assyriska* and *syrianska* groups in the context of the wedding arrangements. Belinda hails from one of the most important Syriac lineages in Södertälje, a family with a long-standing tradition of affiliation with St. Afrem's. Sanharib's family, on the other hand, is staunchly Assyrian nationalist, and Sanharib was a central figure in the Assyriska FF soccer fan club. Given this context, the families determined that the reception would have to take place on "neutral premises." As Sanharib's sister Ishtar told me, "There's no way that Sanharib would get married at Syrianska." With this, she meant the St. Afrem's Church banquet hall near the church. Sanharib's Assyrian nationalism would have been affronted by the ever-present red-and-yellow Syrianska flags there.

Eventually, the couple decided on St. Jacob's Cathedral and its new banquet hall, which opened just months before their wedding. Ostensibly nonaligned, its profile was radically different from that of the adjacent Assyrian Cultural Center, where the Ishtar Gate and Assyriska FF flags were prominently displayed at all times until its renovation and reopening in June 2013 changed this. Today the center features a sign with the English-language words "Yes I Do!" below two intertwined hearts, with an Assyrian flag in neutral white on the side[20] (Figures 4.3 and 4.4). Belinda

FIGURE 4.3. Ishtar Gate stage during a party at the Assyrian Cultural Center, 2009 (before arson and renovation). Photograph by author.

FIGURE 4.4. "Yes I Do!" signage at the Assyrian Cultural Center after renovation, 2015. Photograph by author.

found St. Jacob's especially appealing because she would be among the first brides to use it. With its trendy profile, the space was acceptable to both of them.

In reality, St. Jacob's Cathedral had emerged out of the name conflict, and its banquet hall has an unequivocally Assyrian influence in its ornamentation. Reliefs of Assyrian warriors going into battle adorn the walls and include many motifs that are typically displayed in the living rooms of *assyrier* (Figure 4.5). Belinda and her family were able to overlook the nationalism embedded in these walls to accommodate both her husband-to-be and her desire to use this "fresh" space.

Some observers and members of St. Jacob's parish complained about the quality of the banquet hall's decorations, however, and especially about its small red ceiling lights. Nahrin, who has a special interest in interior design and has obsessively renovated her home, remarked, "It is an Assyrian place," pointing out the contrast to the Christian motifs in the adjoined church. Immediately critical, she said that the quality of the decorations made it look "like a Chinese restaurant." Once, shortly after the space opened, Nahrin and a group of her sisters and cousins discussed the materials. Every one of the nine women took turns knocking on the relief to hear its hollow sound—a test of its poor quality—as they left.

FIGURE 4.5. Interior, St. Jacob's banquet hall during a wedding, 2009. Photograph by author.

The Gift

At Syriac wedding receptions, a jewel-adorned box with a small slit in the center sits on the table of honor throughout the festivities. As guests depart (usually late at night), they offer their congratulations, kissing the bride and the groom on their cheeks. Passing the gift box, they drop into the box an envelope containing a cash present in Swedish kronor and a wedding card. The envelope displays the names of the couple and the guests' own names, "so that it's easy to know who gave what," as Hilma told me. When all the guests have gone, the bride and groom go to their new home together.

When I asked for her advice, Babilonia told me that five hundred kronor would be appropriate for my gift to Sanharib and Belinda, but larger amounts should be given for closer relationships. If one of my closest friends, such as Ishtar, were getting married, she said, I should give one thousand. The circulation of money at the time of a wedding is understood as a system of exchange and is the financial support that allows for the inclusion of hundreds of guests.[21]

Echoing the entanglements and reciprocities that anthropologist Marcel Mauss describes in his classic 1923 theory of gift exchange,[22] a professional wedding planner for one of the Syriac nationalist associations described to me the Syriac tradition of money giving:

> They have a box there for the envelopes with the present money in them. It's up to the person to decide how much they will give. You can give one hundred, one thousand, ten thousand. If it were my sister, I might help her, give her ten thousand. My brother, ten thousand. My cousin, maybe five thousand. My friends two thousand. These are loans, long-term loans. You borrow money over a long period of time. Today, maybe I give you ten thousand. After maybe ten years, my daughter gets married, and you give that back to me by giving it to her. But the money always comes back. It's like a loan, just about. On a Friday or Saturday, you're free from work, and you could go to a discotheque, a restaurant, and sit and drink alcohol, and it will cost one thousand. No, I don't want to do that. I want to go to a wedding with friends, and then I sit and have dinner and drinks for free and give this loan. And it comes back to me. I help you; you help me. It's normal.

Monetary presents do not disappear into the financial black hole of a starry-eyed reception but are logically, carefully calculated. Partygoers are able to enjoy their evenings with exuberant abandon, aware that their gifts will come back to them when their own relatives marry. Meanwhile, the bridal couple and their families know that the sumptuous event, which they are nominally hosting so generously, will actually pay for itself.

On Saturday nights in June and July, all the banquet halls are fully booked as this ritual infrastructure reaches its capacity. In these spaces, many Syriacs are doing the same thing at the same time, just as they do during Assyriska and Syrianska football matches. Even if one can attend a wedding by rote (and bored), the repetition and simultaneity of the experience reinforce values, standards, and cohesion and serve as an opportunity to repay debts to the extended family and to reinforce new traditions in Södertälje's everyday urban social world.

At Last

During the Christmas season that marked her eighth year with Kaveh, Babilonia revealed their involvement to her family, one member at a time. A close friend whose relationship with a Swede had recently dissolved under the pressure of extended secrecy made Babilonia realize the precariousness of her romantic state of limbo. Rather than risking her love, she resolved to proceed. Assuming the worst possible reaction from Babilonia's family, the pair had planned a quick elopement, followed by a long honeymoon in India. As she informed her family, however, several of them encouraged her to plan a regular event on a slightly later date. Babilonia and some of her friends expressed suspicions that this was merely a stalling tactic to give the family time to change her mind, but she eventually agreed to postpone. Her mother and sister did then in fact try to convince her to end the engagement. The ceremony was off and on several times over the following weeks.

Amid great tension, the wedding finally took place about two months later than originally scheduled. Family and friends experienced confusion about how to follow tradition in these unusual circumstances. Women gathered during the week beforehand to discuss whether close friends and family should wear long dresses or shorter ones; many of Babilonia's female relatives ultimately wore knee-length dresses, and almost all the women attending the wedding wore their hair down. Kaveh's family, with their Iranian background, wore the semiformal dresses and suits more typical at Iranian and majority Swedish weddings.

Some women wanted to communicate their happiness for the bride through their own formal dress, while others were concerned about how the community would interpret their propriety if they wore long dresses and professional hairstyles. While most close friends did wear floor-length dresses, several family members capitulated to the dark cloud of disapproval cast by their elders. Even the bride's sister wore a short dress. The bride's youngest brother expressed his feelings more strongly: while normally impeccably styled and groomed, he arrived at the church in jeans and with several days of stubble on his face. His considerable, studied efforts to dress casually signaled his flagrant disrespect for the established dress code that would otherwise have characterized a sister's wedding. Clothing and hair conveyed that some guests attended begrudgingly while others were unsure about whether joy or anger was appropriate for the occasion.

Kaveh had recently converted to Christianity so that they could be married in Babilonia's parish, and the wedding itself followed the protocols and patterns of other Syriac Orthodox nuptials in Södertälje, apart from the small audience, the uncertain facial expressions of Babilonia's family, and the fact that the majority of the proceedings were conducted in Swedish rather than classical Syriac and Suryoyo. When one of Kaveh's guests crossed her legs—a practice considered an affront to God in the space of the Orthodox church—Father Johannes, who was overseeing the wedding, obliquely admonished her in his sermon. She did not notice.

Södertälje's well-developed wedding infrastructure was a particular boon to this star-crossed couple. Without knowing if, and then when, the wedding would take place, Babilonia and Kaveh's entire reception for 180 guests was eventually planned in the space of one week. When we met with some of her other friends to decide on the menu, Babilonia produced a printed list of options from Panorama's wedding planner, sparking a debate that lasted for several hours. In the end, the well-appointed reception included both a Syriac DJ and an Iranian live band, a full dinner including ten appetizers, an army of waiters and waitresses, and an elaborate cake adorned with garlands of fake pearls. Kaveh found the Syriac tradition of presenting bottles of liquor on the table tacky, but they included it nonetheless. Although Babilonia's mother maintained a frown throughout the evening and refused to dance, most of the family's guests behaved as they would at any other Syriac wedding reception. For their first dance, Babilonia and Kaveh used the American singer Etta James's song "At Last," bringing many attendees to tears.

Wedding City

On a Saturday in summer, a cacophony of overlapping rhythms fills the air in Ronna. As a bride on one side of the street steps over the concrete threshold of her parental home to go to the church for her wedding, another group has just begun their call for a different woman on the other side of the street. Happiness and nerves are typically involved whenever people marry, yet spatial practices such as these foreground the link between public spectacle and private expectations in this high-pressure Syriac city.

Dress shops, hair salons, banquet halls, flower designers, and caterers transform the town into the center of a major industry. With preparation before the big day occurring publicly, visibility infuses many aspects of each couple's event. So much of what appears to be merely a family matter includes political overtones and has broader public consequences for the Syriac community. Syriac family trees extend into ancient times, and every new alliance sets the stage for the epic stories of the future.[23] For many Syriac women, a bridal identity begins at an early age; the duty to attend relatives' weddings includes children. As relatives joke about what a beautiful bride a girl of four will eventually make, they also condition the girl to fantasize. She will be queen for a day, a connection exploited by the bridal shop Princessa and its motto, "You are what we are called."

Some Syriacs described Södertälje itself as a "wedding city." Södertälje nuptials, christenings, and parties (such as those held annually for Christmas, Easter, and the Assyrian New Year on April 1) provide a greater degree of showmanship than Syriac events in other towns. Södertälje's professional wedding planners offer the latest on-point trends in event design, and the town's banquet halls are substantially larger and more technologically advanced than those available in other Swedish cities. This wedding city also has social implications beyond these gatherings, with some recommending it as a place where Syriac singles could come to find a partner. I met one woman who had come from Syria before the war on a long-term stay with relatives in the town for exactly that reason. Södertälje thus represents the ultimate site for Syriac spatial practices associated with courtship, where each love story and an infrastructure created through urban design from below remake this peripheral Swedish town into a center where weddings are demonstrations of fashion consciousness and diasporic family reunions.

The Funeral, Take One

In the late spring of 2009, I attended the funeral of Dr. Tomas Hanno, who had died at the age of forty-two from cancer after being diagnosed only a few months earlier. He left behind his young wife, Shamiram, who was also a nurse in his office, and their five children. The events began at the Assyrian Cultural Center at 10:00 a.m. with a secular service focused on his contributions to Assyrian nationalism. Two sets of seats were arranged at a forty-five-degree angle to the Ishtar Gate stage, with an aisle in the middle. As in a church setting, women were mostly on the right, and men sat on the left. The schoolteacher Maria, in her fifties, sat on the right surrounded by female family members, where I joined her.

Prominently displayed in front of the stage was an easel with a photo clearly taken outside Sweden of "Dr. Tomas." The top left-hand corner of the frame was adorned with a black ribbon, symbolizing Tomas's death, and an arrangement of flowers in the shape of the Assyrian flag was placed under the framed portrait. Maria had told me the week before that she was not particularly close to Tomas, so I was surprised that she burst into tears several times. She said she was "emotionally saturated." Clearly, however, showing tears and crying openly was a sign of respect. Tomas was her sister-in-law's brother, and this performance of sorrow conveyed that she was a dutiful member of the family.

After some time, two wooden supports were brought and placed in front of the portrait. The Assyrian flag hung as usual at the back of the stage, with the words "Assyriska FF" on it to represent the soccer team. Maria had mentioned that Tomas was active in the Assyrian Democratic Organization (ADO), which is why they had this special ceremony before the church service. The mourners were mostly quiet until young men arrived, carrying the coffin, causing many people to start crying audibly, increasing in volume over time. Some mourners stood up and motioned to the coffin and then to their hearts as they cried.

A cameraman from Suroyo TV circulated, filming the crying mourners and even holding up the coffin's progress until he was asked to relocate his tripod. Maria's mother was particularly dramatic, standing up and yelling out in emotional anguish, and the cameraman immediately filmed her at close range. Women in the room started ululating, which Maria explained happened when anyone under fifty dies. An emcee then began the proceedings, followed by speeches first from family and then from friends, all men.

Later, the service moved to St. Jacob's Cathedral, where a receiving line to offer condolences formed shortly after a ceremony. Shamiram stared at the floor while also managing to acknowledge people and then completely break down in turn. Almost everyone in the line was crying uncontrollably, although some individuals, such as Tomas's mother, were completely stoic. As the lines formed, women gave condolences to the women, and men comforted the men. After noting that women usually outnumbered men at church services, Maria remarked proudly, "There are almost as many men here as women. Just as many men." The receiving line moved from back to front, and, sitting in the front row, we were among the last to join. Because of the line's duration, we never reached Shamiram.

The ceremony then moved across town to Södertälje Cemetery (Södertälje kyrko-gård), located in the neighborhood of Rosenlund (see Map 5). While Church of Sweden memorial services typically take place in a cemetery chapel, Syriacs have the funeral off-site at one of the Syriac Orthodox churches, in part to accommodate a much larger group of mourners. As we turned the corner to the side of the cemetery grounds, Maria was saying, "It's always so difficult to find parking spots near the cemetery. It was made for Swedes."[24] Having left the church quickly, however, we found ample parking spaces upon our arrival.

The group who came to the cemetery was much smaller than the immense crowd at the church. As we were walking into the grounds, we noticed some hesitation in the group around a car parked on the lane. Shamiram's aunt was ill, and everyone gathered around until an ambulance pulled into the crowd. (The aunt, around forty-five years old, eventually recovered.) Approximately fifty people started to walk toward the grave, and the coffin was lowered into the ground and raised again several times. Maria explained, "They raise and lower the coffin three times. The Father, the Son, and the Holy Spirit."

After this, family members threw roses into the grave. When one fastened on a tree, someone plucked it out and threw it into the hole in the ground. Not all the priests who had presided over the service at the church came to the cemetery. Those who were present departed shortly after the roses were thrown, as people shoveled small, ceremonial amounts of dirt or threw sand or dirt into the grave. Maria cast a pinch of dirt and suggested that I should do the same.

As we returned to the parking lot, I heard some commotion back at the grave site. My view was blocked, but the rumor quickly spread that Shamiram, who had been escorted away a few minutes earlier, had returned, screaming and crying. "The poor thing doesn't want to leave the grave," Maria explained approvingly. While Shamiram was clearly overwhelmed with grief, this dramatic display was considered virtuous behavior from the new widow.

The Funeral, Take Two

When I returned from Dr. Tomas's funeral, I opened the book I had been reading, Nuri Kino and Jenny Nordberg's 2008 fictional crime thriller *Välgörarna: Den motvillige journalisten* (The do-gooders: The reluctant reporter). I was soon shocked by the synchronicity of a scene that took place at the same cemetery in Södertälje that I had just left, during the same time of the year, and with the minimal snow on the ground that had just soaked my boots:

> The funeral train began to move forward slowly, and the mourners lowered their heads and fell silent. The family stepped through the wet snow and clumps of grass to the accompaniment of a regular background noise of blessings from the priests.
>
> When the procession had arrived at the grave, the wreaths were laid on each side, and the bishop and the priests placed themselves on the short end and began to sing psalms. The coffin was lowered slowly into the open, rectangular grave. Yamos and the siblings' cries pierced through Ninos, and he felt how his own tears began to fall. . . .
>
> When everyone had thrown their roses, tossed sand on the lowered coffin, and said "God be with you, go in peace," they walked on together in smaller groups to other graves.
>
> It was in fact important that the dead also felt that they had been able to participate in the funeral. For this reason, every relative's, friend's, or neighbor's grave received a visit and little chat. Everyone mingled and a lot of business other than the funeral was carried out at the cemetery, which became totally dominated by the lively company of funeral-goers.
>
> In his peripheral vision, Ninos saw an older Swedish couple who stood silently before a grave. They had just lit a candle in a lantern and stood completely still in front of the grave without uttering a word, crying, or talking to each other.[25]

One key difference separated my experience from the fictional funeral. In the book, attendees perambulated the cemetery, greeting their deceased family members and sharing the experience of the funeral with them. Rima, Ishtar's mother, explained this as a matter of size: "There are too many of us now. We don't have enough time." Perhaps Kino and Nordberg based their tale on the traditions of the past, when

Syriacs had just come to Sweden. Whatever their reasons, the novel's scene emphasized the importance of burial rituals, and showed how, like the wedding industry,
these have become more elaborate over time.

The Presence of the Dead

In Tur Abdin, reminders of the deceased were inscribed in the local landscape, where
relatives, contemporary and ancient, were always present in prominently positioned
cemeteries. In Bahdi Ecer's epic *I fikonträdets skugga* (In the shadow of the fig tree),
he describes one: "The cemetery was on a hill, a couple of kilometers from the village, and you could see the graves from every house in the village. It was important
that a person should not forget death."[26] In Syriac Södertälje, such microlevel spatial
connections between the living and the dead are not possible. Sharing the town with
other identity groups requires Syriacs to find new ways to express their sorrow and
to pay homage to the departed members of the community. Their graves can no
longer be seen from the town's center. Instead, they are isolated in a city of the dead:
Södertälje Cemetery.

Deaths in Sweden are often announced in the newspaper in a block format and
standard typeface, including the dates and places of birth and death, a list of surviving family members, and the time and location of the funeral. Symbols—such as
a boat for a passionate sailor or a stylized German shepherd for a woman who ran
a kennel—decorate the obituaries, along with a poem or other meaningful phrases.
These sober summaries publicize the passage of loved ones to the larger local community as easily as possible. The funeral agency places the ad using text that the
family has selected. A glance at *LT,* however, reveals virtually no Syriac obituaries.
These pages are instead the domain of the town's majority Swedes, Finns, and Latin
Americans.[27] This newspaper tradition may be unnecessary in a community for
whom all deaths are publicly announced by priests during Sunday services in Södertälje's Syriac Orthodox churches. In the case of significant deaths, announcements
are made in all of them.

In diaspora, however, even local pronouncements from priests are not always sufficient. The funerals of significant community members, like Dr. Tomas, are filmed
and broadcast on Suroyo TV or Suryoyo SAT so they can reach viewers all over the
world. (Assyria TV, which was established in late 2011, after the majority of my
fieldwork ended, mostly avoids such programming, though it occasionally broadcasts the funerals of persons heavily involved in the Assyrian nationalism movement.) When Babilonia's uncle died in the fall of 2008, she spoke proudly about
how Suroyo TV had "honored him" by broadcasting a short segment about his long
life, which began in a village in Tur Abdin and ended in Södertälje. Knowing that
viewers all over the world would learn about his devotion to Assyrian nationalism
somewhat assuaged her family's grief. Satellite television makes local, private events

in Södertälje (whether deaths, births, or weddings) public for global Syriacs. One man explained, "When there's a funeral, the mourners are not just living in Söder-tälje. People come from across Sweden and from outside Sweden." *LT*'s announcements may thus reach too small a community for the cosmopolitan Syriacs. News of the funerals and weddings of Mesopotälje must extend worldwide.

Elias is in his mid-fifties and arrived in the 1970s in Södertälje, where he now lives in a row house with his wife and teenage children. A Chaldean Catholic, he has nonetheless maintained intimate contact with the town's Syriac Orthodox community. A proud curator of the cultural heritage of both *assyrier* and *syrianer* through his work as an archivist, he carefully avoids declaring his allegiances as a proximate outsider. Through his work, he has assembled an extensive collection of Syriac writings and oral histories, allowing him to reflect on how traditions have metamorphosed over time in Södertälje. For example, he recalled:

> I remember that, when someone died in the 1970s or 1980s, we usually went to the dead person's home. The building's elevator [in Ronna] was always occupied: for a whole week, it was filled only with all of these people. Naturally, our native-born friends didn't understand. Okay, on a Sunday, maybe you can go by and visit, but one week, two weeks in a row? Totally inconceivable! So many of them protested and turned to Telgebostäder and others to try to stop it. We understood them also, naturally. Fifty men taking the elevator at one time or in the stairwell together, up and down, up and down. It was horrible for people who didn't have those traditions.

Likewise, the rites of Syriac Orthodox burials also differ radically from contemporary Swedish customs. Most Swedish cemeteries are publicly owned, operated, and managed, and a fee for their upkeep is included in Swedish income taxes. This sum, by law, gives anyone who dies with an official address in a particular municipality the right to a burial place.[28] Since the (Lutheran) Church of Sweden did not separate from the state until 2000, most majority Swedes also assume the church will oversee burials. Independent faith groups or foundations must request permission from the County Administrative Board to create a private burial ground, and they are the only groups allowed to do so.[29]

The new Swedish Burial Law of 2012 states that a person must be "cremated or buried as soon as possible and at the latest within one month of death" unless the Tax Authority gives special dispensation. The ashes of a person who has been cremated must be buried within one year. Notably, the right to a grave is time-delimited: the law requires the allotted time to be either fifteen to fifty years or forever, and it is twenty-five years if not specified. After the contract ends, the person legally responsible (usually a family member) has six months to renew or to remove any personal articles (including tombstones). Otherwise, the body of the original occupant remains, but a new person is buried on top.

During the early twentieth century, new Swedish cemeteries were located on the outskirts of towns rather than adjacent to churches, sometimes owing to a lack of space.[30] Cremations were promoted as hygienic and efficient, a tradition that was further streamlined in the form of the so-called *minneslund* (remembrance garden; literally, "memory grove"). The first *minneslund* appeared in 1959 in Malmö, and they are now a component of nearly all Swedish cemeteries. They usually comprise a small reflecting pool and garden for relatives and friends to sit and contemplate. Cremated remains are interred somewhere in this area, but the exact location is not revealed to the relatives. Echoing the welfare state's emphasis on the community over the individual, this anonymity makes each person part of a permanent collective rather than affixing him or her to a particular site. A *minneslund* burial also eliminates future costs.

Dying in Diaspora: Spatial Practices and the Remaking of Memorial Space

This communitarian view of death and burial practices in Sweden contrasts with Syriac Orthodox gravestones, which often display a small portrait photograph of the deceased. Many graves in Södertälje Cemetery include not only when but where the person was born and died, as well as their affiliation as *assyrier* or *syrianer* (Figure 4.6).[31] Anthropologist Engseng Ho writes about the significant of graves in diaspora:

> Graves, while they are endpoints for migrants, are beginnings for their descendants, marking the truth of their presence in a land. For many diasporas, then, graves are significant places. Abroad, migrants who could no longer be close to their parents can be visited by their own children. Graves provide a point of return in a world where origins keep moving on. A gravestone is a sign whose silent presence marks an absence.[32]

When a tombstone explains that a person was born in the town of Midyat in Tur Abdin and that he or she died in Södertälje, the text succinctly narrates a story of migration for the community, including those members who may merely be visitors from abroad. The grave describes the culmination of the migrant's journey, both an absence from the homeland and a presence in the territory of Sweden at the time of passing.

"Samtal" (Conversation), an episode of the television program *Kunskapskanalen*, broadcast on Swedish public television in 2004, focused on burial rituals.[33] Folklorist and author Bengt af Klintberg talked with the host about a clip showing a Syriac Orthodox funeral in 1993: a deceased bishop was dressed in a white robe and slippers, placed (according to tradition) upright in a chair, and taken into a church. Inside, he was carried through a crowd of mourners, who formed a line to touch the body and pray. As the clip ended, the host said, "Talk about a cultural clash, Bengt!" To which Bengt replied, "Yes, imagine a Swedish burial where the

FIGURE 4.6. Tombstone with Assyrian flag detail and inscription and photograph of the deceased, Södertälje Cemetery, 2009. Photograph by author.

dead person was carried around like that. It would be, like . . . it's very far from our way of commemorating it." In other words, modular, modern Swedish cemeteries anticipate continuous transformation with the arrival of additional bodies over time but conform to specific, restrained expectations about mourning. Since the eighteenth century, plantings, trees, and wall enclosures have mainly encouraged silent contemplation, marking a clear divide between the worldly and the spiritual.[34]

For Syriacs, however, other rules apply, and this extends to the period after the funeral as well, when sharing a meal is also a critical part of the ritual. After Dr. Tomas was interred, the mourners returned to St. Jacob's, where a dinner for three hundred people took place. As Elias described:

> It's those gigantic spaces where churches are parallel to banquet halls that have made it easier. Much easier! This means that the hosts for something like this can celebrate for two or three days and be able to treat the others to food and welcome their friends who are visiting. It's easier and more flexible! In spaces like those, all the problems are no longer problems. In the past it was terrible, I remember. I understood them [the Swedes], but they couldn't understand. I remember that a few people said, "But you can call!" "You can write!" "You can fax!" But that is not our tradition.

Given this requirement to mourn in real time and in real space and over a long period of time, large banquet halls, like the underground associations of the past, have removed the objectionable elements of Syriac ritual practices from majority Swedish view and created an adaptive ritual infrastructure. These flexible, partially blank spaces can be adorned in limitless ways for happy celebrations or melancholy memorial services of a scale, volume, and duration unseen in the surrounding majority Swedish context.

"Cemetery Picnics" on the Day of the Dead

Easter is known as the Big Holiday (*Edo rabo* in Suryoyo) and is the most important religious event of the year for the Syriac Orthodox Church, even surpassing Christmas in its liturgical significance and elaborate ritual expression. The crucifixion and resurrection narrative encapsulates the Syriac Orthodox view of Jesus Christ as simultaneously human and deity. Easter also marks the end of the forty-day Lenten fast. All church members are expected to attend church, and evidence of their visit is provided in the form of the "Happy Easter" stickers given to all who come.

Each church also distributes string bracelets, *siboro* in Suryoyo, for members to wear on their wrists from the Annunciation, celebrated on March 25, exactly nine months before Christmas Day, until Easter Sunday or Easter Monday. Many wear them much longer. Intertwined threads of red and white signify Jesus's humanity (his blood) and divinity, respectively. Mirroring the public display of the cross necklace that signifies a woman's betrothal, this portable symbol telegraphs one's Christian faith to the larger Syriac community. Given its discreet size and location, outsiders may not notice it or may perceive it as merely decorative, yet its absence is likely to be noted by fellow Syriacs, who expect this continuous bodily display. Each individual communicates participation in religious practice through a message that only some residents of Södertälje can read. After removal, bracelets may be returned to the church or burned (today on a stove-top burner rather than over an open fire), often under a pot of rice pudding.

During Holy Week (*Hasho foruqoyo* in Suryoyo, *stilla veckan* in Swedish), which begins with Palm Sunday, significant religious rituals occur almost every day. Maundy Thursday includes the washing of the apostles' feet, acted out with children as the apostles and the bishop as Jesus. On Good Friday (*Zuyoho oseghdto daslibo* in Suryoyo, *Långfredagen* in Swedish), a symbol of Jesus in the form of a cross is placed in a coffin and decorated with flowers for his figurative funeral. The coffin is hung from above, and attendees exit under it, taking a flower. Water, specially treated with bitter herbs to symbolize the water offered to Jesus during crucifixion, is available in small containers for attendees as they depart. After services on Easter Sunday, lunches take place at home, followed by requisite visits to the homes of the extended family.

While Sunday marks the peak of Holy Week, the festivities conclude a day later, on *Thnahto da mithe* (Easter Monday), known as the Day of the Dead[35] in Orthodox Christian communities around the world. Families gather in the space of the deceased—specifically, on top of their graves. Like the tradition of visiting relatives after funerals described in *Välgörarna,* this allows the dead to participate in the Easter holiday and represents the triumph of the spirit over the body. Local priests offer individual blessings while deacons swing censers of burning incense over the graves (Figure 4.7). This is a service—a spatial practice conducted by others—for which family members pay.

Though the blessing rituals may seem to shroud the ritual in the sober cloth of memorial, *Thnahto* is also a major celebratory festival for the Syriac Orthodox community. While the priest's prayer marks the fulfillment of a duty to the dead, the families who participate in this practice do so in large groups. Bringing blankets and other supplies, they set up picnics on their relatives' graves (Figure 4.8). They wait for their turn with the priest while drinking coffee, sharing chocolates and eggs, eating freshly baked bread and cheese, and playing games. One game involves two people each holding a hard-boiled egg and knocking them together; the one whose egg does not break keeps both. Families decorate the graves with lights or flowers before leaving.

FIGURE 4.7. Blessing over a grave on the Orthodox Day of the Dead, Södertälje Cemetery, 2009. Photograph by author.

FIGURE 4.8. Orthodox Day of the Dead picnic, Södertälje Cemetery, 2009. Photograph by author.

The Church of Sweden recognizes its All Saints' Day *(Alla helgons dag)* on the Saturday that falls between October 31 and November 6, and this holiday serves much the same function as *Thnahto.* This somber event involves the solemn lighting of candles and lanterns on the graves of the departed. As night falls (quite early at that time of year), the illuminated cemetery forms a tapestry of light that weaves together the markers of specific individuals into one collective memorial. Little interaction occurs among the mourners.

This contrast in mood may explain why other ethnic groups in Södertälje have reacted negatively when *Thnahto* has taken place in the Södertälje Cemetery. Letters to the editor of *LT* and in the online comments to that newspaper's articles have exhibited wrath over a perceived disrespect for the resting space of the dead. Complaints that the revelers litter and do not clean up after themselves are common, an impression that several Syriacs mentioned they had been trying to work against. Because the picnic tradition is more common in Turkey, some members of the Syriac community who came to Sweden from Syria shared these negative views, describing the event as "tasteless" or "ugly."

The changes to Södertälje Cemetery on *Thnahto* affect not just its appearance but also its ambience, moving in the opposite direction from the majority Swedish All

Saints' Day, even if both holidays involve a metamorphosis that extends beyond the ornamental. As a time-delimited, opportunistic tactic, in de Certeau's sense, *Thnahto* is a performance of respect—involving the dead in a holiday—in a form that confuses those who do not share this tradition. The dolorous home of the lost members of the majority Swedish community is transformed into a raucous, festive Syriac space where the living and the dead interact—a spatial practice that reuses an old site for new purposes.

A Separate Stage? Debating Segregated Cemeteries

Cemetery picnics and the large gatherings there have led some, both majority Swedes and Syriacs, to consider whether Syriac Orthodox Christians should be assigned a specific section of the cemetery or should have a dedicated one of their own. Contentious debates about this question began a little over a decade after the Syriacs started coming to Sweden. In April 1980, *LT* suggested Syriacs would eventually ask for a dedicated space for Orthodox burials. The article's author, Inger Ödebrink, wrote that the burials had not yet posed specific problems in Södertälje, mostly because the group was Christian and could partake in the existing Lutheran cemetery spaces. Ödebrink noted, however, that Muslims and Jews had already asked for their own graves in other places in Sweden and that immigrant burials had been a "problem" in Sweden since 1974.[36] In the article, the municipality's head of cemeteries, Åke Bergström, described the demands of other Syriac groups in Sweden:

> I know that the *assyriska* immigrants in Västerås have demanded their own burial grounds. This is mostly because of the different ceremonies that they have at the cemetery during different holidays, such as Easter, Christmas, etc. But in Södertälje they have not yet gotten to the point of making such demands. The *assyrier* in Södertälje are of course so enormously many more than those in Västerås. For this reason, we in the Cemetery Association are already trying to locate a plot of land to be used exclusively for *assyriska* burials.[37]

This debate led nowhere, however, and the majority of Syriacs, like Dr. Tomas, continue to be buried in Södertälje Cemetery, the town's main cemetery, where mainly Lutheran burials were originally expected.

The debate about segregated cemeteries was reopened in 2009. A March 2009 *LT* article described how an unusually large number of people had died, up to thirty of whom were Syriac Orthodox Christians, while grave diggers had been on vacation during the Swedish Christmas holidays.[38] The Syriac Orthodox liturgy requires burial within three days of a person's death, a speed of interment that the Swedish cemeteries are often unable to accommodate (typically only five graves are dug per week in Södertälje). The Cemetery Board had just approved plans to construct a special Syriac section in another cemetery in Tveta, on the outskirts of Södertälje, to include three hundred graves and one hundred parking places. When the proposal became public, however, representatives from St. Jacob's and St. Afrem's weighed in, a sign that "both archbishops raise[d] an eyebrow."[39]

St. Afrem's archbishop, Benyamin Atas, expressed dismay about the lack of communication from the municipality before the Cemetery Board's decision, stating that he had first learned of the proposal from the article published in *LT*.[40] While signaling his openness to the Cemetery Board's plan, he noted that his own parish had requested permission to bury its dead in a separate space in 1998, a request the municipality had denied. In his view, the Cemetery Board's move would allow the large-scale Syriac Orthodox religious celebrations that had sometimes offended majority Swedes to proceed without incident.

Father Gabriel Barqasho, a priest for St. Jacob's, also expressed surprise at the municipality's silence in the article. Using the language of integration as support, he said, "This is absolutely unnecessary. It will only become yet another exhibit for racism, and it creates segregation, one hundred percent. It will reinforce motivations for vandalism."[41] He acknowledged, however, "The only positive thing is that we would be able to have our 'cemetery picnics' without disturbing others. But we are all Christians. Let us be so in life and in death."[42] The two religious leaders thus offered opposing views not only of the proposal but toward the costs and benefits of creating a Syriac enclave for the dead.

Ultimately, the Cemetery Board voted against the proposal in May 2009, citing the majority opinion of *assyrier* and *syrianer*. In response, Atas agreed:

> This is even better. We don't want to separate ourselves from the other Christians. We would not have said no if we had gotten our own section, but we are not thinking of making trouble because it didn't turn out like that. We must accept the decision and be grateful that the question has been discussed. . . . But it is strange: we are offered this and then don't receive it.[43]

Even so, most Syriac Orthodox graves in Södertälje Cemetery lie in the same section, without the benefit of an explicit declaration or design. As these graves number in the hundreds, a move from Södertälje Cemetery would also require the bifurcation of the group into separate burial spaces. While the Syriac Orthodox and Swedish burial and mourning traditions differ from one another, the cemetery (like the banquet halls) has proven to be a flexible space.

Mourning in Public Space: Funerals for the Global Nation

Singing the Swedish national anthem, "Du gamla, Du fria" (Thou ancient, thou free),[44] requires declaring one's desire to die in that country's territory, with the following sentence repeated twice: "Yes, I want to live, I want to die in the North." Many Syriacs (both young and old) told me that as citizens they sang the anthem gladly but remained silent as others declared their desire to die in the North. Singing the final lines would betray their hybridity and privilege Swedish national space—and an imagined burial in Södertälje Cemetery—over one in the ancestral towns and villages of Tur Abdin.[45]

Ho writes, "Burial is the act of combining a place, a person, a text, and a name at the gravestone,"[46] making the territory in which a body is buried the site of memorial that descendants may visit and revere, but it also serves as a resounding spatial conclusion to that individual's itinerant personal history. He continues, "The nation itself takes its name from the act of giving birth, *nasci*. For migrants, by contrast, place of death is important because it often becomes the site of burial. Tombstones abroad acknowledge the shift in allegiance—from origins to destinations—that migrants take whole lifetimes or more to come to terms with."[47] At the same time, the Swedish practice of limited-time grave leases has the potential to undo this final marriage of a person to a piece of land. This spatial practice threatens the Syriac community's traditional inclusion of the dead in the high and low points of everyday life.

To publicly demonstrate their grief, Syriac Orthodox families are encouraged to wail loudly during funerals, and the high-profile deaths of younger Syriacs require even more dramatic displays of bereavement, where family members sometimes dress as though the funeral were the child's wedding. This happened when a mentally ill middle-aged man stabbed and killed Norba Haddad, a fifteen-year-old Syriac girl, outside her friend's apartment as she was leaving to return home. Her death also resulted in a large demonstration in downtown Södertälje.[48]

The specter of mortality casts a long, dark shadow over cemeteries and intends to limit their use to visits of solitary contemplation or intensive collective mourning at a funeral. Western European cemeteries are rarely considered gathering spaces. Some majority Swedes therefore regard the transformation of Södertälje Cemetery into a social space as inappropriate at best and blasphemous at worst. Syriac funerals and remembrances of the dead are performances of spatial propriety that, like weddings, require showmanship, heavy expenditures, and a traveling series of temporary and permanent Syriac spatial practices. Through rituals of both bereavement and celebration, Syriacs have remade the meaning of these spaces, if temporarily, and transformed Södertälje at large in the process.

Conclusion: The Curtain Is Always Up

To live in Syriac Södertälje is to live in the public eye. For many people, this is a double-edged sword: while it is comforting to reside in the largest community of Syriacs in Sweden, the constant performance of appropriate behavior—the *right* spatial practices—can be suffocating. In her study of Syriac families, anthropologist

Annika Rabo writes about one woman, "The only negative thing she could say about Södertälje is that people maybe impose themselves into each other's lives quite a bit."[49] In this town, private lives are public property, making gathering spaces into a theater where the audience is always watching and always waiting for an error, even as performers and spectators constantly shift roles. In Södertälje, the curtain on this stage is always up.

Many Syriacs spoke of how they had based themselves in other Swedish cities to avoid the unrelenting social pressures of Södertälje's public streets, cafés, banquet halls, soccer matches, churches, and cemeteries. But even from far-flung locales such as Jönköping or Gothenburg, frequent visits to the Syriac capital were a near necessity. Ninorta, a Syriac woman in her early forties, guiltily confessed that she had lived in another town, Norrköping, for seven years after her wedding, specifically to avoid the scrutiny of other Syriacs. She nostalgically described her tremendous psychological relief after many years of exquisitely careful behavior as an unmarried young woman. "But eventually," she said with an exhausted sigh, "I had to return to Södertälje." Ninorta's independence had complicated her attendance at family gatherings and participation in holidays. As her children grew, the logistical challenges crossed a cost-benefit threshold, and she and her family returned to Södertälje. Presence in the town's territory requires each individual to enter—on a daily basis—a complicated intersection of obligation and choice over Syriac spatial practices of chastity, religious observance, happiness, mourning, commitment, fidelity, taste, fashion, and beyond.

Reyner Banham describes "Autopia" as the mobile social world of the Los Angeles freeway in his 1971 *Los Angeles: The Architecture of Four Ecologies,*[50] where exit ramps mark the beginning of domestic space. In similar terms, Babilonia narrated her commute from Stockholm to Södertälje on the highway as a space to see and be seen, where everyone knew who was and was not Syriac. "All the *assyriska* guys drive past fast," she said, explaining how they came up from behind and flashed their lights so she would get out of the way. The closer a vehicle drew to Södertälje, the less private its internal space became. The fleeting sight of a Syriac woman in a car on the E4 highway with a strange man would produce rumors, even if it happened outside the municipality's limits. As Babilonia's story of her fear of being discovered with Kaveh while waiting for the commuter rail suggests, the pressure to practice space correctly begins even on approach to the town.

As this space of performance extends into the crevices of train platforms and travels down highway exit ramps, the spatial practices of weddings and funerals link public perception to private relations in a new Syriac ritual infrastructure that seems to be infinitely expansive. Courtship requires the performance of a woman's chastity, even as it demands her betrothed to exhibit his ability to provide public symbols of wealth in the form of expensive, wearable gifts. Marriage compels each couple to participate in a prescribed ritual in a banquet hall, where the stage sets are as lavish as the event itself is constrained by tradition. Funerals demand the vocal expression of an unlimited grief, which must be acted out in the church, at the cemetery, and at the banquet afterward, and then one must visit this dead—but still present—family member on the Day of the Dead and, when possible, after the funerals of others.

The Syriac community navigates its ritual use of Södertälje's spaces through a form of cultural intimacy that involves loud and very visible ceremonial occupations of urban space, leaving different kinds of traces on the city itself. Södertälje Cemetery was designed for the reflective contemplation of mortality according to Lutheran principles. Syriac spatial practice in this same space vastly exceeds the volume of conversation and the number of visitors imagined, but it does not permanently change its appearance. While some stray chocolate wrappers may be left on the ground and someone may have forgotten to take his blanket home, this use of the space does not alter it physically. Likewise, Million Program public spaces—designed by Swedish welfare-state architects—are today used for a Syriac bride's ritual departure, yet they revert to neutrality when the limousine departs. Here, Syriac standards temporarily remake this Swedish town, reshaping the discourses and norms of the universal citizen of the welfare state for a particularist public.

More critically, perhaps, a new Syriac ritual infrastructure has begun to alter the city in more permanent ways. Syriac banquet halls are revered across the Greater Stockholm region as locations where very large gatherings—for Syriacs, Kurds, Turks, majority Swedes, and others—can take place. The spatial practices that this infrastructure permits remake the city from below in ways that municipal architects, landscape architects, and urban planners never previously imagined. Though the times and spaces of weddings, parties, christenings, and funerals render Södertälje a theater where interior design and clothing, comportment, and display are linked to Syriac social morality, the cumulative effect of these spatial practices radically and enduringly transforms urban spaces. New sounds, sights, and moral codes appear in this hybrid space: a Swedish-Syriac city.

CHAPTER FIVE

Greetings from Hollywood!

Enclaves and Participation "from the Ghetto to the Mansion"

The Nordic dream: a house with white trim and a potato garden. Or at least a garage of your own. We are in Lina Hage in Södertälje. This is a place where house dreams have been realized freely—if not without limits. Here, urban planning rules have not given anyone's fantasy a flat tire. But has Pandora's box been opened? A Småland idyll next to a piece of Mediterranean beach. Stone from far away, like the stones tourists bring home from Crete. Columns that recall the distant homeland's ancient history. I can imagine how the neighbors spend their August evenings. At one house, there's souvlaki on the grill; at another, fermented herring is the rule. This is a lot for the architectural guru to consider.

—PETTERI VÄÄNÄNEN, *Petteri på villovägar* (Petteri goes the wrong way), 2006

IN A MAY 2006 BROADCAST of his Finnish-language road movie–style show on Swedish television, host Petteri Väänänen traveled by motor home to Södertälje, where he visited the neighborhood of Lina Hage (Lina Meadow) (Figure 5.1).[1] His observations reflect the range of fascination, awe, esteem, and disgust with which visitors have reacted to this striking area, which departs radically from the majority of Swedish neighborhoods of single-family homes in its formal variety, materiality, and scale. Planners, architects, residents, and passersby have expressed reactions like Väänänen's, inspiring newspaper articles, field trips, and other forms of both positive and negative attention. Today, the area is an enclave that is almost exclusively the domain of Syriac Orthodox Christian families.

Lina Hage is part of a wave of single-family housing areas outlined since the 1990s in local development plans (*detaljplaner*, sometimes translated as zoning plans or detailed development plans), reflecting a larger trend away from multifamily structures. Independent homeowner initiatives mean that each house is built as a personalized design and through private means. Even if the fantasies of the residents and designers have not been given "a flat tire," as Väänänen says, they must nonetheless adhere to the regulations of the *detaljplan*—which are legally binding if a building

FIGURE 5.1. Östra Lina streetscape, 2011. Photograph by author.

permit is sought—when it comes to building heights, materials, and lot use. In Lina, however, these rules were unusually flexible.

This loosening appears to have taken place as planners made incorrect assumptions about the local market. Here in Lina, Syriacs, rather than the expected middle-class majority Swedes, were the primary purchasers of the plots. As stucco-clad Mediterranean-style homes appeared where Swedish wooden cottages were anticipated, the area became locally famous for its innovative architectural forms and received a new nickname: "Hollywood." Here, each house is a unique composition of elements such as Doric columns, protective lion statues, ornate fountains, and so-called Texas windows. The name "Hollywood" (or sometimes "Beverly Hills") speaks to this collage of international influences and design fantasies, as well as to the residents' wealth.

But how did Lina become Hollywood? In contrast to the designers of postwar Swedish models of multifamily, classless, standardized dwellings, current planners seem to regard Hollywood's houses (and often their residents), to follow anthropologist Mary Douglas, as "matter out of place."[2] For these professionals, the unexpected outcome of the plans has served as a cautionary tale about the dangers of allowing

owners too much freedom to choose forms and materials. Meanwhile, for their owners, the houses represent physical evidence of their hard-won class journey over five
decades in Sweden and the triumphant culmination of a housing career that typically began in the rental apartments of the Million Program. As they pour foundations and place their possessions within custom-designed walls, Syriacs also express
both their intentions to remain in Sweden and their ascendancy from dependent
renters to proud owners.

Segregation is often portrayed as one of Sweden's leading social problems, yet
the construction of luxury enclaves like Hollywood disrupts the easy dichotomies
of ethnic and economic exclusion against which planners have worked since the
Million Program's decline in the 1970s. David Ley and others describe the large-
scale, ornate "monster houses" that immigrants have constructed in Canada and
the United States, and Syriac homes in areas such as Hollywood produce a similar
"moral panic" for planners.[3] The stakes of resident participation in Hollywood question the very terms of equality of the welfare state, disrupting the elements of discrimination that have been built into a planning discourse seemingly wedded to a
spatial logic of immigrant dispersal. Södertälje neighborhoods like Ritorp, the earlier Östra Lina (East Lina), and the more recent Glasberga Sjöstad (Glasberga Lake
City) have required planners to rethink their assumptions, both about segregation
and about the relationship between ethnicity and class.

Making homes, side-by-side, through a planning apparatus that formally seeks
to eliminate segregation, Syriac home owners have created dream houses in Hollywood while also participating in the official building-permit processes. In plain view
of the planners who are charged to separate them (according to the geographic
distribution that integration is said to require), Syriacs have created a suburban
ethnic enclave that is neither underprivileged nor socially isolated. As Swedish ideas
of physical and social control through planning—established during the postwar
period—give way to the influence of new publics prizing hermetic, familial domestic conditions, these residential spaces signal new directions for a Swedish professional-
planning practice that, by necessity, must recalibrate its attitudes to immigrants'
dispersal and enclosure.

Segregation as Crisis, Strategy, or Heritage

In the autumn of 2005, just one month before civil unrest broke out in the suburb
of Clichy-sous-Bois outside Paris, a similar event occurred in Södertälje. What began
as a verbal exchange between teenagers in Ronna Centrum ended with mass protests
and an attack on the police station downtown, an incident that extended the already
long, dark shadows over the area's reputation.[4] The conflict began when a group
of Syriac boys allegedly yelled at a Finnish–Swedish girl, calling her "whore." She
reported the incident to her father, who came to Ronna Centrum with a baseball

bat and threatened the boys. The police arrived, stones were thrown at them, and a police car was vandalized. Tensions flared as riot police turned up in heavy gear and residents yelled at them from their balconies.[5] Later, up to fifteen shots were fired at the police station in central Södertälje with a Kalashnikov AK-47.[6]

Linda, a Syriac civil servant in her thirties, described how a group of young men acted as sentries during the riots, stationing themselves at the neighborhood's ostensible entrance, the "Welcome to Ronna" sign that hangs from a pedestrian bridge on the edge of the neighborhood (Figure 5.2). They denied entry to cars that lacked crucifixes on their rearview mirrors. She said, "When my uncle was stopped by these kids, they asked him why he didn't have one, since he spoke to them in *assyriska* [Suryoyo]." These boys' actions—and the conflict itself—accentuated the separation of Ronna from the rest of Södertälje both geographically and symbolically.

This version of Ronna as both a world apart and a quintessential place of danger reflects the othered identity given to many European neighborhoods with a high concentration of immigrants, such as Slotervaart in Amsterdam or Clichy-sous-Bois. Negative representations define them as "ethnically segregated." Whenever the media

FIGURE 5.2. "Välkommen till Ronna" (Welcome to Ronna) sign, 2011. Photograph by author.

portrays these areas as hotbeds of crime, unemployment, and violence, it does not simply besmirch the reputation of those specific places; it also brings one more witness to the stand to testify against the optimistic grand plans of European welfare-state architects and planners and their aims of building social equity into the spaces of the suburbs. Utopia dies another small death.

Former and current residents of Million Program areas in Södertälje, from Ronna to Geneta to Hovsjö, sometimes share the media's view. Twenty-eight-year-old Gabriella lives in Ronna in a run-down high-rise owned by the Graflund's housing company. When I moved to Ronna in 2009, she sternly warned me, "Don't walk alone at night. After 8:00 p.m., you can't go outside. Ronna is like Texas." She also reminded me that a priest at St. Afrem's Syriac Orthodox Church had told us during a short meeting that Ronna was "like Texas or New Jersey" (comparisons that reflect stereotypes of certain American states as being either the lawless Wild West or the mafia-run society of *The Sopranos*).

Connections between Million Program areas and other unsafe places were also expressed by Hilma, an Assyriska FF fan in her late twenties. As we ambled down the sidewalk in Geneta after a soccer match, avoiding the raucous crowds, she claimed that people from Turkey are "more barbaric" than others. As Syrianska fans vigorously celebrated their win over Assyriska in the streets, Hilma turned and said venomously, "See? Welcome to Turkey!" Some Syriacs who came to Sweden in the 1970s and 1980s described how Ronna had been "ruined" through the recent influx of refugees from Iraq and Syria and told me, "Enjoy your stay in Baghdad!" when I moved there. Whether Södertälje's Million Program neighborhoods are symbolically connected to Texas, New Jersey, Turkey, or Baghdad, they hold a firm position in the Swedish geography of despair, both for those who cannot escape them, like Gabriella (whose rejected asylum claim meant she could not work), or for those whose housing career has taken them elsewhere, like Hilma. Ronna cannot escape its media image.

Geographer Irene Molina argues, "Million Program areas that have a high proportion of immigrants . . . are identified as synonymous with housing segregation, equivalent in many ways to the workers' housing areas from the early twentieth century. These areas *and* their populations are labeled as problems."[7] The ontological transformation of the problem citizen from "member of the working class" to "immigrant" has emerged as a key part of segregation-related initiatives throughout Europe. "Un-European" ethnic enclaves (whatever their character, rich or poor) are portrayed as an existential threat to the European modern project.

Planners and civil servants charged with working against segregation therefore seem to do so in impossible circumstances.[8] During the 1980s and 1990s, renovation programs desperately revitalized Million Program housing with physical changes, often adding new balconies and colorful paint to facades. More recently, efforts have focused on organizing arts programs, using food markets to retool a neighborhood's

cultural influences as resources, or creating stronger geographic linkages between
the peripheries and the central city.[9] But these anxious attempts to create positive
change often appear to be a Sisyphean exercise. Their focus—integration—often
seems elusive, vaguely defined, and, in a sense, already defeated by the unwelcome
concentration of nonmajority Swedes in areas defined as segregated.

Swedish public discourse often refers to immigrants in evolutionary terms as "not
yet integrated." Molina writes that integration "is described as being always on the
way to 'becoming' something, on the way into the society, on the way to being
integrated into some kind of impossible company."[10] Million Program neighborhoods serve as visible reminders of these failures. To accelerate integration, states
and municipalities have tried to ensure that no municipality's piece of the immigration puzzle should be larger than any another's. Most notably, the "Whole of
Sweden" strategy, which began in 1984, forcibly spread asylum seekers around the
country to discourage enclaves and improve their job prospects, though many relocated as soon as they gained refugee status.[11] Ultimately regarded as both inhumane
and ineffective, the policy ended in 1994 with the new policy of *eget boende* (EBO,
"own housing"), which allows asylum seekers free choice about where they live.

Thousands of asylum seekers have arrived from Syria since 2011, and the EBO
policy has led to a pronounced demand for housing, a sudden influx of new students
into Södertälje's schools, and a greater need for municipally funded Swedish for
Immigrants courses. The Social Democratic mayor of Södertälje, Boel Godner,
argued vehemently against EBO when I spoke with her in the summer of 2015:

> I want to abolish EBO. Really. Where refugees end up depends completely on where
> the conflicts are in the world. If there is a war in Syria, then we know that many
> people who are escaping are going to come to Södertälje . . . of the Christians anyway.
> Muslims settle somewhere else in Sweden. And then it will go very well for some
> of them in the best-case scenario when they can choose themselves and live well and
> near relatives and churches. But for those who don't have money or knowledge from
> beforehand, they end up in an environment that is not Sweden and where it is impos-
> sible to learn Swedish.

Godner acknowledged a qualitative difference between some social conditions of
arrival and others, yet her description of segregated areas as "not Sweden" underscores how public discourse instantiates a continuous dichotomy that links undesirable areas to immigrants. Co-opting a term that the national government developed
when the Moderate Party (Moderaterna) held power (from 2006 to 2014), she went
on to say, "It can't be the case that we send people straight to an 'alienation area'
[utanförskapsområde]. All the municipalities need to help each other instead."

While the arrival of thousands of new residents from war zones creates new challenges for the town, Syriac-dominated neighborhoods of single-family homes are far

from socially and economically monolithic. A close look at the problem of segregation in Södertälje illustrates that many areas developed by choice rather than by default, as Sonya Aho describes:

> The family has central importance for the individual in the *assyrisk/syrianska* community. . . . In the homelands, several generations lived under the same roof in large households. In large households, grandparents lived together with the eldest son's family and his married sons and their nuclear families in the same house. Even in the countries of emigration, the generations try to live as close together as possible, preferably in the same house. But if that is not possible owing to the lack of space, one chooses to live as close together as possible to maintain everyday contact.[12]

Izla, in her early thirties, described her ancestral village, where newcomers required permission to move in. She said, "My grandfather decided. If a family came there and wanted to live in the village, it was he who decided, 'Okay, I approve you. You get this place to build a house on.'" This explicit interest in maintaining familial proximity and reducing outside threats was transferred to the new urban environment of Södertälje.

Mirroring the developments of the present, local journalist Stefan Andersson in 1983 analyzed a climate of escalating municipal exasperation toward growing Syriac enclaves:

> One would think that the municipality should have learned its lesson. The *assyrier* obviously have nothing against so-called ghettos. For them, this concentration is nothing negative. And they probably also have their reasons. But what has driven the municipality's conduct when it came to bringing about a dispersal of the *assyrier* has probably been a more or less unconscious fear that the Swedish majority population will lose its cultural dominance.[13]

In Ronna in particular, families who had disbanded in Turkey reunited, as Andersson described: "Within this area [Ronna], the *assyrier* have largely managed to concentrate themselves according to familial relations—in many cases, a single family has managed to monopolize an entire stairwell. This has been a way to get a certain [sense of] safety. But a consequence has also been that more and more Swedes move out of the area."[14] The Million Program's shared circulation spaces, intended to create collective spaces for unrelated citizens, were thereby remade as entrances to new Syriac villages of relatives.

Most urban peripheries in Sweden, and Europe at large, claim residents with a wide range of ethnic identifications and citizenships. Sociologist Loïc Wacquant describes these residents as "urban outcasts,"[15] and cultural geographer Roger Andersson has suggested changing the terms of debate about segregated neighborhoods from "immigrant-dense" *(invandrartäta)* to "Swede-sparse" *(svenskglesa)*; he notes that the absence of majority Swedish residents in these neighborhoods characterizes them much more than the presence of any particular ethnic group.[16]

Quantitative social science research on Swedish Million Program neighborhoods that are segregated by dint of merely being "not Swedish" has demonstrated, time and again, the negative social consequences of being on the margins of both the city and the society. Yet in work on California, Wei Li lauds similarly "multiethnic communities" as dynamic "ethnoburbs."[17] This more recent theorization of immigrant neighborhoods and their spatialization in North America works against the earlier models of "ethnic ghettos" like Chinatown or even the later "suburban Chinatowns" that Timothy Fong and others analyzed in the 1990s.[18] In Sweden, the very diversity of the suburbs has been characterized as a key problem and has made them—like the early-twentieth-century Swedish city more generally—an object of reform under the prevailing spatial logic of distribution. Yet the formation of elective ethnic enclaves in Södertälje represents an unprecedented settlement model that requires both new perspectives and new planning practices.

Detaljplanering and the Limits of Participation

As the Swedish welfare state congealed during the twentieth century, intimate connections between socioeconomic policies and architecture etched a deep groove, dictating the direction of the still-traveling nation. As urban planning transformed into a tool of social engineering, it required new regulations. The building ordinances of 1874 required all densely populated areas to draw up a city plan *(stadsplan)* to direct growth, but only after the 1907 City Planning Act did authorities have effective legal rights to prevent private construction, such as on sites for future streets.[19] Critically, this act also allowed local governments to control the form of future buildings, "such as height, number of floors, etc. . . . [in] perhaps the most important step in the history of Swedish planning legislation."[20]

Even then, outside the plans' boundaries, "shanty towns grew up with substandard sanitation, fire safety, and social conditions."[21] In the postwar period, the 1947 Building Act required municipal plans and bolstered what eventually became known as "the municipal planning monopoly" *(det kommunala planmonopolet),* meaning that "the municipalities could decide where and when plans should be established and what they would include."[22] As the environmental devastation associated with rapid industrialization engendered a new need for planning in the 1950s and 1960s, the building ordinances of 1959 required building committees, providing new power to municipalities to dictate land use, and often aesthetic considerations, even for projects from private developers.[23]

Inconsistencies across the country led to efforts to create national planning regulations, eventually becoming the Planning and Building Law (Plan- och bygglag), usually abbreviated as PBL, with the first version in force from July 1, 1987, to May 2, 2011.[24] A major innovation was the PBL's separation of the *översiktsplan* (master plan) from the *detaljplan*; these replaced other existing types of plans, such as the *generalplan* (master plan), the *stadsplan* (city plan), and the *byggnadsplan* (building plan).[25] While the *översiktsplan* had no direct legal weight and acted as a set of guidelines, the *detaljplan* outlined legally binding rules (valid for five years) and could be vetoed on the basis of guidelines in the *översiktsplan*.[26] The aims of the *detaljplan* were "to provide an overall view regarding appropriate development, to strengthen public control, to clarify rights and obligations, and to rationalize the consideration of individual applications."[27] The *detaljplan* bridged public and private interests as "an instrument for the municipality to realize local building policy and social ambitions, as well as to promote an economic and rational building production."[28] The 1987 PBL also indicated an increasing emphasis on local-level decision making, with the municipal government's right to accept or deny plans having the effect of demoting the representatives of the region or state to a largely consultative role.[29]

Given the power afforded to planning (especially as state rules replaced local ones for building standards in the 1960s),[30] blame for the perceived failures of the Million Program during the 1980s and 1990s shifted from its "monolithic" designs to the centralized decision-making processes of the expert designers and politicians. A key innovation of the 1987 PBL was its attempt to counteract the earlier top-down planning that had characterized the ideological and procedural tenets of the Million Program, as the PBL placed new emphasis on "public interests."[31] For instance, the law required a public review of a proposed *detaljplan* through an exhibition advertised at least a week in advance and continuing for at least three weeks. During this time, members of the public contributed comments and concerns in writing, and these served as the basis for later appeals. Three weeks after approval by the town building committee, and in the absence of appeals, the *detaljplan* took legal effect, allowing applications for compliant building permits.[32] Given the *detaljplan*'s legal status, Swedish planners and building-permit officers often regarded it as a source of comfort in the confusing maelstrom of varying public opinions. The *detaljplan* appeared foolproof, yet Syriac building projects in Södertälje demonstrate the increasing impotence of its underlying cultural assumptions.

When Södertälje's European Union (EU) collaboration project, URBACT/RegGov, focused on Ronna as a so-called deprived area,[33] the label itself justified a need for government intervention. Yet the importance accorded to residents' insights was key: the project should include "participation" *(delaktighet)* and "effectiveness" *(effektivitet),* two institutions of more recent Swedish planning.[34] Gleaning residents' thoughts about the lack of employment opportunities or how to improve safety in public spaces through surveys and workshops—in short, asking residents for their opinions during redevelopments—should, it was argued, produce a new bottom-up alternative to counter the excessively top-down approach of the Million Program.

These methods, however, have frequently been slotted into what is often an already-indolent planning process. During meetings I attended, the EU's German consultant for the project often expressed frustration with the slow pace of Swedish planning vis-à-vis that of partner cities, including Syracuse in Italy, Duisburg in Germany, and Satu Mare in Romania. The other towns, he said, had moved far more quickly to develop their "local action plans."[35] In Södertälje, ideas simply percolated and percolated again. Majority Swedish civil servants from planners to police agreed that Ronna's primary problem was its segregation, but outreach efforts to resident stakeholders led only to further outreach efforts. With Kafkaesque abbreviations and a Byzantine organization, the EU–regional–municipal collaboration seemed to thwart Swedish action, and the German consultant eventually termed the Ronna group a "talking club."

In URBACT/RegGov and Swedish planning more generally, Million Program residents are said to have a valuable voice in a process that has come to be known as "citizen dialogue" *(medborgardialog)*. Residents remain, however, the *beneficiaries* of planning: they are categorized as the occupants of municipal apartments or as the unemployed who must be put to work. After this dialogue, it is planners who will find solutions to problems like illegal gambling or a lack of sports fields. Residents are imagined as informants but never as true collaborators. This people-centered approach also made the creation of slogans such as "Don't worry—be happy—come and live in Ronna!" (in English) appealing but seemed still to instruct residents to adopt a passive position. Those with a "foreign background" are also assumed to be stuck in Million Program areas, without the social and economic capital to move. Though they may freely occupy the category "users" *(brukare),* they are not imagined as designers themselves.[36]

But fifty years after the first Syriacs arrived, many *are* wealthy. As entrepreneurs, the group's restaurant, café, and hair-salon owners are legendary. Many Syriacs are doctors and lawyers, and others have become esteemed specialists with PhDs in fields such as religion, sociology, and Assyriology. With upward mobility, some Syriacs have changed their addresses to reflect an evolving class identity—rejecting Million Program areas just as the majority Swedes did before them. Along the way, they have claimed a position in the planning process that is far more powerful than a mere voice in a citizen dialogue, forcing municipal professionals out of the comfort zones of sanctioned exhibitions or neighborhood workshops. Both groups find themselves in new territory, one increasingly dominated by Syriac enclaves of single-family housing.

The Standard House

The high demand for single-family homes in Sweden was well known before, during, and after the Million Program, appearing as a continuous tradition of passive support—and certainly not discouragement—for this housing type.[37] Single-family homes in fact accounted for 34 percent of the total units produced during the program, although they have received much less scholarly and media attention.[38] While official policies supported the population density and community infrastructure of high- and mid-rise housing as the key to innovative modern lifestyles, six hundred thousand single-family homes were constructed in Sweden from 1950 to 1980.[39] The emphasis on owner-built units limited their market, however, even with available government loans.

Several forces contributed to the reemergence of the single-family house during the late 1960s and 1970s. First, the rise of tract housing developments (*gruppbyggda hus*; literally, "group-built houses") during the 1960s made home ownership a more affordable and therefore viable option for middle-class majority Swedes. By the 1970s, apartment surpluses combined with harsh critiques of Million Program areas reempowered Swedish consumers to demand more single-family homes. Their production increased from 25 percent of new housing in 1970 to 75 percent by 1980.[40] Despite the rejection of the high- and mid-rise products of the Million Program, however, significant limits on heterogeneity remained even for newer single-family homes.[41]

In the mid-1940s, the Swedish government agency known as the National Housing Board (Kungliga Bostadsstyrelsen), with its staff of architects, had initiated the production of prototypes for single-family homes, eventually known as standard houses *(typhus)*. While model drawings *(typritningar)* had existed in Sweden since the late seventeenth century, their use exploded during the 1950s and 1960s.[42] The Housing Board sold 11,848 standard house drawings from 1950 to 1976, and certain types became particularly popular (Figures 5.3 and 5.4). During the early 1950s, the "elastic" Type 167 sold best. As an adaptable duplex, it allowed a family to rent out one floor until it could afford to occupy both.[43]

While the trendiness of new types was reflected in the sales of drawings, the agency ultimately discontinued them in 1964. Leif Jonsson describes their demise: "Through the increased demands, among other things, for handicapped accessibility, established in the new building norms (SBN [*Svensk Bygg Norm,* Swedish Building Norm]) in the year 1975, the model-drawing movement could no longer be used directly for the development of state-leveraged small houses, and their sales died a natural death."[44] The drawings were sold until 1977 and still shape Swedish neighborhoods today. The grim reaper thus did not come for the standard-house movement, since the Housing Board placed greater effort beginning in 1968 on the development of "pattern plans" *(mönsterplaner),* "with the goal of fostering limitations on variation within housing production."[45] Even when the single-family home transformed into an explicit critique of other Million Program models, there remained a strong ideological emphasis on a government-issued average-house plan with scientifically approved, salubrious effects for both home owner and society. With self-effacement

FIGURE 5.3. Cover of Standard House catalog, 1958. Source: *Typritningskatalog* (Stockholm: Kungliga Bostadsstyrelsen, 1958).

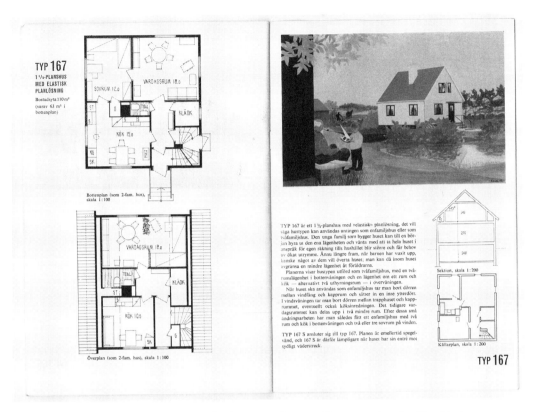

FIGURE 5.4. Type 167, the "elastic" duplex, 1958. Source: *Typritningskatalog* (Stockholm: Kungliga Bostadsstyrelsen, 1958).

a critical component of a national identity focused on a positive attitude toward the interventionist, distributionist welfare state,[46] the single-family house reemerged in "the decade of the small house in Sweden," the 1970s.[47]

During that time, the single-family home enjoyed a position of both ideological and legal support absent since the early twentieth century and posited as a response to the perceived failures of the Million Program, a trend that continues into the present. The hangover after a period of enthusiastic high- and mid-rise housing debauchery has been long lasting. After 1970, loans for houses larger than 125 square meters were allowed in exchange for restrictions on costs, and Jonsson argues, "The intention was to give an increased freedom in the balance between area and standard. The same year, the earlier minimum area for dwellings in small houses was repealed."[48]

In Södertälje in 1974, approximately three thousand people—the largest number in the town's history—waited in the queue for plots of land to build single-family houses.[49] A new municipal housing program for 1974–78 placed the goal for new construction of single-family dwellings at 33 percent of total new housing construction.[50] Yet many of the homes then planned were in multifamily buildings.[51] As elsewhere in Sweden, political parties on the left argued for multifamily dwellings, while those on the right supported single-family units. As one local journalist wrote, "The city of Södertälje has long been criticized for building too few small houses, not the least on the political plane, where the right wing has violently attacked the Social Democrats and the Communists."[52] The minority right-wing parties argued for consumer choice and the romance of the private homestead. With wealthier citizens voting for market-friendlier parties and aiming to live in owner-occupied homes, the neighborhood of Lina Hage became the tinder around which these contentious discussions exploded. This led to a decade-long impasse, a chutes-and-ladders approach that encapsulated the overarching ambivalence about single-family homes in the nation at large.

Home on the Hage

With plentiful available land—including forests and natural water features—city planners of the 1960s had coveted Lina Hage as a prime site for a new neighborhood. Urban historian Göran Gelotte writes that ambitions for Lina were predicated on assumptions of Sweden's infinite economic growth: "The future views were great, and one saw a satellite city with its own grand life in the northern part of Södertälje."[53] Along with Lina Gård (Lina Farm), the area had housed several other industries with expansive grounds (including a brickworks and a distillery) and was close to Ronna.

But this imagined Lina did not receive the optimistic rubber-stamping its forebears had enjoyed. With mostly multifamily housing, Ronna and Geneta had opened to the trumpet calls of a new Swedish modernity in the 1960s, but during the worrying economic downturn of the 1970s, they were increasingly regarded as hubristic mistakes. The pinnacle of the crises and anxieties came when Telgebostäder nearly halted the development of the neighborhood of Hovsjö then under construction; it subsequently became a ghost town where most apartments remained "unrented." It was not too late to do things differently in Lina.

In the early 1970s, a public debate recognized the need for new architectural and urban models that would symbolize a *post*–Million Program era, and proposals for Lina took shape. Large-scale, municipal intervention in the housing market, however, appeared here only in a bruised and battered form, as concerned citizens, dissenting politicians, and even newspaper editors worked ceaselessly against the first Lina proposal. Articles in *LT* detailed the potential and the pitfalls of plans to house twenty thousand to twenty-three thousand residents by 1973. Some referred to environmental problems (a new feature of planning discourse), saying that the development would destroy a well-loved wilderness area; others argued against its large scale.[54] A sharply worded September 1973 article signed by the Center Party (Centerpartiet, historically the representative of agricultural interests) argued explicitly for a reduced population of six thousand to eight thousand inhabitants and a greater focus on single-family houses.[55] Fears of creating yet another Ronna, Geneta, or Hovsjö eventually led to political gridlock.

A revised plan for the section known as Södra Lina (South Lina) finally received approval from the city council in 1979 (Figure 5.5).[56] A collaboration between the municipality's urban design office *(stadsarkitektkontoret)* and the firm of Erskine Arkitektkontor AB, led by Scottish–Swedish architect Ralph Erskine, the plan included twelve new housing zones with 850 dwelling units, a high school and other institutions, recreational spaces and parks, a commercial center, roads for private vehicles, bus routes, and bus stops.[57] While some dwellings were small houses *(småhus),* the vast majority were row houses *(radhus)* and L-shaped buildings *(vinkelhus).* A 1982 *detaljplan* made further specifications. After more than a decade of controversy, Gelotte writes, "Lina Hage was inaugurated in 1983 and, with that, one can say that Telgebostäder's major interventions were finished for the decade."[58]

Despite this new initiative, Södertälje continued to lose population to neighboring communities, where plots for single-family houses were not as scarce. The municipality's panic over this attrition took the form of laments about the decisions of the 1960s, when the town's booming industries had made the creation of

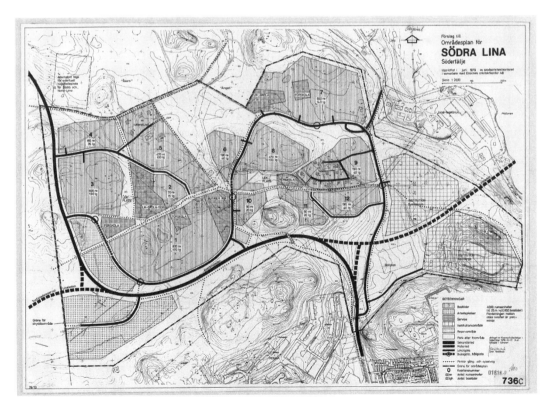

FIGURE 5.5. Södra Lina neighborhood plan, 1979. Collaboration by the Municipal Urban Design Office of Södertälje and Erskine Arkitektkontor AB. Source: Södertälje Kommun.

high- and mid-rises so very logical. Market research indicating the strong preference of the Swedish public for single-family homes—which had been mostly ignored in the context of their specific incompatibility with the common interests of Scania, Astra, and Södertälje—was now reconsidered. The public's desire to live "close to the ground" (see Figure 2.7) became a central theme in the late 1970s, showing the disconnection between official policies and the public opinion.[59] The Syriacs were a growing public with private-house desires of their own, many of which focused on personal expression and living close to family members.

The New Class Journey

In a 1982 episode of the Swedish public television documentary series *Klyftan* (The divide), two officials from the municipality, Agneta and Ingemar, talk while driving through Ronna:

> AGNETA: The concentration of *assyrier/syrianer* happens because they want to live near their relatives, and the Swedes find this hard to understand. When it's usually families with children, it's completely natural that there will be greater wear and tear on the outdoor environment, on the stairwells, and so on. They find this difficult to accept.
>
> INGEMAR: It must also be a shock for all the Swedes when a *syriansk* family moves into a row house area and they notice the incredible family life of the *syrianer*. There are probably relatives running around there all day long, which the Swedes can't understand.
>
> AGNETA: Exactly. There is an energy and activity that we are not accustomed to.
>
> INGEMAR: People say that the *syrianer* are so "isolated" in Södertälje. The Swedish housewives are probably more isolated than the *syrianska* ones.
>
> AGNETA: Yes, or the Finnish ones or the others. . . .
>
> INGEMAR: Have the *syrianer* bought their own homes and settled in a pure Swedish environment *[ren svensk miljö]*?
>
> AGNETA: There are some who have bought, yes. That is definitely beginning. Several live in row houses. In the newest area, Brunnsäng, I know that there are some *assyrisk/syrianska* families who came through the queue for housing plots.
>
> INGEMAR: Has this led to problems in the neighborhood, to protests?
>
> AGNETA: In some cases. It's not that anyone has explicitly protested that they settled there, but it came a while afterward. Many people have come and gone, and, with such small plots, you live densely and close, and they thought it was noisy sometimes.[60]

By the early 1980s, the Syriacs living in rental apartments were increasingly settled, owning businesses, raising children, and affixing their lives to the national space of

Sweden. As they became well established financially and socially, they left the stigmatized Million Program areas.

These patterns reflect those of majority Swedes and earlier immigrant groups like the Finns who came to work in factories, as a Stockholm regional report described: "Many of the people who moved to Södertälje during the Record Years started their housing careers in a room in barracks, in a bachelor hotel, or in an apartment in a multifamily building, which they got through Scania's assistance. In this type of housing, the specific individual has very limited opportunities to make any imprint on the outside environment."[61]

As Agneta of the SVT program outlined, some Syriac families moved first from high- or mid-rises to existing single-family homes, "pattern-built" cottages with large yards. But they could not create Syriac neighborhoods from standardized, repetitive forms in sites where they were not in the majority.

In the early twenty-first century, however, plans were drawn for dedicated plots for single-family homes in a new Lina Hage neighborhood: Murverket, the area that eventually became known as "Hollywood" (or "Beverly Hills" or "Lina Hills," itself a spin on "Beverly Hills"). Although owners were to build the houses individually in this area, planners assumed they would follow the prevailing cultural wisdom of standard house models. Ashur described how an advertisement reflected this supposition:

> Five years ago, it was in the papers that there would be a new area. They did sketches to show how it might look, but those had nothing to do with the way it turned out. They wanted everyone to have the same house. Exactly the same Swedish standard, red cottages with white window frames. I don't think they expected that people would build houses like these.

When numerous Syriacs purchased undeveloped plots in Lina, they understood that they would finally be able to custom design a home. Here, Syriacs have used their prosperity to reshape suburban space through custom-designed houses that reject the homogeneity of both Million Program neighborhoods *and* monolithic areas created with standardized cottages. More than that, building in these areas has afforded them the chance to demarcate the boundaries of a new Syriac neighborhood. In so doing, Syriacs follow the spatial logic of enclosure and hermeticism to which they continued to subscribe after migration to Sweden.

"From the Ghetto to the Mansion in Five Minutes"

When we got to Floravägen after a derby, a car with Syrianska FC flags appeared, and Temra said, "What are they doing on our street? Go away!" and motioned with her hand. As we walked down the street, we heard festive, Turkish-language music coming from the yard of one of her neighbors, and she said, "They can't do that!" As an Assyriska FF fan, Temra thought the citywide celebration of Syrianska's victory was ridiculous, annoying, and much too loud. With dismay, she said that this kind of behavior made her neighborhood of standardized, single-family houses in Geneta increasingly Syriac-exclusive. When they had moved in six years earlier, hers was one of only two Syriac families on the block, but now only two families of majority Swedes remained. She said, "It's a new thing, that all *assyrier* want to own their own house. It happened really quickly that everyone suddenly wanted to move out of the apartments and into single-family houses."

Echoing these sentiments, Sargon, a Syriac hairdresser in his late twenties, told me, "When you travel from Ronna to Lina, you go directly from the ghetto to the mansion in five minutes, from chaos to peace." He grew up in the Million Program neighborhood of Ronna and now lives with his family in the neighborhood of Östra Lina, a move that his family's success in developing restaurants and hair salons in Stockholm facilitated. From the vantage point of his family's class journey—outlined through built form—Sargon thus repeats the media representations of Ronna as a dangerous and unruly environment, despite having grown up there.

One month after the Ronna Riots took place in 2005, Katarina Gunnarsson, a reporter for the popular Swedish radio show *Studio Ett,* returned to Södertälje to interview residents of Lina Hage about their experiences of the conflict.[62] The segment emphasized the perceived contrast between the two neighborhoods, echoing many of the assumptions about Syriac immigrants of the Swedish television broadcast about Ronna twenty-three years earlier:

> KATARINA GUNNARSSON: From here in Lina Hage, it is only seven hundred meters to the immigrant-dense Ronna, but they are like two different worlds, with a road and a forest in between. And now, after the unrest in Ronna and the car that exploded in the parking lot here, it feels like Ronna has come too close, says a mother holding her preschool child's hand and raising her head toward the pastel-colored row houses in Lina Hage. The father and daughter who were harassed over there in Ronna live up there. And she compares the high-rise area Ronna and the row house area Lina.
>
> RESIDENT: Lina is still like Småland [in southern Sweden]. It is small and cozy, and Ronna, that's the real big city. There, you know, large extended families live together. You might have the same last name [on every door] in the entire stairwell. If there's, like, one Swede in every stairwell, that's good.

Until recently, Lina Hage was a Swedish outpost in the center of an immigrant-dominated area, and Ronna was regarded as not only its social but also its physical opposite. This has changed radically, both in older sections of Lina Hage and, eventually, in Hollywood.

One Syriac couple in their thirties, Nahrin and Hannibal, married and moved to an apartment in Lina in the 1990s. Nahrin explained that it was an intentional move away from Syriac Ronna: "Twenty years or so ago, in 1997, everyone lived in Ronna, and Lina was still very beautiful. I mean, there weren't so many immigrants." When the young couple announced their decision to his parents and extended family, however, they were greeted with reservations. Nahrin described the scene:

> His entire family said, "Are you going to live in Lina? It's so far away! It's completely in the wrong direction!" They lived in Ronna, every one of them in Ronna, in the same building. "How can you live so far away? Why do you want to live in Lina?" Like it was the biggest problem ever. "Are you going to take our son away from us?," they asked me. It hadn't been built here [Östra Lina] yet either. Now, all of his uncles live here. Even my in-laws moved here! Everyone, the uncles, the children, the grandchildren. Everyone lives here! And now there's no one left in Ronna.

As Nahrin's story indicates, the transformation of Lina into a Syriac enclave—like Temra's tract-housing neighborhood—has been rapid and remarkable. This metamorphosis has also re-created notions of geographic security for the group, as Ashur described:

> There's safety in having everyone in the same area. When we lived in the high-rises, we always lived near each other. If you wanted something from your brother or sister, they were close by. It's the same thing here. My father lives near his brothers, here and there. It's safe. That's how we lived in Turkey, too, as in a little village. We want to live close to each other. We don't like to live far away from each other, so if it's several kilometers, then that family isn't close to the others. We're going to build two or three houses for my cousins also. So everyone will be here, too.

The spatial proximity afforded in the stairwells in Ronna has given way to a new kind of enclosure in Lina and other newer areas, where the grouping of Syriac houses re-creates a sense of safety lost in migration. Here, Syriac prosperity and a desire to live together take new shape at the scale of the neighborhood, where the individuality of custom-designed homes, paradoxically, signals increased Syriac social cohesion.

Greetings from Hollywood!

One night Temra showed me an area from a distance, but I could see only some amorphous white forms in the darkness. I asked why it was so special. She simply said, "That is Hollywood." She then went on to explain that the owners there built according to unique designs and hoped to outdo one another. Every house was more outrageous than the last. I said Ishtar had suggested that I would be interested in the area, and I had assumed that that was because the area was ethnically mixed. Temra said, "No, that whole area is *assyrier*!" In contrast, she described the area where Nahrin lives as "heterogeneous." Then she laughed, saying, "You know, her next-door neighbors are from Iraq!"

Today's Murverket (Hollywood's official name) was designated as an area for housing as early as the 1979 Erskine *stadsplan*. Meaning "masonry" in Swedish, its name is perhaps fitting for a place that has become synonymous with homes that involve elaborate stonework. As Ashur described, this was not, however, the image presented to the public when the plan was first introduced. In conversation with municipal planners, I learned that the area had been imagined as a semibucolic neighborhood of diminutive wood-frame houses and generous grass lawns with traditional flower beds and the occasional small tree, as seen in similar neighborhoods in Sweden. While they never used this language, the assumption seemed to be that the area would serve as a kind of enclave for majority Swedes who could afford to self-build. Yet it had another destiny.

The *detaljplan* for Murverket, which the Urban Development Committee (Stadsbyggnadsnämnden) had approved in 2001 and which serves as the legal basis for building permits, had few rules for building footprints and heights (Figure 5.6). According to Astrid, a majority Swedish municipal-development engineer:

> The *detaljplan* was not regulated. It stated two hundred square meters over two floors, and, like, *that's it* [in English]. And the plots were between seven hundred and nine hundred, one a little over one thousand square meters. So they were small plots with extraordinarily large building rights. And so it became what it became. And when there's an area that is immigrant-dense, those who want to build there and those who live in the area are mainly *syrianer* and they want . . . for them, stone houses are status: huge stone houses with walls around them.

In retrospect, planners could see that the outcome of these flexible plans might have been anticipated if they had been more adept at understanding the contemporary local market.

Although the Murverket plots could only have 25 percent of their area covered by a building, the maximum size of the houses was set at two hundred square meters. Also, the plan mandated a minimum distance of four meters from the property line to the main building but failed to specify a minimum distance from the plot line to a fence, as Josef, a Syriac building-permit officer, pointed out to me:[63]

> If you go to Murverket, you will notice that everyone wants to use as much of their plot as possible, and I understand why, but then it happens that almost everyone has a stone wall, and they don't really need it. And when the walls are higher, the street feels narrower, and it's not as . . . partially for traffic safety and partially for the feeling

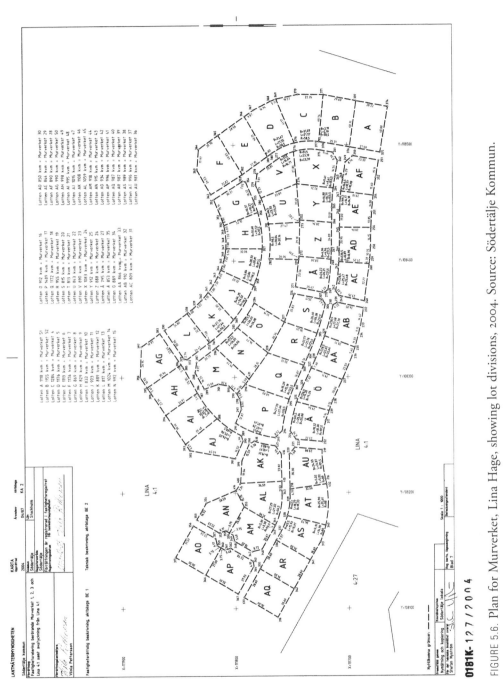

FIGURE 5.6. Plan for Murverket, Lina Hage, showing lot divisions, 2004. Source: Södertälje Kommun.

that it is extremely narrow, the houses are too close. So, now we think that you should try to have at least a meter on each side. And furthermore, we have had some issues with snow removal and such. When they're so close, you can't take, like, take away all the snow.

Stone walls around single-family homes, sometimes shared between neighbors, were also traditional in Tur Abdin, where many of these families have their origins. Creating these enclosures for the family home (often in combination with high shrubbery) may seem structurally unnecessary, merely posing problems for officials like Josef, but they also permit residents to resume familiar ways of defining personal space within a larger collective (Figure 5.7). The walls represent a decision to create a circumscribed domestic sphere materially and, at the same time, contribute to the definition of the larger hermetic social space of this Syriac-dominated neighborhood.

When buyers' views of what a single-family house and its outdoor spaces could become contradicted what City Hall imagined, the freedoms of the plan allowed for an architectural exegesis that seems to have caught its unwitting enablers off guard. Astrid and many other planners indicated that they had expected large lawns and small houses and were surprised when owners maximized house sizes and heights instead. The *detaljplan* did not regulate housing materials, and although it limited single-family homes to two stories, it contained no specific restrictions on building heights. Josef also decried this, saying, "In Lina, there's a house where they built . . .

FIGURE 5.7. Streetscape in Murverket, showing street walls and shrubbery, 2015. Photograph by author.

two stories was the requirement . . . but they made the upper floor extremely high so that it looks like a multifamily house, a three-story building. And we don't want that." Since a building's construction must by law follow its *detaljplan,* the building-permit department had no grounds to deny requests even when they clashed with the planners' larger vision for the neighborhood and its formal and spatial expression. A local backlash emerged in other ways, however.

In Sweden, house or plot purchases are published in the local paper, with the address and the price, leaving no secrets about who will be moving into a neighborhood. As Astrid explained:

> We have a plot queue in Södertälje that we have to sell to. So we send out the information about the *detaljplan,* and then there are showings. The group who came to the showings [for Murverket] was very diverse; they were both Swedes and Finns and *syrianer* and everyone. Then we started to sell, and we sold them, for the most part, to families who had siblings or parents who had purchased houses around each other. There were some Swedes who had bought plots, but they chose to withdraw. They could see, because it's public as soon as we sign the contract. They saw who had bought the plots, and then they drew their own conclusions and decided to back out.

Astrid saw this as an inevitable conclusion for the neighborhood, since the public sales process meant that xenophobic attitudes could be played out in the marketplace. Sales of the plots to one Syriac family after the next produced, by accumulation, a space of enclosure at the urban scale for the group. As his cousin and neighbor Mattias, in his late twenties, looked on, Ashur explained how this affected the neighborhood's social structure:

> In the beginning, there weren't so many *assyrier* who wanted to buy here. My father, my uncle, they wanted to buy. Maybe there were five families of fifty-five. The rest were Swedes. I think that the Swedes became a little bit afraid that there would be too many *assyrier* here, so they sold their land. And people heard, there's an *assyrier,* okay, I can also go there. So it became . . . they heard that it was for sale, for sale, for sale. Eventually, it became the opposite. It became five or six Swedes here, and the rest were *assyrier.*

Transparency in the purchasing process reflects the philosophy of public disclosure characterizing Swedish society, but this information accelerated the creation of an ethnic enclave in Lina, under the noses and with the legal (if not social) approval of planners.

Despite this strong negative reaction among speculative majority Swedish buyers, Hollywood as built remains somewhat hidden from the prying eyes of public opinion and absent from the mental maps of many of the town's majority Swedish residents. Ashur described his experiences with visitors:

I've brought a lot of my Swedish friends here. Not to show them what we've done, just because they were going to come over to my place. Many think, "Oh shit. Who lives here? What's this? Are we allowed to be here? What kind of an area is this?" They haven't heard anything about the area.

The anxious sense that permission to enter might be needed underscores the fact that nonresident majority Swedes believe Hollywood to be potentially off limits, a no-go zone for those who do not belong to its microcommunity and families. Even some Syriac residents of surrounding neighborhoods expressed surprise when I informed them about its existence. On a walk with Gabriella (the resident of Ronna who described it as "Texas"), she simply stopped in the road and stared, saying, "They're rich people who live here. Where are we?" (Figures 5.8 and 5.9). Her reaction indicates that the quality of Hollywood's "segregation" extends beyond mere adherence to the Syriac identity group. Instead it revolves, in part, around questions of class and prosperity, as well as kin relations and settlement in Sweden. Hollywood is not so much an ethnic enclave as an outpost for a new family village of upwardly

FIGURE 5.8. Streetscape in Murverket, with some houses still under construction, 2009. Photograph by author.

FIGURE 5.9. Custom-designed home in Murverket, 2015. Photograph by author.

mobile, well-established Syriacs. As one home owner in Hollywood said, referencing the majority Swedish town beyond the neighborhood, "Södertälje ends here." Such perceptions have also raised questions and suspicions among some majority Swedes about what is happening behind the walls of the houses (and within the boundaries) of Hollywood.

"Anyone Living in a Palace-Like House"

In author and journalist Göran Rosenberg's three-part television documentary from 2005, *Rosenberg: Sveriges val* (Rosenberg: Sweden's vote), he uses Södertälje (his home-town) as a microcosm of the entire Swedish nation.[64] In one segment, Rosenberg walks around in Östra Lina with Staffan Norberg, a government commissioner for Södertälje, who explains his interpretation of the construction methods he sees: "It's very important for these southern European cultures in particular to have a flat lot. And they're keen to build high walls. And that creates some conflicts sometimes with the neighbors in the surrounding area." Rosenberg replies, "They need a building permit, I would imagine, to do things like this." Norberg answers while touching a wall: "Yes, but they don't always seek a building permit. Sometimes there are walls and fences built without a building permit."

The development of communities of luxury single-family houses by members of a group expected to remain in place in Million Program neighborhoods elicits multiple crises: one around ethnic enclavization, another around class, and a third around just how "they" are able to build "that." Although segregation is ostensibly a specific target for elimination among urban planners, the status quo means that efforts to combat it typically focus on Million Program neighborhoods. Ethnically homogeneous yet affluent neighborhoods like Lina fall outside established categories and logics. Syriacs gaining the wealth to build—and to build boldly—disrupts the idea that government intervention is the only way people living in "deprived" areas can advance their standing.

The houses of Östra Lina and Hollywood have also given new fodder to assertions among some majority Swedes that Syriacs not only build without permits but earn the money to do so through illegal means, especially through criminal networks that allow businesses to gain most of their income from the black market. On June 17, 2011, for example, a full-page debate article penned by Carin Götblad, the Stockholm County police chief at the time, appeared in a leading national newspaper and described official law-enforcement efforts against organized crime in Södertälje. Her final line reads, "Anyone living in a palace-like house *[palatsliknande hus]* with almost no declared income should be required to provide a reasonable explanation for how this is possible."[65]

Echoing these sentiments, a 2015 article in the Norwegian newspaper *Aftenposten,* entitled "We Live in the Same Town but Not the Same World," caught the attention of civil servants and residents of Södertälje, as well as of the Swedish national newspapers.[66] Describing the city as a worst-case scenario for integration politics, the article contends that liberal Swedish refugee policies at the national level created social problems and mafia rule at the municipal scale. Online, an accompanying video interview with a concerned criminal inspector shows him driving by Lina Hage and pointing to it and saying, "This over here was only forest. This is where they have established themselves. Grotesque fucking houses. A lot of this was built illegally, I promise you. It is so un-Swedish!"[67]

For county and municipal police representatives and for the critical commentators who discuss these buildings online in anonymous places such as racist Internet forums, the stucco, stained glass, and outdoor monumental staircases of these houses demonstrate the supposed criminality of the city at large, and of the Syriac group in particular. In the aggregate, these neighborhoods are perceived as "no-go zones" where the rule of law has no reach. They have not just awakened envy from within or revealed a new mode of property ownership; they have also become visible symbols of a perceived erosion of control over money, property, and laws, much as the group's everyday wearing of business suits and large purchases of fruits and vegetables did in the 1970s. Negative views label these physical worlds in Södertälje as a "parallel society"—one that is far from integrated. As a moderately wealthy Syriac enclave, Hollywood breaks the uniformity of the Swedish-pattern plan and standard-house models physically and of the segregated, deprived neighborhood socially. With Syriacs thus portrayed as matter out of place in their very ability to make such a neighborhood, Hollywood and other such areas offer a convenient shorthand for xenophobic interpretations of the group's increasing economic and social standing in Sweden.

The Garlic Express

When Gabriella and I entered Hollywood together in 2009, I immediately started taking pictures (Figures 5.10 and 5.11). Many people were outside, especially construction workers. We walked past Ashur's house, past Mattias's house, and into a cul-de-sac, where a group of ten people sat outside having coffee. I said hello and continued walking. Suddenly, a woman from the group approached, speaking to me in Arabic. When she saw that I didn't understand her, she switched to Swedish, "Why are you taking pictures? You don't have the right to go around and take pictures." I explained that I was a researcher, and that Mattias, Ashur, and others had invited me to the neighborhood. She said, "That's fine for them, but I would rather not participate. Is it okay with you if I don't want to participate?" Shaken, Gabriella and I left almost immediately.

FIGURE 5.10. Houses under construction in Murverket, 2009. Photograph by author.

FIGURE 5.11. House under construction in Murverket, 2009. Photograph by author.

When I mentioned the incident to Mattias a few days later, he assessed it quickly: "Ah, she just thinks you're going to steal her ideas." "Her design ideas?" I asked. He nodded, "Well, that or she thinks you're going to rob them later." I also told the story to a Swedish urban planner in her early forties, Julia, who suggested a solution: "We'll take a municipal vehicle and drive up there. We can say it's official business, and you can take as many pictures as you want."

When I returned to take more pictures, however, it was in 2015 in the company of Linda, whose aunt lives in the neighborhood. While Linda knew the purpose of my visit, she expressed concern about being recognized as I used my camera to document the houses as we drove around: "Everyone knows who has which car. They'll wonder why Sabri's wife is taking pictures." Even so, she lamented about the outdoor arrangements of plastic flowers that were now trendy in the neighborhood. Revealing Hollywood's inner dynamics, my attempts to photograph it—from public streets while walking or driving—illustrate its extraordinary cohesiveness while also conveying its residents' fears of theft (of property or ideas), as well as the fact that even civil servants felt they could not trespass there without the symbolic shield of the municipal logo.

The "official," majority Swedish approach to neighborhoods of uniform single-family homes, and not just their Million Program high-rise counterparts, also explains some of these residents' and planners' reactions. Such new and old neighborhoods are portrayed as both social and stylistic poles, where majority Swedish enclaves, following Roger Andersson's logic, are not recognized as counter to integration policies, despite their homogeneity. For example, the neighborhood of Pershagen—on the southern side of Södertälje and characterized by typical Swedish single-family houses modeled on pattern plans—is said to be Ronna's opposite. Ishtar described Pershagen as "the most Swedish place in Södertälje" as she talked about how the Number 754 bus (sometimes pejoratively called the "Garlic Express") started in Pershagen but ended in Ronna, which she called "another world."

The Zelge Fans included this bus line on a prominent banner made for a 2007 Assyriska FF versus Syrianska FC derby. A group of Syrianska fans were shown waiting at a bus stop labeled "754" as a bus with famous Assyriska FF figures on board passed at high speed. Rather than Pershagen and Ronna, however, the bus originated at the Ishtar Gate and traveled on the road to Assyria (a road sign indicated it to be five kilometers away). When the banner was unveiled at the game, a sign reading "Full Speed toward Superettan" was strategically located underneath.

Ishtar had personal experience with the perceived differences between these areas. She had spent much of her teenage years living in Ronna, and her family (who had since moved to central Södertälje) owned and operated a small grocery store in Pershagen for several years. While her descriptions of Ronna were always complimentary, she described her workplace as an alien environment, since, she claimed, "only three or four Assyrian families" lived in Pershagen.[68] The shop itself became the location of many strange encounters with "everyday racisms,"[69] as customers made negative comments about Syriacs under their breath or directly to Ishtar and her siblings and parents. She traveled to the store by car nearly daily, allowing her to compare the spatial priorities of residents of Pershagen and Lina Hage:

> In Pershagen, it's more about the green space. In Lina, it's all about the house. . . . There's hardly any green space. When you build from scratch, you want as big a house as you can get. A Swedish person thinks differently. When you look at the houses in Lina, they remind you of American houses. I think many people tried to imitate that: the American, big houses. Swedish people are more modest. On the outside, it's very Swedish that they don't want to show off. They maybe think, oh, I'll have two or three rooms fewer because then I can have more land outside. But the Assyrians focus on the outside, the appearance. Everybody wants to be the first with their ideas. I think it's nice, but I wonder what Swedish people think. It's almost like it has to be nicer on the outside because other people will see it, too. Everyone wants to have the nicest house.

In Lina, symbols of success and diasporic patriotism are visible in the limestone pavers imported from Turkey or the Assyrian flag included in the cast iron of the entrance gate, borrowing recognizable forms from the past to make a home for the future. From (and within) these private spaces, residents transmit symbolic messages to specific publics, which they also expect to be living in close proximity.

Ashur discussed these differences when talking about the roles of the two main sides of his house. The front faces the residential street that he shares with family and friends, where symbols of his family's devotion to Assyrian patriotism are visible. Any majority Swedish passerby might see the back, so he explicitly chose to have only limited ornamentation there: "You can have an *assyrisk* clock, with the sun; maybe we could have that out here. But with statues and so on, it's better to display them [on the front] to people who like such things" (Figure 5.12). For Ashur, the two sides of the house have two distinct audiences for whom symbolic messages needed to be meticulously, but separately, considered.

Not only form but the diversity of materials used in Hollywood's homes run counter to Swedish notions that neighborhoods should be formally coordinated.[70] For both Million Program blocks and single-family homes in pattern-planned areas, the standardized appearance was intended to erase the class distinctions so clearly visible in nineteenth-century housing. One proposal discussed in meetings for the URBACT/RegGov project included the construction of traditional Swedish red houses in the midst of Ronna's mid- and high-rises as an antisegregation strategy

FIGURE 5.12. Facade with lion statues and column details on a house in Murverket, 2015. Photograph by author.

intended to attract majority Swedes. Building wooden cottages would work against the uniformity of the high- and mid-rise housing of these "concrete suburbs" *(betong-förorter)*. But to propose nostalgic, small houses in Falun red (a dark red that characterizes the region of Dalarna, where the city of Falun is located and where many of the most traditional Swedish crafts and symbols originate) with traditional white window frames is—at the same time—a critique (at least implicitly) of the bold, progressive approaches found in the newer neighborhood of Lina, just a short distance away. If Ronna is Lina's alter ego, such red cottages gesture symbolically to an agrarian, preurban Swedish domesticity and a harmoniously monotonous form, as well as to the idea that bringing majority Swedes (the assumed occupants) into a Syriac enclave would address some of its social problems.

Protect the House

As we walked around outside his house, Ashur described the messages of protection embedded in his ornamental choices of lions, bulls, and other mythological creatures:

> We'll have Assyria here. The Lion Hunter from a picture of an ancient *assyrier*. So it will be a little bit of an American and a little bit of an *assyriskt* house. I haven't decided if it's going to be a lion, the bodyguard for the ancient empire. They always had lions to scare away their enemies. Or else we'll have *taure,* the winged bull, *taure.* They're also the classic *assyriska* "*protect the house*" [said in English]. Then we'll see, maybe we'll have even more *assyriska* themes, but that's what I've thought of so far. We're not completely finished yet. Maybe we'll have a little bit of Babylonian inspiration later, but right now it's the lion or the bull that are going to protect the house.

Beyond these symbolic measures, however, Ashur had carefully incorporated the best in contemporary home-security technologies. He adapted drawings for an open-plan house—which he called "the Texas House"—for even more "protection." He said, "That maybe works in America, but not here. We don't dare to have it so open because of security. There's a lot of criminality in this city." He was especially concerned about his mother, whose chronic illness often kept her at home. He carefully demonstrated the complex system of door and window locks, including seven locks on the front door alone. If a thief broke a door or a window, an electronic security system would respond.

Elaborate security precautions such as those in Ashur's house recall the strategies used in Turkey and Syria to protect the group from menacing outsiders. Syriacs had done their best to re-create such strategies in the Million Program areas, and Hollywood took it a step further. As Ashur described, there was "safety in having everyone in the same area," since this was "like in a little village." He continued:

> It's exactly the same feeling that you had when we lived in Turkey. The entire extended
> family is going to live here soon. I think that's why people choose to live here, too. It's
> not just our extended family, it's other extended families, too, who are coming here to
> be close to each other. We also know them. We like to live close to each other.

Where bars connect the door to the wall today, the stone walls and fortress-like urban
structure of the village existed in the past. Exceeding a mere safety in numbers, this
social structure—deployed through the spatial logic of enclosure—promotes the soft
security of human surveillance.

Here, "eyes on the street"[71] collectively link twenty-first-century Hollywood to
older memories of harassment and persecution abroad, as well as to the spatial strategies employed to combat them. This may also explain some of the negative reactions to my first photo shoot there. Suggesting that some Syriac residents perceive
big northern cities as more dangerous than Middle Eastern ones, with their strong
sense of neighborhood, Mattias's assessment that his neighbor's anxiety stemmed
from her concern about her intellectual property (her design ideas) also indicates
that surveillance is used in the service of privacy in Lina.[72]

With so many eyes on the street, then, are harder security measures such as multiple deadbolts, steel doors, and professional alarm systems really necessary? The
security provided within this re-created Syriac village life has its limits, as Ashur
described:

> Today, it's very important that the houses have good security, that you have an alarm,
> a good door. The door weighs four hundred kilos, so we're well protected. Södertälje
> is a city where you have to protect yourself. This is very new also. Earlier, we thought,
> "No, we don't really need an alarm. I have the neighbor, and he can check things out."
> But we have noticed now that everyone has to have an alarm, a good alarm. And that's
> what we've installed. Every room has protection.

Marking the separation between insiders and outsiders with the latest in technologies for home security promotes a sense of safety for residents, while also flaunting
their new class standing. An expensive, four-hundred-kilo front door, round-the-
clock alarm response, and other public displays of maximum security have a social
value beyond home protection.

Anthropologist Teresa Caldeira, in her work on crime and segregation in São
Paolo, found that individual home owners used modern technologies of security and
lived in gated communities to exhibit their status. She writes, "The use of literal
means of separation is complemented by a symbolic elaboration that transforms
enclosure, isolation, restriction, and surveillance into status symbols."[73] Awareness
of the latest home-security devices casts home owners as savvy consumers while also
telegraphing the messages that Syriac residents have something to protect and prefer

a lifestyle withdrawn from the larger, dangerous world around them. The Securitas alarm-system stickers displayed in the windows of single-family homes boldly demonstrate financial success or aspirations of upward mobility among a population that was historically at the bottom of the Swedish social hierarchy.

One Syriac man in his late forties, Münir, told me that the these houses transmit social messages to majority Swedes and among Syriacs, messages that rest on questions of "status":

> I think this is a way to get some kind of recognition, to say, "Now I'm here," to get a kind of status. Many of the people who have built houses are not exactly high-status civil servants or people with an academic higher education, but are instead many business owners, those who run commercial operations, retail trade, or something like that. And there's not always so much status in that. But you want to show it in some way, "I exist. I'm here." And they do it in a bold way.

In both form and meaning, then, exterior ornamentation, pavers, and the latest in security devices in Hollywood suggest the triumph of a Syriac spatial logic of enclosure over the Swedish logic of distribution that has long sought to separate them. For owners, such choices signify their separation both from other residents of Södertälje and from their own proletarian pasts in the standardized—and then stigmatized—spaces of Million Program apartment blocks. For planners, however, the creation of a zone where outsiders need the shield of a municipal vehicle to enter creates additional anxieties about just what kind of neighborhood the *detaljplan* has permitted and whether it is so safe after all.

Harmony and "Matter out of Place"

While the houses in Lina may be the final postings in housing careers and symbols of success for their residents, many municipal planners dismissed the buildings as "tasteless" *(smaklösa)* or referred to them as "plastered palaces" *(putsade palats)*. Their critiques of the houses extended well beyond a judgment of the appearance of the individual buildings, however, becoming most scathing when they discussed neighborhoods like Lina holistically. For example, one majority Swedish member of the building-permissions department, Lars, told me that he viewed the area as problematic specifically because it lacked stylistic unity:

> It's really exciting. But there's no harmony. When I came to Södertälje in 2007, I thought, "Oh my God, this will be a place where you go on field trips." Now other architects have told me, "I'm going to take my colleagues to Södertälje and look at these areas because they are so exciting. They're so different! They're so *not* Swedish." But there are no links between the small traditional single-family house and

these big white stucco houses. They haven't found a good way to connect them, but it's exciting.

For professionals like Lars, then, the neighborhood has a dual character that stems from its owner-initiated individuality. He finds it both uncomfortably heterogeneous and ambivalently exciting, for instance, when some owners include exterior staircases and others do not (Figure 5.13). At the same time, the buyer–residents and their quest for individual expression have, in his view, failed the makers of the plan through their disregard for "harmonious" connections between the individual buildings. Hollywood separates itself from its surroundings as a conglomeration of difference and distinct personalities. In a time when civil servants like Lars are asked to integrate both immigrants and immigrant-dense areas into the city, Syriacs have intentionally marked their segregation formally and geographically through an urban design from below that sees enclaves and formal individuality in a positive light.

Lars charges that Murverket lacks a sense of being a comprehensive whole, a condition that disturbs planners' agendas. Many older planners were trained in the tenets of a dying functionalism or were at least pedagogically imbued with the notion that grand plans could create social equality. As Magnus, an urban planner in his late twenties, told me, "That we're still trained in the technical colleges shows that the link with social engineering still survives. So it's not surprising that planners can't handle areas like Lina. We wring our hands instead." With such a holistic view of the city and of their own roles in shaping its future, many planners trained in this

FIGURE 5.13. House with exterior staircase in Murverket, 2015. Photograph by author.

way regard the houses—with their at best whimsical and at worst tasteless details and forms and lack of harmony—as chaotic compositions that distress the entire urban environment. Hollywood and its components become bureaucratic "matter out of place."[74] Not only are they disturbing in and of themselves, but they also suggest a loss of municipal control. The houses represent a "danger" to the "purity" (to use Mary Douglas's terms) of the historically established system that dispersed prosperity to all through standardized forms.

In the latest *översiktsplan* (comprehensive plan) for the municipality, ratified in 2014, planners focused in part on how to create more-effective connections between urban zones that are separated from central Södertälje. Mayor Boel Godner voiced her support for this strategy, suggesting that it could go even further to create a single urban zone, as she told me in 2015, so that these "oases" would be linked. In her view, open areas within and adjacent to distinct neighborhoods like Ronna, Hovsjö, and Fornhöjden should be built upon in order to make them denser and to connect them to one another. "It's about not having any more satellites in Södertälje and, instead, densification all the way." For her, doing away with "alienation areas" *(utanförskapsområden)* remained a key aim for future urban planning.[75] No neighborhood should be left behind.

Furthermore, while majority Swedish urban planners often seem to view immigrants as a monolithic block in official documents, the socioeconomic diversity within the Syriac group indicates increasing disparities between the haves and the have-nots in terms that have nothing to do with Swedishness or spatial distribution. The ability of the well established to design and construct their own homes separates them from those who have fewer resources or who simply arrived in the city later, like Gabriella. Complaints about petty theft and even such banal offenses as throwing trash on lawns are now projected onto the new groups by the old ones. More than one Syriac resident of Hollywood connected his or her copious home security devices to the need for protection "from the Iraqis."

As some residents live in areas—such as Ronna or Hovsjö—popularly described as a "concrete ghetto" *(betonggetto),* other Syriacs live in single-family homes that are regarded as near mansions. If social mobility implies physical mobility, the erasure of the hard line drawn since the 1960s between "Swedes" and "immigrants" is here recast in terms that have far more to do with class than ethnicity. Those Syriacs who remain in Million Program housing are increasingly regarded as resource poor, new to the town, or merely unsuccessful.

Conclusion: "Special Areas for Special People"

Wistfully, Ashur said, "Most people like living here because they built their own houses. If you live in another area, you only get to choose your house. You might be happy there for a few years. But here, everyone has built their own house, so they're satisfied, and they want to stay here a long, long, long time." I asked him how long he would remain, and Ashur replied, "Two years," and laughed. Then he continued seriously, "I think we're going to be here our whole lives." His cousin Mattias quickly interjected, "What if you get married? Won't you move?" Ashur said, laughing again, "No, I'll just buy that house," pointing to Mattias's across the street.

The future that Hollywood promises in Sweden is one focused on the redevelopment of a deeply interconnected family life into a new, suburban, Syriac village.[76] Most older Syriacs came from symbiotic village communities of multiple generations of relatives living in extended-family homes and practicing subsistence agriculture. In contrast, Swedish apartments assumed increasing independence from the family, which many elders described as unsettling and isolating. Like the parents of Ashur and Mattias, members of the same Syriac families often buy plots close together in Lina, Ritorp, Glasberga Sjöstad, and other new areas. Thus, while Million Program planners sought to make rental communities of unrelated Swedish citizens, dispersed without regard to previous social ties, Syriacs have explicitly bought land to live permanently near the extended family. With the presence of other relatives in adjacent Million Program areas, staying close by also allows residents to remain connected to family members who have not yet made the same class and geographic journeys.

Residents often described how building in Hollywood created deeper emotional and physical connections to Sweden, even as, perhaps paradoxically, their dream homes are made with design practices and symbols imported from the Middle East and beyond. As Turkish limestone pavers replace the traditional Swedish lawn and an ancient Assyrian winged bull decorates a doorway, immigrants have become residents, bound through their houses to the territory of Sweden and to one another. Like churches and social clubs built elsewhere in the town, these projects illustrate that the Syriacs are now a settler society with a view toward a long-term Swedish future.

As both groups navigate the limits of the *detaljplan,* questions of nationalism, class, and professionalism become the unwritten subtext of whether stucco or wood is a more appropriate building material or why each house has to differ so radically from the next one. For urban planners, however, the Syriacs' choice to self-segregate—to live together in an enclave that forms an "un-Swedish" space at the urban scale—makes Hollywood and other Syriac neighborhoods particularly provocative. Social Democrats wanted to erase inequality, but planners see these areas as instead inscribing difference into the landscape. As Lars told me with exasperation, "We shouldn't build special areas for special people. We just don't do that in Sweden." Murverket's transformation into Hollywood, however, shows that this has happened—despite the plans.

Lars's statement also echoes a belief deeply embedded in the discourse and forms of the Swedish welfare state—namely, that social disparities could be planned away through the erasure of urban and architectural differences and through the distribution of prosperity in a standardized built environment. When these early-twentieth-century tools are used in the service of twenty-first-century integration politics, however, the denial of discrimination may, paradoxically, serve to discriminate. This attitude can be compared to similar efforts across Europe to erase diversity, such as the French policy of *laïcité,* which was originally intended to create a space for religious freedom within the nation-state (and specifically to reduce the influence of the Catholic Church). Recently, it has been used in the anxious and often-xenophobic defense of the secular society—for instance, in the restrictions on veiling among French Muslims.[77] A paradox is thus embedded in such notions of tolerance, which—like integration politics itself—encourage immigrants to retain their difference as long as it remains invisible. Difference is a positive force only when safely diffused as a minority presence among a larger majority Swedish society.

While planners have been trained to prize neighborhood standardization and to regard difference as morally suspect, standardization does not appear to be a salable commodity in the Syriac community. Hollywood and other similar neighborhoods in Södertälje present a suburban landscape that acts as the antithesis to the holistic environments that government-sanctioned 1950s and 1960s standard houses and pattern plans produced and that works explicitly against the dominant rhetoric of achieving integration through geographic dispersal. Because of their proactive roles as owners and designers, the Syriac production of Hollywood has radically exceeded and transformed expectations of immigrant participation and citizen dialogue at the urban scale.

If building for sameness and notions of harmony—via majority Swedishness—is the goal, Hollywood is extraordinarily segregated according to the definitions used in contemporary planning. Yet the residents of this neighborhood and others like it are not the needy refugees portrayed by popular descriptions of immigrants, policy brochures, and governmental research reports. If, as Sargon said, traveling from Ronna to Lina is like going "from the ghetto to the mansion in five minutes," it is nevertheless a class journey that is both consciously traveled and intentionally mapped. Marking the change physically is important for this community, and their desire to live together with other Syriacs distills this combined message of economic success and social separation.

Plots of land for new homes are still being sold across Södertälje, and new enclaves like Hollywood are on the rise. This is happening despite planners' intentions but, intriguingly, it requires their formal approval in the processes of creating a *detaljplan* or approving a building permit. Clients must follow the rules of the plans or receive official exemptions, but these new Syriac neighborhoods ask planners to adapt their professional practice or face their inability to sell plots of land intended to create revenue for the municipality. As planners adapt to the desires of Syriacs—whom they did not expect to be wealthy—the participatory role imagined for the immigrant resident is transcended, and the boundary between planner and resident is increasingly blurred through urban design from below, which requires official approval even as it upends that approval.

As much as the planners regard Million Program neighborhoods as deprived areas to be retrofitted, redesigned, or at least given a new public profile, many residents of Hollywood and other newly constructed neighborhoods, such as Ritorp and the more recent Glasberga, grew up in Ronna, Geneta, Hovsjö, Saltskog, or Fornhöjden and have family members who remain (despite Nahrin's protests to the contrary) in the standardized high- and mid-rise housing there. Some Swedish buyers cited proximity to the forest as one of the most appealing aspects of Östra Lina and considered being close to Ronna a drawback. On the other hand, a number of their Syriac counterparts view a home within walking distance of Ronna (and of their relatives and friends who live there) as a positive feature of the neighborhood, even as they build high walls around their homes. In this sense, civil servants must also rethink their assumptions about what potential buyers value. Being close to disparaged Ronna or Hovsjö might be a selling point for Syriacs who see the social value in being together.

Södertälje's new neighborhoods can also be linked to larger changes in the political and economic structure of Sweden. Even if the welfare state remains an alluring social ideal, the rise to power of the right-wing, market-oriented parties—led by the Moderates and continuing in a diluted form since 2014 under Social Democratic leadership (forced to follow their rivals' budget)—has altered the relationship between the public sphere and public spaces such as municipally owned housing. The new climate has encouraged the sale of municipal apartments *(hyresrätter)* as condominiums *(bostadsrätter)* and has introduced a new housing type in Stockholm: the "owner apartment" *(ägarlägenhet)*. Cultural geographer Brett Christophers outlines how the frictions embedded in the "monstrous hybrid" of the early-twenty-first-century Swedish housing market create more inequalities than the system knows how to absorb, as welfare-state models and market solutions collide without guidance or lucid planning.[78]

On the other hand, the increased emphasis on individual property rights signals, perhaps, a new cultural space within contemporary Swedish urban planning for alternative kinds of neighborhoods. As permitted in Hollywood's *detaljplan,* Syriac innovations completed there reflect a planning process that opens itself to discursively and materially more flexible interventions than were possible during the height of the welfare state and its more rigid forms of spatial control in the 1960s and 1970s. At the same time, these neighborhoods reflect other forms of inequality, such as the difference in housing standards among well-established and more recently arrived immigrants like Gabriella, who wondered with confusion just "who" lived in Hollywood. A socially equitable urban domestic landscape remains elusive.

Pierre Bourdieu writes, "Part of the *inertia* of the structures of social space results from the fact that they are inscribed in physical space and cannot be modified except by a *work of transplantation,* a moving of things and an uprooting or deporting of people."[79] In the case of Södertälje, such a work of transplantation seems to have taken place. Here, official municipal urban planning, where "good democratic [Swedish] citizens"[80] would be developed through independence from the family and a strict focus on sameness, has collided with an immigrant group's need for private family-focused space that, contrary to Swedish political desires, explicitly and intentionally distinguishes them, stylistically, socially, and, especially, geographically. In Hollywood, this has resulted in a hybrid domestic space defined through stone walls that signal exclusion to outsiders but create a sense of safety and cohesion for home owners. Here, residents whom planners group together under the category "immigrants" have gone well beyond the condoned modes of citizen dialogue and participation in the planning and design of this Swedish city.

In Östra Lina, Hollywood, Ritorp, Glasberga Sjöstad, and other up-and-coming neighborhoods, the substantial home-building efforts of the Syriacs have engendered urban design from below as they have reconfigured the neighborhood at large, house by house. Making enclaves by design, they have also remade the relationship between public and private space, giving both a new familial form. Most critical, efforts to build new Syriac suburban villages in Södertälje have required Swedish professional planners to reconsider how to achieve integration in a built environment over which they have decreasing control. Hollywood and its counterparts raise new questions about whether segregated areas and enclaves are the same thing, suggesting that social equality in twenty-first-century Sweden may not require that a neighborhood be formally harmonious and inhabited by any particular social proportions after all.

CHAPTER SIX

Safety in Numbers

Tolerance and Norms in Syriac Design

> Do standards sound boring? Some may consider standards a necessary evil. The word conjures images of rules and regulations. But if the fit of the shoes you are trying on seems unrelated to the size on the label, you'll be irritated for sure. . . . So—it's certainly true that standards are necessary. But evil they are not.
>
> —Swedish Standards Institute website, http://www.sis.se/

THE SWEDISH STANDARDS INSTITUTE (SIS) is a nonprofit organization that oversees standards, mediating between the national government and businesses.[1] Today, for example, the numbers and models they use regulate the building industry, offering insurers a clear set of guidelines for what should be covered. These standards grew out of the research that Swedish architects, planners, social and natural scientists, and politicians conducted during the early and mid-twentieth century. As these professionals worked together to create "building norms" *(byggnormer)* for both dimensions and modules, they explicitly attempted to ensure both quality in product design and equality among citizens. The results of their research, however, such as the *God bostad* (Good housing) publications and Stockholm's *Planstandard 1965,* redefined building construction for houses, apartment blocks, institutional buildings, town centers, and roads through supposedly universal standards that were actually highly culturally specific.[2]

This logic of both welfare-state politics and design persists today, even in a post-welfare-state condition, both as a cultural phenomenon and, more literally, in the form of the standards that the SIS oversees, which today also include standards developed abroad. In housing construction, building norms have long been regulated through a series of government guidelines. During most of the Million Program decade, these were outlined in the national Planverket's *Svensk byggnorm 67* (Swedish Building Norm [SBN] 67), effective from January 1, 1968, until January 1, 1976.[3] These guidelines were said to comprise "partly regulations which are compulsory both for the builders and the authorities, [and] partly of recommendations and directions which are optional."[4] The building norms in SBN were used to evaluate building permit applications.

As building norms embedded in midcentury ideas about modern living have encountered Syriac construction projects in Södertälje, however, they have undergone transformations that often expose the rifts between the idealized models that majority Swedish architects and planners often still pursue and the new social realities that such professionals must increasingly contend with and accept. Alternative dimensions, custom-designed forms, and imported materials have provoked dialogues—sometimes heated—between Syriac clients and majority Swedish planners and contractors. Here, arguments on the intimate scale of cabinet widths, paint colors for doors, window shapes, and emergency exits have generated debates about whether these norms still serve to reinforce the purpose for which they were created: a distributive social equality.

As a practice of welfare-state citizenship, standards were believed to develop a communal spirit and to draw on the innovations of an industrializing society, a connection that architect Uno Åhrén made explicitly in his 1929 essay "Standardization and Personality" (Standardisering och personlighet). Helena Mattsson and Sven-Olov Wallenstein highlight his defense of "a subjectivity rooted in the collective,"[5] making the adoption of standard forms paramount for modern citizens. Adhering to norms thus required submission to cultural codes that were based on a belief in research and in the Swedish nation. Rights but also responsibilities emerged from a new conception of citizenship based on conformism.

Researchers from a range of disciplines worked together to produce what is now popularly labeled the "Swedish Standard": ideal dimensions for kitchens and furniture, and maximum access to sunlight, for example. But that standard also seemed to demand that citizens relinquish the home as a site for personal expression in both decor and socioeconomic status. This renunciation also took on moral dimensions, as the authors of *acceptera* suggested in 1931: "In the past more concern was paid to how a building would appear to others than to one's own needs; in the home individuals wanted to impress guests, in local communities, traveling strangers, both perhaps wanting to boast and appear greater than they were."[6] As mass-produced products took their places in equally standardized Million Program homes, created with SBN building norms, however, choosing individualized forms and materials signified more than merely an affront to the collective spirit. Personalized expression was synonymous with backwardness and worked against the grain of a new and progressive Swedish society.

Political scientist and anthropologist James Scott characterizes standardization as a key component of the toolbox of national modernity.[7] In *Seeing Like a State,* he describes, for example, how states suddenly required surnames for their citizens, producing new condoned and unified identities in the polity. This echoes the distributive rationalities of Sweden's social and spatial agendas, where, following Michel Foucault, the disciplinary regime of the modern state "clears up confusion" and "establishes calculated distributions."[8] As Sweden disseminated good fortune to an expanded middle class through prescribed, standardized forms during the Million Program, this spatial logic also reduced the complexities of everyday life, using building norms to coalesce the nation.

While the aims were certainly noble—to engender a just society where no one would be significantly poorer than anyone else—this esteem for norms has, in many respects, become reified, and the specific products of the mid-twentieth century often continue to be valued, even as demographic and social conditions have changed. Their cultural assumptions often seem to lack validity in contemporary Sweden. Not least, the continuing reverence for and use of dimensions established in mid-century research suggests, if implicitly, that the supposedly homogeneous, majority Swedish society of the booming 1960s remains relevant.[9] With both formal and social repercussions, current plans often reflect this unstated but ostensible continuity. On the one hand, the continuity is visible in the separation of programmed areas. As Sven, one of the head planners in the Södertälje municipal-planning department told me, "There is not a single plan in the entire planning department that is not functionalist." On the other hand, the continuity extends to the social concerns embedded in today's designs, where dimensions, materials, and forms that lie outside the purview of SBN or SIS norms raise suspicions and anxieties about the Swedish future.

Analyzing the "leaky flats" of British mass housing of the 1960s, architectural theorist Katherine Shonfield describes how the ineffective defense of physical and social borders becomes a disturbance of the very science of construction. "Borders hold in what is defined and pure," she contends.[10] Faith in categories, physics, and statistics—that is, in the scientific basis of the decision making that is behind architectural products—creates a sense of safety in numbers that even a leak cannot unsettle. As she writes, "In the context of construction, science's role is to render everything measurable, to attach a number to it, and to make sure each thing keeps to its assigned class."[11] Like both the Swedish philosophy of immigrant "integration" and the notion of zoning in planning, the boundary of the category provides its own unassailable logic. This "order of things," to use Foucault's term, claims an empirical righteousness within which Swedish design has comfortably existed since the mid-twentieth century, despite decades of popular disparagement for the Million Program. Midcentury lessons about taste, size, and texture infiltrate contemporary design processes and interior designs, even in places like the aisles of IKEA, suggesting that questions about beauty and style have long been arbitrated.

New publics like the Syriacs have, however, questioned the justice of these notions of numerical equality and distribution through the building projects they have initiated, commissioned, and designed. If the Swedish Standard is expected to apply not merely in visible exterior spaces such as facades, yards, and front doors but in private interiors that are ostensibly hidden from public view, these schemes have raised questions about how far the tensile strength of the norm can be pushed. When

Syriacs hire majority Swedish contractors or when they propose their plans to the municipality, the fact that a room will not be seen from a public street often has little bearing on how negotiations proceed. Interior design, architecture, and landscaping for houses, churches, and banquet halls, among other buildings, become critical forums for the circulation and negotiation of new ideas about what it means to be modern, what it means to have taste, and, most critically, what it means to be equal. Here, the logics of numbers, borders, and standards in Swedish construction, and their basis in notions of tolerance, have been questioned—and revised.

"That Is Not the Swedish Standard!"

Upon arriving in Sweden, many Syriacs initially enjoyed the safety and high quality of Million Program accommodations, yet the restrictions on personal expression embedded in the system on which this housing was based were quickly apparent to these new residents of the modern Swedish dream. As Million Program neighborhoods came to be scorned in Swedish public discourse, Syriacs found themselves living in housing that left them also negatively categorized as segregated. For those who arrived later, in the 1980s and 1990s, arrival and settlement did not have the same positive connotations as they had for their forebears. Increasing Syriac critiques of these spaces—as an important extension of lifestyle—became a part of everyday conversation, with especially sharp critiques coming from designers among the group.

Imra, an interior design student now in her early thirties, arrived in Sweden at the age of eleven from Istanbul during the 1990s, and her family immediately moved into a two-bedroom apartment in the Million Program neighborhood of Norsborg, not far from Södertälje. She described her sense of disorientation in the neighborhood's outdoor public spaces:

> All the buildings looked the same, in color and in form, even the streets, the parking lots, the entrances to the buildings—everything was the same even in different parts of Norsborg. So, when I, completely new in Sweden, went to school, it was not a problem. I went straight there. But when I was going to go home again, I couldn't find my way home! It was horrible. It was really that all the buildings looked alike and when you're, like, in a totally new country and nervous also because you're a kid. You don't know anyone, you can't speak the language, you don't know anything, and I was completely confused. In the end, I sat somewhere and cried because I couldn't find my way home. No one cared except for one sole woman who came by after a couple of hours and was really nice and let me use her phone to call my dad. And he came and picked me up. It was only five minutes away.

Imra also described how the white materials in her apartment building were already dirty when her family moved in, yet they could not afford to change anything. Her frustrations with the Million Program's uniform approach to design (and the lack of maintenance after construction) was echoed in the thoughts of one Iraqi architect in his sixties, Stefan, who said with disgust that he believed Swedes liked to stack "one cigarette packet on top of another" and call it housing.

The neighborhood of Östra Lina was one of the first places in Södertälje where Syriacs were able to explore their design fantasies. This was certainly true for Nahrin, who today lives in a custom-designed house there with her husband and three children. Her husband Hannibal's successful businesses allowed her to remodel its interior many times, which she described as much more than a pastime. Interior design had long been a way for Nahrin to express her unique identity:

> I have always wanted to work with interior design. I mean since I was little. My mother sewed, so I designed my own comforter, my own curtains, and my own pillows. I didn't like to do things like everyone else, but I can't show it in any other way because I just don't feel free. I felt that I couldn't disobey my father or my mother, but I felt the whole time that I didn't want to be like the *syrianer*. I have my own will. I shrugged my shoulders at everyone, did the opposite. I couldn't show this through going out and smoking and drinking and partying and getting drunk and guys. I show it this way instead. I was too good to defy my parents. The whole time, I thought a whole lot of things, but I never did anything. So, "*mycket snack och lite verkstad*" [all talk and no action], it's called in Swedish. The way I have, like, really shown . . . or at least thought I've shown that I am not like all the other *syrianer* . . . was with design.

To pursue her interest in interiors as a child living with six siblings, she painted curtain rods gold and lamps black to surprise her parents, and she redecorated her bedroom in innovative ways with asymmetrical patterns and bright 1980s colors.

Nahrin, who married at the age of twenty, laughed and said jokingly, "I married because I wanted to design the interior of my house, not because I wanted to get married. I wanted my own house." For her, design was a key means to establishing her independence. The opportunity to build her own house, which she did in Östra Lina in the 1990s, seemed to offer the chance to fulfill long-held dreams. When the construction process began, however, she was surprised to discover that her majority Swedish contractors were resistant to her suggestions. She said:

> There was a lot that I didn't get to do because we built with a Swedish company. And it always has to be standard. "That won't work!" No matter what I said. "No, that won't work." The builders, they said to me, "Why do you have to make everything so complicated? Why can't you have something normal?" I said, "In that case, I would live in an apartment. I am building a house because I want to build it like I want it."

Conflicts between Nahrin and the contractors were especially apparent in questions about dimensions. For instance, she described a discussion of her specifications for a new sink:

> For them, if I ask them to do something, they say, "That is not the Swedish Standard." I heard that a hundred times! Like I said, "Can you place a little bit of tile under the sink, so that it's a little bit higher?" They said, "No, because the pipe is two and a half centimeters long, and if you build with those tiles, it will be three centimeters. It won't reach. And even if I could do it, it wouldn't be covered by insurance if it broke." So everything was a problem! And I didn't get to do what I wanted . . . *many* things!

Nonetheless, Nahrin ultimately prevailed in designing her dream home. The project also inspired others, who asked her for tips on how to work around the Swedish Standard and who even came by to investigate in person. She explained with more laughter, "My house was like a yardstick! Everyone came and measured it! Like the roof, the angle of the roof, the fence, the windows, the heights. Everything that was not the Swedish Standard" (Figures 6.1 and 6.2). In a sense, then, Nahrin's house

FIGURE 6.1. Home in Östra Lina, 2011. Photograph by author.

FIGURE 6.2. Interior of a home in Murverket, 2015. Photograph by author.

became a physical catalog much like the printed *God bostad* pamphlets, but with alternative notions of form and, critically, entirely different dimensions.

Nahrin enviously described how planning regulations for *detaljplaner* had been loosened when other people built custom-designed houses in later years in places like the Lina neighborhood Hollywood (Murverket). She noted that they enjoyed opportunities in their designs that the more strictly regulated plans for Östra Lina had not allowed. She claimed that many Hollywood residents had followed her example, since she had "set their fantasies free." In her view, they would not otherwise have dared to create such audacious houses.

In the Södertälje municipal planning department, however, opinions about new forms and sizes for homes were rather different. Julia, a planner, described how such alternative dimensions worked against cultural codes that she saw as critical to the overall urban image she was charged with creating:

> You can have a very small house—that's fine—but you can't build too large. It doesn't look rational when the others are gigantic stone houses with columns and really flashy and then you see a little Swedish house that looks like, "What is that? Is that a construction barrack?" Then maybe you should have said that the houses should lie within a range of sizes—and they can't be too small either. That's how we should maybe, maybe start thinking a little now, because by tradition we have always said that you can have a maximum size because of the building tradition in Sweden where most

people build very similar houses and there hasn't been a problem to get it to look like a neighborhood where everything corresponds to each other. But now very large differences have developed, and it looks totally strange.

For Julia, such mismatched homes clearly signified the need for more stringent regulations in future *detaljplaner*. To have an area "where everything corresponds," dimensions should be dictated by the plan, not the client.

Similar issues emerged when the parish of St. Jacob's built its new cathedral for one thousand worshippers in the Hovsjö neighborhood. The cathedral's primary architect, Sam Matloub, was labeled "Södertälje's designer" in *LT* in 2008, since he has designed everything from pizzerias to houses to Irish pubs in the town.[12] His design ideas, developed with the faith group, envisioned a behemoth, a white iconic structure befitting its future status as the largest Syriac Orthodox church in Europe.

During *detaljplanering* for the church, Södertälje's planners dealt with a host of seemingly unusual new issues, including an immense need for parking and noise abatement during the facility's projected late-night wedding receptions and parties. One board member also worked with building permits, giving the group professional insights into the potential dilemmas. Nonetheless, heated discussions arose about these concerns and around formal innovations that Matloub and the parish proposed, including the cross-shaped windows and the domed roof over the altar space. Parish priest Father Johannes described the windows as a particularly desirable feature: "In the first place, this is the first church of its kind in the entire world with this kind of architecture. The appearance isn't found anywhere, in any other church. It has these windows, which are in a cross shape. That's important."

The strictures of the standards and majority Swedish building norms were often at odds with the architect's expansive vision. As Father Johannes said:

> Everything built has to be approved according to the Swedish society's needs and demands. That's why we had to put a door where we wanted a window. We always had the Building Permit Department after us about something. Our architect had to do what the municipality wanted a lot of the time. They had so many demands. "You have to do that. You have to do this." He had a lot of work.

Thus, even using custom-designed windows or putting openings in unusual locations in the construction of an institutional building—under the oversight of a civil servant with intimate knowledge of these processes—raised questions about how to reconcile the demands of an alternative public with the accepted protocols of Swedish building norms. When Syriacs design a church with customized details or demand a sink on raised plinths in a private dwelling space, debates concern not just aesthetics but the continued relevance of the norms themselves. For planners, the Swedish Standard has typically been sanctioned as a means to create neighbor-hood (and national) harmony, while Syriacs have often rejected it as a disciplinary imposition on creative freedom.

The Culture of the Couch

Although Hollywood's bucolic location in a semiforested zone in northern Söder-tälje provides a degree of protective cover from the prying eyes of outsiders, the area's individualized architectural expressions have begun to attract attention from the community beyond its boundaries. A thread entitled "Enormous houses in Lina outside Ronna in Södertälje" started in March 2010 on Flashback Forum, a popular Swedish Internet site famous for allowing provocative opinions (including racist and homophobic ones). Participants speculated about the cost of the houses, posted a real estate advertisement for one, and disparaged them, mostly in terms pitting "us" (majority Swedes) against "them" (Syriacs).[13]

The most scathing comments, however, were reserved for the images representing the interiors of Syriac homes. For example, one commentator wrote, "They really love those marble/tile floors. Looks so damned cold and impersonal. And then those obligatory enormous leather couches." Couches and indoor flooring materials are not part of the public streetscape and, one would presume, do little to affect the everyday lives (or views) of majority Swedes in the town. Yet undesirable "enormous leather couches" and other furniture, floor tiles, lighting fixtures, and bathtubs facil-itate new modes of expression for racist sentiments as metonyms for an ostentatious Other whose tastes and patterns of consumption (rather than the physical person) serve as the objects of the posters' scorn and, perhaps, as unacknowledged bitterness that they are not in an economic position to build such homes themselves.

The construction of ornate villas with Turkish limestone stonework and sculptures of Assyrian gods may also be regarded, among certain chauvinists, as disrespectful of the national consensus on appropriate form, explicitly disturbing the notion that class status should not be visible in the built environment. The 1931 Swedish func-tionalist manifesto *acceptera* makes a specific case against traditional building forms: "The homes in the garden cities, whose forms alternate between borrowings from manor houses, farm cottages, Italian villas, and the like, demonstrate how the desire to turn our environment into a stage set has prevented us from coming to terms with our own era and the obvious conditions in which we live."[14] The effect of pre-senting "borrowings" as pernicious follies and considering pastiche to have delete-rious effects is visible in the xenophobic comments of the Flashback participants. Their critiques, with racist undertones, of conspicuous Syriac consumption suggest that the formal ostentation of new homes may also be politically offensive to an older working class in postindustrial Södertälje who lived in and built the welfare state and, more recently, witnessed its fall. Flashback Forum commentators frame their racist consternation in a way that can be read as a refusal to "accept" the symbolic value of this striking architecture.

Syriac motivations to operate outside the Swedish Standard have many facets, including nostalgia for forms from the diasporic past, but they also include a desire to portray prosperity. While we were driving around in Lina Hage one evening, Temra told me as we looked at the houses, "Everything here is motivated by the fact that people are envious." She went on to explain that—as in the theater of wedding receptions—each owner wants to build a bigger and more luxurious house than his or her neighbor. Every structure must be more ornate and eye-catching, and every family must appear wealthier than the last. House design and construction beyond the norms of the Swedish suburban landscape around them offer a new way for Syriacs to express what sociologist Pierre Bourdieu has theorized as "distinction."[15] Like women's dresses at formal events, building design has become a form of communication for those who can read it and a critical marker of taste.

Distinction for majority Swedish planners and local critics, however, is typically embedded in adherence to the Swedish Standard. For them, a failure to conform to these cultural rules suggests a lack of knowledge about where the line between the ugly and the beautiful is drawn. Julia described this:

> We're not used to it [here in the planning department]. I mean most of the people who work here are Swedes from the start, so this looks different than what we are accustomed to and what we grew up with and what we are, like, educated for. I mean, you know, educated during architectural education to be favorable toward. You are, like, brainwashed: "This is beautiful. This is ugly."

When Syriacs combine a (post)modernism that is native more to Turkey than to Scandinavia with elaborate fountains and high stone walls, planners like Julia regard the Swedish Standard as losing ground, even if she also acknowledges its basis in a form of cultural training. By incorporating symbolic references from the past, Syriac architectural projects posit houses, churches, and gathering spaces as stages and thus conflict with tenets dating all the way to *acceptera* and 1931.

In the homes and institutional structures they have recently built in Södertälje, Syriacs ignore these early- and mid-twentieth-century specifically Swedish definitions of modernity to craft their own. They redefine taste from the inside out. Working with designers like Matloub, they develop an architecture of radical difference and thus contradict the standards that have so long been a part of the national ideologies of Swedishness—ideologies reinforced through the formal education received by architectural and planning professionals like Julia. The welfare state used functionalist architecture to erase *economic* counterpublics, but leather couches, marble floors, and cross-shaped windows claim prominent space in the built environment, boldly altering the norms through which equality has long been defined. Syriac aesthetics, in effect, reassert the economic divisions that modernism virtuously tried to eliminate because these aesthetics signify wealth and, in the process, sometimes make poverty among other groups more visible.

Syriacs as Builders

The desire to build within the Syriac community stems not only from everyday interests in putting down roots in a new place or from merely having dreams for a home of one's own but also from an interest in embodying a specific form of cultural heritage. Contemporary Christians from the Middle East, in their new buildings, establish links to pre-Christian groups and to those groups' iconography and achievements in architecture. To work against the Swedish Standard is also to reconnect to sources of historic power and pride.

Many Assyriologists, in positing links between living Assyrians and the ancient Assyrian Empire, cite the work of Austen Henry Layard, a mid-nineteenth-century archaeologist whose work between the Tigris and Euphrates Rivers was focused on ancient Mesopotamia and the Assyrian Empire.[16] While conducting digs at Nineveh (near Mosul, Iraq), Layard spent time with locals who spoke Neo-Aramaic. He concluded that they were the descendants of the ancient Assyrians.[17] This connection has been debated ever since, but the iconography and scale of the palaces and temples Layard uncovered are sources of architectural pride for Assyrian nationalists today.[18]

Interior designs, architectural forms, and even choices about plants and pavers include references that link Syriacs in Södertälje to the long traditions of building in ancient Mesopotamia, Babylon, and beyond. As they connect themselves through symbols to the Assyrians, Aramaeans, Babylonians, and other ancient empires and identity groups in forms and images, they depart from the Swedish Standard and in so doing assert their conspicuous difference from the majority Swedish community through claims of a powerful past beyond the boundaries of Scandinavia. For instance, the Assyrian Association re-created the Ishtar Gate (the eighth gate to the city of Babylon, known for its blue color and decoration with animal forms) inside the Assyrian Cultural Center as the frame for its stage (see Figure 4.3). While arson, water damage, and major renovations ultimately led to the elimination of this feature, the reconstructed gate asserted symbolic cultural links between the modern *assyrier* of Södertälje and the ancient Babylonians in a highly visceral way.

The construction of major new Syriac buildings in diaspora also reasserts the Assyrian Empire's use of architecture as a tool of domination and triumphant settlement. Sonya Aho connects the ancient Assyrians' abilities in the building arts to the successes of contemporary Syriacs:

The temples became institutions that united worship and government, university and court, and not only was the human relationship to the universe and the gods developed within them, but it was also there that problems concerning the management and direction of human societies were solved. As the tangible outcome of this intellectual and spiritual development, single buildings grew to become architectural monuments, and craftspeople began to produce some of the earliest consciously produced artworks. Even today, this legacy in the art of building of that area is evidenced by the *assyrier/syrianer*'s skillful crafts and architecture.[19]

With this logic, Aho alleges a genetic association, connecting the construction projects of the ancient Assyrian Empire to contemporary Syriac buildings abroad as a form of cultural inheritance. Designing according to these imposing paradigms instead of according to the more demure majority Swedish ones becomes a matter of honor and self-respect for a group in exile.

Beyond these references to the ancient world, modern Syriacs in Södertälje also draw upon the buildings and neighborhoods that they more recently left behind in Tur Abdin, northern Syria, and elsewhere during the twentieth and twenty-first centuries. In these, their former homelands, Syriacs have also been known for their prowess in design and construction, as Fuat Deniz notes: "The *assyrier/syrianer* have, beyond agriculture, been dominant in handicrafts, for example, as shoers of horses, potters, well builders, blacksmiths, tailors, and, not least, building engineers. This last profession plays a large role because they built or restored their own churches, mosques, and minarets."[20] Contemporary contributions to the built environment in the Middle East—such as stone houses, churches, and even high- and mid-rise apartment buildings—have also, along with their still-extant ancient counterparts, been objects of specific attack by such groups as the Islamic State in Iraq and Syria. As images of the destruction of these spaces circulate abroad, new Syriac construction projects in Sweden take on increasing importance as the signs of permanent settlement and success.

In his 1981 ethnography of Syriacs, Ulf Björklund also notes that Syriacs living in Midyat before migration were well-regarded builders, a professional identity that followed many of them to Sweden:

> The Christians (here I am thinking mainly of the Miḏyoye [Syriacs from in and around Midyat]) have been and still are very skillful builders, and are also outstanding in the textile and iron goods trades. This market is much larger than the town itself. Miḏyoye have constructed beautiful houses of stone for both Christians and Muslims in the whole of Ṭur ʿabdin. The fact that it was Christians who in many cases built the mosques in the district perhaps indicates the mutual dependence.[21]

In Tur Abdin, certain villages specialized in specific crafts, and many of these processes were done by hand. George, who arrived in Sweden in the early years, described how his own childhood home had been constructed using rough-and-ready methods:

> They made bricks from the earth. They filled a hole with natural stone from the surrounding landscape. They lit leaves, leaves from the trees, and made a fire so it would melt from below. Then it transformed into something like tiny, tiny gravel. And they used it like concrete. Then they built structures out of that combination of limestone and the bricks. They were very strong. In the city, they did it in [commercial] concrete, because they had access to it, but in the small villages, they made it themselves. They didn't have roads, so they couldn't fetch concrete.

Syriacs have carried such grassroots expertise and architectural agility to the diaspora in suburban Sweden. As they pursue the construction of new homes, churches, and community spaces in Södertälje, many everyday Syriacs with dreams of building draw on amateur skills in design and construction, even if they later work with architects, interior designers, and civil engineers to finalize their designs, alter a *detaljplan,* or gain a building permit. Increasingly, however, many of the architects used within the community are design professionals who identify as Syriac (or Chaldean) themselves. For them, producing conspicuously Syriac structures, rather than ones that adapt to external "norms," alludes to both ancient and more recent building achievements abroad.

Breaking the Norm

Today, Imra moonlights for her family's construction company during the summers, fulfilling her long-held dream of being a professional designer. As a child growing up in Istanbul, she enjoyed loitering in her father's architectural office, where he designed numerous buildings, including many skyscrapers, for the town. She longed to become an architect herself after moving to Sweden, but her plans were initially sidelined. "All my friends knew that I wanted to be an architect, but then I put that aside because . . . I don't know, I was maybe affected by others, 'Yeah, but why do you want to be an architect? There are no jobs,' blah, blah, blah. So I nearly started to think, 'Yeah, okay, maybe I'll be a teacher like all the others.'"

Putting her dream on the shelf, Imra worked in cafés for ten years and married a civil engineer. Eventually, she began plans to open a café with her aunt. Her husband pointed out, however, that she seemed far more interested in designing the café's interior than in running it, and he suggested she apply to design schools instead. She did, writing an emotional application essay about her background. Shortly afterward, she began studying interior design at Konstfack, a prestigious art school in Stockholm. For her, this acceptance felt like a coup, but she was shocked to discover that her educators expected her to question and critique many of the Swedish cultural norms she had tried so assiduously to embrace:

I have been, like, divided into two, it feels like. Because when I moved to Sweden when I was eleven years old, the first thing I thought about was trying to adapt myself to this, this society. To adapt to the norms that exist here, to adapt to everything that exists. So, when I started at Konstfack and was told that one should criticize all the norms, it was, like, extremely hard on me!

For Imra, the persistent message she had heard—that, as an immigrant, she was expected to conform and assimilate into Swedish society—collided with the new cultural expectations she encountered in the hypercritical environment of the art school. There, students demonstrated their sophistication and distinction by "breaking the norms for the sake of breaking norms," as she put it.

She quickly learned, however, that breaking the norms in this setting did not overlap with the kind of boundary breaking that Syriacs typically engage in during construction projects in Södertälje. She described her encounter with an assigned book called *Svensk smak* (Swedish taste) and recalled how her instructor had challenged the group: "You have to be critical of norms!" But the text concerned questions about gender norms and assumptions—for example, as she mentioned several times, why a Coca-Cola bottle resembles a woman's body—and had nothing to do with how new groups could influence Swedish design.

Whereas Imra discovered that at Konstfack she was invited to disturb certain norms while not questioning others, architects involved in Syriac projects are often thrilled to have the chance to design something beyond the restrictive Swedish Standard. Syriac clients and designers describe the commissions as sites of escape from the long arm of a planning process that typically appears intractable from the outside.

The threat and promise of such projects typically require unusual negotiations between their proponents and the planners who must move proposals through official channels. Lars, a building-permit officer, tried to explain what "good design" meant in the context of this work:

The important thing is the buildings are good, but it's difficult to put your finger on what that means. Then again, it might be so simple that we just need to make sure that we get sufficiently . . . that we hire . . . that we make sure that we demand that one hires sufficiently good architects. It has in fact been a problem that we haven't demanded that.

The clash for Imra between Syriac desires to stand out versus pervasive attitudes about conformity like Lars's illustrates that the Swedish Standard at times has both cultural and practical resonance. The demand for a "good" architect seems to signify a desire for an architect who understands the norms and abides by them.

In 2005, the national Swedish newspaper *Svenska Dagbladet (SvD)* dedicated three full pages to the development of Östra Lina and the unexpected mixture of styles that had manifested on its streets. One article, "The New Sweden," described how residents had imported building materials and surprised local urban planners with their choice of housing forms.[22] Another, "Great Freedom Was the Plan for Lina Hage," compared the area to older Swedish neighborhoods.[23] Countering negative critiques of the neighborhood, Martin Rörby, then secretary of Stockholm's Beauty Council (Skönhetsrådet),[24] believed that the mixture of styles could be a benefit in the future, while Bengt Andrén, then head of planning for Stockholm's outer belt, noted that several highly esteemed planned areas were initially received with skepticism, even the wildly popular Garden City–inspired neighborhood of Enskede in southeastern Stockholm built in the early twentieth century.[25]

These *SvD* articles also detailed many small conflicts over construction methods, materials, and forms, most of which were conveyed as cultural differences along a dichotomy strictly and discursively divided between "immigrants" and "Swedes." For example, Lotta Lindstam, the city architect *(stadsarkitekt)* for Södertälje at the time, outlined the effects of diverging domestic desires among clientele, stating, "It can be such simple differences as that immigrants are eager to build high walls toward the forest, while Swedes want to have it open."[26] In a publication on Södertälje, a research team from the County Administrative Board wrote, "You can read the aesthetic expression taken from Mediterranean countries and materials that are not traditionally used in Swedish single-family homes *[villor]*."[27] Perceptions of hard lines between ethnicities are here recalibrated to reflect the notion that certain groups always prefer one form of aesthetic expression or one kind of standard.

Simon, an Iraqi architect in his forties who has designed several churches both in Sweden and abroad, described his frustrations with the way norms—and fear of the new—could sometimes be used to derail a project:

> Democracy [in Sweden] has gone very far . . . a little further than it should have gone. An old lady who is seventy-eighty years old comes along and says, "No, I don't want this!" Then a hundred like that come. And then it's all over—there will be no project.

The Chaldean Cultural Center Virgin Mary Church, for which he had participated in initial designs, had seen its first proposal fail when the municipality discovered a major pipe in the middle of a proposed site. As he fought both to find financing and to convince planners, backers, and the faith group itself of the viability of the project on a site at the entrance to the Million Program neighborhood Hovsjö, the ziggurat form of the building raised eyebrows (Figure 6.3). In a 2015 version of the design by architects working for the Catholic Diocese of Stockholm (now the major financial backer), this was replaced by a shedlike wooden structure (Figure 6.4).[28] Simon explained that he had "tried to forget" his first design, as it was too painful for him; he simply wanted the project built. While motivated by financial considerations, the new design also conformed to majority Swedish tastes—which

FIGURE 6.3. Original design, then known as the Chaldean Catholic Cultural Center (Kaldeiska Katolska Kulturcentrum), 2010. Source: Södertälje Kommun.

FIGURE 6.4. Redesigned building, known as Chaldean Cultural Center Virgin Mary Church (Kaldéiskt Kultur Centrum Jungfru Maria kyrka), 2015. Source: BAU Arkitekter.

he regarded as powerful—and submission to this norm gave the project a greater chance of being completed.

The Swedish Standard defines the normal by defining norms; Irene Molina goes one step further, writing, "Normality could now be rounded off to the concept Swedishness."[29] While economic considerations come into play, planners like Lars and, in effect, representatives of the Catholic Diocese of Stockholm treat departures from these spatial logics as possible offenses against an established order and as threats to the cultural codes of conduct, even as their intentions are benevolent, being ostensibly meant to facilitate social equality through conformism. Breaking the norms may disrupt the urban environment and its image, especially when they are occurring in aggregate.

From Parlor to Family Room and Back Again

Despite setbacks, the role of Syriac designers within Södertälje has also evolved greatly since the early days when a suburban Stockholm firm was hired to design St. Afrem's, the first Syriac Orthodox church in the town, which opened in 1983. As Syriac designers expand their presence in design processes, they mark, little by little, a major victory, especially for foreign-trained architects such as Simon, Sam, Stefan, and Imra's father, whose education in the field was initially not recognized as valid for such employment in Sweden but who later found opportunities to work. These designers have also been asked to slot themselves into a career for which a consensus also exists about standard modes of professional praxis. This has historical dimensions as well.

Given the important role of architects and planners in the development of the welfare state, Swedish esteem for these professionals increased significantly during the 1940s and 1950s. For designers, a new social role emerged, revising the notion of the "good commission" from the high-end luxury home for elites to the creation of a total social world. In a 1976 television documentary shown on one of Sweden's public channels and entitled *Arkitekter berättar* (Architects tell), various architects discussed this shift.[30] Architect Sune Lindström pointed out that designing a leasehold apartment block *(hyreshus)* had previously held no glamour for architects and that the typical professional education had included instruction in how to design rooms so that a maid would not disturb the hiring family. With the Million Program, however, these designers were responsible not just for the outposts of the elite but for the form of the new classless nation. They also worked for a far wealthier and more powerful client: the Swedish state.

For these midcentury architects, home interiors were to complement the utopian goals of the Million Program strictly. Measurements for new homes were aligned with prescriptions about the character of their spaces. For example, the *allrum* (family room; literally, "everything room") would be the site of dining, pantry, work, and living-room functions and was introduced in 1951.[31] In the multipurpose space of the *allrum,* families would watch television and eat together, the mother/housewife would do housework, and children, if applicable, would play. The *finrum* (parlor), an unwanted vestige of a class society, would be eliminated.

The *vardagsrum* (living room), the ideological counterpart to the *allrum* rather than the *finrum,* was therefore incorporated into planning for Million Program dwellings, with only the *vardagsrum* being mentioned in the 1964 edition of *Good Housing.* Yvonne Hirdman describes its social role for families as stemming from earlier functionalist doctrines:

> Here, the functionalist architects united themselves with earlier liberal reformers' demands: to remove the kitchen as the focus of the family's everyday life and instead locate family life in the so-called *vardagsrum.* This meant a fight against *finrummet,* the Swedish parlor, which despite need and poverty stood and exuded dignity in unheated houses. But one did not live in the parlor, and it was this unnecessary waste of space that naturally irritated the angry young people who could not accept its symbolic value.[32]

Eliminating the *finrum* in favor of the *vardagsrum* in Million Program homes, then, served as one more spatial strategy to reduce the differences between socioeconomic classes. Its removal jettisoned what had been a significant symbol of the separation between haves and have-nots.

Despite minimalist housing, however, many families took extreme measures to maintain the *finrum,* even reducing space for other functions.[33] Intentions to engineer social behaviors through floor plans were frustrated, as Leif Jonsson writes: "The apartments were built also, but, in the housing use investigation that was later conducted, one could state that the *allrum*—contrary to what the architects had imagined—was being used in most cases in the same way as the traditional *vardagsrum.*"[34] Nonetheless, the flexible *vardagsrum* consolidated household functions in a manner considered more rational, while also reflecting the rising importance of the television as a central feature of family leisure time, an active role that contrasted with the museum-like role of the *finrum.* As the single-family home experienced renewed life in the 1970s and 1980s, living-room spaces were often labeled *vardagsrum* or *allrum* interchangeably.

Individually designed Syriac houses signal a radical departure not only from rental units, where the standards of 1960s Swedish modernity paradoxically affixed social life to the so-called open plan, but even from the single-family houses of the Million Program period, which often predicated their designs on similar principles (Figure 6.5). On one visit, Hollywood resident Ashur showed me the interior spaces of his home while talking about the importance of this *"finrum,"* where he and his parents and sister regularly entertained extended family members. In their

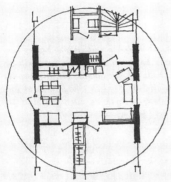

Bild 24 A och B. Exempel på kök-allrum. Huset ligger i detta fall i sluttande terräng och har sin entré i undervåningen. Kontakten mellan kök och entré är ju inte idealisk, men husmodern har dock utsikt åt entrésidan och från allrummet finns direkt förbindelse med uteplatsen på den bakre och högre belägna delen av tomten.

Den som vill förlägga huvudmåltiderna till ett annat utrymme än köket klarar sig med ett lite mindre kök än annars, eftersom matplatsen i köket kan begränsas till vad som erfordras för de strömål som alltid förekommer i hushåll med barn. Vardagsmatplatsen för hela familjen — som med tanke på dukning, servering och avdukning bör ha direkt kontakt med köket — kan ordnas i ett större vardagsrum, i ett särskilt matrum eller gärna i en ljus hall.

De flesta husmödrar med barn håller emellertid styvt på att de vill ha ett kök med en matplats som är tillräckligt stor för hela familjen, inte bara för att detta underlättar hushållarbetet utan också av trevnadsskäl. De föredrar med andra ord ett kök som inte bara utgör en funktionsduglig "verkstad" utan också är någorlunda rymligt och har en trivsam rumskaraktär. Husmodern kan också bättre ha tillsyn över de minsta barnen om de får plats att uppehålla sig och leka i köket.

26

FIGURE 6.5. Example of a combined kitchen–*allrum* in a single-family home. Source: Kungliga Bostadsstyrelsen, *God bostad i småhus,* 26.

custom-designed home, ornate furniture, a raised floor level, and decorative columns marked the entrance to this space, which was intended to project an image of stately visits and formal clothing.

When I noticed a second living room nearby with a comfortable couch, armchairs, and a television set, Ashur explained that this "*allrum*" was where he and his immediate family members or friends gathered and talked on less-festive occasions. Most newly constructed Syriac houses include both an *allrum* for watching television and talking with the nuclear family and a separate *finrum* to accommodate family members on special occasions (Figure 6.6). As Ashur told me, gesturing to the one and then the other, "Here you drink water, there you drink whiskey."

Reserved for special occasions, the *finrum* remains the domain of extraordinary events, yet Syriacs have many of these, and regularly. Ashur pointed out the platform upon which this space was located, saying:

This room is a little higher than the others. When we have visitors, relatives, friends, and so on, when people come, we usually use it. Sometimes it's often, sometimes

FIGURE 6.6. Interior of a Syriac home in Östra Lina (the family's *finrum*), 2011. Photograph by author.

there's nothing in here for a whole month. When they come, then the baklava and cookies come out, and then we roll *[då kör vi]*.

Despite its intermittent use, Ashur and other Syriacs designing homes in Södertälje nonetheless regard the *finrum,* which was not allowed in standardized Million Program apartments, as a vital part of a house's design. As Ashur noted:

> Old houses in Sweden don't have a room like this. They have only the living room, which is the *allrum, vardagsrum,* for everything. If you go to all the houses here [in Hollywood], everyone has two rooms now, separated. We have a separate set of furniture for only the family and not for guests and meetings and things like that, family gatherings.

The resurgence of the *finrum* in neighborhoods like Hollywood allows the practices of Syriac collective family life to take a central position in the Syriac home, even as it coexists with a typically Swedish *allrum.* Rather than a contrast, then, the doubling of family gathering spaces reasserts the hybridity of both the owners' spatial histories and their requirements for a successful social life in the domestic environment.

The Million Program's focus on the central familial gathering space of the *vardagsrum* also affected the role and size of the kitchen, recalibrating the apartment's center of gravity. As Hirdman argues about the functionalist kitchens that inspired later planners, "The small kitchens could also be legitimized on the basis of a rationalized housework: the kitchens should be small, effective laboratories where the small space saved steps and generated exact, rehearsed movements."[35] While other housework could be done in an *allrum,* Million Program kitchens emphasized small eat-in spaces where women would cook alone and children would not be present for safety reasons.

By 1972, most kitchens included streamlined sizes for cabinets and shelves and stainless steel countertops with a raised edge to prevent spills.[36] The standards outlined in the *God bostad* manuals and in *Svensk Byggnorm 67* were by then pervasive:

> The interior design of kitchens in the majority of Swedish houses is "standardized," which means that the individual cabinets are manufactured with dimensions set by Building Standardization (BST) and with certain given quality requirements for materials and workmanship. The report is presented in the form of standard fliers sold by the Swedish Standards Institute (SIS). Standardization has been undertaken for many reasons: to make products cheaper through long production runs of the same units, to make products from different manufacturers interchangeable and possible to complement, to facilitate design and construction, and to obtain a certain quality control of the products.[37]

With norms set for products, interior forms, and floor plans, the Swedish home took a shape that remains recognizable today, even as new market-friendlier forms of governance have taken hold.

In this sense, a government-approved universal—developed through a science of the real—successfully infiltrated the domestic realm, allowing the state to shape its citizens' most intimate interior spaces. Iraqi architect Stefan described this with exasperation: "That's what the Swedes did a lot in the 1960s. It was boring. Not just cigarette packets outside but also inside, within the house, they made tons of hallways everywhere to divide it up. There was no *spice* [said in English]. There was no life in that. It's like a hospital." He noted that many of the homes he had designed for Syriacs in Södertälje operated according to a different rationale:

> They come to me, and they say to me, "Stefan, you know how we live. You know that we live in a different way. For us, food is very important." They want to have a large kitchen. In Sweden, they don't put large kitchens in small homes. They all eat at restaurants; everyone eats lunch at restaurants. And in the evening, the Swedes just eat sandwiches. Here [the Syriacs] cook tons of food, and they also have parties. Sometimes, twenty or thirty people come, relatives. They are all supposed to sit together and eat. So the dining table has to be a very long dining table. There will be forty, fifty people coming when his daughter gets married. They all need to sit in a *finrum,* and it has to be a big *finrum.* Not this 4 by 4; that won't work. So, I work to make it possible to change the dining table, so you can extend it for twenty people or have just six. So, it is a big house, but it is also flexible, not just for six people. *That's it* [said in English].

While typically used for far more than sandwich production, the Swedish Standard kitchen pales in comparison with those custom-designed for the Syriac community, which must accommodate the large-scale cooking of Middle Eastern cuisine needed for baptisms, major holidays, and large family gatherings (such as when visitors come from abroad). Whereas Million Program kitchens emphasized linearity (in order to make the housewife's work, assumed to be done alone, as efficient as possible), Syriac kitchens might include islands with stools and are often square, allowing many people to gather and work on food preparation or simply to socialize. One kitchen serves the needs of an efficient individual; the other accommodates a different form of modernity centered on family exchange and the frequent visitors associated with a diasporic life.

To explain what motivated young Syriac couples to invest in their own homes, Imra described not only the strictures of the Million Program's spatial planning for everyday social life but also its sheer limits on size:

> In Turkey, in Midyat, even if you aren't so extremely wealthy, you always had a large house. There were often several families living together, but there was often an

enormous amount of space. You wanted to have airiness, to have space around you. In Million Program areas, okay they weren't small buildings, but they are nonetheless extremely well planned. Kitchen, living room . . . I mean, you are not supposed to have any extra space because it should, like, be sufficient. Yeah, one person gets so many square meters and not more. That's what they want to get away from.

Whether driven to work against the inner divisions of corridors or the open plan that reduced the formal function of the living room, Syriacs have often sought new models when considering how to allocate sleeping, eating, and living spaces in private homes.

This is not to say that the Swedish Standard has been entirely replaced in the Syriac designs of the new Södertälje. On the contrary, as in Ashur's home, the *allrum* still appears alongside its *finrum* counterpart, and extra-large Syriac kitchens often use fixtures and equipment developed through Swedish research. Interior design for alternative publics thus illustrates a dialectical relationship between Swedish building norms and the conspicuously different desires of Syriac families. Their homes include forms from early- and mid-twentieth-century research, today's SIS and Boverket, the villages and cities of the Middle East, and even homes seen on American and British interior design shows. These spaces reflect the hybridity both of their use and of their occupants' identities. But do they also conform to a norm of their own?

A Syriac Standard

Shortly after Nahrin married in the 1990s, she discovered that a young Syriac wife was not expected to have unusual opinions about home furnishings, especially since her fiancé's father would be buying them as a wedding present. She realized this could be a problem when he took her shopping:

It was the classic, you know. He said, "I know an Italian woman. We'll go there and buy furniture." I sat with my heart going, dugdugdugdugdug, shitshitshitshitshit. Then he shows me these enormous Italian beds that have a built-in radio and such disgusting lamps. Everyone had those Italian ones, with the really ugly lacquer. They're shiny, super-plastic, hard plastic that looks like marble, pink, and extremely ugly. And he says, "These over here are gorgeous!" And I say, "Mmmm . . ." You're a little shy when you're engaged. So I say, "I'll think about it." He says, "Why? Gabriel and Ninve bought them! George and Izla bought them! Everyone has them. They're gorgeous!"

And of course that's exactly what I don't want: what everyone has! We all marry the same year, and everyone buys them because they're a sure thing. He says to me, "If George bought them, they're good and beautiful. So why should we take a chance on something else?"

So I feel really ill and even have some mild anxiety attacks. My sister tells me, "But just say something! Say something!" It continues like this for several weeks. I want to say something to him, but I don't dare, and I start to feel really terrible. Then he orders everything, and it's due to arrive, and Hannibal and I are at a Swedish place and look at a catalog. And they have genuine stone, thick, you know, rock with glass. That was really trendy then! And leather, black leather chairs. "Hannibal, look how incredible they are! Please cancel, cancel, cancel!" He thinks they're amazing, and Hannibal also wants to impress. So, he agrees to call and cancel the order at the last minute and buy the other ones.

While Syriac designs often question the Swedish Standard, Nahrin's story illustrates that there are, nonetheless, limits on material forms of expression within the group. While she was able to convince her husband-to-be that they should buy trendy furniture rather than "the sure thing," the encounter demonstrates that everything is not on the table. Nahrin's vision worked not only against majority Swedish norms but against an evolving "Syriac Standard" that emerged in Södertälje in the 1990s.

Imra recollected that most clients for whom she had drawn up architectural plans for homes demurred when she offered her interior design services: "You know, they want to have a house that actually isn't their own original design that they have come up with, but instead like something they have seen in Lina Hage or somewhere. They want to do the same thing, just a little bit differently." She noted that while their feelings about the exteriors and shapes of their homes are progressive and daring, Syriacs are quite conservative about their interiors. There, she said, "I don't have power as an interior designer."

In the households of both *assyrier* and *syrianer,* images of the Virgin Mary and Jesus are common, along with depictions of the family tree over many centuries, offering a glimpse into the separations between different "clans."[38] In the households of Assyrian nationalists, as in the Assyrian Cultural Center and St. Jacob's Cathedral, Christian iconography often sits side-by-side with Assyrian imperial symbols and motifs, such as the ever-present image of Ashurbanipal going into battle on a war chariot (Figure 6.7). Another popular piece is a painting of a hand holding the Assyrian flag, which emerges from the ground in front of the burning city of Nineveh; it is meant to signify the tenacity of the Assyrian nation. Some choose to display the national flags of Sweden and other countries to convey their hybrid sense of patriotism (Figure 6.8). While each house is said to manifest its owners' personalities and to illustrate the distinction of each family, from the edge of the street to the wall hangings in the bathroom, the range of interior influences in new Syriac homes is actually quite narrow.

Stefan is a Chaldean Catholic and originally from Baghdad, and he described how this Syriac Standard sometimes affected commissions for institutional buildings.

FIGURE 6.7. Interior in remodeled gathering space for youth, Assyrian Cultural Center, 2015. Photograph by author.

He had immigrated to Italy in 1959, where he studied architecture at the Sapienza University of Rome under the esteemed modernist architect Pier Luigi Nervi. Stefan's success in major competitions was tempered as Mafia threats prevented the projects from being realized, and he moved to Sweden in 1969 to join relatives, bringing his Italian wife and children with him. His architectural education was not recognized in his new country, so he worked for several years in low-skilled jobs and as a teacher, but he soon began to design again, specializing in restaurants. He claimed to have imported the first kebab machine to Sweden after seeing it at a restaurant exposition in Germany.

Stefan described the radical church design he had developed for a Syriac group in another part of Sweden:

The problem with the *syrianer* is that they are extremely traditional. You can build a modern house for them, and they accept that. But the church, for them, that's tradition, that's history. You can't change it. You understand me. This is extremely important. You cannot make a super-modern church for *syrianer*. Young people like these projects, but the old people, they don't like them. They say, "That doesn't look like a church. There's no *campanile,* tower, there's no cross, nothing." And the windows, no strange windows. They have to be the regular ones. So they don't accept modern architecture for churches, unfortunately.

FIGURE 6.8. Swedish and Syriac flags inside a Murverket home, 2015. Photograph by author.

Despite the architect's frustrations with this earlier commission, a church he had recently designed in Södertälje clearly exhibits eclectic stylistic influences, distinguishing itself both from Syriac Orthodox churches in Syria and Turkey and from most Swedish Lutheran churches.

Stefan claimed a pathbreaking role for himself, arguing that no Swedish architect would have been able to handle such a commission:

> If they went to a Swedish architect, he [*sic*] would never do it like this. That you would make a restaurant in a church, a dancing room in a church, that's impossible. He wouldn't understand. A Swedish architect, he doesn't understand. It wouldn't work. That many people in a church? They don't believe it. A Swedish church takes two hundred people, one hundred and fifty, but not seven hundred, eight hundred.

Designers like Stefan view as straw men the critical strictures on space and on which functions may appear adjacent to which others. He sees these regulations as unnecessarily rigid, even as he also concedes the limitations and embedded moral imperatives within what appears to be another important frame of reference, the Syriac Standard. He claims a position for himself that, in his view, a Swedish architect trained in Swedish norms could not develop. Sharing the perspective of many planners (and perhaps even echoing the sentiments of some commentators on Flashback Forum), however, he also adheres to the notion that clear divisions exist between the design standards of majority Swedes and Syriacs. Both the Swedish and Syriac Standards have curbed his ability to express himself fully in design commissions, suggesting that, while formally contradictory, they are more similar in motivation than either group may wish to acknowledge.

Conclusion: The Swedish Standard and Its Discontents

On a 2005 episode of the Swedish home-makeover show *Från koja till slott* (From shack to castle), the home chosen for renovation belonged to a Syriac family living in Södertälje, the Makdissis. They had occupied the space, a predesigned home, for twelve years.[39] Discussing their constraints with the interior designers, daughter Helena mentioned the differences between her and her siblings' tastes and those of her parents as expressed in the house: "It is not just one style. For the most part, it's *syrianskt,* but we try to make it a little more modern. But that doesn't work because Mom always wants her *syrianska.*"

Her sister Alexandra added, "You're very worried when you're sitting on furniture like this. You're afraid that it will break, or that you'll spill something on the carpet or something." By the end of the program, the designers have replaced almost all the contents of the house with modernist-looking pieces, evoking strong reactions from all family members. Alexandra commented, "The relatives are sure going to be a bit surprised because no one we know has furniture like this. They usually have the *syrianska* style instead. But their children will be delighted."

While a Syriac Standard based in part on inherited models from Syria, Turkey, Iraq, or Lebanon may be appealing to the older generations, younger Syriacs (like the Makdissi daughters, Imra as a professional designer, and Nahrin with her interest in interior design) find new ways to express themselves stylistically outside these norms. Following Hirdman, this new generation of Syriacs may, like their functionalist architect and reformist majority Swedish forebears of the early twentieth century, view the Syriac Standard and its design products with the eyes of "angry young people who could not accept their symbolic value."[40] These progressive Syriacs' views of the future disturb the hard boundaries between majority Swedish and traditional Syriac that other planners, residents, and designers have often interpolated into decisions about form.

Shonfield writes, "In matters of tolerance, statistics are irrelevant, for tolerance by definition must be able to accommodate even the most extreme circumstances."[41] For her, tolerance itself is a fiction or "constructional mystification."[42] The clashes over definitions of taste and distinction during the process of planning and design in Södertälje suggest that Swedish norms of the mid-twentieth century are, like the British flats to which Shonfield refers, leaking. Returning to Scott's discussion about universal standards as a technology of state power and Foucault's notions of discipline as distributive, the Swedish spatial logic that created standards has accepted and maintained them as a means both to create a collective and to eliminate both inequality and particularism. SIS emphasizes this, writing in 2011:

> There is a great deal that divides us in this world. Political ideas, national ambitions, religious beliefs, a lack of knowledge, and common human weakness, which make conflicts smolder and create divisions all over the place. SIS operates in the other direction. Together with companies, organizations, researchers in Sweden and abroad, we work for that which unites, that which we have in common.[43]

Thus, even today, when the welfare state is being radically altered through a market-oriented political leadership, the rise of privatization, and international migration, Sweden continues to emphasize a safety in (the use of) numbers developed through research and analysis, as Hirdman writes, "to set life right."[44]

A welfare-state cult of the quantitative persists, and the Swedish Standard assumes the social benefits of dimensional homogeneity. But as Syriac counterpublics have produced new architectural and interior forms, these spatial practices have simultaneously questioned whether this particular standard is still a way to generate equality—this time ethnic and religious rather than socioeconomic—among citizens. Planners and residents seem to disagree about whether uniformity in measurements makes things just, and they disagree about whether the interior of a house, a church, or a banquet hall is really a fair place for a regulatory regime—or a Syriac architect or interior designer—to flex its muscles. Hybrid Syriac designs also demonstrate just how an intentional blending of forms and references operates as a mix within a system that seeks to erase, distribute, or contain it.

Some journalists and government officials have labeled Syriacs "model" immigrants because of their unique prowess in starting small businesses and because of the success of their soccer teams. Conversely, other journalists and government officials portray Syriacs negatively as instigators of corruption, black-market business practices, and other illicit activities. This dual attitude becomes overt when Syriacs commission new buildings that depart from the Swedish Standard, as evidenced in discussions on Flashback Forum and among majority Swedish designers and planners like Lars and Julia. An individual or group that can initiate a construction project is suspected for its very ability to pay for a church, house, or restaurant renovation. Often, the formal expression of these buildings is interpreted as evidence of illicit dealings.

From the perspective of many Syriacs, however, the conspicuous use of imported building materials, the stonework, the Doric columns—which materially shift their designs away from Swedish norms—represent evidence of their advanced taste and their rejection of the impositions of the stringent Swedish Standard (and its apparent distribution both domestically and abroad through the IKEA chain of stores). The inclusion of fountains or lion statues in a front yard and the use of luxurious materials inside offer evidence of an owner's distinction, just as specialized Orthodox Church spaces and innovative banquet halls with nationalist symbols convey a new and luxurious community space for a successful and settled group. Intriguingly, this design sensibility is increasingly paired with a Syriac Standard that regulates these same spaces in other ways according to strict notions of distinction, even if the designs are perceived in places like Flashback Forum and City Hall as lacking both taste and restraint.

When Simon designed his first iteration of the Chaldean Cultural Center Virgin Mary Church in Hovsjö, he regularly encountered suspicions from both the majority Swedish and the more settled Syriac communities of Södertälje during the group's search for a site:

> It was the residents who said no to the church project. First, because [those building the church] are Iraqis. There's a conflict also, a hidden conflict, between the newly arrived Iraqis and all the people who were in Södertälje earlier. You know, people don't want just anyone, just any new group to come, to have power, and to run a large neighborhood.

As the Swedish Standard has given way to a new Syriac Standard, newly arrived groups are gaining power to develop further variations on this theme. For those embedded in established social systems, whether majority Swedish or Syriac, new definitions of taste appear to be a threat against the hegemony of their divergent spatial logics.

For majority Swedish planners, however, groups other than their own often appear to be monolithic. Some civil servants described projects from both older and newer arrivals as upending the rule of law through which standards are maintained, even as these professionals sometimes did not distinguish between their choices of typology, material expressions, or social backgrounds. Lars told me, for example, "Immigrants affect our work greatly because they have another culture. They have another culture when it concerns questions of design, but they also have another culture when it concerns how one negotiates. A building permit is not complete because you've received a building permit but is instead a negotiation." In this sense, Lars saw only two categories as actors on the Swedish landscape: immigrants and Swedes.

City planners have attempted in other ways to reestablish control in new plans as they confront their concerns about their loss of hegemony over the city. Astrid, the majority Swedish development engineer, described an effort in the planning of Ritorp to outlaw so-called Mexi-brick *(mexitegel),* a white masonry material promoted in the late 1960s that is now considered tacky (Figure 6.9). She said, "I heard about an owner who had shaped plaster to look like Mexi-brick. Then we have to ask what the point is. If it still looks like Mexi-brick, then you might as well have Mexi-brick." Most land buyers in Södertälje are now Syriacs, and planners are now acknowledging their influence as a large and powerful market. As Astrid said, "You have to see what people want, or else we won't be able to sell the land."

Likewise, in the newer Södertälje neighborhood of Glasberga Sjöstad, the *detaljplan* originally specified that only three types of housing were to be allowed. Syriac designers and home owners have largely read this as another attempt to control their formal desires in favor of the Swedish Standard. Here, however, planners quickly discovered that they were powerless to regulate an expansive and affluent Syriac clientele. Over time, the rules of the plan proved untenable, and Syriacs now design their own houses much as they have in Hollywood, since other buyers were few and far between. One planner in her thirties, Frida, told me this was possible only because many Syriacs had applied for exceptions from the *detaljplan*'s regulations and had had their applications approved, repeatedly. The planning process has had to roll with the times and the community, as urban design from below has exhibited its power and as Syriacs demonstrated their "cultural intimacy"[45] with the planning processes.

Imra regarded these attempts at rigid control as a lost opportunity on the part of the municipality's planners:

Glasberga Sjöstad was of course planned as a Garden City. It was supposed to be only, like, wooden houses, small houses, pitched roofs. It wasn't supposed to have anything

Sydländskt vackra vita väggar

FIGURE 6.9. Advertisement for Ytongbolagen's *mexitegel* (Mexi-brick), as published in
Arkitektur 9 (1966): xix.

else—definitely not! That's where I can start to criticize and wonder how you plan a city when you plan in Södertälje? I don't think they thought it through when they put so many limits on what people could do. They couldn't sell the land, and people started threatening, "If I don't get to design my house then I'm not buying that!" So they were forced to accept it in the end. So, now, now you can build whatever you want in Glasberga Sjöstad when they could have planned it from the beginning, you know, like allowed a greater range of possibilities. Instead, they could have planned from the beginning, "Yes, but you have these alternatives," so that they could have managed it better from the municipality's side, and people could have actually had a few opportunities to make choices. You can't, like, demand that everyone has to have the same house. No one wants that.

In Glasberga, exceptions to the rules are less exceptional than the rules themselves, because clients refuse to purchase plots upon which they cannot build as they dreamed. Here, negotiations indicate how impotent a *detaljplan* becomes when it diverges from the social conditions in which it is meant to exist. In Imra's view, planners could have controlled the designs if they had allowed more elasticity from the start rather than attempting a draconian approach that left everyone frustrated.

Even so, from the perspective of planners like Lars, the extraordinary flexibility with which Syriacs have viewed not only materials, dimensions, and forms but also the regulatory apparatuses of planning itself creates new challenges for Swedish urban professionals. The rules on which officials thought they could rely—promised in the Planning and Building Law—are instead the starting point for negotiations with unforeseeable results.

Geographer Allan Pred and others discuss how crimes by majority Europeans and immigrants are described differently in the media. Immigrant criminals today are often assumed to be terrorists and are always immediately taken to represent their ethnic groups as a whole. Majority Swedish, French, or German criminals are, on the other hand, typically regarded as having individual mental problems.[46] As in synecdoche, the part stands for the whole, and the construction of structures that work against the accepted norms recalls debates about racist rhetoric around individual crimes.

What is merely a question of taste and distinction (or conformity) for Syriacs or, more recently, Chaldeans becomes evidence of an unbearable transgression for majority Swedish civil servants when urban design from below meets the leaky flat of the Swedish *detaljplan*. If tolerance must accommodate even the most extreme circumstances, the universal, one-size-fits-all approach to design in cities like Södertälje finds renewal in Syriac projects that deviate from this standard, while producing and adhering to new norms—sometimes equally rigid—of their own.

The New Periphery

In a class of its own, the largest *assyriska* colony in Sweden is in Södertälje—about four thousand people. The longer time goes on, the more this colony has closed itself off from the world around it. There is a tendency that the *assyrier* are now in the process of developing a community within a community.

—STEFAN ANDERSSON, journalist for *LT, Assyrierna*, 1983, 66

WITH A DASH OF SWEDISH FLAVOR added to the International Style, the recipe to blend social engineering and modernist design began with the functionalist treatise *acceptera* in 1931 and moved to the Million Program in the 1960s and 1970s. Along the way, it created a new national identity that hinged on norms as means to create social equality among citizens. Following Stockholm's Social Democratic leader Harry Sandberg, good housing would nurture good citizens and a good society. Designers and policy makers used modernism to construct a new progressive nation, as they did in parallel in France, the United Kingdom, the Netherlands, Denmark, and elsewhere. The drastic scale of Sweden's operations vis-à-vis its small population and aims to distribute modernism to all—not just to the needy—meant, however, that these interventions had far greater effects there than in other places. The discourses linking modern living to democracy and justice, however, regarded the sine wave of the public sphere as having a limited depth. Notably, these discourses also omitted a conception of social change.

Since the early 1970s, however, the borders that the makers of Swedish national policy had curiously imagined were impermeable have been challenged through international forces: global economic crises; the rise of neoliberalism, privatization, and deregulation; and, critically, the introduction of New Swedes through labor migration, refugee reception, and family reunification. Today, the nationalist dimensions of universalist, modernist designs have become questionable, both in Sweden and in Europe at large. Architects, interior designers, landscape architects, and urban planners operate in a new, fluid, ever-changing climate where national identity can no longer be reductive. To strive for sameness is a lost cause in a borderless European Union or as the Islamic State in Iraq and Syria gains territory and sends refugees fleeing before it or when the economic fortunes of Greece or the United States affect Europe at large.

Domestically, a strange friction chafes at the nation-state itself as Swedish policies of integration and multiculturalism produce hopes that immigrants will disperse around the country while simultaneously retaining particularist cultural markers. Immigrants are allowed to be different but are also meant to be not too concentrated, not too loud, and especially not too visible. In this view, any building projects that nonmajority Swedes propose add salt to the wound: they articulate difference materially and change the physical territory of Sweden permanently. Whenever controversies erupt in Södertälje, Paris, Berlin, or London over bell towers or minarets, or even over how private the interior of a mosque or church and conversations there should be, questions of multiculturalism, diaspora, migration, regulation, the state, and the very redefinition of national and European identities lurk under the surface.

In Södertälje, in the wake of these crashing and colliding forces, a new process of city making has been working against the vestiges of a long, languid, mid-twentieth-century modern project. Syriac interventions in the town suggest that European models of nationalist planning both as ideal and as professional practice are in the process of being replaced. In 1983, Syriacs completed their first major construction project with the inauguration of St. Afrem's Syriac Orthodox Church in Geneta. An achievement in and of itself, this project also catalyzed a chain of events that have radically transformed the Geneta neighborhood at large spatially, not merely in the social terms usually associated with the rise of immigration in European cities.

In Geneta, Million Program planning originally produced linear housing, wide lawns, and a full-service town center, all within a semicircular road around the neighborhood (Figure C.1). Today, however, an aerial view illustrates the radical changes made to the neighborhood since then (Figure C.2). In areas zoned for open space or industry in the 1960s, Geneta now has a large church, a series of strip malls, a major soccer arena, and practice fields, among other "unplanned" uses. The Syriacs' discrete design projects—developed through official planning and building-permit approvals—slowly accumulated to alter Södertälje's physical shape at the urban scale, a development that I label "urban design from below." In the process, these projects have required planners and designers to consider whether a universalist, normalizing approach to design is really still the best way to create social equality in a changing Sweden.

In 2009, Michael Sorkin predicted the "end(s) of urban design," suggesting that current models have arrived at a "dead end."[1] Conversely, optimistic theories of the "non-plan"[2] or "guerilla urbanism"[3] follow in the tradition of advocacy planning, arguing that citizens may be tapped for their insights or observed for their practices, helping designers build more inclusively. The power of design, however, remains with the professionals. Michelle Provoost and Wouter Vanstiphout's theory of "ditch urbanism" radically reenvisions the role of residents. Even so, ditch urbanists adopt an "oppositional" approach that requires them to "keep their master plans, visions, and ambitions tucked away" from "the powers that be."[4]

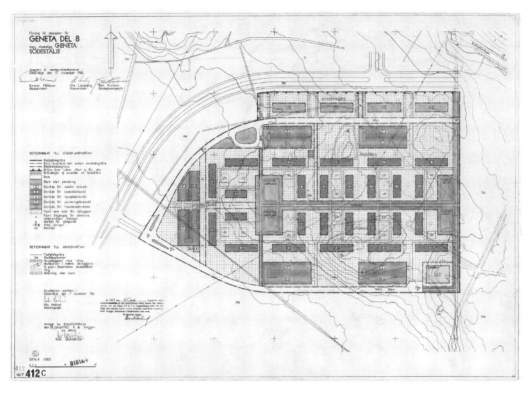

FIGURE C.1. Plan for Geneta Section 8, 1966. Source: Södertälje Kommun.

In Geneta and in Södertälje at large, a new Syriac–Swedish city has been made not through a dystopic retreat of professional design or solely through the resistance of urban "weapons of the weak"[5] hidden from municipal planners and professional designers. Instead, Syriacs have constructed new building types, with new forms and materials, and sometimes in unexpected places with the nominal (if at times grudging) approval of architects, planners, development engineers, and building-permit officers. These projects have all occurred in the light of day, since Syriac projects have obtained official building permits, legally changed *detaljplaner,* and even remade whole neighborhoods.

In design, *from above* and *top-down* typically connote official plans: the sanctioned reshapings of space that anthropologist Michel de Certeau calls "strategies"[6] and sociologist Henri Lefebvre describes as "representations of space."[7] Architectural and urban historian Abidin Kusno provides a related definition: "Urban design is understood not simply as a method of representing cities . . . but is used rather as a technique for turning cities into fields of social, cultural, and national identity production that generates a particular form of modernity."[8] In a technology of power in the service of utopian nation building, mid-twentieth-century Swedish architects

FIGURE C.2. Aerial view of Geneta, 2010. Source: Södertälje Kommun.

and planners blended the morphologies of welfare-state social agendas with functionalist spatial ideologies and science in a radically top-down approach.

Meanwhile, *from below* and *bottom-up* within both urban theory and practice usually refer to grassroots efforts, often taking the form of community activism or advocacy planning, what Sorkin calls "an enduring culture of opposition."[9] Historically, nondesigners' interventions in the city have frequently been cast as the deeds of mere "users." Like de Certeau's tactics, their measures are thought to have no specific or long-term impact on the physical form of the city, even if they are organized. Yet John Chase, Margaret Crawford, and John Kaliski's notion of "everyday urbanism" emphasizes the way nondesigners' temporary takeovers of space—as in yard sales or street vending—have become, apparently, permanent.[10] The Syriacs' interventions expand this scope. Their spatial practices have in many cases become buildings, and their slow accretion of alternative spaces has produced new centers of gravity that City Hall did not imagine.

A process traditionally regarded as inherently top-down—urban design—has occurred through piecemeal interventions from below as urban plans have been slowly, but significantly, altered. This innovation potentially points the way to viewing other European histories of an ostensibly top-down urban design through a less unidirectional lens, as progressions in which the user becomes a maker and where processes of negotiation and dialogue, while occurring through official channels, are paramount. As both a cause and a symptom of larger changes and challenges for the Swedish nation and others in Europe, urban design from below happens building by building, house by house, and permit by permit. Its results, however, are comprehensive.

From Edge to Center

The neighborhood of Geneta occupies land once dedicated to a *prästgård,* or retreat center, for the Lutheran parish priests of the Church of Sweden. This history is reflected in such street names as Klockarvägen (Church Bell Ringer's Road), the neighborhood's main road, and Prosten Linders Väg (Parson Linder's Way), named for a leading priest of the bygone district.[11] Urban plans to transform the area to a New Town were adopted in the 1960s. The first housing, approved in 1965 and 1966, comprised primarily row houses and single-family houses. Multifamily structures— especially of three and eight stories—appeared in the plans of 1967 and 1968. High-rise buildings appeared at the center, with new service roads, including Klockarvägen, Fritidsvägen, and Holmfastvägen, encircling the neighborhood.[12] Spatial delineation in Geneta, with hard edges between programmed zones, offers clear evidence of its planners' functionalist inspirations. This new satellite of Södertälje was also sited farthest from the town's historic center.

When Geneta Centrum opened in 1969, it closely followed predecessors like Ronna Centrum, with "service" spaces for a post office, a grocery store, and a library situated around an open square. Later, the brick construction of St. Mikael's (Lutheran) Church appeared, completing the small, enclosed square of the town center. Like Ronna Centrum, Geneta Centrum was intended to become a focal point for the community, and plots across the street were designated for additional commercial spaces.

While its ring road delineated the neighborhood, Geneta's flat topography and porous boundaries offered wide views over fields and trees to the west, opening out over Lake Måsnaren and the Södertälje Golf Club.[13] In this periphery, a space between Klockarvägen and the community border was left open and eventually zoned for parkland in the 1972 Geneta Section 12 *stadsplan* (Figure C.3).[14] After the construction of St. Afrem's Syriac Orthodox Church in this unplanned strip in 1983, the Syriacs quickly began a larger process that transformed this transit and buffer zone into a new commercial center.

In May 1974, a new indoor space for squash opened at Klockarvägen 108. The company advertised in *LT.* The head of the town council, Lennart Andersson, remarked on its potential, "We have so many people who have moved in other parts of the country and from outside the country. But in the bathhouse, on the golf course, and in other similar places, you always have a chance to meet your fellow

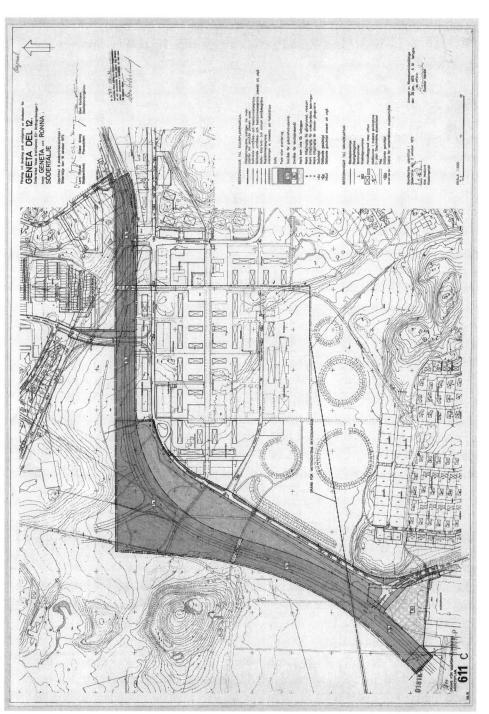

FIGURE C.3. Plan for alteration and expansion of Geneta Section 12, 1972. Source: Södertälje Kommun.

humans."[15] Such optimism for the role of squash did not last, however, and the facility eventually closed. St. Afrem's purchased the property, conveniently located next to the church.

In 1986, the group remodeled the former squash center as a social venue to complement the church. The Nyköping firm of Birgir Østling Byggkonsult AB adapted the simple shed into a meeting space and banquet hall for three hundred people,[16] and an exception was made from the plan of the block, which had been designated for commercial activities. Thirty-seven new parking spaces (rather than the sixty-nine that the St. Afrem's group had requested) and an additional 608 square meters of building area were approved in 1994. This required an official revision to the *detaljplan*. The Geneta local municipal board wrote, "Previously, there were complaints from neighbors on Klockarvägen concerning disturbances in the form of loud music on weekends and during parties. To remedy this, it was recommended that the ventilation system be replaced and the windows along Klockarvägen be locked."[17] Increasing use of the space for large social events meant further aural annexation.

In the aftermath of the Syriacs' initial innovations, the municipality drafted a new plan for the remainder of the parkland strip in 1986. The new plan called for commercial spaces, although Telgebostäder, the owner of Geneta Centrum, stipulated that food could not be sold there, writing, "The rationale for the restriction is so as not to have an establishment in competition with the shops in the *centrum*."[18] St. Afrem's Church itself submitted a letter arguing against the new development.

Despite their own objections, Syriacs eventually constructed numerous new businesses in the strip. Benjamin, a Syriac author in his sixties, described this:

> In Geneta, there were many Syriacs, and one was able to buy the area, or able to buy land there at least. Everything was close to the [Syriac] community in Geneta. It was located outside the [majority Swedish] community, which is better. I mean, as we say, it's "not in the people's eye." You can be out there and be as many people as you want without disturbing others.

Through this process of silent negotiation, moving to a peripheral strip allowed Syriacs to develop social structures without attracting negative attention.

For instance, a broadcasting station for the Suryoyo SAT television channel projects to eighty-three countries from Klockarvägen 104. The channel began in 2006 and includes programming in Suryoyo, English, Turkish, and Arabic.[19] Shows such as *Bible Contest* and *The Land of Ancestors* offer education, solidarity, and propagandizing from this nondescript brick building. Likewise, the headquarters of the Syrianska Federation occupies space there from which it publishes the national journal *Bahro Suryoyo*. Also occupying office spaces are the Syriac Youth Organization and the Syriac Universal Alliance, organizing member groups around the world in Australia, the United States, Belgium, Austria, Holland, Germany, Switzerland, and the United Kingdom. From this generic building in marginal Geneta, a diaspora is being organized and marketed for the twenty-first century (Figure C.4).

Other businesses include the Mona Lisa Banquet Hall (Mona Lisa Festvåning) at Klockarvägen 118, offering a gigantic party room, a large kitchen, and high-tech sound equipment for weddings and parties. Just below it is an indoor playground, Funhouse, with services catering to Syriac children and staff members who speak Suryoyo (Figure C.5). Despite the early demand for regulations to discourage commercial competition for Geneta Centrum from Telgebostäder, several boutiques occupy otherwise-nondescript storefronts on the strip, today owned entirely by St. Afrem's Church and Syriac family companies such as Jakob's Furniture (Jakobs Möbler) and Louay's Furniture (Louays Möbler)—furniture stores that import much of their stock from abroad—and florists, caterers, and dress shops that offer products required at Syriac weddings and christenings.

Nahrin laughed as she talked about the Syriac businesses in Geneta and referred to a cartoon published in the free magazine *NEWZ Södertälje*:

> They show two neighbor women. One of them asks, "Should we go and shop at IKEA?" The other responds, "Not on my life! They are racists. Everything is called "Emil Shelf" [referring to the male Swedish name Emil]. There's nothing that's called the "Metin Shelf" [a typical Syriac name]. Then they joke, "They're racists at IKEA! We'll go and buy our furniture at Jakobs Möbler in Geneta."

Through the filter of humor, Nahrin described the commercial enclave that has emerged in Geneta as an explicitly Syriac alternative to supposedly universalist Swedish retail environments like IKEA. This unplanned center—designed from below—offers an escape from the perceived racism of mundane commercial transactions taking place in sanctioned shopping centers elsewhere.

In contrast, Geneta Centrum—intended to be the *center* of the neighborhood—"is completely dead," according to Ishtar and others (Figure C.6). Its depopulated space has only a few surviving businesses. Winter winds whip through the small square in front of St. Mikael's Church, where the private housing company Graflund's receives visitors looking for apartments, and the bell on the door of the Tempo convenience store chimes only occasionally. In this sense, the construction of St. Afrem's catalyzed a shift, relocating the geographic and commercial centers of gravity and remaking a disused edge space into a linear alternative to the *centrum*. Such forms of alternative, diasporic modernity also work against the notion of the monolithic Swedish national identity imagined in the 1960s and 1970s and still operating through the perplexing oppositions of the integration discourse of the twenty-first century.

The Syriac enclave on Klockarvägen is now dominant and clearly visible as an urban zone (Map 6, compare with Figures C.1 and C.2), where the area originally

FIGURE C.4. Signage for Syriac businesses at Klockarvägen 104, Geneta, 2009. Photograph by author.

FIGURE C.5. Mona Lisa Banquet Hall, Funhouse, and furniture store (now Louay's Furniture) at Klockarvägen 118, 2009. Photograph by author.

FIGURE C.6. Geneta Centrum, 2008. Photograph by author.

zoned for open space is now filled with Syriac programming. These changes become much more than merely an unplanned city. Here, Syriacs have built in the aftermath of Swedish nationalist planning, but they have sought approvals and changes to zoning through official channels and plans. These forms of urban design from below have also affected other areas.

For instance, when conceiving the plans for Geneta in the 1960s, planners dedicated several areas to sports. The *stadsplan* for Geneta Section 9 included four areas for tennis, soccer, ice hockey, and (in one) volleyball and basketball, to be surrounded by 2.5-meter-high, circular earthen berms (see Figure 3.12). City architect *(stadsarkitekt)* Gunnar Påhlman and urban designer *(planarkitekt)* Olle Landberg described the rationale for the berms aesthetically, writing, "The purpose of these is in part to attain a feature of interest in the open landscape and in part to provide wind protection."[20] Smaller areas for shot put, sprints, high jump, and long jump were also on offer. The aerial view of the same area today (see Figure C.2) shows that modifications have undermined these formal gestures. A practice field for Södertälje's top division soccer teams, planned in 2003, erodes the area designed

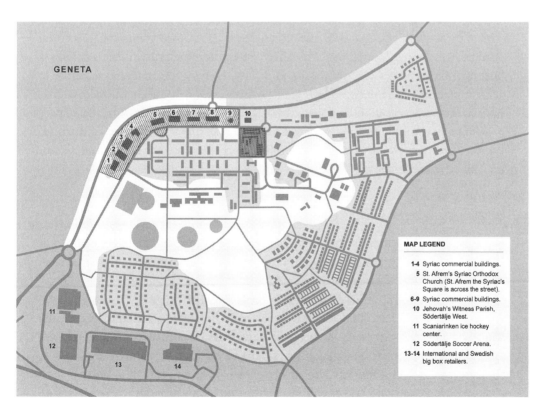

MAP 6. The Geneta neighborhood with key projects, new Syriac commercial and social district *(dot hatch),* and the original Geneta Centrum *(line hatch).* Graphic design by Eliza Hearsum.

for tennis courts, even as the circular area dedicated to soccer in the original plan lies disused.

Like the nearby Syriac commercial strip, the site chosen for the Södertälje Soccer Arena was originally designated as "land that cannot be built upon" in the 1968 Geneta Section 11 plan.[21] The site is located at the edge of the E20 freeway and Strängnäsvägen, adjacent to a major big-box shopping area. The 1968 plan referred to the nearby future construction of the Scania Rink (Scaniarinken), which was built in the 1970s. Soccer was to be an activity to take place temporarily in parking lots when they were not in use.

Today, this stretch of road witnesses lively postmatch celebrations, in which private cars honk their horns and pedestrians shout in small groups, waving flags. Fans might be greeted by the parish priest in front of St. Afrem's or by older women sitting together at picnic tables on the lawn of a housing estate to cheer on the supporters. What was intended as a mere circulation space in the 1960s has instead become a space for unscripted spatial practices. The soccer arena and practice fields have not just made the separatist, functionalist circles of the original plans irrelevant; they have also recalibrated a road, making a new public space.

As Geneta's centers of gravity have shifted, Syriacs have, in effect and in dialogue with official planners, designed the urban realm from below through piecemeal changes. No longer a satellite for Swedish industrial modernity, Geneta is now a hub for this contemporary Syriac–Swedish city. Defying bureaucrats' attempts to achieve planning hegemony, today's Geneta also suggests that their efforts to diffuse immigrants' concentration have been thwarted. No longer an edge, this Syriac space provides a new dimension to the flattened social and spatial landscapes of the mid-twentieth-century Swedish modernist project: both a linear town center and an ethnic and religious enclave.

Equality and Difference in the Built Environment

Segregated suburbs have become the dystopias of Europe in the twenty-first century, a contrast to representations of ethnic enclaves elsewhere, where names such as "Little Italy" or "Chinatown" cover them in a patina of Old World nostalgia.[22] When Swedish neighborhoods are called "Little Baghdad" or when one Stockholm subway line is labeled "the Orient Express," one hears the shrill and judgmental sound of social problematics. Some politicians regard multiculturalism as creating a comfortable space for difference, but, as Allan Pred argues, planners' attempts to "desegregate" neighborhoods reveal this tolerance to be ambivalent at best.[23]

Many debates around late-twentieth- and early-twenty-first-century immigration to Europe have portrayed equality and difference as difficult, if not impossible, to harmonize. Doomsday scenarios and tales from the dangerous European suburban front lines have been prolific: sociologists decry the failures of integration through statistical examinations of labor-market entry, journalists offer sensationalist articles about suburban criminality, and architects and planners are hired to refurbish "deprived" areas. The European suburb is made complicit in painting ever-darker strokes of gray onto this image of the city. In these views, both places and people disturb the national balance: their unassailable, unerasable difference makes the battle to create post-welfare-state equality impossible. In Sweden, segregation constitutes a crisis for a country whose politics were predicated on positive egalitarianism and notions of tolerance.

Arguing that governments have been unable or unwilling to solve segregation, anti-immigration political parties have notoriously had increasing success across Europe. The ultra-right-wing Sweden Democrats (SD) had their best showing yet in the national election of September 2014, garnering 12.9 percent of the vote. In the wake of the Syrian refugee crisis, some public opinion polls showed support for the SD at more than 20 percent during 2016 and 2017, and sometimes the SD had the second-largest level of support in coalition-ruled Sweden. Their advertising campaign in the Stockholm subway in 2015—in English and directed at tourists—falsely claimed that foreign beggars on Sweden's streets belonged to criminal gangs. Outrage against SD produced a major demonstration. SD leaders express nostalgia for a Sweden that never was, even as the menu for their 2010 election-watch party included, without hint of irony, both bulgur and pizza. If this anecdote suggests that "newness enters the world"[24] benignly through food (such that SD did not recognize their consumption of immigration-related goods), then perhaps the built environment is the next frontier.

The story I have told is a very different one. Territory—even on the municipal scale—has long been a source of conflict, but historically it has also provided treasured opportunities for new groups to make themselves seen. According to Lefebvre, "*(social) space is a (social) product*";[25] if so, immigrants who build are redefining the European cities around them rather than merely accepting the desperate conditions of social alienation that supposedly define Million Program areas and others like them. In Södertälje, what looks like segregation has sometimes actually occurred by design, as Syriacs have intentionally developed enclaves and exclusive architectural and urban spaces for their own use and by their own design, in new neighborhoods, on urban edges, and in industrial zones. Through urban design from below, Syriacs have questioned Swedish urban-planning philosophies that regard spatial segregation and social integration as opposites. New suburban landscapes like these are doing critical work in redefining European space, national identity, and architecture and planning practice today.

This process of Syriac design began earlier than the building efforts of many of the group's more recently arrived counterparts across Europe. Their establishment in Sweden occurred early by comparison. Lacking a unified homeland (or even a common passport), the stakes for them have also been high: should their settlement in Sweden fail to take root, Syriacs have no specific nation-state to which to return, and recent developments in Syria and Iraq make any thoughts of Middle Eastern repatriation appear impossible. Syriacs therefore readily invest in a Swedish future: a legacy including both communal and private spaces and affiliated institutions.

The controversial development of Södertälje's urban periphery also serves as a litmus test for the role of faith in questions of equality, given that Muslim immigrants to Europe have all too often been assigned the role of twenty-first-century invaders in a metaphorical religious war. In light of increasing Islamophobia, the recent rise of the Islamic State in Iraq and Syria, and xenophobic rhetoric against refugees that is often articulated in terms of religion, this close examination of the case of the Syriacs of Södertälje removes the razor-thin veneer of objections based in doctrinal differences. Religion is apparently not the determining factor for racist arguments against new architecture and urbanism.[26] From protests over a mosque built in Gothenburg in 2011 to the 2009 Swiss referendum that prohibits minaret construction to attempts to block St. Afrem's Church in Geneta in 1983, buildings created by immigrants—especially those considered "foreign" in form and purpose—have been equal targets of complaint and suspicion in Europe.[27]

This mistrust resurfaced recently in Södertälje when Elafskolan (the Elaf School), a Swedish–Assyrian elementary school, opened in a renovated downtown space in the fall of 2014, despite objections from many majority Swedes. About the school, which serves as an intervention into the public school system with a separatist agenda, Boel Godner, the Social Democratic mayor of Södertälje, told me, "I hate it. I think things like this are terrible because it becomes like a religious school. That is segregation for real. I talked with them when they were about to start up, and I said, 'I think this is completely wrong—no, no, no!'" While Godner's political work often focuses explicitly on making Södertälje a place where immigrants can live successfully, with this she articulates strong concerns—like those raised about ethnic or national groups that concentrate in specific housing areas—about institutional enclaves like this one. Tensions about what it means to worship separately, to celebrate separately, or to study separately are brokered through the granting and denying of building permits and the tightening and loosening of restrictions in urban plans. In these views, equality is constructed through uniformity, not through the creation of space for difference.

As creative solutions place party venues with late-night services in sites originally zoned for industry or respond to demands for houses with appearances that majority Swedish civil servants would rather not accommodate, however, the planning process scientifically developed in the mid-twentieth century has been forced toward a more organic position, to see and accept social and spatial change. All within a small geographic area, a Syriac bridal couple examines a banquet hall, her dress, and possible flower arrangements; a television station uses the "first Aramaic keyboard ever produced" (as one television station worker explained); and a Syriac Orthodox bishop sits in the VIP box at the municipal soccer arena to watch a match. These functions, and their adjacencies, were never imagined or included in the urban plans of the 1960s and 1970s.

If Södertälje's position as a suburb (if not by name, then by role) makes its territories less precious than those of nearby Stockholm, the commercial, social, and recreational spaces on its edges—in Geneta, Ronna, Lina Hage, Hovsjö, and beyond—afford even more freedom for change than does its historic downtown. Questioning such orderings, Syriacs have created new urban spaces and practices that erase functionalist separations, giving way to a mixture of religious, commercial, residential, and institutional spaces, sights, and sounds. As Syriacs have redrawn these "representations of space," to use Lefebvre's term,[28] they have done so from an extra-architectural domain that has typically been bracketed in design, even within practices such as advocacy planning that seek to tap into residents' wishes and demands.

In their challenges to the "visible modernity"[29] of the Swedish welfare state, particularly in the guise of the Million Program, Syriac changes simultaneously create new symbolic buildings (churches, houses, banquet halls, cultural associations, soccer arenas, strip malls, schools, and more) and new centers of gravity, drawing energy and interest to sites that were never imagined as social spaces. This adheres to Crawford's observation that "streets, sidewalks, vacant lots, parks, and other places of the city, reclaimed by immigrant groups, the poor, and the homeless, have become sites where public debates about the meaning of democracy, the nature of economic participation, and the public assertion of identity are acted out on a daily basis."[30]

In Södertälje, Syriac spatial practices of urbanism have taken on more significant forms, with lasting effects through the construction and use of purpose-designed buildings resulting, over time, in a significant urban metamorphosis. Many of the group's advances and challenges in constructing this new Syriac–Swedish city were even playfully represented in a new board game released in 2016, Suryopol'y, based on Monopoly (Figure C.7). Finding room for flexibility in rigidly regulated Swedish planning to create Syriac spaces—both physical and social—negotiates tensions, as building permits are accepted or declined and as *detaljplaner* are changed or retained. In the process, the requests for these changes and the decisions that result broker larger shifts in planning practices, in the shape of the city, and in the meaning of equality. Even in the expanded space that Syriacs have created, the vestiges of a midcentury belief in equality through sameness in the built environment remains. One man's story illustrates some of the continuing challenges.

New Swedish Landmarks

Ninos owns the prominent Gulf gas station at the corner of Robert Anbergs Väg and Enhörnaleden in Ronna and has lived in Sweden for over two decades. He

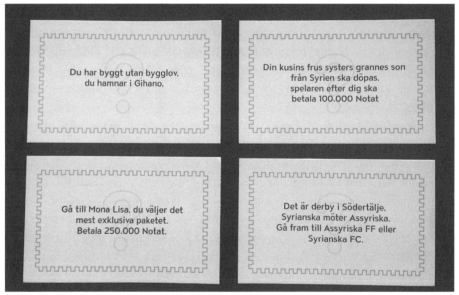

FIGURE C.7. A board game released in 2016, Suryopol'y (based on Monopoly) features properties such as Lina Hills (one of Murverket's nicknames) and the option to buy churches, including St. Afrem's. Game cards give instructions such as those shown: "You have built without a building permit. Go to hell." "Your cousin's wife's sister's neighbor's son from Syria is going to be christened, the player after you will pay 100,000 Bill." "Go to Mona Lisa [Banquet Hall], you choose the most exclusive [wedding] package. Pay 250,000 Bill." "There is a derby in Södertälje. Syrianska will play Assyriska. Go forward to Assyriska FF or Syrianska FC." The game was produced by the group Ett Folk (One People). Photograph by author.

worked at the station for several years before purchasing and renovating it, most notably by adding the adjacent Roros Pizzeria Grill and Kebab eatery. This restaurant offers both indoor and outdoor seating to its clientele, who primarily come from the adjacent high-rise housing blocks or are passing motorists.

When I visited Ninos at the station (then affiliated with Royal Dutch Shell) on a hot summer day in 2009, we talked about his plans while seated in the loud, pungent space of a service garage. With wistful frustration, he explained his dream to remake this urban corner, the main entrance to the Ronna neighborhood, into a multifunctional space that would include not only the Roros restaurant but a children's play area, a rooftop dining terrace, picnic tables, and special lighting already imported from Syria (Figure C.8):

> Originally, I intended to build two levels over there, so that there would be outdoor seating upstairs. It would be a summer place on the roof, so that people could go up the stairs and sit over there and see everything a little better. But the municipality didn't want that. We only got to build one floor and 160 square meters. I wanted to have about 200 to 220. So I made a little eatery next to the station, so that people could fill their tanks, wash their cars, and then sit in the peace and quiet and eat. There's outdoor seating. People coming from the beach in the afternoon can sit over there, sunbathe,

FIGURE C.8. Plans for a multiservice gas station, restaurant, and recreational center in Ronna, 2009. Photograph by author.

and have an ice cream or cup of coffee. I thought I would make a small playground for children there, so that families could come and eat and their children could play outside. But I didn't get everything I wanted. They said it wasn't safe.

The municipality granted Ninos permission to construct only a small portion of this imagined empire, citing planners' concerns about mixing children's recreation with the dangers of gasoline. Furthermore, vandals had destroyed five picnic tables that Ninos had managed to place on the site. This curbed his ambitions with a simmering resentment at the damage, which he regarded as a sign of envy among local neighbors.

Ninos's achievement was nonetheless significant because Roros was the first Ronna restaurant with an alcohol license to appear outside Ronna Centrum. Of these predecessors, one interested observer said, "There are not so many people who will go there because there are a lot of alcoholics who sit there. No regular person or regular woman would go there and order a pizza. They yell at her and say a lot of ugly things. No one dares to go in." While Voigt's original 1964 plan did not envisage "service" anywhere but the *centrum*, Ninos was undeterred, questioning the official town center's hegemony for neighborhood social life.

The multiplex's hybridity is also mirrored in the materials and colors Ninos selected for Roros. The gas station and the restaurant occupy opposite sides of the building; the internationally recognized, colorful design of the Gulf service station ends and is replaced abruptly with beige stonework (Figure C.9). Imported from Syria before the civil war, these stones give the restaurant a distinctive color and character, contrasting with the multicolored but monolithic high-rise housing behind them. About the stones, Ninos explained:

> First and foremost, there are no beautiful stones in Sweden, and the ones they have are expensive. They only have ordinary stone in Sweden, just reddish, coarse stones. I realized that bringing an entire container of stones from Syria would be cheaper than to buy them here. Here they cost, let's say, fifteen kronor per stone. Over there, they cost only two kronor per stone. So why should I pay fifteen kronor? And they just don't look good. Secondly, this is a restaurant. It's not a warehouse, not just an auto repair shop where you should have sheet metal or wood on the facade. It should be clear that this is a restaurant, and a slightly upscale restaurant at that. And that's why I chose stones from Syria. They keep the warmth in the winter and they're cool in the summer. They're gorgeous. They look fantastic from outside.

By using two materials for the facade, Ninos was able to signal that the one building housed two functions: the Gulf station and the restaurant. Importing materials from the Middle East to suburban Scandinavia, Ninos altered the material landscape of the city and reinvented the form of the generic Gulf station. More than that,

FIGURE C.9. Roros restaurant with imported Syrian stone facade, 2015. Photograph by author.

Ninos's combination of functions that once were separated has permitted a new hybrid alternative to Ronna Centrum to emerge. This mini-*centrum* of Syriac extraction tests both the hegemony of the original urban plan for Ronna and the current logics of urban design in operation in Södertälje.

Ninos's imagination exceeded the plans he had dared to present to the municipality. During a visit to Germany, a Virgin Mary and Jesus statue that greeted him upon his arrival in a village inspired an idea to construct something similar in Ronna. He explained, "I have a thought that I should make a Mary and Jesus statue, make it a little nicer here on the corner, so that you can see that there are Christians who live here. . . . There are many *syrianer* and Christians who live here in Ronna, and they believe in God at all times, I mean in Jesus." He was at great pains to emphasize that this statue was intended not to work against any other religious group but, instead, to portray the character of the neighborhood as a predominantly Christian one.

While Ronna's planners saw its *centrum* as complete, Ninos reenvisions his gas station both as a new service node for the area and as a prime location to announce the area's ethnic and religious difference from the majority Swedish city around it. Furthermore, while the Million Program explicitly intended to separate functions and standardize the urban environment, the Ronna Gulf station, like the strip in Geneta, places commerce and recreation close to industry. In proposing his hybrid gasoline station, car wash, and restaurant, Ninos thus challenges the prevailing Swedish planning wisdom and offers a new vision of European modernity.

Despite the setbacks, Ninos's dream remains: he still keeps the images of the statues from Germany and other sources of urban inspiration close at hand in his Gulf office. Perhaps as Syriacs make further headway in their urban dialogue with the official planners of Södertälje, their urban design from below will permit a statue of the Virgin Mary to greet those arriving in the Ronna neighborhood. Perhaps Ninos's multiplex will, eventually, shift the center of gravity away from Ronna Centrum, just as the Klockarvägen strip in Geneta has done for its affiliated *centrum*.

Utopia on the Margins

In Södertälje, Syriac occupations, changes, and designs have elbowed their own spaces and definitions of equality into what was scientifically and nobly planned to be "both a rational and a critical utopia"[31] that would expand the middle class and erase income inequalities. The Swedish urban landscape designed to improve living conditions removed the detritus of disorder associated with nineteenth-century industrialization as it standardized forms and separated functions, but it also omitted any notion of cultural or social change to the nation. The cherished Swedish urban-planning philosophies of the postwar period, as elsewhere in Europe, were intended to generate both a "particular form of modernity"[32] and a "project of legibility"[33] that was assumed to be universal but that appeared increasingly static.

In Södertälje, urban design—a practice and scale of space making traditionally defined as occurring exclusively from above—has transpired, piece by piece and building by building, from below to create space (social and material) for difference. Reshaping a city through its own official planning processes, this form of urban design emerges not from planners' computers but from Syriacs' individual, piecemeal efforts. People whom planning discourse typically portrays as mere *users* of urban space are now its creators. Inheriting a functionalist urban order and working within the constraints of contemporary planning, urban design from below—itself a semantic paradox—creates space for new programs and new publics to enter and remake the urban scene.

Unlike practices that are usually described as "insurgent," Syriac building projects are formal changes to the city, made through the official means of building permits and official plans and with the full awareness and participation of professionals.[34] In this sense, Syriacs follow Herzfeld's notion of "cultural intimacy," selectively participating in official Swedish planning structures while also crafting their own ideological and physical spaces.[35] These sites are, furthermore, made in the interest of creating something more than what journalist Doug Saunders terms an "arrival city," or a new community focused on making a "place of transition" for transactions around belonging.[36] Instead, these are spaces for and about the present and the long-term future, one that Syriacs assume will take place in Sweden.

As a new paradigm for European urban design more generally, urban design from below works slowly. In contrast to the Million Program, which sliced its way through the landscape in just ten years, Syriac spatial practices of urbanism have evolved methodically since the building of their first church in 1983. As Dolores Hayden writes, "Change over time can be traced in incremental modifications of space as much as in an original city plan or building plan."[37] Nonetheless, alternative publics such as immigrants traditionally are seen as having only temporary effects on cities. In the case of Sweden this is especially curious, considering that Syriac projects do not evince the "morphological modesty"[38] of so many urban measures from below.

The Syriac spatial metamorphosis of Södertälje has not emerged from one-off measures, resistance, or reaction but via accumulated action through legitimate, formal planning channels. While Syriacs have not produced a master plan for their own Mesopotälje, they have nonetheless had a vigorous, interventionist approach to urban form, allowing their spatial needs to infiltrate the official plans—in costly, permanent, and paradoxically comprehensive ways. As professional designers adapt their assumptions about form, location, and clients, Ninos and his compatriots do not limit themselves to conventional definitions—for example, of the town center or of which building materials should be juxtaposed. Likewise, Syriac projects work against the omnipresent Swedish notion that immigrants should not live, gather, or celebrate together, as the majority-Swedish building-permit officer Lars said, in "special areas for special people." They have nonetheless done so, by design.

As immigrants arrive and claim space in Europe, the Syriac case may indicate a way out of the supposed nightmare of segregation. In Sweden, as elsewhere in Europe, ethnic enclaves are often seen as the enemies of equality, as solely negative forces to be eradicated through urban redevelopments. Many emerging Syriac territories in Geneta, Ronna, Lina Hage, and beyond, however, do not match these portrayals of poor, downtrodden, "immigrant-dense" European neighborhoods.

Even so, tilting the lens to see these developments in a different light will require a philosophical change. Assuming their hegemony, planners may not be ready to acknowledge the shifts that are undeniably occurring and that are visible in the aerial views with which they work every day. This appears to be one of the main roadblocks in adopting a new and more inclusive form of planning practice. Even so, the construction of new buildings that Syriacs have desired, commissioned, and often designed continues to alter radically both the politics and the design of the urban environment—and with at least the nominal approval of those who hold official power.

As newcomers interact with the restrictive urban landscapes and urban regimes in which they arrive, not only do they bring with them memories of the places and societies of past homelands, but they also initiate new sites of negotiation over the future of cities and of European countries and their national identities. Rather than bringing a dystopic end to urban design, informal activism, or change after planning, immigrants—mostly nonprofessionals—redefine urban planning from *within* its existing structures. As in Södertälje, other cities will offer opportunities to redefine European urban space and, with it, Europe itself. On the suburban periphery, in the satellites of the satellites, the semidisposable, marginal, segregated areas of the past are giving way to the most important architectural and urban spaces of the European future.

Acknowledgments

The roots from the trees are now penetrating the frame of the ship itself, it won't be long before these hoisted sails cease to be needed, the wind will just have to catch the crown of the trees and the caravel will set off for its destination. It is a forest that sails and bobs upon the waves, a forest where, quite how no one knows, birds have begun to sing.

—JOSÉ SARAMAGO, *The Tale of the Unknown Island*

Saramago's *The Tale of the Unknown Island* has been a source of inspiration for me since I was a master's student in architecture and planning at work on a thesis about temporary housing for refugees. How can a ship also be an island? This seemingly paradoxical condition—combining entrenched settlement with continuous mobility—has become the major theme of my research through more recognizable keywords: migration, diaspora, architecture, and urban planning.

When I first met members of Zelge Fans during the summer of 2007, Södertälje was, to me, merely an industrial Swedish town on the margins of Stockholm County. I wanted to know more about why it had gotten attention for its "national team without a country," Assyriska FF, but it was also a place known in the media to be "segregated." The Zelge Fans—dedicated, excited, and knowledgeable—quickly explained that Södertälje was actually a global capital known as Mesopotälje. Over the next few weeks, I followed them to the stands of Södertälje Soccer Arena, on bus trips to away matches, and to late-night sessions spray-painting match banners and flags, and I met people visiting from Germany, Syria, and the United States.

I began to understand that Södertälje was both a ship and an island, like the one described in Saramago's story. There, people put down roots through physical changes, but mobility and faraway places are always on the horizon (in discussions, in architectural forms and imported building materials, and in the constant arrival of new residents). A reproduction of the Babylonian Ishtar Gate around a performer's stage at a social club, a handmade flag bearing an image of the ancient Assyrian king Ashurbanipal in the stands at a soccer match, and the Syriac Orthodox crosses dominating the silhouette of a suburban skyline were among my first clues.

The Zelge Fans introduced me to this fascinating place. In the process, they gave me abundant reasons to choose Mesopotälje as the site for this research, and I am tremendously thankful for that. I am particularly indebted to Paul Barsoum, Sargon Barsoum, Ninos Rhawi, Bobil Sharro, and Ninos Sharro, and I thank the Assyriska Fotbollsförening for similar support. Special thanks to the endlessly resourceful and always positive Danielle Barsoum, who also assisted me with research.

At Södertälje Kommun, I thank the planners and building-permit officers of the municipal planning department and the members of the URBACT team for my internship there and for the insights they shared. Thank you to Merja Olofsson for help with archival materials and to Ebba Löndahl-Åkerman for assistance with images. I am grateful for the time that the two "mayors" of Södertälje, Boel Godner and Anders Lago, made for our terrific discussions. Many thanks to Jessica Andersson and Gunilla Gottvall at the Södertälje City Archive *(Stadsarkivet)* and to Jan Bet-Şawoce of the Mesopotamia Library, Södertörn University. I am also grateful to Lennart Andersson, Göran Gelotte, Hanna Gelotte, and Nils Linder for sharing their insights into the history of Södertälje, and to the late Ulf Björklund, who generously described his experiences there in the 1970s and 1980s. A special thank you to Will Day and Rüstem Tasdemir for driving me around southeastern Turkey while sharing ideas and reflections and coffee and tea.

To those informants whose names cannot be mentioned in order to preserve their anonymity, I express deep gratitude for helping me see how and why a periphery on the periphery became a capital. I am particularly indebted to those whom I have here given the pseudonyms Ashur, Babilonia, Gabriella, Ishtar, Jakob, Julia, Katrin, Linda, Magnus, Maria, Nahrin, Sanharib, Sargon, Simon, and Sven. The time and conversations that we shared changed my perspectives not just on Södertälje but on city making and on the spatial dimensions of migration more generally.

I started this journey well before I ever set foot in Södertälje, and I had four special guides. Margaret Crawford shaped my thinking about the city, challenging me to question doomsday narratives and helping me develop a "theory smorgasbord" to analyze this unusual place. Her sharp comments always sliced through the layers of my confusion, and her super sense of humor helped me keep my "antenna up." Likewise, Michael Herzfeld provided unceasingly meticulous, generous, and perceptive attention both to this project and to my development as a scholar. He treated me as a colleague from our very first meeting and was always available for a pep talk, English grammar lesson, or Vietnamese food, and his own research and theories have been foundational for this project.

Eve Blau taught me to remember and value what I observed in the built environment—to foreground the background. Her innovative methodologies for exploring the materiality of social change were critical for helping me see what was happening in Södertälje and are now a fixture of my tool kit. Mary Steedly encouraged me to believe in my writing and in myself as an anthropologist. Not only did I first learn about ethnography from her, but I am enormously grateful for the time we spent talking about this project and in an independent study on publics and public spaces that was instrumental to it. These four advisers also supported my pursuit of a joint PhD and collaborated across departmental boundaries to facilitate it.

For their generous financial support of this project over the decade of its development, I thank the American–Scandinavian Foundation, the Graham Foundation for Advanced Studies in the Fine Arts, the Graduate School of Arts and Sciences at Harvard University, the Graduate Student Council at Harvard University, the Krupp Foundation of the Center for European Studies at Harvard University, the Philanthropic Educational Organization, and the Society of Architectural Historians. This vital assistance enabled me to have the time and space to think through the complexities of this field, to write and edit my many drafts, and to reshape words and images into this book.

A number of people supported me as I took the project from its adolescent dissertation form into maturity. Thank you to everyone at the University of Minnesota Press and especially Pieter Martin for his encouragement and patience. His thoughtful insights were crucial in helping me distill the essence of the project and fit it into a larger scholarly landscape. Thanks also to Ana Bichanich, Anne Carter, Kristian Tvetden, and Laura Westlund for their guidance and to Caitlin Newman for help with grant applications. I am also grateful to the two anonymous reviewers who provided invaluable feedback that enriched the text immeasurably. Thank you to Kathy Delfosse and Chris Davey, who vastly improved the quality of the text during different phases of the endgame. Thank you to Eliza Hearsum for crafting maps that made Mesopotälje's complex local and global geographies legible. Thank you Diana Witt for developing a thoughtful index. I am very appreciative of Brian Palmer's great advice at the end of the project.

For reading chapters and providing thoughtful comments and invaluable suggestions, I thank Cynthia Browne, Brady Burroughs, Brett Christophers, Alison Cool, Kenny Cupers, Mats Franzén, Catharina Gabrielsson, Jeanne Haffner, Julie Kleinman, Anna Knight, Johan Lindquist, Steve Moga, Mariana Mogilevich, Irene Molina, Andrea Murray, Juno Salazar Parreñas, Annika Rabo, Helen Runting, Erik Sigge, Sara Westin, and Helena Wulff. Particular thanks to Ulf Hannerz for perceptive comments on an entire early manuscript and to Justin Parscher and Gary Mack, who read and edited several dissertation drafts.

I am tremendously grateful for feedback I received on presentations drawn from this research at conferences, symposia, and workshops over the many years it has been in progress. Thank you especially to Roger Andersson, Ted Bestor, Teresa Caldeira, Lieven De Cauter, Catherine Fennell, Farha Ghannam, Janina Gosseye, Dianne Harris, Hilde Heynen, James Holston, Ann Legeby, Heidi Moksnes, Rayna Rapp, Ananya Roy, Erik Stenberg, Moa Tunström, Rosemary Wakeman, Charlotta Widmark, and Andrew Wiese. Over the years, this project required more than a little coordination and organization, and I greatly appreciate the friendly support I received on that front from Barbara Elfman, Susan Farley, Marianne Fritz, Susan Hilditch, Kerstin Larsson, Maria Morner, Cris Paul, and Amy Zug.

The project could not have been completed without the stimulating time I have spent at the Graduate School of Design and Department of Anthropology at Harvard University, the School of Architecture and the Built Environment at KTH, the School of Architecture and Planning at MIT, and the Institute for Housing and Urban Research (IBF) at Uppsala University. I have always felt encouraged in my interdisciplinarity in these invigorating environments and in the company of supportive and gifted colleagues. Particular thanks go to Erica Allen-Kim, Pelle Backman, Lara Belkind, Naor Ben-yehoyada, Ina Blind, Matz Dahlberg, Alex Fattal, Hélène Frichot, Rania Ghosn, Brian Goldstein, Katja Grillner, Anthony Guma, Terry Hartig, Jennifer Hock, Ebba Högström, Timothy Hyde, Fyllio Katsavounidou, Ateya Khorakiwala, Helena Mattsson, Anna Miller, Diana Ramirez, Bill Rankin, Göran Rydén, Meike Schalk, Paul Schlapobersky, Claudio Sopranzetti, Olga Touloumi, Florian Urban, and Kathy Wheeler. Thank you also to Engseng Ho, Karen Jacobsen, and Ajantha Subramanian for fantastic seminar courses that laid the groundwork for this research. Thank you to the members of the Sensory Ethnography workshop and the Political Ecology Working Group (especially Namita Dharia and Andrew Littlejohn) at Harvard University, who helped me reflect on the earliest incarnations of this project.

My first research in Sweden was conducted with the support of the Fulbright U.S. Student Program, and I remain grateful for that invaluable experience, to colleagues at IBF, and to the friends who expanded my thinking about Sweden then (and afterward): Stephanie Kissam, Nathan Lauster, and Ursula Lindqvist. Likewise, my advisers for earlier projects, Joseph Siry and Ann Pendleton-Jullian, encouraged my initial thinking about connections between the spatial and the social. I thank my students, especially those with whom I had the chance to discuss this project in more depth as thesis advisees and in the seminar "Making Space 'Real.'" I have learned so much from you.

When I started this research, the Syriacs had been in Södertälje for forty years; they are now celebrating a half-century since their arrival. Through fieldwork, drafts, dissertation, and more drafts, I have been sustained by great friends. Special thanks to two supportive and generous people who also inspired me with their creative and socially engaged ways of thinking about the city: Jeanne Haffner and Mariana Mogilevich. Thank you to Rebecca Ross and Kirsten Weiss, who both helped me find my way through this project while being mutually supportive in our respective rhizomatous conditions. Thank you to Alison Cool, Gabriella Körling, and Andrea Murray, who, as both great friends and great anthropologists, all aided me in navigating the personal and professional challenges of fieldwork and much more.

Thank you to friends in Sweden who helped me keep on keeping on at critical moments: Laura Almenberg, Åsa Back, Danielle Barsoum, Tina Dunker, Anna Hjalmarsson, Aralia Issa, Robert Österbergh, Helen Runting, Ryan Tebo, and Annett Walter. And thank you to friends based elsewhere who provided moral support (often accompanied by helpful questions about the project) whenever we had the chance to meet: Paula Allen, Michele Auer, Kenny Cupers, Bridget Hanna, Max Hirsh, Matt Lasner, Abena Osseo-Asare, and Ioana Urma. I am grateful to Ilnaz Samoudi Asli and Anna Dreber Almenberg for their humor and generosity (even though they "took all my money" at poker), distracting me when I needed it most. Thank you to Maria Hansson and Anna Knight who, in different ways, calmed me and helped me find ways to combine motherhood and scholarship comfortably. I have been very fortunate to have the support of Sara Westin, whose social conscience and scholarly innovation inspire me and who was a compassionate friend during the many challenges of the final stages. Thank you to Jennifer Oster Bleich, who has been in my life almost as long as my parents and whose keen eye for beauty and boundless positive energy pushed me onward.

For many reasons, including and well beyond the development of this book, I appreciate the support and love of my family. Thank you to my parents, Connie and Art Smith and Gary and Nancy Mack, who have all taught me to value education and supported me during what at times probably appeared to be an endless period of schooling. They challenged me to question convention and to analyze diverging perspectives, and they patiently and lovingly guided me toward and through this project (and elsewhere). I dedicate this book to them.

Thank you to my extra parents, Leila and Kjell Eriksson, who have made research possible after parenthood as incredible grandparents. Thank you to my sister, Jessica; my brother, Jeremy; my stepbrothers, Geoff, Drew, Gavin, and Dustin; and their families. Thank you to my grandparents, whose jokes, songs, stories, and recipes will always be with me. My gentle grandfather Earl Naylor and I shared a love of baseball that carried over to my work on soccer fandom and to Assyriska FF and Södertälje. Though he did not live to see the completion of this project, I thank him deeply for that.

Thank you and love to Kim Eriksson, who always challenges my assumptions while offering perceptive insights, gives me a soundtrack for my days, and makes delicious dinners while doing it. To our children, Holger and Ingrid, I am grateful to have the chance to see the world (and its cities) in new ways through you, sometimes in crayon or chalk. I am so lucky to know you.

Notes

1. The majority of my fieldwork was conducted using Swedish as the primary language. All translations of statements made by informants and translations of Swedish source literature are mine.

2. In the interest of protecting informants' anonymity, all of their names (except those of public figures) are pseudonyms, some personal details have been changed, and the dates on which communications with them took place are not provided.

Introduction

1. I use the term *Syriac* to refer to the two groups who are known in Swedish as *assyrier* and *syrianer* and who, in Sweden, are predominantly members of the Syriac Orthodox Church. They are termed *Suryoyo* (sg.; pl., *Suryoye*) in their everyday language, called Turoyo or Suryoyo (a branch of Neo-Aramaic that itself has many different and contested names). Throughout the book, I describe the complications and conflicts surrounding the terms used for Syriacs and their factions and surrounding the historical and contemporary politics of the Swedish words *syrianer* and *assyrier* (the former exists only in Swedish and is an ethno-religious designation; the latter is equivalent to the English word *Assyrians*—that is, a reference to ancient Assyria, and so, in this case, to people claiming descent from that group—and is an ethno-nationalist designation). The double-barreled *assyrier/syrianer* is most frequently found in recent Swedish literature as a means of avoiding the conflicts inherent in choosing one or the other. While other authors have chosen to use "Assyrians/Syriacs" as the English translation of *assyrier/syrianer,* I do not consider Syriacs to be a full translation of *syrianer.* First, the term *syrianer* exists only in Swedish, and second, the Syriac Orthodox Church is primarily known in Swedish as the *Syrisk-* (that is, not *syriansk,* the adjective form of *syrian*) *ortodoxa kyrkan* (although even here matters are not clear-cut, as some factions have in fact used *Syriansk ortodoxa kyrkan*). Further complicating this is the fact that some *syrianer* also identify as Aramaeans *(araméer)* and that some *assyrier* are not Syriac Orthodox but are instead members of other Christian denominations, such as Chaldean Catholic or Syriac Catholic (though those denominations, like the Syriac Orthodox Church, use the classical Syriac language in their liturgy). Moreover, in English, the terms *Syriac* and *Syrian* are used interchangeably to refer to the group's Orthodox Church. I favor the former to avoid

271

confusion with nationals of the country of Syria, who also figure in this story. I therefore use *Syriac* as shorthand, recognizing its significant limitations. When I refer to the subgroups as separate categories or quote from informants or Swedish sources, I use the emic Swedish words *assyrier* (sg. and pl.) or *syrian* (sg.; pl., *syrianer*) to create an equivalence that English translations do not allow. The term *Syriac* is especially appropriate for use in this book, given that the majority of my fieldwork was conducted among members of the Syriac Orthodox Church, notwithstanding other affiliations.

2. The group consisted mainly of Syriac Orthodox Christians, but "some belonged to families which had embraced Protestantism, and there were possibly some Syrian Catholics. There was also a very tiny minority of Nestorians." Björklund, "North to Another Country," 58. Footage of the plane arriving and passengers disembarking is available at https://www .svt.se/nyheter/lokalt/sodertalje/jean-och-farida-massi-flyttade-till-sodertalje?.

3. Since all migration to Sweden at this time was considered "labor migration," the Labor Market Board oversaw most of it. In 1969, the Swedish government established the State Immigration Board (Statens Invandrarverk), which in turn became the Migration Board (Migrationsverket) in 2000 and later changed its English name to the Migration Agency. For more on the sequence of events and details of the original selection process, see Björklund, "North to Another Country," 57–58.

4. Sweden's accounting of its immigrant population has been conducted according to country of origin rather than according to ethnic or religious designations. Since Syriacs hail from varied states across the Middle East, identifying exactly how many live in Sweden is difficult, but estimates as of 2012 were 90,000 to 120,000. According to a statistician for the municipality, Syriacs in Södertälje were approximately 26 percent of the town's May 2011 population of 86,246 (which had risen to 94,631 by December 31, 2016). Estimates range from a low of 12,000 (14 percent) to a high of at least 30,000 (35 percent). In his 2006 dissertation, "Vems är historien?," Kenneth Nordgren posits the number of Syriac Orthodox Christians in residence across Sweden as around 45,000, based on a 2001 estimate available in Brock, *Den dolda pärlan*. He also offers several other authors' descriptions of the size of the group since their arrival, from 8,000 to 10,000 in 1977 (see Ornbrant, *Möte med välfärdens byråkrater*) to 40,000 in the late 1990s (see Pripp, *Företagande i minoritet*) to up to 80,000 in Sweden and 16,000 in Södertälje in 2004 (see Cetrez, "Meaning-Making Variations in Acculturation and Ritualization"). For more historical estimates of the number of Syriac Orthodox Christians in the diaspora, see Nordgren, ibid., 69–71. While the official statistics make assumptions based on country of origin, more liberal accountings are based on church membership records. By contrast, the population of Syriacs in the sending region of Tur Abdin is estimated at 2,500. See Atto, "Hostages in the Homeland, Orphans in the Diaspora," 4. For an official presentation of Södertälje's demographics, see Södertälje Kommun, *Facts about Södertälje,* or, for the very latest, the website sodertalje.se.

5. Several writers claim to have coined the name *Mesopotälje,* including Syriac journalist, novelist, and filmmaker Nuri Kino. See Merit Wager, "En dag i Mesopotälje," *Svenska Dagbladet,* June 25, 2007; and Nuri Kino, "Mesopotälje in the News Again," Assyrian International News Agency, February 3, 2009, http://www.aina.org/guesteds/20090301191747.htm. In light of the ongoing Islamic State massacres of Christians in Syria and Iraq, Wager filmed Kino in May 2015 telling the story of his own grandmother's escape from the genocide in Turkey one hundred years earlier, in 1915. See "The Root: A Century of Genocide," YouTube video, http://www.youtube.com/watch?v=2kS6pG7h3Y4.

6. A 2015 documentary film, *Förvaret (Detained: Where Dreams End)*, concerned the treatment and conditions of soon-to-be-deported asylum seekers in Swedish detainment camps (where they live under lock and key). The directors, Shaon Chakraborty and Anna Persson, offered a prime example of the contrast between the public face of Swedish humanitarian policies and their practice in the often-unseen spaces of refugee processing. The influx of Syrian asylum seekers to Sweden in 2015 and 2016 further exacerbated rising tensions around Sweden's capacity to integrate them.

7. Claire Soares, "Welcome to Mosul-on-Stockholm," *Independent*, July 15, 2007, http://www.independent.co.uk/news/world/europe/welcome-to-mosul-on-stockholm-5333994.html.

8. For more on the history of Södertälje before World War II, see A. Nordström, *Södertälje stads historia*, vol. 1; A. Nordström, *Södertälje stads historia*, vol. 2; and Gelotte, "Stadsplaner och bebyggelsetyper i Södertälje intill år 1910."

9. Gelotte, *Södertälje som badort*.

10. These companies have been top sources of employment in the town and have generated prodigious regional commuter traffic. Scania AB was founded in Södertälje as Scania-Vabis in 1891. After a merger with Saab, it was known as Saab-Scania AB from 1968 to 1995. Astra AB was founded in Södertälje in 1913 and became AstraZeneca after merging with the British company Zeneca Group PLC in 1999. AstraZeneca is headquartered in the United Kingdom but has its main production facility in Södertälje (where 35 percent of its medicines are made). See AstraZeneca's website at http://www.astrazeneca.se/om-oss/verksamheten-i-sverige/Sodertalje.html.

11. For more on this, see Gelotte, Dahlström Rittsél, and Ulfstrand, *Nästa hållplats Södertälje*.

12. Ibid., 8.

13. Björklund, "North to Another Country," 58.

14. Gelotte, Dahlström Rittsél, and Ulfstrand, *Nästa hållplats Södertälje*, 3. Of the town's official population of 94,631 people on December 31, 2016, 52 percent were defined as having a "foreign background," meaning "people who are either born abroad or born domestically but with two parents who were born abroad." See the website of Södertälje Kommun for more: https://www.sodertalje.se/kommun-och-politik/statistik-och-nyckeltal/snabbstatistik-sodertalje/.

15. R. Andersson, "Socio-spatial Dynamics," 408.

16. Dawod, "Uppstickarlaget," 5.

17. The major refugee crisis in the wake of several years of civil war in Syria and the turbulence in Iraq has had deep reverberations in Sweden. The atrocities of Bashar al-Assad's government, al-Qaeda, and the Islamic State (including its systematic brutality and such major actions as its takeover of Mosul in the summer of 2014) have particularly affected religious minorities. These push factors, along with the reluctance of other European governments to accept refugees, have been key for recent discussions of Swedish immigration and foreign policy. In 2013, Sweden granted permanent residency (and the right to family reunification) to all refugees from Syria who had previously been granted temporary permits. In 2014, Sweden was the recipient of the second-largest number of asylum applications in the European Union, and the most per capita. Newcomers to Södertälje from Syria and Iraq mostly identify as Christian but add further dimensions to the already complex *assyrier* and *syrianer* issue. They belong variously to the Syriac Orthodox, Asyrrian Church of the East,

Nestorian (Church of the East), Chaldean (Catholic), or Protestant denominations but may also identify as *assyrier* or as *araméer*. While these groups use classical Syriac for biblical readings, Iraqis often use Arabic during church sermons, while priests for the Syriacs who arrived from Turkey, Lebanon, and Syria (at least in the early years) typically speak to them in Suryoyo. The recently arrived Syrian and Iraqi groups differ sharply from the Syriacs who came to Södertälje before the recent crises, since they were mostly protected minorities under Bashar al-Assad's and Saddam Hussein's governments in Syria and Iraq. Those who came later are more likely to refer to themselves as *assyrier/syrianer and* Syrian or Iraqi, a compound understanding of their identities that those coming earlier are much less likely to use. See Cecilia Wikström and Ninos Maraha, "Glöm inte de kristna i Irak," *Newsmill,* October 4, 2011.

18. See Ivar Ekman, "The Reach of War: Iraqi Refugees Find Sanctuary in Sweden," *New York Times,* January 16, 2007; and Ekman, "Södertälje Journal: Far from War, a Town with a Well-Used Welcome Mat," *New York Times,* June 13, 2007. The potential for such generosity to end was also present as Iraqis arrived. See Mary Jordan, "Iraqi Refugees Find Sweden's Doors Closing: Immigrants Overtax System, Critics Say," *Washington Post,* April 10, 2008. While the arrival of Iraqis raised many questions for Sweden's welfare state, the doors "closed" more radically when Sweden resumed border controls with Denmark in the context of Syrian war-refugee migration in early 2016. See Andreas Önnerfors, "These Denmark–Sweden Border Controls Turn Back the Clock to a Pre-Europe Age," *Guardian,* January 4, 2016.

19. "Assyrian Football in Sweden," segment on *Sportsworld,* Al Jazeera English, August 21, 2007, YouTube video, https://www.youtube.com/watch?v=qVRjKJwKKk8.

20. After Sweden provided permanent residency to Syrians holding temporary permits in 2013, the country received 81,301 asylum seekers in 2014 and then broke its record with 162,877 persons in 2015. Unprecedented numbers of asylum seekers, critiques of national policy, and the rise of the anti-immigration Sweden Democrats, however, led to a new and much-debated law that took effect in July 2016. This law limits residence permits to three years for those asylum seekers whose applications are approved under the 1951 United Nations Convention on Refugees definition and to just thirteen months for those who are acknowledged to be "[in] need of subsidiary protection." For more on the arrival of Syrian refugees, see Christopher Harress, "Syrian and Iraqi Refugees Are Half the Population of This Swedish City," *International Business Times,* July 3, 2014; and Joanna Kakissis, "Sweden's Tolerance Is Tested by Tide of Syrian Immigrants," *National Public Radio Morning Edition,* December 5, 2014. For the 2016 law on residence permits, see https://www.riksdagen.se/sv/dokument-lagar/dokument/svensk-forfattningssamling/lag-2016752-om-tillfalliga-begransningar-av_sfs-2016-752 and the Swedish Migration Agency website, https://www.migrationsverket.se.

21. Following the lead of many recent journalists and scholars who immigrated to Sweden or have parents who did, I use the term *majority Swedes* in lieu of more static, unsatisfying, and exclusionary alternatives such as *ethnic Swedes* or *native-born Swedes.*

22. Quoted in Einar Haakaas and Frode Sætran, "-Vi bor alle i samma by, men ikke i same verden," *Aftenposten,* May 15, 2015, http://www.aftenposten.no/nyheter/iriks--Vi-bor-alle-i-samme-by_-men-ikke-i-samme-verden-8021162.html.

23. The neighborhoods were Ronna, Geneta, and Lina. See Anders Johansson and Linda Hjertén, "Polisens hemliga rapport: Här är Stockholms läns farligaste områden," *Aftonbladet,* February 3, 2016, http://www.aftonbladet.se/nyheter/krim/article22190105.ab.

24. Rakel Chukri, "Vi syrianer är bäst i klassen," *Expressen,* September 20, 2005, http://www.expressen.se/debatt/vi-syrianer-ar-bast-i-klassen.

25. For example, Bowen, *Why the French Don't Like Headscarves*; Mandel, *Cosmopolitan Anxieties*; and Silverstein, *Algeria in France.*

26. Magnusson Turner, "Invandring och segregation"; Molina, "Stadens rasifiering"; Pred, *Even in Sweden*; and Bleich, *Race Politics in Britain and France.*

27. Christophers, "A Monstrous Hybrid."

28. Low, *Behind the Gates*; and Herzfeld, *Evicted from Eternity.*

29. Crawford, "Contesting the Public Realm," 4. See also Crawford and Cenzatti, "On Public Spaces, Quasi-Public Spaces, and Public Quasi Spaces."

30. For a seminal take on this, see Hannerz, *Exploring the City.*

31. Sandercock, *Toward Cosmopolis,* 27, 30.

32. Khakee, "Politics, Methods, and Planning Culture"; Khakee and Johansson, *Staden och invandrarna*; Kings, "Till det lokalas försvar"; and Olsson, "Den självorganiserade staden."

33. Ghannam, *Remaking the Modern,* 180.

34. Herzfeld, *Cultural Intimacy.*

35. Williams, *The Country and the City,* 12.

36. Sieverts, *Cities without Cities.*

37. Bourdieu, *Distinction.*

38. Kusno, "Violence of Categories," 45n2. See also Kusno, *The Appearances of Memory.*

39. Agamben, "We Refugees."

40. I also draw on anthropologist Liisa Malkki's work on how the spaces of the "town" and the "refugee camp" engendered differing notions of national belonging among Hutu refugees in Burundi. Malkki illustrates an intriguing relationship between the material dimensions of settlement and self-perception for nations in exile. See Malkki, *Purity and Exile*; and Malkki, "Speechless Emissaries."

41. Brah, *Cartographies of Diaspora.*

42. Rabo, "'Familjen betyder allt' eller 'Vi blir snart lika kalla som svenskarna,'" 216–17.

43. Rakel Chukri, "Vi syrianer är bäst i klassen." This is also quoted in Rabo, "'Familjen betyder allt' eller 'Vi blir snart lika kalla som svenskarna,'" 206–7.

44. Nuri Kino quoted in Haore Sulaiman, "Arbetarstad som blev huvudstad," *Dagen,* August 4, 2009, http://www.dagen.se/arbetarstaden-som-blev-huvudstad-1.183181.

45. Habermas, *The Structural Transformation of the Public Sphere.*

46. Fraser, "Rethinking the Public Sphere," 19.

47. Ibid., 7.

48. Ibid., 11.

49. Ibid., 14.

50. See Erdentug and Colombijn, "Urban Space and Ethnicity."

51. Warner, *Publics and Counterpublics.*

52. Ibid., 88.

53. Ibid., 122 (my emphasis).

54. de Certeau, *The Practice of Everyday Life*; and Lefebvre, *The Production of Space.*

55. Chase, Crawford, and Kaliski, *Everyday Urbanism.*

56. Olalquiaga, *Megalopolis,* xx (emphasis in the original).

57. Holston, *Insurgent Citizenship*; and Miraftab, "Insurgent Planning."

58. Lefebvre, *The Production of Space,* 52–53.

59. See, for example, Crane, *Mediterranean Crossroads*; Haffner, *The View from Above*; Mumford, *The CIAM Discourse on Urbanism*; and Vidler, *The Scenes of the Street, and Other Essays*.

1. Standards and Separatism

1. Björklund, "North to Another Country," 57.

2. For more on their expectations of this new Christian environment, see ibid.; and Atto, "Hostages in the Homeland, Orphans in the Diaspora." The larger research program from which Atto's project comes, concerning the formation of a Syriac Orthodox Christian identity, is described in ter Haar Romeny, "From Religious Association to Ethnic Community."

3. This first group of Syriac immigrants consisted of thirty-three families and thirty-nine single individuals, with thirteen people over the age of forty-five and ninety-six people under the age of twenty. See *Bahro Suryoyo*, "Ankomsten," 19; and Björklund, "North to Another Country," 57–58.

4. The State Immigration Board (Statens Invandrarverk, now the Swedish Migration Agency, Migrationsverket) was established in 1969, though the Labor Market Board retained responsibility for asylum seekers until 1985.

5. Svanberg and Tydén, *Tusen år av invandring,* 404.

6. In the 1960s, migrants to Sweden were labeled *utlänningar* (aliens or foreigners) or *främlingar* (foreigners or strangers), but by the 1970s the preferred term had become *invandrare* (immigrants). For more on shifts in institutions and labels, see Hammar, "Sweden." Svanberg and Tydén, *Tusen år av invandring,* 334, argue that public debates about immigration and terminology became heated with the publication of an article by David Schwartz, "Utlänningsproblemet i Sverige," published October 21, 1964, in the national newspaper *Dagens Nyheter*. In 1973 Schwartz founded the journal *Invandrare & Minoriteter* and served as its editor until 1996.

7. Björklund, "North to Another Country."

8. Members of the current community talk about this group as their pioneers or pilgrims, and the First Plane has acquired a mythical status equivalent to that of the *Mayflower*. The Second Plane, which arrived only weeks later with another group of Syriacs, is mentioned less frequently.

9. Hyresgästföreningen, *Hyresgästföreningens historia,* 13.

10. For analyses of how urban planning became the preferred solution to these problems, see Hall, "Urban Planning in Sweden"; and Hall and Vidén, "The Million Homes Programme."

11. I. Johansson, *Stor-Stockholms bebyggelsehistoria,* 262–65. "In 1870, less than 10% of the population lived in localities with more than 200 inhabitants. At the turn of the century, the figure was about 36%, in 1930 about 50%, and in 1970 about 80%." Fraenki, *Swedish Urban Planning,* chap. 1: 15.

12. Per Albin Hansson's "Folkhemmet, medborgarhemmet" speech was delivered four years before he became prime minister. He shrewdly co-opted the term *folkhem* from non-socialist politicians. For more on this choice of phrasing, see Isaksson, *Per Albin*.

13. In Swedish, definite articles are enclitic, or attached to the end of a word, so *folkhem* can be translated as "people's home," while *folkhemmet* is "the people's home."

14. The entire "Folkhemmet, medborgarhemmet" speech is available in Berkling, *Från Fram till folkhemmet*, 227–34.

15. Hansson led the Social Democrats from 1928 to 1946 and was prime minister from 1932 to 1946. The Nazi use of *Volk* made *folk* uncomfortable in the aftermath of World War II. The term had previously been ambiguously used to signify both ethnos and demos in Sweden. Hansson's successor, Tage Erlander, used the phrase "welfare society" *(välfärds-samhälle)* or "the strong society" *(det starka samhället)* instead. While *folkhem* is no longer the term used to denote the welfare state in contemporary Sweden, I use it as a key metaphor highlighting the continuing assumption of a strong Swedish welfare state during the 1960s, devoted to planning and with a hardy collectivist streak, which began with this term but outlasted it ideologically. Today the word *folkhem* has a nostalgic feel. Current political discourse focuses instead on the "welfare state."

16. Frykman and Löfgren, "På väg"; and Hirdman, *Att lägga livet tillrätta*.

17. Headey, *Housing Policy in the Developed Economy*, 13.

18. Arvidsson, Berntson, and Dencik, *Modernisering och välfärd*.

19. For more on prevailing ideas about the future during the 1960s, see Hall, "Urban Planning in Sweden," 194.

20. Hirdman, *Att lägga livet tillrätta*, 88–89.

21. Childs, *Sweden: The Middle Way*. An American journalist, Childs coined this term to describe a balance between the economic and political extremes of the Soviet Union and the United States.

22. Frykman and Löfgren, "På väg," 20.

23. For more, see Österberg, "Vardagens sträva samförstånd"; Rojas, *Sweden after the Swedish Model*; and Trägårdh, "Svenskhet och civilitet."

24. Österberg, "Vardagens sträva samförstånd," 144.

25. Frykman and Löfgren, "På väg," 98.

26. Social pressures to conform were pervasive, extending even into the home, as described in Frykman and Löfgren, *Culture Builders*, covering the period from 1880 to 1910.

27. Alva Myrdal won the Peace Prize in 1982 and Gunnar Myrdal took the prize in economics in 1974. Gunnar Myrdal had argued as early as 1931 that the Swedish state should develop its citizens through a modernized built environment.

28. Myrdal and Myrdal, *Kris i befolkningsfrågan*, 135. In 1941, Alva Myrdal further developed ties between nationalism, social progress, and the built environment in *Nation and Family*. She argues that housing should be a social right.

29. For details on the development of Swedish laws related to building and urban planning during the twentieth century, see Hall, "Urban Planning in Sweden," 196–206.

30. For an overview of the professionalization of urban planning in Europe, see Choay, *The Modern City*.

31. Ebenezer Howard developed the Garden City concept in *To-Morrow, a Peaceful Path to Real Reform* (1898), renamed as *Garden Cities of To-Morrow*. Its Swedish dissemination is explored in Rådberg, *Den svenska trädgårdsstaden*.

32. Svedberg, "Funktionalismens bostadsprogram," 42.

33. For a detailed description of the proceedings of the CIAM group from inception to dissolution, see Mumford, *The CIAM Discourse on Urbanism*.

34. Holston, *The Modernist City*, 41.

35. The plan resembled his 1925 Plan Voisin, which proposed the replacement of most of the buildings in central Paris with cruciform high-rise buildings.

36. Råberg, *Funktionalistiskt genombrott*; and Svedberg, "Funktionalismens bostadsprogram," 54–58. CIAM member Uno Åhrén promoted these ideas in the 1930 Stockholm Exhibition. See Åhrén, *Arkitektur och demokrati*. For an overview of Swedish architectural history during the twentieth century, including all the periods mentioned in this chapter, see Caldenby, *Att bygga ett land.*

37. Rådberg, *Drömmen om atlantångaren,* 18.

38. Rådberg, *Funktionalistiskt genombrott*; Rådberg, *Drömmen om atlantångaren,* 52–53; and Rudberg, "1940–1960."

39. Pred, *Recognizing European Modernities,* 100. The Svenska Slöjdförening and the city of Stockholm organized the event, with Gunnar Asplund the main architect.

40. Hitchcock and Johnson curated the International Exhibition of Modern Architecture, held in 1932 at the Museum of Modern Art.

41. Pred, *Recognizing European Modernities,* 111. Cited in the text as having appeared in *Social Demokraten,* May 25, 1930.

42. Ibid., 153–54.

43. Åhrén is widely credited with having imported functionalism to Sweden after his involvement in the Paris Exhibition of 1925. There he admired Le Corbusier's Pavillon de l'Esprit Nouveau and then joined CIAM. As Lucy Creagh points out, Åhrén found inspiration in Le Corbusier's focus on "collective conditions" rather than "personal expression" in housing design, which meshed well with the political climate in Sweden during the interwar period. See her "An Introduction to *acceptera.*"

44. Åhrén et al., *acceptera,* 180 (emphasis in the original).

45. See Hirdman, *Att lägga livet tillrätta,* esp. 92–101.

46. For more, see Rudberg, *Stockholmsutställningen 1930*; Rudberg, "Utopia of the Everyday"; and Pred, *Recognizing European Modernities.*

47. Mattsson and Wallenstein, *1930/1931,* 49. The text they analyze is Uno Åhrén's 1929 "Standardisering och personlighet." Mattsson explores a similar theme in her essay "Designing the Reasonable Consumer."

48. Åhrén et al., *acceptera,* 198 (emphasis in the original). Sven Markelius's pioneering 1935 Collective House in Stockholm (in collaboration with Alva Myrdal) sought to emancipate women from housework and child rearing; it included a group kitchen and collective day care. For more, see Caldenby and Walldén, *Kollektivhus*; Markelius, "Kollektivhuset"; and Vestbro, *Kollektivhus från enkökshus till bogemenskap.*

49. Åhrén et al., *acceptera,* 217.

50. With the participation of many well-known architects such as Josef Frank, Walter Gropius, Le Corbusier, and Bruno Taut and with the leadership of Ludwig Mies van der Rohe, the Weissenhof Estate (Weißenhofsiedlung) in Stuttgart represented a key such housing model. In this project, the architects designed individual houses in one area as part of the German Werkbund's *Die Wohnung* (The Housing) exhibition of 1927. This project signified a crucial development in the creation of CIAM. See Pommer and Otto, *Weissenhof 1927 and the Modern Movement in Architecture.*

51. Magnusson Turner, "Invandring och segregation," 14.

52. SOU 1956:32, 120.

53. Popenoe, *The Suburban Environment,* 35. See also Perry, *The Neighborhood Unit.* For a thorough analysis of the rise of the neighborhood unit in Swedish urban planning, see also Franzén and Sandstedt, *Välfärdsstat och byggande.*

54. The neighborhood-unit plans include six critical elements: size, borders, open spaces, institutions, shops, and an internal traffic system. Also known as New Towns, the model has been strongly associated with the British housing areas that emerged out of the New Town Act of 1946. Perry places commerce at the periphery, but, as Mats Franzén and Eva Sandstedt note, "in *Sweden* on the other hand, *the shops are brought to the centrum* as a rule." Franzén and Sandstedt, *Välfärdsstat och byggande,* 159 (emphasis in the original).

55. Åström, *Svensk stadsplanering,* 73. The Building Act of 1947 "brought in essential changes in the relationship between the rights of society and the individual land owner. The concept of urban development was permitted only where society considered it appropriate, and only in accordance with a town plan or building plan adopted and ratified in advance." Fraenki, *Swedish Urban Planning,* chap. 2: 4.

56. Ten kilometers northeast of central Stockholm, Vällingby comprised eight thousand dwelling units, with 90 percent in multifamily housing and most municipally owned. For more on Vällingby's design, see Hall, "Urban Planning in Sweden," 219–221; Pass, "Vällingby and Farsta"; and Sax, *Vällingby.*

57. Popenoe, *The Suburban Environment,* 74; and Rudberg, "1940–1960," 98.

58. Deland, "The Social City," 9. Thomas Hall notes, "With hindsight we can also see that it was a little illogical to try to counteract commuting while also building the latest type of transport system nicely scaled to commuting requirements." Hall, "Urban Planning in Sweden," 220–21.

59. Rudberg, "1940–1960," 74 and 76.

60. Parr, "Modern Kitchen, Good Home, Strong Nation."

61. Hald, Holm, and Johansson, *Swedish Housing*; and P. Holm, *Swedish Housing.*

62. Hald, Holm, and Johansson, *Swedish Housing.*

63. See Roos and Gelotte, *Hej bostad,* 8–9; Sax, "Hem för miljoner," 10; and Sigge, "Architecture's Red Tape."

64. Arnstberg, *Miljonprogrammet,* 39.

65. See Tunström, "The Story." For more on the debates that continue around the Million Program today, see B. Johansson, *Miljonprogram*; and Broms Wessel, Mack, and Anstey, *Future People's Palace.*

66. See Stenberg, "Building the Dream." He notes that they remain a quarter of the four million Swedish housing units available today.

67. SOU 1965:32. Holm was later appointed director general of Planverket, the Swedish National Board for Planning and Building.

68. The period from approximately 1960 to 1975 is known as "the Record Years," thanks to the strong economy and record-breaking construction. Lisbeth Söderqvist cites the 1969 documentary film *Rekordåren* by Lena Ewert and the Swedish Film Institute as the likely source of the term, noting that the period remains ambiguously defined. See her "Rekordår och miljonprogram flerfamiljshus i stor skala," 11.

69. Hall and Vidén, "The Million Homes Programme," 303; and Söderqvist, "Rekordår och miljonprogram: Flerfamiljshus i stor skala," 12.

70. Mattsson, "Where the Motorways Meet," 169.

71. Sax, "Hem för miljoner," 8. In his polemic on using Million Program structural systems in renovation projects, architect Erik Stenberg notes that the process was nonetheless complex, involving numerous actors (for example, twenty-three different construction companies in the adjacent Stockholm suburbs of Rinkeby and Tensta). See Stenberg, "Building the Dream."

72. Hall, "Urban Planning in Sweden," 224.

73. Kungliga Bostadsstyrelsen, *God Bostad* (1960), 19.

74. Hirdman, *Att lägga livet tillrätta.*

75. T. Andersson, *Utanför staden.*

76. Original footage of Sandberg's speech can be seen in the television documentary "Goda bostäder fostra goda medborgare," an episode of *Arkitekter berättar,* shown on the Swedish channel TV1 on September 2, 1976.

77. Lars-Erik Borgegård and Jim Kemeny use "good democratic citizens" to describe the overall focus of postwar housing policy in their "Sweden," 35.

78. Merry, "Spatial Governmentality and the New Urban Social Order." Merry critiques neoliberalism, but her conclusions apply equally well to the Swedish welfare state.

79. Foucault, *The History of Sexuality,* vols. 2 and 3.

80. Wirtén, *Där jag kommer från,* 126.

81. The eugenics movement had leading Swedish politicians from all the major political parties advocating for the sterilization of anyone who lacked "good" genetic material in the 1930s. The Swedish Racial Hygiene Society was established in Stockholm in 1909, and the Swedish state's Institute of Racial Biology opened in Uppsala in 1922. In their *Kris i befolkningsfrågan* (Crisis in the population question), even the Myrdals argued for the sterilization of "less worthy" members of the population. Until public debates in the 1990s, this dark side of Social Democracy was largely obscured. Journalist Maciej Zaremba argues that the *folkhem* is a racist trope, granting full citizenship rights only to certain "desirable" individuals. See his *De rena och de andra.* Frykman and Löfgren further observe that, in the *folkhem,* "the identity of the self was built up with the help of a symbolic inversion: 'the others' are as black as we are white, as rough as we are fine, as ill-mannered as we are polite, as careless as we are tidy. . . . This is where a view developed of the people, of the workers, of the proletariat as a lesser kind of people: more primitive, less cultivated." Frykman and Löfgren, "På väg," 28. See also Runcis, *Steriliseringar i folkhemmet.*

82. Tunström, "The Story."

83. Ecer, *I fikonträdets skugga.* This "emigrant epic" *(utvandrarepos)* is based on Ecer's own family history and was published, intriguingly, as a "multiethnic paper" in a research series by Uppsala University.

84. Van den Boogart, *The Capitulations and the Ottoman Legal System.*

85. Braude, "Foundation Myths of the Millet System."

86. Atto, "Hostages in the Homeland, Orphans in the Diaspora," 14. The millet system can be linked to the later certification of minorities in the Treaty of Lausanne, the peace treaty between Turkey and several European states signed on July 24, 1923, which were intended to protect Christians in Turkey and Muslims in Greece. Syriacs were notably absent from these arrangements. Ibid., 88–97.

87. S. Andersson, *Assyrierna,* 67. Writing at a time of great hostility between *assyrier* and *syrianer,* Andersson uses *assyrier* to denote his support for that faction in response to his

assessment that Swedish authorities harbored unfair suspicions about them, a choice he explains in the book. Ibid., 8–9.

88. Findlay, *Turkey, Islam, Nationalism, and Modernity.*

89. Özoğlu, *From Caliphate to Secular State.*

90. *Seyfo* continues to be a critical rallying point for Syriacs, and protests, public lectures, and memorials often occur in Södertälje and other diasporic outposts. *Seyfo* later came to describe both the attacks during World War I and those during the Simele massacre in Iraq in 1933. For more on the history of *Seyfo,* see Courtois, *The Forgotten Genocide*; Gaunt, *Massacres, Resistance, Protectors*; and Gaunt, *Seyfo.* For an analysis of *Seyfo* in Sweden, see Nordgren, "Vems är historien?," 105–30.

91. Gaunt, *Massacres, Resistance, Protectors,* 2006. Sweden officially recognized the events as "genocide" by parliamentary vote in March 2010. This prompted the Turkish government to withdraw its ambassador, Zergün Korutürk, though she returned two weeks later.

92. See "Islamic State Video 'Shows Destruction of Nimrud,'" *BBC News,* April 12, 2015, http://www.bbc.com/news/world-middle-east-32273672.

93. Benjamin told a similar story, although his account placed more blame on the increasing conflicts between Kurds and Turks. He described the changes to his previously completely Christian village, saying, "The Christians left the village because there were disturbances in the 1970s. The greatest part of the violence was between Kurds and Turks, but we were caught in the cross fire. Often, Kurds came to the village, and they would say that they wanted money. They said they would kill us if they didn't get it. Then, the state or the police would come to the village and ask, 'Why did the Kurds come? Are you working with them?' So we were threatened by the state, too."

94. The italicized words were said in Arabic in a conversation otherwise conducted in Suryoyo and English between Jakob, a mutual friend, and me.

95. Atto, "Hostages in the Homeland, Orphans in the Diaspora," 199.

96. Björklund, "North to Another Country," 64.

97. Ibid., 112.

98. For instance, Atto, "Hostages in the Homeland, Orphans in the Diaspora"; Björklund, "North to Another Country"; Pripp, *Företagande i minoritet*; and Rabo, "'Familjen betyder allt eller 'Vi blir snart lika kalla som svenskarna.'"

99. Smith, "Civic Nationalism and Ethnocultural Justice in Turkey," 443.

100. S. Andersson, *Assyrierna,* 17.

101. Hollerweger, *Living Cultural Heritage Turabdin,* 14.

102. Ibid., 16.

103. Hollerweger also writes, "*Mor* in Syriac corresponds to the English word 'Saint.' It is also used as a title of honour for bishops," and "the place of burial of saints, patriarchs and bishops is named in Syriac *Beth Kadishé* ('The House of Saints')." Ibid.

104. S. Andersson, *Assyrierna,* 17.

105. Deniz, *En minoritets odyssé,* 142. The author cites Björklund's "North to Another Country" here.

106. For a rich account of the cultural heritage and dangers of this landscape in the 1990s, see Dalrymple, *From the Holy Mountain.*

107. Hollerweger, *Living Cultural Heritage Turabdin,* 173.

108. Atto, "Hostages in the Homeland, Orphans in the Diaspora," 100–103; and Smith, "Civic Nationalism and Ethnocultural Justice in Turkey."

109. Scott, *Seeing Like a State,* 64–71.

110. Deniz, *En minoritets odyssé,* 134. The Syriac Orthodox Church did retain a degree of juridical autonomy over its members.

111. Björklund, "North to Another Country," 64.

112. Björklund, a Swede writing in English in the early 1980s, uses Swedish welfare-state terminology by employing *neighborhood unit* to describe these enclaves, translating the official community structures of Sweden onto his Turkish fieldwork context.

113. Björklund, "North to Another Country," 64–65.

114. Emil Çelebi, "Midyat: City of Stone," 2001, Christians of Iraq, http://www.chris tiansofiraq.com/midyat2.html.

115. Björklund, "North to Another Country," 79. All the parenthetical notes are Björklund's own commentary.

116. For a complete list of the villages of Tur Abdin by language, see Svanberg, *Invandrare från Turkiet.*

117. The monastery's website is Deyrulzafaran Manastiri, http://www.deyrulzafaran.org/turkce.

118. For a history of the city, see Palmer, *Monk and Mason on the Tigris Frontier.*

119. Hollerweger, *Living Cultural Heritage Turabdin,* 94.

120. "An Outpost of Aramaic Speakers: The Battle for Mor Gabriel," *Economist,* November 3, 2012, http://www.economist.com/news/europe/21565655-battle-mor-gabriel-outpost -aramaic-speakers.

121. Media coverage included Andrew Higgins, "Defending the Faith: Battle over a Christian Monastery Tests Turkey's Tolerance for Minorities," *Wall Street Journal,* March 7, 2009. This article mentions the active role of Swedish parliamentarian Yilmaz Kerimo, a Syriac, in negotiations between the Turkish state and Mor Gabriel. During the conflict, Turkey appeared keen to project an image of tolerance, which lasted at least until its highly publicized 2013 violent crackdown on those protesting the demolition of Gezi Park in Istanbul.

122. Björklund, "North to Another Country," 35.

123. Ecer, *I fikonträdets skugga,* 128.

124. Atto, "Hostages in the Homeland, Orphans in the Diaspora," 108–9.

125. Ecer, *I fikonträdets skugga,* 128.

126. Atto, "Hostages in the Homeland, Orphans in the Diaspora," 151. For more on how exiled Syriac Orthodox Christians framed their identities in Syria in the early twentieth century, see Sato, "Selective Amnesia."

127. For more on how different political regimes shifted Syria's borders, see Rooke, "Tracing the Boundaries."

128. Following the dissolution of the Ottoman Empire, the territories of modern-day Syria and Lebanon became French mandates. Lebanon gained independence in 1943; Syria in 1946. The seat of the Syriac Orthodox Church was in Tur Abdin at the Dayro Zafaran monastery until 1933.

129. For more on the fluidity and politics of these borders, see Brandell, *State Frontiers;* and Karpat, "Millets and Nationality."

130. Rabo, "Change on the Euphrates." For a comparison of land policies, see Warriner, *Land Reform and Development in the Middle East.* An overview of the political structure of the Syrian peasantry is found in Batatu, *Syria's Peasantry, the Descendants of Its Lesser Rural Notables, and Their Politics.*

131. The population of the town of Hasakah in the 2004 Syrian census was 254,622, while Qamishli's population at that time was 232,258. These numbers differed sharply from those of the 1994 census, when the populations were 119,798 and 144,286, respectively.

132. While ADO was regarded as a terrorist group by Swedish authorities during the 1970s and 1980s and members often distanced themselves publicly from the organization, a fiftieth-anniversary party for the group, with hundreds in attendance, was held in Södertälje in 2007.

133. Anderson, *Imagined Communities,* 7.

134. "About ADO," ADO World, n.d., http://www.ado-world.org/en/about-ado/ (emphasis in the original).

135. For more on ADO, see Deniz, *En minoritets odyssé,* 186–87. He argues that "the organization has played a major role for the group's ethnic consciousness, and many people suggest that it was thanks to ADO that the assimilation of the group in Syria and Lebanon could be prevented. ADO also played another important role in that it inspired the founding of the organization ADR among *assyrier* in Iraq. Later, ADO developed branches in West Germany, Sweden, and the United States." Ibid., 187.

136. The divide is far from strict, yet a larger percentage of self-identified *assyrier* came from Syria and of *syrianer* from Turkey. Thus, the development of this split can be partially read as a hangover from political structures abroad. The State Immigration Board assigned linguist Bengt Knutsson to conduct an investigation, hoping that he would find a truth that would resolve the ongoing conflicts. His 1982 *Assur eller Aram* increased animosities instead.

137. When I studied the Syriacs' common language, Suryoyo, with Maria, a Syriac Orthodox Christian who had grown up in Qamishli, she disparaged Otto Jastrow's Suryoyo-German textbook, where the language is labeled Turoyo. The textbook was translated to a Suryoyo-Swedish version by Karol, a Chaldean Catholic who had emigrated from Tur Abdin. Although both Maria and Karol identified as *assyrier,* Maria felt that Karol's interpretation was too "Turkified," since he used Turkish letters and some Turkish words where she used an Arabic replacement. Maria ultimately suggested doing away with the book. Karol had himself changed many translations based on Kurdish from the first (German) version. These politics of language connect latent differences to diverse Syriac political and linguistic contexts.

138. Björklund, "North to Another Country," 50. See the volume edited by Pacini, *Christian Communities in the Arab Middle East,* for detailed overviews of the various Christian groups in the region.

139. Björklund explains that the sectarian violence between Christians and Muslims that erupted in Lebanon in 1958 made it "difficult or impossible at least for Syrian Orthodox immigrants to acquire Lebanese citizenship." Björklund, "North to Another Country," 29.

140. Nordgren, "Vems är historien?," 61.

141. See note 77.

142. See Narrowe, *Under One Roof,* for a summary of the shift from assimilation to integration in Sweden. For an analysis of the theoretical implications, see Diaz, "Choosing Integration."

143. *Bahro Suryoyo,* "Ankomsten," 19.

144. Björklund, "North to Another Country," 60.

145. Aho, *Assyrier/Syrianer,* 25.

146. Deniz, *En minoritets odyssé,* 251.

147. Ecer, *I fikonträdets skugga,* 137.

148. Agamben, "We Refugees."

149. Sweden's income inequality increased more than that of any other member of the Organisation for Economic Co-operation and Development in recent decades, according to a study published in 2013. See "Klyftor växer snabbast i Sverige," *Svenska Dagbladet,* May 15, 2013, http://www.svd.se/nyheter/inrikes/klyftor-vaxer-snabbast-isverige_8172016.svd. See also Christophers, "A Monstrous Hybrid."

150. Foucault, *Discipline and Punish,* 220.

151. Ibid., 219.

152. Björklund, "North to Another Country," 60–61 (ellipsis points in the original). Björklund describes how the small Syriac group needed to simulate internal conflicts in order to convince the Swedish authorities to disperse them.

153. *Bahro Suryoyo,* "Ankomsten," 19.

2. Visible Cities, Invisible Citizens

1. Bosco, "Ronna Centrum invigs: Hypermodernt köpcity. Sluträkning: 4,7 milj. kr.," *Länstidningen,* November 30, 1965, 7.

2. Ibid.

3. Currently, the Swedish term *centrum* denotes both mid-twentieth-century modernist town centers like these and shopping centers or malls of more recent vintage.

4. Björklund, "North to Another Country," 5.

5. Gelotte, Dahlström Rittsél, and Ulfstrand, *Nästa hållplats Södertälje,* 8.

6. Saab-Scania first recruited workers from Greece in 1960 and then from Finland. Afterward, many more immigrants arrived on their own. See Margit Silberstein's 1981–82 series in the Swedish national newspaper *Svenska Dagbladet* for more: "'Gräns' mitt i Södertälje," December 30, 1981, 1; "Rashat och protestlistor: En gräns delar torget," December 30, 1981, 8; "Hantverk tillbaka," December 30, 1981, 8; "På Orient Café: 'Rädda för att visa oss i samhället,'" January 3, 1982, 8; "På raggarnas gård: Tror att invandrarna skall 'ta over,'" January 3, 1982, 8; "Polisutredning visar: Begår inte fler brott än andra," January 3, 1982, 8; "Skolan där varannan elev är invandrare: Barnen lär sig förstå sina kamrater bättre," January 7, 1982, 8; "Södertälje för 20 år sedan: Industrin ropade efter arbetskraft," January 11, 1982, 7; "Det var lättare tidigare att umgås med svenskar," January 11, 1982, 7; and "Framtiden osäker: Klarar inte ordna jobb," January 11, 1982, 7. Describing ethnic divisions as a "border in the middle of Södertälje," Silberstein focused on "Södertälje as an 'immigrant city'" that had transformed from a Swedish "small town" to "a city in the world" over the previous twenty years.

7. Gelotte, Dahlström Rittsél, and Ulfstrand, *Nästa hållplats Södertälje,* 20–21. Swedish policy makers also prized the expeditious Million Program techniques because they made workers available for other jobs more quickly.

8. For an overview of how Scania and the Million Program were complementary partners in the urban development of Södertälje after 1945, see ibid.

9. For more on this, see ibid., 11–15. Scania and Astra were the primary beneficiaries, and a full 20 percent of all housing went to the Industry Group in the early 1950s. This is detailed in Södertälje Drätselkammare, Bostadsnämnden.

10. For example, "Illegalt invandrade assyrier fortsätter strömma till Södertälje," *Länstidningen,* December 8, 1977, 1; and Per-Erik Persson, "Massinvasion av assyrier: Kommunen hårt ansträngd," *Länstidningen,* September 19, 1975, 8.

11. This particular group did not exist until mid-1979.

12. Mattsson, "Where the Motorways Meet," 170.

13. Taylor, "Modern Social Imaginaries"; and Taylor, *Modern Social Imaginaries.*

14. For more on Ronna, see the histories of housing and urbanism in Södertälje by historian Göran Gelotte: *Telgebostäder genom fyra årtionden*; and *Södertälje kommuns historia,* vol. 3.

15. In Swedish, *Telge* and *Tälje* may be pronounced identically. Politicians discussed whether this housing authority should be wholly municipal or half-privatized. By a vote of twenty-three to fifteen, the former was selected. For more, see Gelotte, *Telgebostäder genom fyra årtionden,* 19–20.

16. Gelotte, Dahlström Rittsél, and Ulfstrand, *Nästa hållplats Södertälje.*

17. Gelotte, *Telgebostäder genom fyra årtionden,* 32.

18. Voigt ultimately resigned from his position as city architect owing to a conflict of interest with his own urban design and architecture firm, but he remained responsible for overseeing Ronna's construction.

19. The "neighborhood unit" used a five-minute walking distance from the town center to the home as the key determinant of plan size. Helena Mattsson describes how collaborations between politicians and industrial leaders crafted an unusual symbiosis between structures for citizenship and for retail activities in Swedish urban development. This image of a dual, civic and commercial Swedish welfare state—"a corporatist democracy"—contrasts with more typical descriptions of an entirely utopian, social project. For more, see Mattsson, "Where the Motorways Meet."

20. In 1955, an entire report on laundry was produced (368 pages in length). See SOU 1955:8.

21. For an analysis of the evolution of the idea of "service" in the Swedish welfare state from the 1940s to the 1980s, see Franzén and Sandstedt, *Välfärdsstat och byggande.*

22. SOU 1955:28.

23. For a related discussion of the role of youth centers, see Mack, "Love in the Time of Pinball."

24. A full analysis of the relationship between Social Democratic government research and *centrum* planning in Sweden is available in Franzén and Sandstedt, *Välfärdsstat och byggande.*

25. Rådberg, "Doktrin och täthet i svenskt stadsbyggande 1875–1975," 376. He notes that the idea was first presented in a booklet by the Greater Stockholm tenant organization in March 1968; it stipulated a maximum distance of two hundred meters from the *centrum* to individual apartment blocks, with each neighborhood unit comprising two thousand to three thousand residents. See also Hyresgästföreningen, *Boendemiljön.*

26. *Din egen stad,* "Vi bygger och bor."

27. Heineman, "Introduction," 12.

28. Kungliga Bostadsstyrelsen, *God bostad i dag och i morgon.*

29. Franzén and Sandstedt, *Välfärdsstat och byggande,* 34–35. For more on the government's specific recommendations, see the seven individual reports: SOU 1968:38; SOU 1970:68; SOU 1971:25; SOU 1971:26; SOU 1971:27; SOU 1971:28; and SOU 1973:24. See also the brochures HSBs Riksförbund, *Service i bostadsområden*; and Hyresgästföreningen, *Boendemiljön.*

30. The report states that "almost one-third of Swedish households were composed of five or more people" in 1920. Based on statistics from 1965, however, the authors argue that

"multigenerational families, which also include relatives and employees, have almost completely disappeared," and "households with three or more children number only one out of seven or approximately 160,000 households." See SOU 1968:38, 8.

31. The first report notes, "210,000 mothers of 350,000 children at the age when care is needed work at home but would prefer to be gainfully employed—part-time or full-time—if child care could be arranged." SOU 1968:38, 8.

32. SOU 1968:38, 9–10.

33. Westerman, "Nya stadscentra," 267.

34. Ågren, "Thinking in Terms of Service," 130–31.

35. See I. Johansson, *Stor-Stockholms bebyggelsehistoria,* for a more detailed account of this process in the Stockholm region.

36. In the 1980s, political will shifted back to the proximity principle *(närhetsprincip),* significantly altering municipal governance structures. Neighborhood administrative bodies were created in 1988. Ronna oversaw its own management until 1998, when these bodies were closed and recentralization took place.

37. David Popenoe notes that the "hierarchical network" of new service-based developments during the Million Program led to "distinct neighborhoods," especially because of the clear separation of pedestrians from automobile traffic. See Popenoe, *The Suburban Environment,* 37.

38. Franzén and Sandstedt, *Välfärdsstat och byggande,* 34–35. They cite SOU 1970:68, *Boendeservice 2.*

39. SOU 1955:28.

40. Foucault, *The Order of Things.*

41. Herzfeld analyzes Linnaeus's classifications of people as an "anthropological taxonomy" of Americans, Asians, Europeans, and Africans in *Anthropology through the Looking-Glass,* 96–98.

42. This can be connected to what political scientist Will Kymlicka theorizes as "multicultural citizenship." See Kymlicka, *Multicultural Citizenship.* For more on the policy of integration in Sweden, see Ålund and Schierup, *Paradoxes of Multiculturalism*; Rojas, *I ensamhetens labyrint*; and SOU 1996:55.

43. Legislation quoted in Svanberg and Tydén, *Tusen år av invandring,* 365.

44. Legislation quoted in Svanberg and Tydén, *Tusen år av invandring,* 365.

45. Pred, *Even in Sweden,* 70.

46. McIntosh, "Impossible Presence."

47. Sawyer, "Routings."

48. For more on popular portrayals of the "immigrant-dense suburb" and the destructive power of this imagery, see Ericsson, "Belägrade människor–belägrade rum." Some attempts to use demographics in a positive light have been made, such as a 2006 housing exhibition in the Million Program Stockholm suburb of Tensta, which sought to counter the neighborhood's negative reputation by highlighting its diversity. The accompanying brochure, however, informed visitors that in Tensta, "chocolate brown children play in sandboxes," and the exhibition showed the apartment of a fictional Italian–Somali family as containing little more than bundled sticks and an Alessi toilet-paper holder.

49. Molina, "Stadens rasifiering," 93.

50. The controversial anthropologist Unni Wikan argues that the Norwegian welfare state has encouraged immigrants to become dependents of the state. See Wikan, *Generous Betrayal.*

51. Silverstein, "Immigrant Racialization and the New Savage Slot." For an anthroplogical perspective on the othering of immigrants in Germany, see Mandel, *Cosmopolitan Anxieties.*

52. For more on this, see Widgren, *Svensk invandrarpolitik.*

53. Most information in this section comes from the Swedish Migration Agency's website, Migrationsverket, http://www.migrationsverket.se.

54. The limits of the original convention (originally for refugees escaping Nazi persecution) were broadened in 1967 through the United Nations Protocol Relating to the Status of Refugees.

55. They came from places like Eritrea, Iran, Iraq, Kosovo, Lebanon, Somalia, Syria, and Turkey, as well as from the member countries of the former Eastern Bloc.

56. In 2016, the number was over 1.78 million out of a total population of almost 10 million, or 17.9 percent. For more, see Statistics Sweden, "Summary of Population Statistics 1960–2016," http://www.scb.se/en/finding-statistics/statistics-by-subject-area/population/pop ulation-composition/population-statistics/pong/tables-and-graphs/yearly-statistics--the -whole-country/summary-of-population-statistics/.

57. Regional variations within Sweden constitute another recognized form of difference. This is especially pronounced in the case of the Sami population.

58. Franzén and Sandstedt, *Välfärdsstat och byggande.*

59. All terms in circulation from the 1960s to the 1980s (*utlänning, främling,* and *invandrare*), are exclusionary, and Svanberg and Tydén suggest *nysvenskar* (New Swedes) as a more benign label than *invandrare* (immigrant), which is otherwise most commonly used. See their *Tusen år av invandring,* 383. Recent scholarship within the Internationell migration och etniska relationer (IMER) network—focusing on immigration research in Sweden—has employed *invandrade* (immigrated) in place of *invandrare* (immigrant) in an attempt to distinguish between the action of the former and the stasis of the latter. *Invandrade* also works against the controversial category *utländsk bakgrund* (foreign background), used to describe those born in Sweden to two parents who were born abroad.

60. Kusno, "Violence of Categories."

61. For example, see SOU 1972:40.

62. I. Johansson, *Stor-Stockholms bebyggelsehistoria,* 107.

63. Hedman, *Den kommunala allmännyttans historia,* 16.

64. I. Johansson, *Stor-Stockholms bebyggelsehistoria,* 114.

65. Several articles described this mass exodus, such as Per-Erik Persson, "Varning till Sveriges industrier: Finländarna vill åka hem igen," *Länstidningen,* August 2, 1973, 1, 11; and "Stora språkproblem bland finländarna: Många vill hem," *Länstidningen,* November 16, 1973, 1, 12.

66. In my 2009 conversation with Södertälje urban historian Göran Gelotte, he confirmed that this semantic play was intentionally used to downplay the significance of these vacant spaces. In November 1976, 1,398 apartments went unrented. See "Fortfarande 1398 tomma lägenheter!" *Länstidningen,* November 12, 1976, 3.

67. Examples of such articles include "Rekordmånga tomma lägenheter nu igen!," *Länstidningen,* May 24, 1974, 1; Lorenz Berglund, "Fyra milj. hyresförlust. Kolonilotter räddning?," *Länstidningen,* May 24, 1974, 1, 4; "Drygt var fjärde lägenhet i Hovsjö fortfarande tom!," *Länstidningen,* April 9, 1976, 3; "Ännu 1380 lägenheter outhyrda i Södertälje," *Länstidningen,* October 4, 1976, 5; and "Fortfarande många outhyrda lägenheter," *Länstidningen,* June 3, 1977, 5, which put the number at 1,328.

68. Ingegerd Asp-Lundström, "Geneta, Saltskog och Ronna förbättras för två och en halv miljon," *Länstidningen,* April 21, 1975, 5. The cost of renovations would be divided between the municipality and the Swedish state.

69. Geographically isolated, Hovsjö was designated to become the site of a major regional hospital. It was cleared of trees in preparation for construction and then abandoned when another location, in the town of Huddinge and closer to Stockholm, was chosen.

70. GNY, "Att stoppa Hovsjö kostar för mycket," *Länstidningen,* July 31, 1974, 10.

71. See Asplund, *Farväl till funktionalismen!* Another scathing account was penned by Sune Lindström in *PLAN* in 1977 with the title, "Hur kunde det gå så illa?" (How could it go so wrong?).

72. The suburban Swedish dialect containing words from languages such as Turkish, Kurdish, Spanish, and Arabic is sometimes referred to as *miljonsvenska* (Million Swedish), referring to its use in Million Program neighborhoods.

73. For more on the rise of segregation in Södertälje, see Hajighasemi, *Att bryta den beständiga segregationen.* A more general overview of the shifts in population is offered in Blomé and Azmier, *Södertälje!*

74. See Björklund, "North to Another Country," 60–63, for a detailed description of how Södertälje became the group's center.

75. See Blomdahl's *Folkrörelserna och folket* for a detailed overview of the connections between *folkrörelser* and *föreningar.*

76. Franzén and Sandstedt, *Välfärdsstat och byggande,* 229.

77. Several SOU publications address the importance of the association for Swedish public life, including one entitled *Ju mer vi är tillsammans* (The more we are together). See SOU 1987:33.

78. This was part of a larger Swedish policy to encourage immigrants to develop associations. See Lundberg and Svanberg, "Turkish Associations in Metropolitan Stockholm."

79. For an early 1980s perspective on immigrant organizations at the national level *(riksförbund),* including how they were financed, see Bäck, *Invandrarnas riksorganisationer.* This support continues. For example, a 2014 article detailed state financial backing for youth organizations, with ten million Swedish kronor going to groups in Södertälje that year. See Monika Nilsson Lysell, "Miljoner till föreningar i Södertälje," *Länstidningen,* January 17, 2014, http://lt.se/nyheter/sodertalje/1.2348746-miljoner-till-foreningar-i-sodertalje.

80. Svanberg, *Invandrare från Turkiet,* 48.

81. Svanberg and Tydén, *Tusen år av invandring,* 367. Immigrant associations exploded in the second half of the twentieth century, but they began earlier. The first was a Finnish association in Stockholm in 1898; an Italian association appeared in 1909 in Nacka. In 1989, the State Immigration Board and Labor Market Department copublished a brochure detailing the major organizations. The revised edition, published in 1990, included thirty-eight groups, including the Assyrian Federation of Sweden (Assyriska Riksförbundet) and the Syrianska Federation (Syrianska Riksförbundet). See Hansson, *Invandrarföreningar.* In 2015, the Assyrian Federation of Sweden claimed ten thousand members, with thirty member organizations (http://www.assyriskariksforbundet.se). The Syrianska Federation, together with the Syrianska Aramaean Youth Federation (Syrianska Arameiska Ungdomsförbundet), cited a membership of over twenty thousand (http://syrianska.org).

82. Deniz, *En minoritets odyssé,* 241.

83. The Finlandia Association was described as "one of the most active in Södertälje" in 1974, during the time when its members had begun to return to Finland. See "Föreningen Finlandia—En av de aktivaste i hela Södertälje," *Länstidningen,* April 16, 1974, 4. This article appeared adjacent to a story about members of the local government visiting Finland on a field trip: GNY, "Södertäljepolitiker i österled studier i invandrares hemland," *Länstidningen,* April 16, 1974, 4.

84. The Assyrian Federation of Sweden eventually took a space in nearby Norsborg in the municipality of Botkyrka. See "Assyrisk förening får lokal," *Länstidningen,* January 5, 1977, 3.

85. Hansson, *Invandrarföreningar,* 13.

86. Ibid., 10.

87. *Hujådå* maintains a strong Web presence today at http://www.hujada.com. The site largely publishes articles about Assyrian nationalism, information about upcoming events, advertisements for Syriac products (such as wedding paraphernalia), and appeals regarding Syriac issues (such as monastery land holdings in Turkey and the fight against the Islamic State in Syria and Iraq).

88. "Våra assyrier/syrianers bakgrund," *Ditt Södertälje* 4, October 1980.

89. "Illegalt invandrade assyrier fortsätter strömma till Södertälje."

90. For example, "Assyrier i massor till Södertälje," *Länstidningen,* September 19, 1975, 1; Persson, "Massinvasion av assyrier"; "Ny invandrarvåg av assyrier," *Länstidningen,* March 24, 1976, 1; Sture Ankarstrand, "Assyriska invandringen nu större än någonsin," *Länstidningen,* March 24, 1976, 4; "Illegalt invandrade assyrier fortsätter strömma till Södertälje"; and Sture Ankarstrand, "1 500 assyrier smugglades in . . . Invandringen till Södertälje fortsätter," *Länstidningen,* December 8, 1977, 3. The "spontaneous immigration" of thousands of Syriacs to Sweden also became national news, as evidenced by articles like "Illegala invandringen av assyrier regeringsfråga," *Länstidningen,* October 17, 1975, 1, and the article from the Swedish news service TT, "Oreglerad invandring bör stoppas," *Länstidningen,* December 23, 1975, 7.

91. Persson, "Massinvasion av assyrier."

92. Germany had had bilateral agreements with other countries earlier, including Italy in 1955, but the Turkish agreement quickly became the most significant.

93. Persson, "Massinvasion av assyrier."

94. Sture Ankarstrand, "Anna-Greta Leijon till Södertälje: Blir läger lösningen av assyriefrågorna?" *Länstidningen,* October 17, 1975, 5. This article also includes a vocabulary list, including *utvisning* (deportation), stating, "Foreign citizens can be deported out of the country as a result of antisocial lifestyles, such as alcoholism, immoral living, etc."

95. "Ny invandrarvåg av assyrier."

96. Lorenz Berglund, "Ny stödgrupp vädjar: Låt assyrierna stanna!" *Länstidningen,* February 19, 1976, 20.

97. "Döda oss hellre än utvisa oss!," *Länstidningen,* February 19, 1976, 1.

98. "Avvisad assyrier: Regeringen splittrar våra familjer," *Länstidningen,* July 16, 1976, 1. See also the longer article in the same issue, "Nya avvisningar av assyrier: 'Varför vill regeringen splittra vår familj?'" *Länstidningen,* July 16, 1976, 4.

99. See Ornbrant, *Möte med välfärdens byråkrater.* Syriacs regarded the Swedish lawyer Kjell Jönsson as having had an instrumental role in this effort, and they even wrote a song

about him. The story and the lyrics are included in Björklund, "North to Another Country," 117–18.

100. Roland Cox, "Vi får stanna! Både glädje och besvikelse hos Assyriska Föreningen," *Länstidningen,* November 15, 1976, 7.

101. Rumors surfaced that the Assyrian Federation of Sweden had intentionally organized migrations. See Stefan Andersson, "Assyrieföreningen underkänner 'forskar'-rapport—Grundlösa anklagelser," *Länstidningen,* March 10, 1977, 3.

102. The actual term is *Gågatan.*

103. Kramer, *Unsettling Europe,* 97–98.

104. Several other documentaries on the Syriacs were produced for television and radio. For example, "Nya svenskar" (New Swedes), an episode of *ZOOM* on SVT in 1980, followed a Syriac girl in a "Turkish" family in Södertälje. Another, *Var kommer du ifrån—Vart är du på väg?* (Where do you come from—Where are you going?), aired on SVT in the fall of 1981 and included interviews with Syriacs in Tur Abdin, claiming that only elderly Christians remained.

105. Greeks provoked similar reactions from majority Swedes. Michael Herzfeld discusses the poet Andreas Nenedakis's experiences of this in *Portrait of a Greek Imagination.*

106. *Hanna—Assyrier i Södertälje,* SVT.

107. Silberstein, "Rashat och protestlistor."

108. Ambjörnsson and Janke, *Bråket på Bristol.*

109. Ibid.

110. A 1977 article described the need for two associations because of "religious tensions," naming a second association as the "Svensk-Suryoyoyoortodoxföreningen [*sic*]" and describing their plans to rent a former bank in Geneta Centrum for thirty thousand Swedish kronor per year. See "Assyrisk förening får lokal." The municipal Committee for Recreational Activities referred the case to the town council for financial help.

111. S. Andersson, *Assyrierna,* 71. He writes that more than fifty Syriac companies were active in Södertälje by 1980, with seventy by 1982. Ibid., 72.

112. This word can be translated as "toughs" and corresponds roughly to the British "Teddy Boys" of the same period.

113. Ambjörnsson and Janke, *Bråket på Bristol.*

114. "Lördagsnattens kravaller bara början: Polisen fruktar fortsatt rasbråk," *Länstidningen,* June 20, 1977, 4. See also "Här började rasbråket . . . Nu talas om hämnd," *Länstidningen,* June 20, 1977, 4. The conflict, I was told, happened to coincide with a United Nations meeting in Stockholm. An article published almost seven months later described how "the *raggare* riots in Södertälje in the summer of 1977 destroyed a great deal of Sweden's good reputation in international circles. . . . This was not without observing a certain schadenfreude from certain quarters." See Paul Neptune, "LT på besök i FN-skrapan i New York: Raggarbråket i Södertälje gav eko i FN," *Länstidningen,* February 1, 1978, 3. This tarnished Sweden's self-image as a "peace broker, opinion builder, and country on the forefront concerning questions of human rights." Ibid. Neptune mentioned that Kaj Sundberg, part of the Swedish delegation at the UN, argued that the international media had increased tensions by erroneously describing the events as "race riots" rather than "*raggare* riots." *LT* did the same, however.

115. See "Rasismens terror-natt," *Länstidningen,* August 25, 1980, 1; Sture Ankarstrand, "Det var sån här terror vi flydde från," *Länstidningen,* August 25, 1980, 4; Ankarstrand, "Hur

förberedd var vandaliseringen?," *Länstidningen,* August 25, 1980, 9; and Janne Holmström, "Det här gjorde vi bra, säger raggarna," *Länstidningen,* August 25, 1980, 5.

116. Other observers suggested that Syriacs should be forcibly redistributed around Sweden. High school student Yıldız Töker recounted his dismay about *raggare* power over public space in Södertälje for the *syrianska* magazine *Bahro Suryoyo* in May 1980, writing, "On Friday and Saturday nights, immigrant women almost don't dare to go out because they're afraid that they'll be attacked by the *raggare.*" See his "Att vara invandrare," 7.

117. Ambjörnsson and Janke, *Bråket på Bristol.*

118. In conversations with Syriacs, I heard about alternative versions, including "Södertälje belongs to the *assyrier!*" and "We're taking Södertälje!"

119. Ambjörnsson and Janke, *Bråket på Bristol.*

120. I could find no other records of the *raggare*'s rental of a clubhouse in Ronna Centrum, and other Syriacs discounted his story.

121. The Assyrian Association remained in Ronna until its move in the 1990s to a larger space in the Hovsjö industrial district, a remodeled former gardening center. This structure was partially destroyed in late September 2009 in an arson attack after a derby match between Södertälje's two major soccer teams, Assyriska FF and Syrianska FC. A protest on October 4, 2009, used the slogan "Stand up for Södertälje" *(Stå upp för Södertälje).* Despite pouring rain and cold temperatures, hundreds took part, including local politicians and musical artists. The marketing director of Assyriska FF, Robil Haidari, addressed the crowd at Politician Square. In a melancholy tone, he said, "They burned our *folkhem,*" using the most potent metaphor of Swedish Social Democratic politics.

122. Avermaete and van den Heuvel, "Obama, Please Tax Me!," 2.

123. Ardalan Samimi, "Vård på flera språk i Ronna," *Länstidningen,* July 28, 2011, http://lt.se/nyheter/sodertalje/1.1299939-vard-pa-flera-sprak-i-ronna.

124. Statistics Sweden, "Andel personer med utländsk bakgrund, 2016 jämfört med 2015," March 21, 2017, http://www.scb.se/hitta-statistik/statistik-efter-amne/befolkning/befolkningens-sammansattning/befolkningsstatistik/pong/tabell-och-diagram/topplistor-kommuner/andel-personer-med-utlandsk-bakgrund/; and "Andel utrikes födda 2016 jämfört med 2015," March 21, 2017, http://www.scb.se/hitta-statistik/statistik-efter-amne/befolkning/befolkningens-sammansattning/befolkningsstatistik/pong/tabell-och-diagram/topplistor-kommuner/andel-utrikes-fodda/.

125. Claire Soares, "Welcome to Mosul-on-Stockholm," *Independent,* July 16, 2007.

126. Nuri Kino, "Mesopotälje in the News Again," Assyrian International News Agency, February 3, 2009, http://www.aina.org/guesteds/20090301191747.htm; and Merit Wager, "En dag i Mesopotälje," *Svenska Dagbladet,* June 25, 2007.

127. See chapter 5 for more on this incident and how the nearby neighborhood of Lina Hage has developed a public identity that is said to contrast with Ronna's.

128. See the final report from 2011, Södertälje Kommun, "It's Time for Ronna!" Scathing critiques of this project have come from within, given that nothing from the initiatives was implemented and hopes were raised unnecessarily, despite an introduction to the report that ends, "Now the work begins!"

129. Nisha Besara, "Ronna—Sveriges Chinatown," *Aftonbladet,* February 14, 2006.

130. Ibid.

131. Bhabha, *The Location of Culture,* 3 (my emphasis).

132. Borgegård and Kemeny, "Sweden," 35.

3. Making Mesopotälje

1. Clifford, "Diasporas"; and Clifford, *Routes.*

2. Ho, *The Graves of Tarim.* His first chapter, beginning on page 3, has this phrase as its title. He explains, "The diaspora is a society in which the absent are a constant incitement to discourse about things moving. We may call the diaspora 'the society of the absent' as a convenience and a theoretical position because in it, discourses of mobility appear as both cause and effect and are inseparable from diasporic life, saturating its internal social space." Ibid., 19.

3. Brah, *Cartographies of Diaspora.*

4. Gilroy, *The Black Atlantic.*

5. See Ghosh, "The Diaspora in Indian Culture."

6. Werbner, "The Place Which Is Diaspora," 119.

7. A one-day conference entitled "Diaspora Cities: Urban Mobility and Dwelling" emphasized these connections and was held at Queen Mary, University of London, on September 16, 2009. See http://www.ucl.ac.uk/urbanlab-archive/en2/index.php?page=1.3.0 &listnumber=1&getlistarticle=60&listrange=archive.

8. Erik Sandberg and Nuri Kino refer to Assyriska FF as a "national team without a country" in the title of their 2005 documentary film series, *Assyriska—Landslag utan land.*

9. Ho, *Graves of Tarim,* 20.

10. Cetrez, *Syrisk-ortodoxa kyrkan.*

11. Rabo, "'Without Our Church We Will Disappear.'"

12. This can be compared to Pnina Werbner's description of religious practices in apartments among Pakistani Muslims living in the United Kingdom. See Werbner, *The Migration Process.*

13. Björklund, "North to Another Country," 63.

14. Ibid.

15. Damascus has been the official headquarters of the Syriac Orthodox Church since 1959, but Beirut has been, in part, its shelter during the Syrian civil war in the 2010s.

16. Björklund writes, "At that time a discussion was being held in Sweden about financial support from the state for 'immigrants' churches.' The Swedish YMCA (the KFUM) was the organization which argued most strongly for the immigrants' churches. In 1971 an agreement was reached whereby the Syrian Orthodox priest was appointed for two years (from 1st July 1971) by the KFUM, the money for his stipend being provided by the Swedish Immigration and Naturalization Board." Björklund, "North to Another Country," 63.

17. Ibid.

18. For more on the order of events, see Wannes, *Syrisk-ortodoxa kyrkan.*

19. Sture Ankarstrand, "Det var sån här terror vi flydde från," *Länstidningen,* August 25, 1980, 4.

20. In the 1980s, the construction of new churches continued in Turkey, despite the loss of the Christian population. In a Swedish television program from 1981, residents of one village discussed church construction as a form of protection from external threats and as a way to maintain a local presence. One man said, "We have expanded the church so that they will protect us and so that our saints will have mercy and help us. We believe that if we build the church, we will be able to stay here." See TV1's *Var kommer du ifrån—Vart är du på väg?*

21. Maria Morris, "Syrisk-ortodoxa kyrkan: Vi vill ha en tomt av kommunen," *Länstidningen,* July 11, 1980, 4.

22. Several articles concerning the church were published in *Länstidningen* on March 20, 1979, including Ida Dahlgren, "Syrisk-ortodoxa kyrkan: Tung doft av rökelse och orientalisk sång," 16; Dahlgren, "Religionsfrihet i Sverige är viktig för George," 16; Dahlgren, "Fakta om syrisk-ortodoxa kyrkan," 16; and "Näst största kyrkan finns i rivningshus," 1.

23. "Kyrka för invandrare," *Länstidningen,* June 30, 1975, 2. Articles published in June 1977 described the visit of the patriarch of the Syriac Orthodox Church, who came from Damascus to Södertälje and held services in the church "behind the police station." Maria Morris, "Patriarken av Damaskus ledde syrisk gudstjänst med rökelse, bön och sång," *Länstidningen,* June 14, 1977, 18; and "På knä för patriarken," *Länstidningen,* June 14, 1977, 1. These articles labeled the group *syrier* rather than *assyrier* or *syrianer,* probably in response to the patriarch's sermon, which included a warning that they "absolutely cannot use the word *assyrier.* They must call themselves *syrier,* and the church is called *syrisk-ortodox.*" Morris, "Patriarken av Damaskus ledde syrisk gudstjänst med rökelse, bön och sång." The church is described as having a "Spartan interior design, with only a few small paintings," with men on the ground level and women and children in the balcony (ibid.).

24. "Kyrka för invandrare."

25. "Näst största kyrkan finns i rivningshus." Dahlgren's adjacent article, "Fakta om syrisk-ortodoxa kyrkan," states that the Syriac Orthodox Church had 2,300 members in Södertälje, 8,000 in Sweden, and 2.5 million around the world; it also mentions a "church building fund," a portion of the forty thousand Swedish kronor that the church collected from members in 1978.

26. Ida Dahlgren, "Hasse Mattsson till husvilla syrianer: Ni kan väl skaffa en ny kyrka i Stockholm," *Länstidningen,* March 22, 1979, 3.

27. Stefan Andersson, "Svårt hitta kyrka för assyrierna," *Länstidningen,* November 29, 1979, 10.

28. Morris, "Syrisk-ortodoxa kyrkan."

29. They noted that since they worship "while standing," less room would be needed. S. Andersson, "Svårt hitta kyrka för assyrierna."

30. Morris, "Syrisk-ortodoxa kyrkan."

31. Ulf Sundblad, "Invandring bör spridas över landet," *Länstidningen,* May 30, 1980, 3.

32. Morris, "Syrisk-ortodoxa kyrkan."

33. Stockholm had been suggested even earlier, but the Syriacs specifically asked to build a church in the Södertälje neighborhoods of Ronna or Geneta "where the most of the parish's members live." See Dahlgren, "Hasse Mattsson till husvilla syrianer."

34. S. Andersson, "Svårt hitta kyrka för assyrierna."

35. Quoted in Morris, "Syrisk-ortodoxa kyrkan."

36. Quoted in ibid.

37. Ibid.

38. Quoted in ibid. Site studies solved the parking problems. Initially, the plan called for sixty-four parking places, but ample space for more remained on the site.

39. Ankarstrand, "Det var sån här terror vi flydde från"; Janne Holmström, "Det här gjorde vi bra, säger raggarna," *Länstidningen,* August 25, 1980, 5; and "Rasismens terror-natt," *Länstidningen,* August 25, 1980, 1.

40. The church as built has a prominent sign on its facade that labels it "S:t Afrem Syrianska Ortodoxa Kyrkan," reflecting the parish's preference for *syriansk* over *syrisk* as the

translation of *Syriac*. I will continue to refer to it as St. Afrem's Syriac Orthodox Church in the remainder of the text.

41. They sought space for one thousand. Morris, "Syrisk-ortodoxa kyrkan."

42. Atto, "Hostages in the Homeland, Orphans in the Diaspora," 179, n332. Christian stonecutters from Midyat were so widely known that many had been commissioned to work on mosques in Turkey, Syria, and Iraq (ibid.).

43. "Byggnadslov för nybyggnad av klockstapel, kv. Hundäxingen 7, Klockarvägen 110, Södertälje," April 24, 1985. The building permit was signed by Dan Björklund.

44. In February 1992, the Stockholm County Administrative Board received and approved an application to bury the recently deceased archbishop, Mor K. Jacoub Kas Georges, on the grounds of the church (Number 212-1992-934). They then approved a permit to construct a physical grave in October 1993 (Number 212-93-32436). The Södertälje Municipal Planning Department provided a building permit for a one-story grave of 37.8 square meters on the north side of the existing church later that month (Diary Number 93–787). This was followed by other proposals for parking spaces and additional burial spaces.

45. For more on the complexities concerning ethnicity and naming in Sweden, see Björklund, "North to Another Country," especially 138–52; and Bertil Nelhans's introduction to Nelhans, *Assyrier*. Deniz offers a background and historical overview of the terms *assyrier, suryoyo, syrianer,* and *araméer* (Deniz, *En minoritets odyssé,* 117–20) and a detailed explanation of name-related conflicts (ibid., 282–90). Atto also explores these themes in "Hostages in the Homeland, Orphans in the Diaspora," esp. chap. 7.

46. Roland Petterson and Janne Holmström, "De tog farväl av Aslan Noyan," *Länstidningen,* October 1, 1980, 7.

47. *Varför mördades Aslan Noyan?,* SVT2.

48. An *LT* article two years earlier had declared, "The organization is being run from Södertälje." See Janne Holmström and Roland Thunström, "Så är ADO uppbyggt: Verksamheten styrs från Södertälje," *Länstidningen,* September 24, 1980, 5.

49. *Varför mördades Aslan Noyan?*

50. Deniz, *En minoritets odyssé,* 209.

51. *Varför mördades Aslan Noyan?*

52. Ibid.

53. *Suryoye* is the plural form of *Suryoyo,* referring to a group or an individual with this background, respectively. Suryoyo is, as noted, also an emic term for the Neo-Aramaic language that members of the group speak. Having applied a recognizably Swedish term—*assyrier*—to all Middle Eastern Christians who had come to Sweden since 1967, the conflicts over names were troubling for a Swedish state that suddenly realized that it had contributed to them. The State Immigration Board thus commissioned research, including Ulf Björklund's report *Från ofärd till välfärd,* developed into his dissertation "North to Another Country." See also Knutsson, *Assur eller Aram.* While Swedish authorities had assumed that classical Syriac was the everyday language of the group, Knutsson's report clarified that the language was used exclusively in liturgy and that the Neo-Aramaic dialect Suryoyo was used in conversation, though Syriacs who grew up in Kurdish-dominated villages in Turkey, or speaking Arabic in Syria or Iraq, might not speak Suryoyo.

54. *Hujådå,* "Namnkonflikten."

55. Ibid.

56. As noted, the *assyrier* link themselves to the ancient Assyrian empire, a pre-Christian civilization. Today the *syrianer* typically claim links to the ancient *araméer* (Aramaeans). See, for example, the website of St. Afrem's Syriac Orthodox Church for more: http://www.stafrem.se/page.php?p=19.

57. For more on the chronology of these events, see Deniz, *En minoritets odyssé,* 282–84.

58. *Hujådå,* "Namnkonflikten."

59. As quoted in 1980 in *Bahro Suryoyo,* "Nationalitet" (emphasis in the original). The journal is today the official publication of the Syrianska Federation. The text suggests that the patriarch concedes the existence of Assyrian and other ethnicities but separates them from the religious designation.

60. I received this form from an informant. One corner includes a stamp that states, "Södertälje Sverige 1975" and "Syriska Ortodoxa kyrkan." Presumably, the date refers to the establishment of the church in the town. While the form included threats to both Assyrians and Aramaeans, today, many *syrianer* actively link themselves to Aramaean groups. As the name used by Syriacs in Germany and other European countries, this linkage provides transnational power.

61. Çakır, "Historia," 6.

62. "Ansökan om bygglov i Almen 8 i Södertälje," January 24, 1991. This letter is sealed with the official stamp of Father Gabriel Isik (priest) and signed by him, Avgun Bahe (chairperson), Nail Davidson, Semun Tastekin, and Yusuf Büyükbalik.

63. Syrisk-ortodoxa kyrkans ärkestift, "Ansökan om organisationsnummer," November 8, 1990.

64. Ibid. See also Södertälje Kommun, Byggnadsnämnden, Byggnadsärende, Almen 8, "Förhandsförfrågan: Ombyggnad av bottenvåning till local för religiös/kyrklig verksamhet," March 6, 1991.

65. For more, see Atto, "Hostages in the Homeland, Orphans in the Diaspora," 347–48.

66. I heard varying reports about the total cost, ranging from 4.5 to 8.3 million kronor.

67. Hollerweger, *Living Cultural Heritage Turabdin.*

68. The parish originally aimed to house the burial spaces in the basement of the church building, but the County Administrative Board (Länsstyrelsen) denied their application on the grounds that they had not paid off the mortgage for the church building. The detached site for the burial space, with a unique local development plan, evaded this regulation. Josef pointed out to me that Swedish churches would never face this problem, given their secure finances, "which is why they have so many cemeteries outside."

69. See Levitt, *God Needs No Passport,* for a related discussion about how immigrant groups in the United States use large spaces as megachurches for temporary worship.

70. Syriac journalist and activist Nuri Kino created a five-part documentary for Swedish television with Erik Sandberg, called "Assyriska: National Team without a country." Sandberg and Kino, *Assyriska: Landslag utan land.*

71. As its early incarnation was deemed by Al Jazeera's *Sportsworld* during the broadcast.

72. Dawod, "Uppstickarlaget." In Turkey in 2009, I saw an Assyriska FF banner at the cash register in Midyat, and almost every Syriac I met there mentioned the teams.

73. Every recent World Cup has sparked the publication of new books on soccer and national identity, and scholarly attention has increasingly focused on immigrant teams across Europe.

74. Such as Bromberger, "Football as World-View and as Ritual."

75. For example, I was in Gällivare in the summer of 2008 to attend the Viva World Cup, a tournament for "national" teams not recognized by FIFA (Fédération internationale de Football Association) and including teams from Padania, Provence, Kurdistan, and Sami-land and a team called Aramaeans Suryoye. The coach of this last team told me he did not regard Syrianska as the Syriac national team, since it paid non-Syriacs to play. Instead, he argued that his team, comprising only Syriac players, was the true national team.

76. Sandberg and Kino, *Assyriska: Landslag utan land*.

77. Dawod, "Uppstickarlaget."

78. For example, a 1976 article stated that Assyriska FF usually had two hundred to three hundred spectators. See Maria Morris, "Glädjeyra runt fotbollsplanen," *Länstidningen,* October 25, 1976, 4. Morris described the scene: "When the *assyrier* play soccer, there is life and speed on the field. And when they make a goal, yes, there is no end to the cheers of celebration. In other words, they treat the game with verve and pleasure." She also noted, however, that "many *assyrier* sit in their cars and watch the match. They honk their horns for several minutes. This is a dreadful noise."

79. "Fotboll och slagsmål," *Länstidningen,* May 30, 1980, 3.

80. Intriguingly, during conversations with early arrivals, I was told that either they or one of their family members had founded the Assyriska FF team. I came to understand that this meant they had played with the team early on, a claim that gave them status, given the team's later successes. The actual founder of the team is acknowledged to be the man now known as "Mr. Assyriska," Melek Bisso. In 2007, a cartoon version of his highly recognizable face was prominently displayed on a banner that the Zelge Fans had prepared for a derby.

81. Media coverage attests to this rapid advance. One match summary described how Assyriska defeated Bårsta 4–2 and was already doing well in the division to which it had just advanced, Division VI. Patrik Österblad, "Div VI och VII," *Länstidningen,* April 28, 1980, 24. On the same page, summaries of other Syriac teams' matches were included; they were then playing in Division VII (Suryoyo was defeated by Finlandia 0–7, and Midyat lost to Hölö/Mörkö 2–11).

82. The field is artificial turf and measures 105 by 68 meters.

83. "Historien om den moderna Zelge," Assyriska team website, September 11, 2008, http://www.assyriska.se/index.php?id=27&articleID=1250&page=85&filter_year=0&filter_text=. Sharro seems to self-reference ethnic stereotyping often found in Swedish media representations of immigrants.

84. *Zelge* means "sun ray" in Suryoyo and refers to the rays on the Assyrian national flag. *Gefe* means "wings" in Suryoyo and refers to the wings on the Syrianska flag, which are modeled after an Aramaean symbol. See Syrianska Riksförbundet i Sverige, "Syrianer—en nation i förskingring" for more on the latter.

85. The Zelge Fans sometimes offered regular updates to fans through their Web-based Zelge TV programming, connecting to fans beyond the boundaries of not only the town but Sweden. For more, see my 2008 ethnographic film about the Zelge Fans, *Assyriska until We Die . . . .*

86. In September 2007, I was shooting video for my film. As match host, Syrianska FC controlled the stadium during the match, and I had asked for permission to film but had been denied via a text message from the board. The Zelge Fans assumed this to be retribution

for a declined request from the Syrianska side during Assyriska's home derby match earlier in the season. I accompanied the Zelge Fans to film their preparations hours before kickoff. A light rain was falling, and as I stood trying to shield my camera with an umbrella over my shoulder, a representative of Syrianska ran across the field to me. She said the police would be called if I did not remove my camera from the stadium immediately.

87. Assyriska FF advanced to Superettan at the end of the 2007 season, but Syrianska FC took one additional year to reach that division.

88. The May 2007 derby match between Assyriska FF and Syrianska FC had an audience of over 7,000, despite the arena's official capacity of 6,700.

89. Roland Pettersson, "För högt buller från arenan," *Länstidningen,* June 20, 2011.

90. Barthes, *What Is Sport?,* 57–58.

91. This was covered closely in the media at the time. See, for instance, Sara Sjöström, "Gator ska döpas efter stans minoriteter," *Länstidningen,* December 15, 2008.

92. The patriarch declared he would only visit religious sites in Södertälje during his stay in 2015, avoiding the hornet's nest of the name conflict and its expression in the rivalries between the federations and associations. Linda, a Syriac who identifies as an *assyrier* and is in her thirties, explained proudly that the Hovsjö site made this easier than did the one in Geneta, since "the fence between St. Jacob's and the Assyrian Cultural Center divides the religious from the nationalist. At *Syrianska* [and at St. Afrem's in Geneta], everything is mixed together in one place." She explained, however, that the Syriac Orthodox Church's flag, originally placed on the Assyrian Cultural Center's site, had to be moved.

93. The St. Jacob's group considered this site, but neighbors' complaints about the proposed clearance of the forest and about late-night parties and weddings made them reconsider.

94. The original design, in a ziggurat form, was created by a member of the congregation; it could not proceed owing to a lack of financing, although ground was broken in 2011. A June 2015 SVT broadcast outlined the new plans for a smaller church, accommodating three hundred worshippers. See the SVT article *Planer för kaldeisk kyrka i Hovsjö,* http://www.svt .se/nyheter/lokalt/sodertalje/planer-pa-kaldeisk-kyrka-i-hovsjo.

95. The former Tax House was sold by St. Jacob's to Coptic Christians for 11.5 million Swedish kronor and is now known as St. Mina's Coptic Orthodox Church. More recently, Somali and Palestinian Muslim groups have begun worshipping in spaces in Södertälje, but they have experienced vandalism in this town where, in contrast to most other Swedish cities, immigrants are predominantly Christian. See Roger Stigell and Katrin Hellström, "Hatbrott mot muslimers lokaler i Södertälje," *Länstidningen,* September 12, 2014, http://lt.se /nyheter/sodertalje/1.2633788-hatbrott-mot-muslimers-lokaler-i-sodertalje.

4. "Södertälje Is a Theater"

1. de Certeau, *The Practice of Everyday Life*; and Lefebvre, *The Production of Space.*

2. Deniz, *En minoritets odyssé,* 313–17.

3. Herzfeld, *Cultural Intimacy.*

4. Veblen, *Theory of the Leisure Class.*

5. Description of *iamjustagirl* from http://www.ticnet.se/, an online ticket sales agent.

6. For a detailed discussion of Syriac endogamy in Sweden, see Deniz, *En minoritets odyssé,* 257–65.

7. Rabo, "'Without Our Church We Will Disappear,'" 192.

8. Jane Jacobs coined the term "eyes on the street" to describe a similar monitoring function, intended to bolster public safety in Greenwich Village. See her *The Death and Life of Great American Cities.*

9. Aho, *Assyrier/Syrianer,* 46.

10. Some such incidents have resulted in a woman's death, including the high-profile killing of Fadime Sahindal, a Kurdish woman, by her father. For more, see Wikan, *In Honor of Fadime*; and Kurkiala, *I varje trumslag jordens puls.*

11. Many informants expressed outrage, despair, or anger about the show, since it seemed to parody the group. The couples portrayed were said to be "extreme" examples, and the narrator, owner of a kiosk in Södertälje, appeared to reinforce negative stereotypes about Syriacs specifically and immigrants generally. *Mitt stora feta syrianska bröllop,* TV3.

12. See Simone, "People as Infrastructure"; and Larkin, "The Politics and Poetics of Infrastructure."

13. Bondeson, *Seder och bruk vid bröllop.*

14. Ibid., 48.

15. Frykman and Löfgren, *Culture Builders.*

16. Hairstyling is also a common profession among Syriacs, suggesting that hair services may be provided through reciprocal economic transactions. Aho describes hairstyling as "the absolutely most common profession that youth choose." Aho, *Assyrier/Syrianer,* 40.

17. For the websites of Princessa and Svanens Hus, see http://princessa.se/ and http://www.svanenshus.se/, respectively.

18. Deniz, *En minoritets odyssé,* 314.

19. While the *assyrier* have numerous options, the *syrianer* typically limited themselves to a few dances, especially to *katfothe* and *hurse.*

20. When two arsons in 2009 and 2010, together with water damage, required its renovation, the Assyrian Association decided to make the cultural center into a more "neutral [and therefore marketable] space," as the director told me in 2015. New exterior decorations with Assyrian imperial themes added in 2017 belied this, however.

21. Underscoring its superficial understanding of these events, the program *Mitt stora feta syrianska bröllop* implied that weddings on this scale were possible only because Syriacs had black-market sources of income.

22. Mauss, *The Gift.*

23. For more on how Syriacs are connected to larger families, and their historical importance in connection to their migrations, see Björklund, "North to Another Country."

24. During weddings and major holidays, parking spaces are always at a premium, as was mentioned many times by both church officials and city planners working on the design and planning of the new or renovated Syriac Orthodox, Chaldean, and Coptic churches in Södertälje.

25. Kino and Nordberg, *Välgörarna,* 159.

26. Ecer, *I fikonträdets skugga,* 81.

27. Syriac birth announcements sometimes appear alongside majority Swedish counterparts. The free municipal paper *Södertälje Posten* offers family announcements like this without charge.

28. This is specified in the addendum (1999:306) to the burial law *Begravningslag* (1990:1144). See http://rkrattsbaser.gov.se/sfsr?bet=1990:1144 for a list of legal changes to the

1990 law. For more on the public burial infrastructure developed during the second half of the twentieth century, see SOU 1961:5; SOU 1987:16; and SOU 1997:42.

29. The burial or cremation is to be paid for by the estate of the deceased, and no funeral costs are covered. For members of the Church of Sweden, however, these costs are covered.

30. Kjell Lundquist notes that Martin Luther suggested suburban cemeteries during the Reformation but that the idea was not implemented for more than two hundred years. Luther explicitly intended to change cemeteries "from a marketplace and common to a place for Christian worship and contemplation. A person shall not visit the cemetery merely to observe the vanity in everything worldly but to meditate there about death and resurrection." Lundquist, "Från beteshage till trädgård," 17.

31. Historically, Swedish graves often included men's professional titles on their gravestones.

32. Ho, *The Graves of Tarim*, 3.

33. "Samtal," SVT.

34. One of the first to promote these ideas was the German landscape theorist C. C. L. Hirschfeld in his *Theory of Garden Art*, published in five volumes from 1779 to 1785.

35. See their Facebook page for additional details: http://www.facebook.com/StJacobkat ederal. The information originally came from the group's website, at http://www.morjacob .se/ but now (when this book was published) mostly defunct.

36. Inger Ödebrink, "Invandrarbegravningar inget problem i Södertälje," *Länstidningen*, April 8, 1980, 10. The text does not mention why 1974 was a key date in this debate, and I could find no further information.

37. Ibid.

38. Linda Asmar's article was originally entitled "Assyrier/syrianer får egen del på kyrko-gård," but the title was changed to "Syrisk-ortodoxa får egen del på kyrkogård" the next day. This probably reflects the critique that the issue concerned the religious group (Syriac Orthodox Christians) rather than the identity group (*assyrier* or *syrianer*). See Linda Asmar, "Syrisk-ortodoxa får egen del på kyrkogård," *Länstidningen*, March 4, 2009.

39. Linda Asmar, "Barqasho är kritisk till syrisk-ortodox gravplats: Syrisk-ortodoxa kyr-kan önskar att de blivit tillfrågade," *Länstidningen*, March 17, 2009.

40. Ibid.

41. Ibid.

42. Linda Asmar, "Kyrkor får inga egna gravplatser," *Länstidningen*, May 30, 2009.

43. Ibid.

44. Text by Richard Dybeck, 1844; the music is "Folkmelodi från Västmanland."

45. Repatriations of the remains of Syriacs to Turkey and Syria—especially of the elderly who had grown up there—were becoming more common until the Syrian civil war.

46. Ho, *The Graves of Tarim*, xxiii.

47. Ibid., 3.

48. My first apartment was two blocks from the scene, and several friends expressed relief when I moved from there to Ronna, since they would no longer need to visit the tainted street. Another incident involved four adolescent boys who had been at a volleyball tourna-ment and died together in a car accident. Ishtar described how everyone left school to march to the cemetery. Their adjacent gravestones, with spires and volleyball themes, united them forever in death.

49. Rabo, "'Familjen betyder allt' eller 'Vi blir snart lika kalla som svenskarna,'" 217.

50. Banham, *Los Angeles*.

5. Greetings from Hollywood!

1. *Petteri på villovägar,* SVT2.

2. Douglas, *Purity and Danger.* Douglas describes cultural taboos around dirt. See Herzfeld's "Spatial Cleansing" for another relevant discussion of the relationship between physical space and "matter out of place."

3. Ley, "Between Europe and Asia."

4. For a full description and the sequence of events, see Johan Edgar, "Jättebråk urartade i kravaller," *Aftonbladet,* September 12, 2005.

5. Residents and the media later criticized the police for their disproportionate reaction. See Johan Edgar, "Polisen slog till för hårt," *Aftonbladet,* September 12, 2005.

6. Bosse Brink, "Två anhållna för skotten i Ronna," *Svenska Dagbladet,* September 20, 2005.

7. Molina, "Den rasifierade staden," 63 (emphasis in the original).

8. See Bradley, Tunström, and Broms Wessel, *Bor vi i samma stad?* for an interesting analysis of ethnic segregation and its articulation as a problem in contemporary urban planning.

9. In her esteemed thesis, urban-design researcher Ann Legeby used methods from "space syntax" to analyze how Södertälje's Million Program areas remain disconnected from the central city. See Legeby, "Urban Segregation and Urban Form."

10. Molina, "Intersektionella rumsligheter."

11. For more on this, see R. Andersson, "The Geographical and Social Mobility of Immigrants"; and Murdie and Borgegård, "Immigration, Spatial Segregation and Housing Segmentation of Immigrants in Metropolitan Stockholm, 1960–1995." For an analysis of how this has affected internal migrations after the reception period, see R. Andersson, "Invandrarnas rörlighet."

12. Aho, *Assyrier/Syrianer,* 30.

13. S. Andersson, *Assyrierna,* 70.

14. Ibid.

15. Wacquant, *Urban Outcasts.*

16. R. Andersson, "Skapandet av svenskglesa bostadsområden," 125. Andersson recommends that the analytical scale should be increased to include the "segregated" neighborhood *and* its surroundings, in order to adopt a more holistic view (ibid., 154). Susan Bickford argues that physical space has a key role in creating social boundaries and argues that a focus on a "regional democratic public" and "overlapping" rather than functional separation could increase diversity in publics and spaces. Bickford, "Constructing Inequality," 368–69.

17. Li, *Ethnoburb.*

18. Fong, *The First Suburban Chinatown.*

19. See Åström, *Svensk stadsplanering;* Fraenki, *Swedish Urban Planning;* and Hall, "Urban Planning in Sweden" for more on the development of Swedish planning laws over time. Hall describes the 1874 ordinances as "the beginning of a new era," since they focus on "the large cities of the industrial age" instead of smaller towns. Hall, ibid., 179. See also Boverket, "Plan- och bygglagstiftningens utveckling," September 24, 2014, http://www.bover ket.se/sv/PBL-kunskapsbanken/Allmant-om-PBL/lag--ratt/plan--och-bygglagstiftningens -utveckling/.

20. Hall, "Urban Planning in Sweden," 180.

21. Fraenki, *Swedish Urban Planning,* chap. 2: 3.

22. Boverket, "Plan- och bygglagstiftningens utveckling."

23. Fraenki, chap. 2: 4. The Building Statute of 1959 also, in a sense, necessitated the professionalization of city planning, although no degrees in planning were offered at Swedish universities until the 1970s. The Municipal Reform of 1971 consolidated the scale of operation, combining smaller townships, villages, and other areas into a smaller number of larger municipalities *(kommuner)*.

24. The PBL was submitted as a bill to the Swedish Parliament in 1985 (Proposition 1985/86:1). The law (Plan- och bygglag [1987:10]) went into effect on July 1, 1987. While many revisions were added over time, a new PBL (Plan- och bygglag [2010:900]) took effect on May 2, 2011, replacing the 1987 law. The 1987 law was in effect during the development of the single-family housing areas in Lina Hage and is the law discussed in detail in this section.

25. Boverket, "Plan- och bygglagstiftningens utveckling." See also Hall, "Urban Planning in Sweden," 198–99. Each municipality now needed a master plan that also delineated "the way in which the municipality intends to safeguard national interests." Fraenki, *Swedish Urban Planning,* chap. 5: 2.

26. The *översiktsplan* also replaced the *markdispositionsplan* and *kommunöversikt,* both of which were previously created under the National Board of Physical Planning and Building, or Statens Planverk. See Hall, "Urban Planning in Sweden," 199–200. This agency was merged with the National Housing Board to become the National Board of Housing, Building, and Planning (Boverket) in 1998.

27. Fraenki, *Swedish Urban Planning,* chap. 6: 1.

28. Boverket, *Boken om detaljplan och områdesbestämmelser,* 11. The "permitted content" of the *detaljplan* was as follows: (1) "the siting, design, and construction of buildings"; (2) "the plot ratio above and below ground level"; (3) "the use of buildings"; (4) "vegetation, the design of the land, and the position of the ground surface"; (5) "protection regulations and prohibition of demolitions"; (6) "the size and siting of parking areas"; (7) "earmarking of land on a development site for public traffic, public pipelines, and cables of energy installations"; (8) "modernisation requirements"; (9) "the use and design of public places"; (10) "fencing and exits to public places"; and (11) "temporary use of land or buildings." Fraenki, *Swedish Urban Planning,* chap. 6: 11.

29. Under the 1987 PBL, the flow of the planning process for a *detaljplan* under normal circumstances was as follows: (1) master planning *(översiktsplanering)*; (2) program consultation *(programsamråd)*; (3) plan consultation *(plansamråd)*; (4) exhibition *(utställning)*; (5) passage *(antagande)*; (6) review *(prövning)*; (7) legal force *(laga kraft)*. Appeals are forwarded to the County Administrative Board (Länsstyrelsen), and, if appealed again, to the Land and Environment Court (Mark- och miljödomstolen) and the Land and Environment Superior Court (Mark- och miljööverdomstolen). The County Administrative Board has power "only if a municipal plan is thought to threaten environmental and other national interests, or if plans touch on intermunicipal interests, or if a development is considered unsuitable from the point of view of health or safety." Hall, "Urban Planning in Sweden," 202. A decision of the County Administrative Board becomes valid three weeks later, in the absence of a further appeal, while a state-level decision goes into effect immediately (PBL 5:31).

30. Boverket, "Plan- och bygglagstiftningens utveckling."

31. Boverket, *Boken om detaljplan och områdesbestämmelser,* 8.

32. Ibid., 127. In the absence of a *detaljplan,* a proposed building is evaluated in accordance with chapter 2 of the PBL.

33. See the UrbAct website, http://urbact.eu/reggov, for further information. This is part of a program entitled RegGov, or "Regional Governance of Sustainable Integrated Development of Deprived Urban Areas."

34. Boverket, *Boken om detaljplan och områdesbestämmelser,* 21.

35. The neighborhood of Hovsjö was the initial choice for the project, but the conflict of interest with the Telge Hovsjö group made the neighborhood less desirable for the EU intervention.

36. In 2009, I was invited to present on the construction of St. Jacob's Cathedral at a workshop in Hovsjö and was surprised when my talk was described as giving "the users' perspective" *(brukarperspektivet).* Abdul Khakee critiques this approach, writing, "Planners think the local people interfere with a well-ordered process and that active groups do not represent the interests of the community in which they live. . . . No wonder the methods planned to allow local people to take part in planning have not satisfied them: most comprise forms of one-way communication, including hearings, meetings, and exhibitions." Khakee, "Politics, Methods, and Planning Culture," 279.

37. Jonsson, *Från egnahem till villa,* 21.

38. Hall and Vidén, "The Million Homes Programme," 304.

39. Jonsson notes that this has often been omitted from studies of twentieth-century Swedish housing. Jonsson, *Från egnahem till villa,* 17. From 1935 until the early 1990s, nonprofit municipal housing corporations had an advantage over other developers in securing Swedish state support. In 1991 a parliamentary decision eliminated this, reshaping housing construction after 1992.

40. Hall, "Urban Planning in Sweden," 228–29.

41. Jonsson distinguishes between the early-twentieth-century owner-occupied house *(egnahem),* used for both living and working and often part of a farmstead, and the later detached house *(villa),* used solely for dwelling. Explaining that *egnahem* and *villa* had ideological resonance, "the term single-family home *[enfamiljshus]* is intended to serve as a more value-neutral structural concept, which in itself includes both the *egna hem* and the *villa."* Jonsson, *Från egnahem till villa,* 13–14. The type received other designations, such as in *Good Housing in Small Houses,* where the Housing Board refers to "houses in the garden," meaning everything from the single-family home to the row house; "that is to say, the most attractive housing types for families with children." See Kungliga Bostadsstyrelsen, *God bostad i småhus,* 3.

42. See Jonsson, *Från egnahem till villa,* 53–71.

43. Ibid., 64.

44. Ibid., 69.

45. Ibid., 70.

46. Daun, *Swedish Mentality.*

47. Hall, "Urban Planning in Sweden," 228. Furthermore, "as interest on loans was tax deductible, the progressive tax system meant that the higher income-earners enjoyed a greater tax benefit." Ibid., 229.

48. Jonsson, *Från egnahem till villa,* 35.

49. Lorenz Berglund, "Kärvt idag, men. . . . Nästa år blir det lättare att komma över småhus!" *Länstidningen,* February 8, 1974, 4.

50. Ibid.

51. "Dubbelt fler bostäder byggs i flerfamiljshus," *Länstidningen,* February 8, 1974, 4.

52. Berglund, "Kärvt idag, men."

53. Gelotte, *Telgebostäder genom fyra årtionden,* 77.

54. For example, see "Vitbok om Lina," *Länstidningen,* September 21, 1973, 2; and Kerstin Weyler, "Varför ska man bygga i Lina egentligen?" *Länstidningen,* November 9, 1977, 4.

55. "Centerpartiet: Planera efter människors behov: Lina-planen måste göras om!" *Länstidningen,* September 11, 1973, 5.

56. Wolfgang Hansson, "Omarbetat förslag för Södra Lina: Kommunen tog intryck av kritik från de boende," *Länstidningen,* June 27, 1979, 3.

57. Erskine's office had been involved for several years and had even held meetings with concerned town dwellers in 1977. See Weyler, "Varför ska man bygga i Lina egentligen?"

58. Gelotte, *Telgebostäder genom fyra årtionden,* 81. Comparing the 1979 *stadsplan* to the area's form as built reveals the omission of several planned housing areas and two institutional zones.

59. For more on the Södertälje Municipal Council's positions about living at ground level, see "Fullmäktige: Oenighet om Lina—Nu är det byggklart," *Länstidningen,* February 26, 1980, 16.

60. "Klyftan 4: Södertälje—Stad i världen," SVT.

61. Gelotte, Dahlström Rittsél, and Ulfstrand, *Nästa hållplats Södertälje,* 33.

62. "En månad sedan upploppet i Södertälje," SR.

63. The *detaljplan* for Hollywood also specifies use. Under "Degree of Utilization," the legend on the plan states, "Apart from the main building, a maximum of two sheds/garages may be built, for a total of 50 m² per lot." Under "Placement, Layout, and Design," the legend reads, "The attic may not be designed to exceed this number of stories. In the case of an underground level, the main building may only be built to one story"; and "P1 This regulation concerns freestanding, single-family houses: The main building shall be placed at least 4.0 m from the property boundary. The shed/garage shall be placed at least 1.5 m from the property boundary and at least 6.0 m from the street."

64. *Rosenberg: Sveriges val,* part 1, *Nationen,* TV4.

65. Carin Götblad, "Så ska vi stoppa den grova brottsligheten i Södertälje," *Dagens Nyheter,* June 17, 2011. Widely discussed and reposted extensively on social-networking sites, the article elicited a sharp response a few days later from a group calling itself (in English) the Assyrian-Chaldean-Syriac Association (ACSA). Their representatives stated, "Götblad bunches an entire ethnic group together with criminals." See Özcan Kaldoyo and Olle Wiberg, "Götblad buntar ihop en hel folkgrupp med kriminella," *Dagens Nyheter,* June 21, 2011.

66. Einar Haakaas and Frode Sætran, "—Vi bor alle i samme by, men ikke i samme verden," *Aftenposten,* May 15, 2015, http://www.aftenposten.no/norge/--Vi-bor-alle-i-samme -by_-men-ikke-i-samme-verden-61348b.html.

67. Ibid.

68. She said this in English, hence my use of "Assyrian."

69. Pred, *Even in Sweden.*

70. See also Thompson's *Rubbish Theory* for a parallel example in a London neighborhood where Greek Cypriots added new ornamentation to previously sedate buildings.

71. Jacobs, *The Death and Life of Great American Cities.*

72. See Friedl, *Vasilika,* for a related discussion of how Greek village houses were constructed to impede prying.

73. Caldeira, *City of Walls,* 259.

74. Douglas, *Purity and Danger.*

75. See also "Södertälje: Immigration the Swedish Way," Radio Sweden, December 26, 2012.

76. Compare with Gans, *The Urban Villagers.*

77. Bowen, *Why the French Don't Like Headscarves.* For another analysis of the paradoxes embedded in bureaucratic rhetoric, see Kapferer, *Legends of People, Myths of State.*

78. Christophers, "A Monstrous Hybrid."

79. Bourdieu, "Site Effects," 124.

80. Borgegård and Kemeny, "Sweden," 35.

6. Safety in Numbers

1. SIS is one of three organizations that the national government has directed to oversee standards in Sweden under the umbrella of the Sveriges Standardiseringsförbund (the Swedish Standards Council). The other two cover telecommunications (ITS, Svenska informations- och telekommunikationsstandardiseringen) and electricity (SEK, Svensk Elstandard).

2. Kungliga Bostadsstyrelsen, *God bostad* (1960); Kungliga Bostadsstyrelsen, *God bostad i dag och i morgon*; and Stockholms Stadsbyggnadskontor, *Planstandard 1965.*

3. Updates to these norms were developed frequently. An overview of the different publications, categories of regulation, and rubrics used for them since 1947 is available on the website of Boverket (National Board of Housing, Building, and Planning): http://www.boverket.se/sv/lag--ratt/aldre-lagar-regler--handbocker/aldre-regler-om-byggande/.

4. Statens Planverk, *Svensk Byggnorm 67,* 519 (their translation).

5. Mattsson and Wallenstein, *1930/1931,* 49. See also Åhrén, "Standardisering och personlighet."

6. Åhrén et al., *acceptera,* 187–88.

7. Scott, *Seeing Like a State,* 64–71.

8. Foucault, *Discipline and Punish,* 219.

9. See Stenberg, "Building the Dream," for more on this mismatch.

10. Shonfield, *Walls Have Feelings,* 33.

11. Ibid., 40.

12. Shamiram Demir, "Sam är Södertäljes formgivare," *Länstidningen,* August 4, 2008.

13. The title of the thread was "Enorma villor i Lina utanför Ronna i Södertälje." See https://www.flashback.org/t1314970.

14. Åhrén et al., *acceptera,* 238.

15. Bourdieu, *Distinction.*

16. For instance, the exhibition *Art and Empire: Treasures from Assyria in the British Museum,* held at the Boston Museum of Fine Arts from September 21, 2008, to January 4, 2009, devoted considerable space to Layard.

17. Some of his findings were published in a two-volume book. See Layard, *Nineveh and Its Remains.*

18. See Leick, *Mesopotamia.*

19. Aho, *Assyrier/Syrianer,* 8.

20. Deniz, *En minoritets odyssé,* 155.

21. Björklund, "North to Another Country," 43.

22. Karolina Andersson, "Det nya Sverige," *Svenska Dagbladet,* October 23, 2005, 18–19.

23. Karolina Andersson, "Stor frihet var planen för Lina Hage," *Svenska Dagbladet,* October 23, 2005, 20.

24. The Beauty Council reviews plans and makes recommendations about aesthetics; it comprises thirteen members, twelve of whom are elected officials. The thirteenth member is elected by the other twelve.

25. K. Andersson, "Stor frihet var planen för Lina Hage." The Planning and Building Law outlines specific desirable visual characteristics for both buildings and public spaces and states, "Now it even applies that buildings must have an exterior form and color that are aesthetically pleasing, suitable for the buildings as those that appear to have a good overall effect." The text remains unclear about how these considerations will be adjudicated. See Boverket, *Boken om detaljplan och områdesbestämmelser,* 8–9.

26. K. Andersson, "Stor frihet var planen för Lina Hage."

27. Gelotte, Dahlström Rittsél, and Ulfstrand, *Nästa hållplats Södertälje,* 33.

28. For more, see *Planer för kaldeisk kyrka i Hovsjö,* SVT.

29. Molina, "Den rasifierade staden," 65.

30. "Goda bostäder fostra goda medborgare," SVT.

31. The idea of a multipurpose room emerged in a competition entry for the residential area Baronbackarna, in Örebro, in 1951. Ekholm and White, the winning architects, described the *allrum*: "An effort has also been [made] to seek to facilitate the housewife's housework and, to this end, a unit of workroom–kitchen–laundry room has been developed, with features that actually correspond to the old large kitchen. . . . Kitchen and laundry–bathroom have an intimate connection, separated only by means of a glass wall. This arrangement facilitates the housewife's work; when she stays in the laundry room, she can keep an eye on the pots on the stove simultaneously. The work room next to the kitchen fulfills a versatile function; other than at mealtimes, it is designated to be used for sewing (the mother avoids having to remove the work from the dining table at mealtimes), ironing, homework, children's play, etc." Quoted in L. Holm, "Bostadens form som ideologisk spegel," 91. See also Rudberg, "1940–1960," 90–91.

32. Hirdman, *Att lägga livet tillrätta,* 103–4.

33. Rudberg, "1940–1960," 78.

34. Jonsson, *Från egnahem till villa,* 192.

35. Hirdman, *Att lägga livet tillrätta,* 103.

36. Konsumentinstitutet, *Köksstudier,* 39–40. See also chapter 1 for more details.

37. Konsumentinstitutet, *Köksstudier,* 62.

38. For more on the relationship between the family and the clan, as well as the traditional structures, see Björklund, "North to Another Country"; and Björklund, "Kulturell och social bakgrund och invandring till Sverige."

39. "Familjen Makdissi i Södertälje har problem," TV3.

40. Hirdman, *Att lägga livet tillrätta,* 104.

41. Shonfield, *Walls Have Feelings,* 42.

42. Ibid., 46.

43. SIS website, http://www.sis.se/. The website text has since been changed but reflects similar sentiments.

44. Hirdman, *Att lägga livet tillrätta.*

45. Herzfeld, *Cultural Intimacy.*

46. Pred, *Even in Sweden.*

Conclusion

1. Sorkin, "The End(s) of Urban Design," 155.
2. Hughes and Sadler, *Non-plan.*
3. Hou, *Insurgent Public Space.*
4. Provoost and Vanstiphout, "Facts on the Ground," 196.
5. Scott, *Weapons of the Weak.*
6. de Certeau, *The Practice of Everyday Life.*
7. Lefebvre, *The Production of Space.*
8. Kusno, "Violence of Categories," 15.
9. Sorkin, "The End(s) of Urban Design," 159.
10. Chase, Crawford, and Kaliski, *Everyday Urbanism,* 1999.

11. A 1980 article series in *LT,* "Sån't är livet" (That's life), focused on the history of each neighborhood in Södertälje. When Geneta's turn came about, the area's name was said to have emerged from a play on words, "G'en att äta!" meaning loosely, "Give something to eat!" The story continued, "This is what [King] Karl XI is said to have told his chaplain, Mårten Buller, and thrown him a bun when he demanded a higher salary. Mårten Buller lived in the Geneta rectory, and that's how the name Geneta is said to have emerged." See "Sån't är livet: Geneta: Ett ortsnamn som förbryllar," *Länstidningen,* December 17, 1980, 9.

12. For more on the first steps, see Gelotte, *Telgebostäder genom fyra årtionden,* 51.

13. Södertälje Golfklubb is an eighteen-hole golf course designed by Nils Sköld and established in 1955.

14. An early plan study envisioned commercial structures here.

15. "Squashhallen invigd och intresset ökar," *Länstidningen,* May 13, 1974, 4.

16. Further renovations included an expanded entry door, additional emergency exits, a stage, and a new kitchen area, as detailed in the building-permit application. See the building-permit application "Ansökan bygglov Klockarvägen 108," 1993, Diary Number 930803.

17. See the building-permit application Geneta kommundelsnämnd, Tjänsteutlåtande 940601, 1994. Södertälje had decentralized authority to various *kommundelsnämnder* (local municipal boards).

18. See the building plan "Förslag till ändring av stadsplanen för kvarteret Hundäxingen vid Klockarvägen inom Geneta i Södertälje," Plan 0181K-P891B, 1986.

19. See their website for more: http://suryoyosat.com. A subsidiary station is located in Gütersloh, Germany.

20. See the building plan "Förslag till stadsplan för Geneta Del 9 inom stadsdelen Geneta i Södertälje," Plan 0181K-P430B, 1968.

21. See the building plan "Förslag till stadsplan för Geneta Del 11 inom stadsdelen Geneta i Södertälje," Plan 0181K-P431B, 1968.

22. Some more recent U.S. enclaves are steeped in lesser degrees of nostalgia and greater controversy, as detailed in works such as Fong, *The First Suburban Chinatown*; Saito, *Race and Politics*; and Davis, *Magical Urbanism.*

23. Pred, *Even in Sweden,* 100.

24. Bhabha, *The Location of Culture.*

25. Lefebvre, *The Production of Space,* 26 (emphasis in the original).

26. Naures Atto writes, "An elderly female respondent who visited her relatives in Sweden explained to me that for several years she had attended the Roman Catholic Church in

Germany, since there was no Syriac Orthodox church in the neighborhood. One day a German lady came up to her and asked her: 'Are you reading the Koran?' The Assyrian/Syriac woman was unpleasantly surprised by this question and answered her: 'No, I am reading the Bible; why else would I come to your church?'" Atto, "Hostages in the Homeland, Orphans in the Diaspora," 251.

27. See, for example, Cesari, "Mosques in French Cities." Xenophobic social-media groups based in Sweden focus their attention on defending the national terrain against immigrant architectural influence. The Facebook group "NO THANKS! To mosques in Sweden" (NEJ TACK! Till moské i Sverige) is one example. Links offer insights into their paranoid rationale: "If Muslims build a mosque in a foreign country, they express something with that. What they say is not only: 'In this house of God, we will henceforth pray.' They say also: 'This country, in which this mosque has been established, is henceforth our country. And in this country, we will remain.'" "Klokt om moskéer," n.d., http://www.bgf.nu/islam/moske.html.

28. Lefebvre, *The Production of Space.*

29. Ghannam, *Remaking the Modern,* 176.

30. Crawford, "Contesting the Public Realm," 6.

31. Holston, *The Modernist City,* 85.

32. Kusno, "Violence of Categories," 15.

33. Scott, *Seeing Like a State,* 80.

34. See Holston, *Insurgent Citizenship*; and Miraftab, "Insurgent Planning."

35. Herzfeld, *Cultural Intimacy.*

36. Saunders, *Arrival City,* 10.

37. Hayden, *The Power of Place,* 15.

38. Sorkin, "The End(s) of Urban Design," 173.

Bibliography

Agamben, Giorgio. "We Refugees." European Graduate School, Media and Communications Division, 1994. http://www.egs.edu/faculty/agamben/agamben-we-refugees.

Ågren, Ingegerd. "Thinking in Terms of Service." In *New Towns and Old: Housing and Services in Sweden,* edited by Hans-Erland Heineman and translated by Keith Bradfield, 128–73. Stockholm: Swedish Institute, 1975.

Aho, Sonya. *Assyrier/Syrianer: Ett folk utan land.* Södertälje: Södertälje kommun, n.d.

Åhrén, Uno. *Arkitektur och demokrati.* Stockholm: Kooperativa förbundets Bokförlag, 1942.

———. "Standardisering och personlighet." *Svenska Slöjdföreningens tidskrift,* 1929, 44–50.

Åhrén, Uno, Gunnar Asplund, Wolter Gahn, Sven Markelius, Gregor Paulsson, and Eskil Sundahl. *acceptera.* In *Modern Swedish Design: Three Founding Texts,* edited by Lucy Creagh, Helena Kåberg, and Barbara Miller Lane and translated by David Jones, 140–339. New York: Museum of Modern Art, 2008 (*acceptera* originally published 1931).

Akcan, Esra. *Architecture in Translation: Germany, Turkey, and the Modern House.* Durham, N.C.: Duke University Press, 2012.

Ålund, Aleksandra, and Carl-Ulrik Schierup. *Paradoxes of Multiculturalism.* Brookfield, Vt.: Gower, 1991.

Anderson, Benedict. *Imagined Communities.* Rev. ed., New York: Verso, 1991 (originally published 1983).

Andersson, Roger. "The Geographical and Social Mobility of Immigrants: Escalator Regions in Sweden from an Ethnic Perspective." *Geografiska annaler B* 1 (1996): 3–25.

———. "Invandrarnas rörlighet. Om mobilitet och integration i ett geografiskt perspektiv." In *Nordplan Rapport 1996: Etnicitet, Segregation och Kommunal Planering,* edited by Kerstin Bohm and Abdul Khakee, 6–39. Stockholm: Nordplan.

———. "Skapandet av svenskglesa bostadsområden." In *Den delade staden,* rev. ed., edited by Lena Magnusson Turner, 119–60. Umeå: Boréa Bokförlag, 2008 (*Den delade staden* originally published 2001).

———. "Socio-spatial Dynamics: Ethnic Divisions of Mobility and Housing in Post-Palme Sweden." *Urban Studies* 35, no. 3 (1998): 397–428.

Andersson, Stefan. *Assyrierna: En bok om präster och lekmän, om politik och diplomati kring den assyriska invandringen till Sverige.* Stockholm: Tidens Förlag, 1983.

Andersson, Thorbjörn. *Utanför staden: Parker i Stockholms förorter.* Stockholm: Stockholmia Förlag, 2000.

Arnstberg, Karl-Olov. *Miljonprogrammet.* Stockholm: Carlsson Bokförlag, 2000.

Arvidsson, Håkan, Lennart Berntson, and Lars Dencik. *Modernisering och välfärd: Om stat, individ och civilt samhälle i Sverige.* Stockholm: City University Press, 1994.

Asplund, Hans. *Farväl till funktionalismen!* Stockholm: Byggförlag, 1980.

Åström, Kell. *Svensk stadsplanering.* Stockholm: Byggmästaren, 1967.

Atto, Naures. "Hostages in the Homeland, Orphans in the Diaspora: Identity Discourses among the Assyrian/Syriac Elites in the European Diaspora." PhD diss., University of Leiden, 2011.

Avermaete, Tom, and Dirk van den Heuvel. "Obama, Please Tax Me! Architecture and the Politics of Redistribution." *Footprint* 5, no. 2 (2011): 1–3.

Bäck, Henry. *Invandrarnas riksorganisationer.* Report 24. Stockholm: Delegationen för invandrarforskning, 1983.

Bahro Suryoyo. "Ankomsten." 1, no. 11 (November 1979): 19, with continuation on 16.

———. "Nationalitet." 2, no. 1 (January 1980): 3–4.

Banham, Reyner. *Los Angeles: The Architecture of Four Ecologies.* New York: Harper and Row, 1971.

Barthes, Roland. *What Is Sport?* Translated by Richard Howard. New Haven: Yale University Press, 2007 (originally published in French in 1961).

Batatu, Hanna. *Syria's Peasantry, the Descendants of Its Lesser Rural Notables, and Their Politics.* Princeton: Princeton University Press, 1999.

Berggren, Henrik, and Lars Trägårdh. *Är svensken människa? Gemenskap och oberoende i det moderna Sverige,* rev. ed. Stockholm: Norstedts, 2015 (originally published in 2006).

Berkling, Anna Lisa, ed. *Från Fram till folkhemmet: Per Albin Hansson som tidningsman och talare.* Selections and introduction by Anna Lisa Berkling. Foreword by Tage Erlander. Solna: Metodica Press, 1982.

Beṯ-Şawoce, Jan, ed. *Om assyriers, araméers, kaldéers, syriers ursprung: En översikt av några huvudlinjer inom forskningen 1.* Södertälje: Bokförlaget Nsibin, 2008.

Bhabha, Homi. *The Location of Culture.* New York: Routledge, 1994.

Bickford, Susan. "Constructing Inequality: City Spaces and the Architecture of Citizenship." *Political Theory* 28, no. 3 (2000): 355–76.

Björklund, Ulf. *Från ofärd till välfärd: En kristen minoritetsgrupps migration från Mellersta Östern till Sverige.* Stockholm: Liber Förlag/Allmänna Förlaget, 1980.

———. "Kulturell och social bakgrund och invandring till Sverige." In *Assyrier/syrianer tipskatalog: Några fakta om gruppen och några exempel från kommunal verksamhet.* Stockholm: Kommunförbundet, 1982.

———. "North to Another Country: The Formation of a Suryoyo Community in Sweden." PhD diss., Stockholm University, 1981.

Bleich, Erik. *Race Politics in Britain and France: Ideas and Policymaking since the 1960s.* Cambridge: Cambridge University Press, 2003.

Blomdahl, Ulf. *Folkrörelserna och folket: Med utblick mot framtiden.* Stockholm: Carlsson Bokförlag, 1990.

Blomé, Gunilla, and Rakel G. Azmier. *Södertälje! Människor, miljöer och händelser.* Södertälje: Södertälje kommun, 1986.

Blücher, Gösta. "Miljonprogrammet—Så här var det." 2008. http://www.arkitekt.se/s33917.

Bondeson, Lars. *Seder och bruk vid bröllop.* Stockholm: Verbum, 1988.

Borgegård, Lars-Erik, and Jim Kemeny. "Sweden: High-Rise Housing for a Low-Density Country." In *High-Rise Housing in Europe: Current Trends and Future Prospects,* edited by Richard Turkington, Ronald van Kempen, and Frank Wassenberg, 31–48. Delft, Netherlands: Delft University Press, 2004.

Boudon, Philippe. *Lived-In Architecture: Le Corbusier's Pessac Revisited.* Translated by Gerald Onn. London: Lund Humphries, 1972 (originally published in French in 1969).

Bourdieu, Pierre. *Distinction: A Social Critique of the Judgement of Taste.* Translated by Richard Nice. Cambridge, Mass.: Harvard University Press, 1984 (originally published in French in 1979).

———. "Site Effects." In *The Weight of the World: Social Suffering in Contemporary Society,* translated by Priscilla Parkhurst Ferguson, 123–29. Stanford: Stanford University Press, 1999 (*The Weight of the World* originally published in 1993; original English translation published in 1999 by Polity Press).

Boverket. *Boken om detaljplan och områdesbestämmelser.* Karlskrona: Boverket, 2002 (earlier editions published in 1987, 1993, and 1996).

Bowen, John R. *Why the French Don't Like Headscarves: Islam, the State, and Public Space.* Princeton: Princeton University Press, 2007.

Bradley, Karin, Moa Tunström, and Ola Broms Wessel, eds. *Bor vi i samma stad? Om stadsutveckling, mångfald och rättvisa.* Kristianstad: Pocky, 2005.

Brah, Avtar. *Cartographies of Diaspora: Contesting Identities.* New York: Routledge, 1996.

Brandell, Inga, ed. *State Frontiers: Borders and Boundaries in the Middle East.* New York: I. B. Tauris, 2006.

Braude, Benjamin. "Foundation Myths of the Millet System." In *Christians and Jews in the Ottoman Empire: The Functioning of a Plural Society,* edited by Benjamin Braude and Bernard Lewis, 69–88. New York: Holmes and Meier, 1982.

Brock, Sebastian P. *Den dolda pärlan: Syrisk ortodoxa kyrkan och dess gamla arameiska arv.* Vol. 3, *Vid tvåtusenårskiftet det syrisk ortodoxa vittnet.* Rome: Trans World Film, 2001.

Bromberger, Christian. "Football as World-View and as Ritual." *French Cultural Studies* 6, no. 18 (1995): 293–311.

Broms Wessel, Ola, Jennifer Mack, and Tim Anstey, eds. *Future People's Palace.* Stockholm: Arvinius Förlag, forthcoming.

Çakır, Feridun. "Historia." *Bahro Suryoyo* 1, nos. 6–7 (June–July 1979): 6–11.

Caldeira, Teresa. *City of Walls: Crime, Segregation, and Citizenship in São Paulo.* Berkeley: University of California Press, 2000.

Caldenby, Claes, ed. *Att bygga ett land: 1900-talets svenska arkitektur.* Stockholm: Byggforskningsrådet, 1998.

Caldenby, Claes, and Åsa Walldén. *Kollektivhus: Sovjet och Sverige omkring 1930.* Stockholm: Statens Råd för Byggnadsforskning, 1979.

Cesari, Jocelyne. "Mosques in French Cities: Towards the End of a Conflict?" *Journal of Ethnic and Migration Studies* 31, no. 6 (2005): 1025–43.

Cetrez, Önver A. "Meaning-Making Variations in Acculturation and Ritualization: A Multi-generational Study of Suroyo Migrants in Sweden." PhD diss., Uppsala University, 2005.

———. *Syrisk-ortodoxa kyrkan: En religiös och kulturell symbol.* Jönköping: Assurbanipals Bokförlag, 1998.

Chase, John, Margaret Crawford, and John Kaliski, eds. *Everyday Urbanism.* New York: Monacelli Press, 1999.

Childs, Marquis W. *Sweden: The Middle Way*. New Haven: Yale University Press, 1936.

Choay, Françoise. *The Modern City: Planning in the 19th Century*. New York: G. Braziller, 1969.

Christophers, Brett. "A Monstrous Hybrid: The Political Economy of Housing in Early Twenty-First Century Sweden." *New Political Economy* 18, no. 6 (2013): 885–911.

Clifford, James. "Diasporas." *Cultural Anthropology* 9, no. 3 (1994): 302–38.

———. *Routes: Travel and Translation in the Late Twentieth Century*. Cambridge, Mass.: Harvard University Press, 1997.

Courtois, Sebastien de. *The Forgotten Genocide: Eastern Christians, the Last Arameans*. Translated by Vincent Aurora. Piscataway, N.J.: Gorgias Press, 2004.

Crane, Sheila. *Mediterranean Crossroads: Marseille and Modern Architecture*. Minneapolis: University of Minnesota Press, 2011.

Crawford, Margaret. "Contesting the Public Realm: Struggles over Public Space in Los Angeles." *Journal of Architectural Education* 49, no. 1 (1995): 4–9.

Crawford, Margaret, and Marco Cenzatti. "On Public Spaces, Quasi-Public Spaces, and Public Quasi-Spaces." *Modulus* 24 (1998): 14–21.

Creagh, Lucy. "An Introduction to *acceptera*." In *Modern Swedish Design: Three Founding Texts*, edited by Lucy Creagh, Helena Kåberg, and Barbara Miller Lane, 126–39. New York: Museum of Modern Art, 2008.

Dalrymple, William. *From the Holy Mountain: A Journey among the Christians of the Middle East*. New York: Henry Holt, 1998.

Daun, Åke. *Swedish Mentality*. Translated by Jan Teeland. University Park: Pennsylvania State University Press, 1996 (originally published in Swedish in 1989).

Davis, Mike. *Magical Urbanism: Latinos Reinvent the U.S. City*. New York: Verso, 2000.

Dawod, Nivette. "Assyrianer." *Gringo Grande* 5 (2006): 40–42.

———. "Uppstickarlaget." *Gringo Grande* 5 (2006): 46–50.

de Certeau, Michel. *The Practice of Everyday Life*. Translated by Steven F. Rendall. Berkeley: University of California Press, 1984 (originally published in French in 1980).

Deland, Mats. "The Social City: Middle-Way Approaches to Housing and Suburban Governmentality in Southern Stockholm, 1900–1945." PhD diss., Stockholm: Institute of Urban History, 2001.

Deniz, Fuat. *En minoritets odyssé: Det assyriska exemplet*. Rev. ed. Örebro: Örebro University, 2001.

Deniz, Fuat, and Antonios Perdikaris. *Ett liv mellan två världar: En studie om hur assyriska ungdomar som andra generationens invandrare i Sverige upplever och hanterar sin livssituation*. Örebro: Örebro University, 1990.

Diaz, Jose Alberto. "Choosing Integration: A Theoretical and Empirical Study of the Immigrant Integration in Sweden." PhD diss., Uppsala University, 1993.

Din egen stad. "Vi bygger och bor: Hur ett nytt område kommer till," June 1965, 14–17.

Ditt Södertälje. "Situationen i Libanon och Syrien," October 1980, 5.

———. "Statligt program: Utflyttning från Södertälje ger assyrier/syrianerna bättre möjligheter," October 1980, 3.

———. "Våra assyrier/syrianernas bakgrund," October 1980, 4–6, 14.

Douglas, Mary. *Purity and Danger: An Analysis of Concepts of Pollution and Taboo*. New York: Routledge, 1966.

Ecer, Bahdi. *I fikonträdets skugga: Ett syrianskt utvandrarepos*. Uppsala Multiethnic Papers 22. Uppsala: Centrum för multietnisk forskning, Uppsala University, 1991.

Erdentug, Aygen, and Freek Colombijn. "Urban Space and Ethnicity." In *Urban Ethnic Encounters: The Spatial Consequences,* edited by Aygen Erdentug and Freek Colombijn, 1–24. New York: Routledge, 2001.

Ericsson, Urban. "Belägrade människor–belägrade rum: Om invandrargöranden och förorter." PhD diss., Uppsala University, 2007.

Findlay, Carter Vaughn. *Turkey, Islam, Nationalism, and Modernity: A History, 1789–2007.* New Haven: Yale University Press, 2010.

Fong, Timothy. *The First Suburban Chinatown: The Remaking of Monterey Park, California.* Philadelphia: Temple University Press, 1994.

Foucault, Michel. *Discipline and Punish: The Birth of the Prison.* Translated by Alan Sheridan. New York: London: Penguin Books, 1991 (originally published in French in 1975).

———. *The History of Sexuality.* Vol. 2, *The Use of Pleasure.* Translated by Robert Hurley. New York: Pantheon Books, 1985 (originally published in French in 1984).

———. *The History of Sexuality.* Vol. 3, *The Care of the Self.* Translated by Robert Hurley. New York: Pantheon Books, 1986 (originally published in French in 1984).

———. *The Order of Things: An Archaeology of the Human Sciences.* New York: Pantheon Books, 1970 (originally published in French in 1966).

Fraenki, Claes. *Swedish Urban Planning.* Translated by L. J. Gruber. 2nd ed. Härnösand: Härnö-förlaget, 1993 (originally published in Swedish in 1991).

Franzén, Mats. "Problemet segregation: En orättvis jämförelse." In *Den delade staden,* rev. ed., edited by Lena Magnusson Turner, 25–50. Umeå: Boréa Bokförlag, 2008 (*Den delade staden* originally published 2001).

Franzén, Mats, and Eva Sandstedt. *Välfärdsstat och byggande: Om efterkrigstidens nya stadsmönster i Sverige.* Uppsala: Arkiv Förlag, 1981.

Fraser, Nancy. "Rethinking the Public Sphere: A Contribution to the Critique of Actually Existing Democracy." In *The Phantom Public Sphere,* edited by Bruce Robbins, 1–32. Minneapolis: University of Minnesota Press, 1993.

Friedl, Ernestine. *Vasilika: A Village in Modern Greece.* New York: Holt, Rinehart, and Winston, 1962.

Frykman, Jonas, and Orvar Löfgren. *Culture Builders: A Historical Anthropology of Middle-Class Life.* New Brunswick, N.J.: Rutgers University Press, 1987.

———. "På väg—Bilder av kultur och klass." In *Modärna tider: Vision och vardag i folkhemmet,* edited by Jonas Frykman and Orvar Löfgren, 20–139. Lund: Etnologiska sällskapet, 1985.

Gans, Herbert. *The Urban Villagers: Group and Class in the Life of Italian-Americans.* New York: Free Press of Glencoe, 1962.

Gaunt, David. *Massacres, Resistance, Protectors: Muslim-Christian Relations in Eastern Anatolia during World War I.* Piscataway, N.J.: Gorgias Press, 2006.

———. *Seyfo: Folkmordet på assyrierna: När—var—hur.* Stockholm: Assyriska Ungdomsförbundet i Sverige, 2011.

Gelotte, Göran. *Södertälje kommuns historia.* Vol. 3. Södertälje: Kultur- och Fritidskontoret, 2004.

———. *Södertälje som badort.* Södertälje: Östra Södermanlands Kulturhistoriska Förening, 1974.

———. "Stadsplaner och bebyggelsetyper i Södertälje intill år 1910." PhD diss., Stockholm University, 1980.

———. *Telgebostäder genom fyra årtionden: En krönika om stiftelsens tillkomst och utveckling 1948–1988.* Södertälje: Telgebostäder, 1988.

Gelotte, Hanna, Eva Dahlström Rittsél, and Anna Ulfstrand. *Nästa hållplats Södertälje.* Stockholm: Länsstyrelsen i Stockholms Län, 2006.

Ghannam, Farha. *Remaking the Modern: Space, Relocation, and the Politics of Identity in a Global Cairo.* Berkeley: University of California Press, 2002.

Ghosh, Amitav. "The Diaspora in Indian Culture." *Public Culture* 2, no. 1 (1989): 73–78.

Gilroy, Paul. *The Black Atlantic: Modernity and Double Consciousness.* Cambridge, Mass.: Harvard University Press, 1993.

Habermas, Jürgen. *The Structural Transformation of the Public Sphere: An Inquiry into a Category of Bourgeois Society.* Translated by Thomas Burger and Frederick Lawrence. Cambridge, Mass.: MIT Press, 1989 (originally published in German in 1962).

Haffner, Jeanne. *The View from Above: The Science of Social Space.* Cambridge, Mass.: MIT Press, 2013.

Hajighasemi, Ali. *Att bryta den beständiga segregationen: Fallet Södertälje.* Huddinge: Södertörns Högskola, 2005.

Hald, Arthur, Per Holm, and Gotthard Johansson, eds. *Swedish Housing.* Translated by Burnett Anderson. Stockholm: Swedish Institute, 1949.

Hall, Thomas. "Urban Planning in Sweden." In *Planning and Urban Growth in the Nordic Countries,* edited by Thomas Hall, 167–246. New York: E. and F. N. Spon, 1991.

Hall, Thomas, and Sonja Vidén. "The Million Homes Programme: A Review of the Great Swedish Planning Project." *Planning Perspectives* 20 (July 2005): 301–28.

Hammar, Tomas. "Sweden." In *European Immigration Policy: A Comparative Study,* edited by Tomas Hammar, 17–49. Cambridge: Cambridge University Press, 1985.

Hannerz, Ulf. *Exploring the City: Inquiries toward an Urban Anthropology.* New York: Columbia University Press, 1980.

Hansson, Sune. *Invandrarföreningar.* Rev. ed. Norrköping: Statens Invandrarverk; Arbetsmarknadsdepartementet, March 1990 (originally published in 1989).

Hayden, Dolores. *The Power of Place: Urban Landscapes as Public History.* Cambridge, Mass.: MIT Press, 1995.

Headey, Bruce. *Housing Policy in the Developed Economy: The United Kingdom, Sweden, and the United States.* London: Croom Helm, 1978.

Hedman, Eva. *Den kommunala allmännyttans historia: Särtryck av underlag till utredningen om allmännyttans villkor* (SOU 2008:38). Karlskrona: Boverket, 2008.

Heineman, Hans-Erland. "Introduction." In *New Towns and Old: Housing and Services in Sweden,* edited by Hans-Erland Heineman and translated by Keith Bradfield, 7–21. Stockholm: Swedish Institute, 1975.

Herzfeld, Michael. *Anthropology through the Looking-Glass.* Cambridge: Cambridge University Press, 1987.

———. *Cultural Intimacy: Social Poetics in the Nation-State.* New York: Routledge, 1997.

———. *Evicted from Eternity: The Restructuring of Modern Rome.* Chicago: University of Chicago Press, 2009.

———. *Portrait of a Greek Imagination: An Ethnographic Biography of Andreas Nenedakis.* Chicago: University of Chicago Press, 1997.

———. "Spatial Cleansing: Monumental Vacuity and the Idea of the West." *Journal of Material Culture* 11, nos. 1–2 (2006): 127–49.

Hirdman, Yvonne. *Att lägga livet tillrätta: Studier i svensk folkhemspolitik.* Stockholm: Carls-son Bokförlag, 1989.

Hirschfeld, Christian Cay Lorentz. *Theory of Garden Art.* Philadelphia: University of Penn-sylvania Press, 2001 (originally published in five volumes from 1779 to 1785).

Ho, Engseng. *The Graves of Tarim: Genealogy and Mobility across the Indian Ocean.* Berkeley: University of California Press, 2006.

Hollerweger, Hans. *Living Cultural Heritage Turabdin.* Linz, Austria: Friends of Turabdin, 1999.

Holm, Lennart. "Bostadens form som ideologisk spegel." In *Bostadspolitik och samhällsp-lanering,* edited by Alf Johansson and Gunnar Myrdal, 67–96. Stockholm: Tidens Förlag, 1968.

Holm, Per. *Swedish Housing.* Stockholm: Swedish Institute, 1957.

Holston, James. *Insurgent Citizenship: Disjunctions of Democracy and Modernity in Brazil.* Princeton: Princeton University Press, 2008.

———. *The Modernist City: An Anthropological Critique of Brasília.* Chicago: University of Chicago Press, 1989.

———. "Spaces of Insurgent Citizenship." In *Cities and Citizenship,* edited by James Hols-ton, 155–73. Durham, N.C.: Duke University Press, 1999.

Hou, Jeffrey, ed. *Insurgent Public Space: Guerrilla Urbanism and the Remaking of Contempo-rary Cities.* New York: Routledge, 2010.

Howard, Ebenezer. *Garden Cities of To-Morrow.* London: Swan Sonnenschein, 1902.

HSBs Riksförbund. *Service i bostadsområden.* Stockholm, 1966.

Hughes, Jonathan, and Simon Sadler, eds. *Non-plan: Essays on Freedom, Participation, and Change in Modern Architecture and Urbanism.* Boston: Architectural Press, 1999.

Hujådå. "Namnkonflikten," 1 (1978–79): 37.

Hyresgästföreningen. *Boendemiljön: Ett miljöpolitiskt handlingsprogram för och av hyresgäst-föreningen i Storstockholm.* Stockholm: Hyresgästernas Riksförbund, 1968.

———. *Hyresgästföreningens historia.* Stockholm: Hyresgästföreningen, 1999.

Isaksson, Anders. *Per Albin.* Part 3, *Partiledaren,* and Part 4, *Landsfadern.* Stockholm: Wahl-ström och Widstrand, 2002.

Jacobs, Jane. *The Death and Life of Great American Cities.* New York: Random House, 1961.

Johansson, Bengt O. H. "Det stora bostadsbyggandet: succé och baksmälla." In *Funktion-alismens genombrott och kris: Svenskt bostadsbyggande 1930–1980,* 101–20. Stockholm: Arki-tekturmuseet, 1980 (originally published in German in 1976 and in Hungarian in 1978).

Johansson, Birgitta, ed. *Miljonprogram—Utveckla eller avveckla?* Stockholm: Forskningsrå-det Formas, 2012.

Johansson, Ingemar. *Stor-Stockholms bebyggelsehistoria: Markpolitik, planering och byggande under sju sekler.* Stockholm: Gidlund i Samarbete med Byggforskningsrådet, 1987.

Jonsson, Leif. *Från egnahem till villa: Enfamiljshuset i Sverige 1950–1980.* Stockholm: Statens Institut för Byggnadsforskning, 1985.

Kapferer, Bruce. *Legends of People, Myths of State: Violence, Intolerance, and Political Culture in Sri Lanka and Australia.* Washington, D.C.: Smithsonian Institution Press, 1998.

Karpat, Kemal H. "Millets and Nationality: The Roots of the Incongruity of Nation and State in the Post-Ottoman Era." In *Christians and Jews in the Ottoman Empire: The Func-tioning of a Plural Society,* edited by Benjamin Braude and Bernard Lewis, 141–69. New York: Holmes and Meier, 1982.

Khakee, Abdul. "Politics, Methods, and Planning Culture." In *Remaking the Welfare State: Swedish Urban Planning and Policy-Making in the 1990s,* edited by Ingemar Elander, Abdul Khakee, and Sune Sunesson, 275–96. Aldershot, U.K.: Avebury, 1995.

Khakee, Abdul, and Marcus Johansson. *Staden och invandrarna: Om mångfaldens förutsättningar i Örebro.* Umeå: PfMI, 2003.

Kings, Lisa. "Till det lokalas försvar: Civilsamhället i den urbana periferin." PhD diss., Stockholm University, 2011.

Kino, Nuri, and Jenny Nordberg. *Välgörarna: Den motvillige journalisten.* Stockholm: Norstedts, 2008.

Knutsson, Bengt. *Assur eller Aram: Språklig, religiös och nationell identifikation hos Sveriges assyrier och syrianer.* SIV Rapport No. 4/82. Norrköping: Statens Invandrarverk, 1982.

Konsumentinstitutet. *Köksstudier: Hushållsstorlek, inredningsmängd, förvaringsmöjligheter.* Stockholm: Konsumentinstitutet, 1972.

Kramer, Jane. *Unsettling Europe.* New York: Penguin Books, 1980.

Kungliga Bostadsstyrelsen. *God bostad.* Stockholm: Kungliga Bostadsstyrelsen, 1954.

———. *God bostad.* Stockholm: Kungliga Bostadsstyrelsen, 1960.

———. *God bostad i dag och i morgon.* Stockholm: Kungliga Bostadsstyrelsen, 1964.

———. *God bostad i småhus.* Stockholm: Nordiska Bokhandeln, 1956.

———. *Typritningskatalog.* Rev. ed. Stockholm: Bostadsstyrelsen, 1958.

Kurkiala, Mikael. *I varje trumslag jordens puls: Om vår tids rädsla för skillnader.* Stockholm: Ordfront Förlag, 2005.

Kusno, Abidin. *The Appearances of Memory: Mnemonic Practices of Architecture and Urban Form in Indonesia.* Durham, N.C.: Duke University Press, 2010.

———. "Violence of Categories: Urban Design and the Making of Indonesian Modernity." In *City and Nation: Rethinking Place and Identity,* edited by Michael Peter Smith and Thomas Bender, 15–50. New Brunswick, N.J.: Transaction, 2001.

Kymlicka, Will. *Multicultural Citizenship.* New York: Oxford University Press, 1995.

Laclau, Ernesto. "Universalism, Particularism, and the Question of Identity." *October* 61 (1992): 83–90.

Larkin, Brian. "The Politics and Poetics of Infrastructure." *Annual Review of Anthropology* 42 (2013): 327–43.

Layard, Austen Henry. *Nineveh and Its Remains: With an Account of a Visit to the Chaldæan Christians of Kurdistan, and the Yezidis, or Devil-Worshippers; and an Inquiry into the Manners and Arts of the Ancient Assyrians.* New York: G. P. Putnam, 1849.

Le Corbusier. *The Athens Charter.* Translated by Anthony Eardley. New York: Grossman, 1973.

Lefebvre, Henri. *The Production of Space.* Translated by Nicholson Smith. Oxford: Basil Blackwell, 1991 (originally published in French in 1974).

Legeby, Ann. "Urban Segregation and Urban Form: From Residential Segregation to Segregation in Public Space." Licentiate thesis, Kungliga Tekniska Högskolan, 2010.

Leick, Gwedolyn. *Mesopotamia: The Invention of the City.* New York: Penguin Books, 2001.

Levitt, Peggy. *God Needs No Passport: Immigrants and the Changing American Religious Landscape.* New York: New Press, 2007.

Ley, David. "Between Europe and Asia: The Case of the Missing Sequoias." *Cultural Geographies* 2 (1995): 185–210.

Li, Wei. *Ethnoburb: The New Ethnic Community in Urban America.* Honolulu: University of Hawai'i Press, 2008.

Lindström, Sune. "Hur kunde det gå så illa? Dialog fackmän—allmänhet viktigast." *PLAN* 31, no. 4 (1977): 203–5.

Low, Setha. *Behind the Gates: Life, Security, and the Pursuit of Happiness in Fortress America.* New York: Routledge, 2003.

Lundberg, Ingrid, and Ingvar Svanberg. "Turkish Associations in Metropolitan Stockholm." Uppsala Multiethnic Papers, no. 23. Uppsala: Center for Multiethnic Research, Uppsala University, 1991.

Lundquist, Kjell. "Från beteshage till trädgård—Kyrkogårdens historia." In *Kyrkogårdens gröna kulturarv,* edited by Eivor Bucht, 12–34. Stad & land 103. Alnarp: Movium/inst för landskapsplanering, Sveriges Lantbruksuniversitet, 1992.

Mack, Jennifer. *Assyriska until We Die . . . .* Film, 2008. The Zelge Fans divided this into three parts, available on YouTube: Part 1, http://www.youtube.com/watch?v=NbQSPTq8Vlg&t=291s; Part 2, http://www.youtube.com/watch?v=mynDdJ5Zr5g&t=278s; and Part 3, http://www.youtube.com/watch?v=jXKQhjCSO5E&t=431s.

———. "Love in the Time of Pinball." In *Walls That Teach: On the Architecture of Youth Centres,* edited by Susanne Pietsch and Andreas Mueller, 75–84. Delft, Netherlands: TU Delft and JapSam, 2015.

———. "New Swedes in the New Town." In *Use Matters: An Alternative History of Architecture,* edited by Kenny Cupers, 121–37. New York: Routledge, 2013.

———. "Urban Design from Below: Immigration and the Spatial Practice of Urbanism." *Public Culture* 26, no. 1 (2014): 153–85.

Magnusson Turner, Lena. "Invandring och segregation." In *Den delade staden,* edited by Lena Magnusson Turner, 9–24. Umeå: Boréa Bokförlag, 2008 (*Den delade staden* originally published in 2001).

Malkki, Liisa. *Purity and Exile: Violence, Memory, and National Cosmology among Hutu Refugees in Tanzania.* Chicago: University of Chicago Press, 1995.

———. "Speechless Emissaries: Refugees, Humanitarianism, and Dehistoricization." *Cultural Anthropology* 11, no. 3 (1996): 377–404.

Mandel, Ruth. *Cosmopolitan Anxieties: Turkish Challenges to Citizenship and Belonging in Germany.* Durham, N.C.: Duke University Press, 2008.

Markelius, Sven. "Kollektivhuset: Ett centralt samhällsproblem." *Arkitektur och samhälle* 1 (1932): 53–64.

Mattsson, Helena. "Designing the Reasonable Consumer: Standardization and Personalization in Swedish Functionalism." In *Swedish Modernism: Architecture, Consumption, and the Welfare State,* edited by Helena Mattsson and Sven-Olov Wallenstein, 74–99. London: Black Dog, 2006.

———. "Where the Motorways Meet: Architecture and Corporatism in Sweden." In *Architecture and the Welfare State,* edited by Mark Swenarton, Tom Avermaete, and Dirk van den Heuvel, 154–75. New York: Routledge, 2014.

Mattsson, Helena, and Sven-Olov Wallenstein. *1930/1931: Den svenska modernismen vid vägskälet = Swedish Modernism at the Crossroads = Der schwedische Modernismus am Scheideweg.* Stockholm: Axl Books, 2009.

Mauss, Marcel. *The Gift: Forms and Functions of Exchange in Archaic Societies.* Translated by W. D. Halls. London: Routledge, 1990 (originally published in French in 1923).

McIntosh, Laurie. "Impossible Presence: Race, Nation, and the Cultural Politics of 'Being Norwegian.'" *Ethnic and Racial Studies* 38, no. 2 (2015): 309–25.

Merry, Sally Engle. "Spatial Governmentality and the New Urban Social Order: Controlling Gender Violence through Law." *American Anthropologist* 103, no. 1 (2001): 16–29.

Miraftab, Faranak. "Insurgent Planning: Situating Radical Planning in the Global South." *Planning Theory* 8, no. 1 (2009): 32–50.

Molina, Irene. "Den rasifierade staden." In *Den delade staden,* edited by Lena Magnusson Turner, 51–83. Umeå: Boréa Bokförlag, 2008 (*Den delade staden* originally published 2001).

———. "Intersektionella rumsligheter." *Tidskrift för genusvetenskap* 3 (2007): 7–21.

———. "Stadens rasifiering: Etnisk boendesegregering i folkhemmet." PhD diss., Uppsala University, 1997.

Mumford, Eric. *The CIAM Discourse on Urbanism, 1928–1960.* Cambridge, Mass.: MIT Press, 2000.

Murdie, Robert A., and Lars-Erik Borgegård. "Immigration, Spatial Segregation, and Housing Segmentation in Metropolitan Stockholm, 1960–95." *Urban Studies* 35, no. 10 (1998): 1869–88.

Myrdal, Alva. *Nation and Family: The Swedish Experiment in Democratic Family and Population Policy.* New York: Harper, 1941.

Myrdal, Alva, and Gunnar Myrdal. *Kris i befolkningsfrågan.* Stockholm: Albert Bonniers Förlag, 1934.

Narrowe, Judith. "Under One Roof: On Becoming a Turk in Sweden." PhD diss., Stockholm University, 1998.

Nelhans, Bertil, ed. *Assyrier—Vilka är dem? En tvärvetenskaplig rapport.* Gothenburg: Gothenburg University, 1977.

Nordgren, Kenneth. "Vems är historien? Historia som medvetande, kultur och handling i det mångkulturella Sverige." PhD diss., Karlstad University, 2006.

Nordström, Alf. *Södertälje stads historia.* Vol. 1. Stockholm: Södertälje Drätselkammare, 1968.

———. *Södertälje stads historia.* Vol. 2. Stockholm: Södertälje Drätselkammare, 1968.

Nordström, Ludvig. *Lort-Sverige.* Stockholm: Kooperativa Förbundets Bokförlag, 1938.

Olalquiaga, Celeste. *Megalopolis: Contemporary Cultural Sensibilities.* Minneapolis: University of Minnesota Press, 1992.

Olsson, Lina. "Den självorganiserade staden: Appropriation av offentliga rum i Rinkeby." PhD diss., Lund University, 2008.

Ornbrant, Birgitta. *Möte med välfärdens byråkrater: Svenska myndigheters mottagande av en kristen minoritetsgrupp från Mellersta Östern.* Stockholm: Liber Förlag, 1981.

Österberg, Eva. "Vardagens sträva samförstånd: Bondepolitik i den svenska modellen från Vasatid till frihetstid." In *Tänka, tycka, tro: Svensk historia underifrån,* edited by Gunnar Broberg, Ulla Wikander, and Klas Åmark, 126–46. Stockholm: Ordfronts Förlag, 1993.

Özoğlu, Hakan. *From Caliphate to Secular State: Power Struggle in the Early Turkish Republic.* Santa Barbara: ABC Clio / Praeger, 2011.

Pacini, Andrea, ed. *Christian Communities in the Arab Middle East: The Challenge of the Future.* Oxford: Clarendon Press, 1998.

Palmer, Andrew. *Monk and Mason on the Tigris Frontier: The Early History of Ṭur ʿAbdin.* Cambridge: Cambridge University Press, 2009.

Parr, Joy. "Modern Kitchen, Good Home, Strong Nation." *Technology and Culture* 43, no. 4 (October 2002): 657–67.

Pass, David. "Vällingby and Farsta—From Idea to Reality: The Suburban Development Process in a Large Swedish City." Ph.D. diss., Kungliga Tekniska Högskolan, 1969.

Perry, Clarence. *The Neighborhood Unit, a Scheme of Arrangement for the Family-Life Community.* Regional Plan of N.Y., Regional Survey of N.Y. and Its Environs. Monograph 1, vol. 7. New York, 1929.

Pommer, Richard, and Christian F. Otto. *Weissenhof 1927 and the Modern Movement in Architecture.* Chicago: University of Chicago Press, 1991.

Popenoe, David. *The Suburban Environment: Sweden and the United States.* Chicago: University of Chicago Press, 1977.

Pred, Allan. *Even in Sweden: Racisms, Racialized Spaces, and the Popular Geographical Imagination.* Berkeley: University of California Press, 2000.

———. *Recognizing European Modernities: A Montage of the Present.* New York: Routledge, 1995.

Pripp, Oscar. *Företagande i minoritet: Om etnicitet, strategier och resurser bland assyrier och syrianer i Södertälje.* Botkyrka: Mångkulturellt Centrum, 2001.

Provoost, Michelle, and Wouter Vanstiphout. "Facts on the Ground: Urbanism from Midroad to Ditch." In *Urban Design,* edited by Alex Krieger, 186–97. Minneapolis: University of Minnesota Press, 2009.

Råberg, Per G. *Funktionalistiskt genombrott: Radikal miljö och miljödebatt i Sverige, 1925–1931.* Stockholm: Arkitekturmuseet, 1972.

Rabo, Annika. "Change on the Euphrates: Villagers, Townsmen, and Employees in Northeast Syria." PhD diss., Stockholm University, 1986.

———. "'Familjen betyder allt' eller 'Vi blir snart lika kalla som svenskarna': Assyrier/syrianer i Södertälje." In *Globala familjer: Transnationell migration och släktskap,* edited by Marita Eastmond and Lisa Åkesson, 205–29. Riga, Latvia: Gidlunds, 2007.

———. "'Without Our Church We Will Disappear': Syrian Orthodox Christians in Diaspora and the Family Law of the Church." In *Family, Religion, and Law: Cultural Encounters in Europe,* edited by Prakash Shah with Marie-Claire Foblets and Mathias Rohe, 181–94. Farnham, U.K.: Ashgate, 2014.

Rådberg, Johan. *Den svenska trädgårdsstaden.* Stockholm: Statens Råd för Byggnadsforskning, 1994.

———. "Doktrin och täthet i svenskt stadsbyggande 1875–1975." PhD diss., Kungliga Tekniska Högskolan, 1988.

———. *Drömmen om atlantångaren: Utopier & myter i 1900-talets stadsbyggande.* Stockholm: Atlantis, 1997.

Rojas, Mauricio. *I ensamhetens labyrint: Invandring och svensk identitet.* Stockholm: Bromberg, 1993.

———. *Sweden after the Swedish Model: From Tutorial State to Enabling State.* Stockholm: Timbro, 2005.

Rooke, Tetz. "Tracing the Boundaries: From Colonial Dream to National Propaganda." In *State Frontiers: Borders and Boundaries in the Middle East,* edited by Inga Brandell, 123–39. New York: I. B. Tauris, 2006.

Roos, Britta, and Hanna Gelotte. *Hej bostad: Om bostadsbyggande i Storstockholm 1961–1975.* Stockholm: Länsstyrelsen i Stockholms Län, 2004.

Rudberg, Eva. "1940–1960: Bostadspolitik med förändrade förutsättningar." In *Funktionalismens genombrott och kris: Svenskt bostadsbyggande 1930–1980,* 65–99. Stockholm: Arkitekturmuseet, 1980 (originally published in German in 1976 and in Hungarian in 1978).

———. *Stockholmsutställningen 1930: Modernismens genombrott i svensk arkitektur.* Stockholm: Stockholmia Förlag, 1999.

———. "Utopia of the Everyday: Swedish and Un-Swedish in the Architecture of Functionalism." In *Utopia and Reality: Modernity in Sweden 1900–1960,* edited by Cecilia Widenheim, 150–73. New Haven: Yale University Press, 2002.

Runcis, Maija. *Steriliseringar i folkhemmet.* Stockholm: Ordfront Förlag, 1998.

Saito, Leland. *Race and Politics: Asian Americans, Latinos, and Whites in a Los Angeles Suburb.* Urbana: University of Illinois Press, 1998.

Sandercock, Leonie. *Toward Cosmopolis: Planning for Multicultural Cities.* New York: John Wiley and Sons, 1998.

Sato, Noriko. "Selective Amnesia: Memory and History of the Urfalli Syrian Orthodox Christians." *Identities: Global Studies in Culture and Power* 12 (2005): 315–33.

Saunders, Doug. *Arrival City: How the Largest Migration in History Is Reshaping Our World.* New York: Vintage Books, 2012.

Sawyer, Lena. "Routings: 'Race,' African Diasporas, and Swedish Belonging." *Transforming Anthropology* 11, no. 1 (2002): 13–35.

Sax, Ulrika. "Hem för miljoner." In *Miljonprogram i Stockholm: En utställning om byggandet, boendet och människorna,* edited by Ulrika Sax, 8–22. Stockholm: Stockholm Stadsmuseum, 2000.

———. *Vällingby—Ett levande drama.* Stockholm: Stockholmia Förlag, 1998.

Scott, James C. *Seeing Like a State: How Certain Schemes to Improve the Human Condition Have Failed.* New Haven: Yale University Press, 1998.

———. *Weapons of the Weak: Everyday Forms of Peasant Resistance.* New Haven: Yale University Press, 1985.

Shonfield, Katherine. *Walls Have Feelings: Architecture, Film, and the City.* New York: Routledge, 2000.

Sidenbladh, Göran. "Grannskapsplanering: Dess innehåll och form." *PLAN* 2, no. 3 (1948): 112–16.

Sieverts, Thomas. *Cities without Cities: An Interpretation of the Zwischenstadt.* Translated by Daniel de Lough. New York: Spon Press, 2003 (originally published in German in 1997).

Sigge, Erik. "Architecture's Red Tape." PhD diss., Kungliga Teknika Högskolan, forthcoming.

Silverstein, Paul. *Algeria in France: Transpolitics, Race, and Nation.* Bloomington: Indiana University Press, 2004.

———. "Immigrant Racialization and the New Savage Slot: Race, Migration, and Immigration in the New Europe." *Annual Review of Anthropology* 34 (2005): 363–84.

Simone, AbdouMaliq. "People as Infrastructure: Intersecting Fragments in Johannesburg." *Public Culture* 16, no. 3 (2004): 407–29.

Smith, Thomas W. "Civic Nationalism and Ethnocultural Justice in Turkey." *Human Rights Quarterly* 27, no. 2 (2005): 436–70.

Socialstyrelsen. *I utlandet Sverige: En presentation av kristna flyktingar från Mellersta Östern och Turkiet.* Stockholm: Socialstyrelsen, 1976.

Söderqvist, Lisbeth. "Rekordår och miljonprogram: Flerfamiljshus i stor skala: En fallstudiebaserad undersökning av politik, planläggning och estetik." PhD diss., Stockholm University, 1999.

Södertälje Drätselkammare. Bostadsnämnden, protocol no. 1 1951, appendix A, "Överenskommelse." Södertälje: Municipality of Södertälje, 1951.

Södertälje Kommun. *Facts about Södertälje.* Södertälje: Södertälje Kommun, 2011.

———. "It's Time for Ronna! Utvecklingsplan för Ronna, Ett projekt inom URBACT II/ RegGov." Södertälje: Södertälje Kommun, April 5, 2011.

———. *Välkommen till Södertälje: En bok till den nyblivne södertäljebon.* Stockholm: Norstedts, 1978.

Södertälje Rotary. *Södertälje: En orientering.* Södertälje: Axlings Bok- och Tidskriftstryckeri, 1947.

Sorkin, Michael. "The End(s) of Urban Design." In *Urban Design,* edited by Alex Krieger, 155–82. Minneapolis: University of Minnesota Press, 2009.

Statens Planverk. *Svensk Byggnorm 67: Föreskrifter, råd och anvisningar till byggnadsväsendet utfärdade med stöd av 76 § byggnadsstadgan, BABS 1967.* Repr. Stockholm: Statens Planverk, 1968.

Stenberg, Erik. "Building the Dream." In *Future People's Palace,* edited by Ola Broms Wessel, Jennifer Mack, and Tim Anstey. Stockholm: Arvinius Förlag, forthcoming.

Stockholms Stadsbyggnadskontor. *Planstandard 1965.* Stockholm: Stockholms Stadsbyggnadskontor, 1965.

Svanberg, Ingvar. *Invandrare från Turkiet: Etnisk och sociokulturell variation.* Uppsala: Center for Multiethnic Research, 1985.

Svanberg, Ingvar, and Mattias Tydén. *Tusen år av invandring: En svensk kulturhistoria.* 3rd ed. Stockholm: Dialogos, 2005 (originally published in 1992).

Svedberg, Olle. "Funktionalismens bostadsprogram—En bakgrundsskiss." In *Funktionalismens genombrott och kris: Svenskt bostadsbyggande 1930–1980,* 41–63. Stockholm: Arkitekturmuseet, 1980 (originally published in German in 1976 and in Hungarian in 1978).

Syrianska Riksförbundet i Sverige. "Syrianer—en nation i förskingring," 2004. http://www .saaf.info/syrianer.pdf.

Taylor, Charles. "Modern Social Imaginaries." *Public Culture* 14, no. 1 (2002): 91–124.

———. *Modern Social Imaginaries.* Durham, N.C.: Duke University Press, 2004.

ter Haar Romeny, Bas. "From Religious Association to Ethnic Community: A Research Project on Identity Formation among the Syrian Orthodox under Muslim Rule." *Islam and Christian–Muslim Relations* 16, no. 4 (2005): 377–99.

Thompson, Michael. *Rubbish Theory: The Creation and Destruction of Value.* Oxford: Oxford University Press, 1979.

Töker, Yıldız. "Att vara invandrare." *Bahro Suryoyo* 2, no. 5 (May 1980): 7.

Trägårdh, Lars. "Svenskhet och civilitet: Om dygd, kärlek och oberoende i svensk politisk kultur." In *Civilt samhälle kontra offentlig sektor,* edited by Lars Trägårdh, 11–34. Stockholm: Studieförbundet Näringsliv och Samhälle, 1995.

Tunström, Moa. "The Story." In *Future People's Palace,* edited by Ola Broms Wessel, Jennifer Mack, and Tim Anstey. Stockholm: Arvinius Förlag, forthcoming.

van den Boogert, Maurits H. *The Capitulations and the Ottoman Legal System: Qadis, Consuls, and Beraths in the 18th Century.* Boston: Brill, 2005.

Veblen, Thorstein. *The Theory of the Leisure Class: An Economic Study in the Evolution of Institutions.* New York: Macmillan, 1899.

Vestbro, Dick Urban. *Kollektivhus från enkökshus till bogemenskap.* Stockholm: Swedish Building Research Council, 1982.

Vidler, Anthony. *The Scenes of the Street and Other Essays.* New York: Monacelli Press, 2011.

Wacquant, Loïc. *Urban Outcasts: A Comparative Sociology of Advanced Marginality.* Malden, Mass.: Polity, 2008.

Wannes, Süleyman. *Syrisk-ortodoxa kyrkan: Bildandet, ankomsten och utvecklingen i Sverige.* Linköping: Self-published, 2008.

Warner, Michael. *Publics and Counterpublics.* Cambridge, Mass.: Zone Books, 2002.

Warriner, Doreen. *Land Reform and Development in the Middle East: A Study of Egypt, Syria, and Iraq.* 2nd ed. London: Oxford University Press, 1962.

Werbner, Pnina. *The Migration Process: Capital, Gifts, and Offerings among British Pakistanis.* New York: Berg, 1990.

———. "The Place Which Is Diaspora: Citizenship, Religion, and Gender in the Making of Chaordic Transnationalism." *Journal of Ethnic and Migration Studies* 28, no. 1 (2002): 119–33.

Westerman, Allan. "Nya stadscentra." *Arkitektur* 8 (1965): 267–76.

Widgren, Jonas. *Svensk invandrarpolitik.* Lund: Liber Förlag, 1982.

Wikan, Unni. *Generous Betrayal: Politics of Culture in the New Europe.* Chicago: University of Chicago Press, 2002.

———. *In Honor of Fadime: Murder and Shame.* Chicago: University of Chicago Press, 2008.

Williams, Raymond. *The Country and the City.* London: Hogarth Press, 1973.

Wirtén, Per. *Där jag kommer från: Kriget mot förorten.* Stockholm: Bonniers Förlag, 2010.

Zaremba, Maciej. *De rena och de andra: Om tvångssteriliseringar, rashygien och arvsynd.* Stockholm: Dagens Nyheter, 1999.

Swedish Government Official Reports (Statens Offentliga Utredningar, SOUs)

SOU 1955:8. *Tvätt.* Bostadskollektiva kommitténs betänkande III. Stockholm: Socialdepartementet.

SOU 1955:28. *Samlingslokaler.* Bostadskollektiva kommitténs betänkande IV. Stockholm: Socialdepartementet.

SOU 1956:32. *Hemmen och samhällsplaneringen.* Bostadskollektiva kommitténs slutbetänkande. Stockholm: Socialdepartementet.

SOU 1961:5. *Begravningsplatser och gravar.* Förslag av tillkallad sakkunnig. Stockholm: Justitiedepartementet.

SOU 1965:32. *Höjd bostadsstandard.* Betänkande avgivet av Bostadsbyggnadsutredningen. Stockholm: Inrikesdepartementet.

SOU 1967:18. *Invandringen. Problem och handläggning.* Utlänningsutredningsbetänkande II. Stockholm: Inrikesdepartementet.

SOU 1967:30. *Höga eller låga hus?* Betänkande avgivet av Bostadsbyggnadsutredningen. Stockholm: Inrikesdepartementet.

SOU 1968:38. *Boendeservice 1.* Fakta och synpunkter sammanställda av den statliga Servicekommittén. Stockholm: Inrikesdepartementet.

SOU 1970:68. *Boendeservice 2. Mål, finansiering av lokaler, utvecklingsprojekt.* Betänkande avgivet av Servicekommittén. Stockholm: Inrikesdepartementet.

SOU 1971:25. *Boendeservice 3. Kommunstudien.* Studie utgiven av Servicekommittén. Stockholm: Inrikesdepartementet.

SOU 1971:26. *Boendeservice 4. Projektstudien—en redovisning av aktuella serviceanläggningar.* Studie utgiven av Servicekommittén. Stockholm: Inrikesdepartementet.

SOU 1971:27. *Boendeservice 5. Totalkostnadstudien—en diskussion av ekonomiska konsekvenser av några former av boendeservice.* Studie utgiven av Servicekommittén. Stockholm: Inrikesdepartementet.

• SOU 1971:28. *Boendeservice 6. Strukturstudien—tio uppsatser om samhällsförändringar som påverkar boendeservice.* Studie utgiven av Servicekommittén. Stockholm: Inrikesdepartementet.

SOU 1972:40. *Konkurrens i bostadsbyggandet.* Betänkande avgivet av Byggkonkurrensutredningen. Stockholm: Inrikesdepartementet.

SOU 1973:24. *Boendeservice 7. Verksamheter. Planering och organisation. Ekonomiska frågor. Exempel.* Studie utgiven av Servicekommittén. Stockholm: Inrikesdepartementet.

SOU 1974:17. *Solidarisk bostadspolitik.* Betänkande av Boende- och bostadsfinansieringsutredningen. Stockholm: Bostadsdepartementet.

SOU 1974:69. *Invandrarutredningen 3. Invandrare och minoriteter.* Huvudbetänkande av Invandrarutredningen. Stockholm: Arbetsmarknadsdepartementet.

SOU 1987:16. *Begravningslag.* Betänkande av Arbetsgruppen för översyn av begravningslagstiftningen. Stockholm: Civildepartementet.

SOU 1987:33. *Ju mer vi är tillsammans. Ett förslag som öppnar vägen för utökad föreningsmedverkan i kommuner och landsting.* Betänkande från 1986 års folkrörelseutredning. Stockholm: Civildepartementet.

SOU 1996:55. *Sverige, framtiden och mångfalden.* Slutbetänkande från Invandrarpolitiska kommittén. Stockholm: Arbetsmarknadsdepartementet.

SOU 1997:42. *Begravningsverksamhet. Staten och trossamfunden.* Betänkande av Begravningssamhetskommittén. Stockholm: Kulturdepartementet.

SOU 1998:25. *Tre städer. En storstadspolitik för hela landet.* Slutbetänkande av Storstadskommittén. Stockholm: Socialdepartementet.

SOU 2008:38. *EU, allmännyttan och hyrorna.* Betänkande av Utredningen om allmännyttans villkor. Stockholm: Finansdepartementet.

Radio and Television Broadcasts

Sveriges Radio (SR, Radio Sweden)

Ambjörnsson, Siri, and Emma Janke, producers. *Bråket på Bristol—Sveriges första raskravaller.* January 26, 2008.

Gunnarsson, Katarina, reporter. "En månad sedan upploppet i Södertälje." Segment on *Studio Ett.* October 20, 2005.

Södertälje: Immigration the Swedish Way. December 26, 2012. http://sverigesradio.se/sida/artikel.aspx?programid=2054&artikel=5389357.

Sveriges Television (SVT, Swedish Public Television)

"Goda bostäder fostra goda medborgare." Episode of *Arkitekter berättar.* TV1. September 2, 1976.

Hanna—Assyrier i Södertälje. TV1. September 6, 1980.

"Nya svenskar." Episode of *ZOOM.* TV1. November 26, 1980.

Var kommer du ifrån—Vart är du på väg? TV1. October 2, 1981.

"Klyftan 4: Södertälje—Stad i världen." Episode of *Utbildningsradio.* TV1. February 2, 1982.

Varför mördades Aslan Noyan? SVT2. March 19, 1982.

"Samtal." Episode of *Kunskapskanalen.* January 11, 2004.

Sandberg, Erik, and Nuri Kino, directors. *Assyriska—Landslag utan land.* Produced by Erik Sandberg, Oscar Hedin, and Nuri Kino. Five-part documentary. SVT2. October 24–November 21, 2005.

Petteri på villovägar. SVT2. May 22, 2006.

Planer för kaldeisk kyrka i Hovsjö. June 14, 2015. http://www.svt.se/nyheter/regionalt/sodertalje/planer-pa-kaldeisk-kyrka-i-hovsjo.

TV3 (Sweden)

"Familjen Makdissi i Södertälje har problem." Episode of *Från koja till slott.* February 7, 2005.

Mitt stora feta syrianska bröllop. Series. October 17–December 11, 2011.

TV4 (Sweden)

Rosenberg: Sveriges val. Part 1, *Nationen.* December 28, 2005.

Rosenberg: Sveriges val. Part 2, *Välfärden.* January 4, 2006.

Rosenberg: Sveriges val. Part 3, *Demokratin.* January 11, 2006.

Index

JENNIFER MACK is a researcher at KTH School of Architecture and the Built Environment in Stockholm, Sweden, and at the Institute for Housing and Urban Research (IBF), Uppsala University.